WORLD CUP
GUIDE

EDITED BY BILL FRINDALL

A Guide to the Sixth World Cup Tournament

HEADLINE

First published in 1996
by HEADLINE BOOK PUBLISHING

Cover photographs: Left – Allan Donald of South Africa;
right – Brian Lara of West Indies (both by Patrick Eagar)

10 9 8 7 6 5 4 3 2

ISBN 0 7472 4648 3

Typeset by
Letterpart Limited, Reigate, Surrey

Printed and bound in Great Britain by
BPC Paperbacks Ltd
A member of The British Printing Company Ltd

HEADLINE BOOK PUBLISHING
A division of Hodder Headline PLC
338 Euston Road
London NW1 3BH

CONTENTS

EDITORIAL NOTES

My first thanks are fairly obviously due to Headline for agreeing to publish this Guide and for doing so under the prestigious *Playfair* label. The concept took root during the Australasian World Cup tournament of 1991-92 when, having just installed a fax machine, I was inundated with requests from Down Under for statistics on the teams and for records of the four previous competitions. This wee tome is my cunning plan to forestall similar problems. It has also replaced a massive binder of papers and a large amount of computer disk space. *Playfair's* luggage-friendly format will not only benefit media folk as they battle through cricket's most testing itinerary, in an area not noted for its transport reliability ratings, but hopefully should prove a boon to those following this remarkable circus via radio, television and the press. The Wills World Cup, as this sixth tournament will be known, is the biggest cricketing bonanza ever conceived. It involves more participating teams (12), more host countries (3) and more grounds (26) than any of its predecessors. The more cynical have already observed that, unless the three associate ICC members (Holland, Kenya and the Emirates) can exceed their wildest aspirations, the first 30 matches of this competition are devoted to reducing the nine full members by just one. Life was so much easier in 1975 and 1979 when there were only six Test-playing countries and a grand total of 15 matches played over as many days was sufficient to produce the winner.

The fate of recent England cricketers portrayed on the cover of the *Playfair Cricket Annual* has prompted me, as sole bestower of that dubious accolade, to attempt to inflict some damage on some of England's opponents. Although Headline reduced my original assembly of players most threatening to Michael Atherton's dreams to just two, I am sure he will approve of the final choice of Allan Donald and Brian Lara, two outstanding cricketers who have done much to secure Warwickshire the unprecedented and astonishing tally of five trophies in two seasons. In Lara's case, my unfortunate jinx seems to have worked prematurely and it remains to be seen if he either receives a summons to the World Cup or chooses to obey it. Writing this on the day after the England captain's epic innings at The Wanderers, I am not sure that Lara's epithet of 'the world's greatest batsman' is beyond dispute. After all, his two record-breaking innings were, unlike Atherton's, not exactly team motivated and his performances on some testing pitches in India last winter produced 198 runs in six innings. Atherton scored over 1000 Test runs in 1995 and against the attacks of Australia, West Indies and South Africa, a phenomenal feat.

Many people have contributed to this book and have done so under the daunting schedule imposed by having to put it to bed before the Christmas hiatus. It would certainly not have been accomplished without Ian Marshall's unflappable expertise in the publisher's office, nor without the enthusiastic co-operation of Chris Leggett and his team at Letterpart. I am also indebted to my wife Debbie, who, notwithstanding the demands of five marauding cats, 17 gold fish (the village pond ran dry in the summer; to date they have managed to decline the advances of the cats), and the imminent delivery of a 'beardless wonder', has supported, dogsbodied, researched and proof-checked with great distinction.

My thanks are also due to Vic Isaacs (scores and records), Wendy Wimbush (World Cup Cricketers index), Allan Miller (Australia), Andrew Samson (South Africa), Tony Cozier (West Indies), Cheryl Styles (New Zealand), Rajesh Kumar and Mohandas Menon (India), John Ward (Zimbabwe), Alex de la Mar (KNCB, Holland), Harilal Shah (Kenya) and Vikram Kaul (UAE), Shilpa Patel (BBC Radio) and Justine Erim (BSkyB). Clive Hitchcock (ICC) has been a benevolent source of vital data, as has Philip Bailey, compiler of the incomparable ACS Yearbooks.

Let us hope that this World Cup produces an abundance of entertaining cricket and close finishes – but not too many new records . . .

Bill Frindall
Urchfont

4

THE WILLS WORLD CUP PREVIEW

International limited-overs cricket has developed from a fun-and-frolic fill-in to cheer disappointed spectators at a washed out New Year's Test match 25 years ago into a highly marketable industry which, according to reports emanating from Lahore, venue for the final, is expected to net the organisers a cool £40 million in sponsorship deals and TV rights. This contrasts remarkably with the figure of under £2 million which accrued from the last World Cup hosted by the sub-continent nine years ago.

These vast spoils will be divided equally between the Boards of India and Pakistan with the third host country, Sri Lanka, left out in the cold. Although represented on the six-member Pak-Indo-Lanka Committee (PILCOM), the Sri Lankans declined to commit any money at the bidding stage. Thus, despite hosting four of the 37 matches, they are not entitled to a share of the profits.

Attracting financial support has proved to be the least of the organisers' problems. Anyone who has travelled in that part of the world will be only too aware of the logistical difficulties involved in moving oneself from one city to another. Multiply that by twelve squads of 14 players, each with its coach and manager, thread them continuously from one country to another, add a massive number of journalists and supporters and you have the chaotic framework for a Tom Sharpe classic. In India this has been compounded by their Board's eagerness to please as many of the state cricket associations as possible, their solution being to stage each of their 17 matches on different grounds. Apart from the resulting logistical problems, this appeasement has meant that 17 venues have to be brought up to international standard in terms of playing, media and spectator facilities. The ghastly tragedy at Nagpur during a limited-overs international between India and New Zealand on 26 November, when a wall collapsed causing 12 deaths and a further 61 serious injuries, illustrated only too graphically the scope for disaster at grounds unused to accommodating vast crowds.

PILCOM have addressed the problem by employing a specialist company, IMG from England, to advise them on every facet of ground organisation so, hopefully, all will be well on the day. It will have to be all right on the night as well for some of the matches will be staged under floodlights, a novelty introduced to World Cup cricket in Australia four years ago. All 37 matches will employ coloured clothing, white balls and black sightscreens.

Sadly, major sporting events are increasingly susceptible to political interference and it cannot have escaped general notice that all three host countries have seen serious internal unrest in recent months. Riots in Karachi, civil war in Jaffna and death threats if Pakistan play in India cannot be shrugged off as troubles which will disappear once the tournament gets underway and everyone becomes involved with the cricket.

PILCOM can hardly be expected to deal with their governments' difficulties and they are determined that this will be the best as well as the biggest World Cup pageant. The gala opening ceremony in Calcutta on 11 February, three days before the opening match, will be a hi-tech affair organised by an Italian company, Half Moon Image Consultants. They had a little net practice six years ago when they choreographed a similar curtain-raiser for the soccer World Cup there. The company's chairman, Gianfranco Lunette, has promised a display which will 'reflect the passage of the world in a manner that could certainly be described as 'hi-tech'. But in doing so, we would not lose sight of the glorious tradition of the subcontinent. The entire ceremony is being conceived in such a manner that it portrays a synthesis of the past, present and the future – a bridge between tradition and modernity.' Hopefully he will seek advice from Dr Simone Gambino, *Presidente of the Associazione Italiana Cricket*, who succeeded in having his country promoted to Associate Membership of the ICC last July. If the logistical and political problems can be overcome, the sixth World Cup promises to be the cricketing extravaganza of the century.

WORLD CUP MATCH RESULTS

GROUP A MATCHES

Feb	Venue		Score		Score	Winners	Award
16	Hyderabad (I)	WEST INDIES	....	ZIMBABWE	....	....	....
17	Colombo (RPS)	SRI LANKA	....	AUSTRALIA	....	....	....
18	Cuttack	INDIA	....	KENYA	....	....	....
21	Gwalior	INDIA	....	WEST INDIES	....	....	....
21	Colombo (SSC)	SRI LANKA	....	ZIMBABWE	....	....	....
23	Vishakhapatnam	AUSTRALIA	....	KENYA	....	....	....
25	Colombo (RPS)	SRI LANKA	....	WEST INDIES	....	....	....
26	Patna	ZIMBABWE	....	KENYA	....	....	....
27	Bombay	INDIA	....	AUSTRALIA	....	....	....
29	Poona (Pune)	WEST INDIES	....	KENYA	....	....	....
Mar							
1	Nagpur	AUSTRALIA	....	ZIMBABWE	....	....	....
2	Delhi	INDIA	....	SRI LANKA	....	....	....
4	Jaipur	AUSTRALIA	....	WEST INDIES	....	....	....
6	Kanpur	INDIA	....	ZIMBABWE	....	....	....
6	Kandy	SRI LANKA	....	KENYA	....	....	....

GROUP A RESULTS TABLE

	P	W	L	NR	Points	Hundreds Batsman	Score	Four Wickets Bowler	Analysis
AUSTRALIA	.....	.....	.....	.....	.....	.....		.....	
INDIA	.....	.....	.....	.....	.....	.....		.....	
KENYA	.....	.....	.....	.....	.....	.....		.....	
SRI LANKA	.....	.....	.....	.....	.....	.....		.....	
WEST INDIES	.....	.....	.....	.....	.....	.....		.....	
ZIMBABWE	.....	.....	.....	.....	.....	.....		.....	

QUARTER-FINALS

Mar	Venue	Country		Score	Country		Score	Winners	Award
9	Faisalabad	A1	....	....	B4	....	....	....	....
9	Bangalore	A3	....	....	B2	....	....	....	....
11	Karachi	B1	....	....	A4	....	....	....	....
11	Madras	B3	....	....	A2	....	....	....	....

Hundreds		Four Wickets	
Batsman	Score	Bowler	Analysis
....	....	....	....
....	....	....	....
....	....	....	....
....	....	....	....

RECORD THE WILLS WORLD CUP STATISTICS

GROUP B MATCHES

Feb	Venue		Score		Score	Winners	Award
14	Ahmedabad	ENGLAND	....	NEW ZEALAND	....	....	....
15	Rawalpindi	SOUTH AFRICA	....	UAE	....	....	....
17	Baroda	HOLLAND	....	NEW ZEALAND	....	....	....
18	Peshawar	ENGLAND	....	UAE	....	....	....
20	Faisalabad	SOUTH AFRICA	....	NEW ZEALAND	....	....	....
22	Peshawar	ENGLAND	....	HOLLAND	....	....	....
24	Gujranwala	PAKISTAN	....	UAE	....	....	....
25	Rawalpindi	ENGLAND	....	SOUTH AFRICA	....	....	....
26	Lahore	PAKISTAN	....	HOLLAND	....	....	....
27	Faisalabad	NEW ZEALAND	....	UAE	....	....	....
29	Karachi	PAKISTAN	....	SOUTH AFRICA	....	....	....
Mar							
1	Lahore	HOLLAND	....	UAE	....	....	....
3	Karachi	PAKISTAN	....	ENGLAND	....	....	....
5	Rawalpindi	SOUTH AFRICA	....	HOLLAND	....	....	....
6	Lahore	PAKISTAN	....	NEW ZEALAND	....	....	....

GROUP B RESULTS TABLE

	P	W	L	NR	Points	Hundreds Batsman	Score	Four Wickets Bowler	Analysis
ENGLAND	....	.....	....	.....	.....	....	....	....	....
HOLLAND	....	.....	....	.....	.....	....	....	....	....
NEW ZEALAND	....	.....	....	.....	.....	....	....	....	....
PAKISTAN	....	.....	....	.....	.....	....	....	....	....
SOUTH AFRICA	....	.....	....	.....	.....	....	....	....	....
UAE	....	.....	....	.....	.....	....	....	....	....

SEMI-FINALS AND THE FINAL

Mar	Venue	Country	Score	Country	Score	Winners	Award
13	Calcutta	....	....	....	....	....	....
		Winner of Faisalabad Q-F	*Winner of Bangalore Q-F*				
14	Chandigarh	....	....	....	....	....	....
		Winner of Karachi Q-F	*Winner of Madras Q-F*				
17	Lahore	....	....	....	....	....	....

Hundreds		Four Wickets	
Batsman	*Score*	*Bowler*	*Analysis*
....	....	....	....
....	....	....	....
....	....	....	....
....	....	....	....

THE GROUNDS

The 37 matches which comprise the programme for the Wills World Cup tournament will be staged at 26 venues in India (17), Pakistan (6) and Sri Lanka (3). The following are the records and best performances for all limited-overs internationals at those venues.

INDIA

AHMEDABAD (Sardar Patel Gujarat Stadium, Motera)

Wednesday 14 February – England v New Zealand (Group A) – opening match.

7 Limited-Overs Internationals

Highest Total	227-8	(50 overs)	India v Sri Lanka	1989-90
Lowest Total	100	(28.3 overs)	India v West Indies	1993-94
Highest Score	83	A.P.Gurusinha	Sri Lanka v India	1989-90
Best Bowling	3-9	C.L.Hooper	West Indies v India	1993-94

BANGALORE (M.Chinnaswamy Stadium)

Saturday 9 March – Second Quarter-Final (3rd in Group A v 2nd in Group B)

6 Limited-Overs Internationals

Highest Total	252-7	(50 overs)	India v New Zealand	1987-88
Lowest Total	170	(41.4 overs)	India v England	1992-93
Hundreds (1)	121	R.L.Dias	Sri Lanka v India	1982-83
Best Bowling	5-35	P.W.Jarvis	England v India	1992-93
	5-41	J.Srinath	India v England	1992-93

BARODA (IPCL Sports Complex)

Saturday 17 February – New Zealand v Holland (Group A)

4 Limited-Overs Internationals (3 at Moti Bagh Palace Stadium)
Records for all Baroda internationals:

Highest Total	282-8	(47.1 overs)	India v New Zealand	1988-89
Lowest Total	141	(36.3 overs)	Sri Lanka v India	1986-87
Hundreds (3)	115	S.R.Tendulkar	India v New Zealand	1994-95
	108*	M.Azharuddin	India v New Zealand	1988-89
	108	K.R.Rutherford	New Zealand v India	1994-95
Best Bowling	5-27	G.F.Labrooy	Sri Lanka v India	1986-87

8

BOMBAY (Wankhede Stadium)

Tuesday 27 February – India v Australia (Group B)

7 Limited-Overs Internationals

Highest Total	299-4	(40 overs)	India v Sri Lanka	1986-87
Lowest Total	135	(44.2 overs)	Zimbabwe v India	1987-88
Hundreds (3)	115	G.A.Gooch	England v India	1987-88
	108*	M.Azharuddin	India v Sri Lanka	1986-87
	104	H.P.Tillekeratne	Sri Lanka v West Indies	1993-94
Best Bowling	5-22	W.K.M.Benjamin	West Indies v Sri Lanka	1993-94

CALCUTTA (Eden Gardens)

Sunday 11 February – Opening Ceremony
Wednesday 13 March – First Semi-Final (Faisalabad Q-F winners v Bangalore Q-F winners)

12 Limited-Overs Internationals

Highest Total	279-7	(50 overs)	Pakistan v India	1989-90
Lowest Total	123	(40.1 overs)	West Indies v India	1993-94
Hundreds (2)	123	K.Srikkanth	India v Pakistan	1986-87
	107*	D.L.Haynes	West Indies v Pakistan	1989-90
Best Bowling	6-12	A.Kumble	India v West Indies	1993-94
	5-29	A.A.Donald	South Africa v India	1991-92

CHANDIGARH (Punjab Cricket Association Stadium, Mohali)

Thursday 14 March – Second Semi-Final (Karachi Q-F winners v Madras Q-F winners)

5 Limited-Overs Internationals (4 at Sector 16 Stadium)

Records for all Chandigarh internationals:

Highest Total	251-8	(50 overs)	Australia v New Zealand	1987-88
Lowest Totals†	221	(49.2 overs)	India v South Africa	1993-94
	170-6	(50 overs)	Bangladesh v India	1990-91
Hundreds (2)	126*	G.R.Marsh	Australia v New Zealand	1987-88
	104*	N.S.Sidhu	India v Bangladesh	1990-91
Best Bowling	3-23	T.A.P.Sekhar	India v England	1984-85

† Lowest total for which the whole team was dismissed and lowest total when the overs were complete.

9

CUTTACK (Barabati Stadium)

Sunday 18 February – India v Kenya (Group B)

8 Limited-Overs Internationals

Highest Total	266-5	(50 overs)	Australia v Zimbabwe	1987-88
Lowest Total	148-9	(50 overs)	Pakistan v England	1989-90
Hundreds (2)	104	A.D.Jadeja	India v West Indies	1994-95
	102	R.J.Shastri	India v England	1984-85
Best Bowling	3-19	G.A.Gooch	England v Pakistan	1989-90

DELHI (Feroz Shah Kotla)

Saturday 2 March – India v Sri Lanka (Group B)

9 Limited-Overs Internationals

Highest Total	289-3	(50 overs)	India v New Zealand	1994-95
Lowest Total	172	(40.5 overs)	India v Australia	1984-85
Hundreds (4)	109	R.J.Shastri	India v South Africa	1991-92
	107	K.C.Wessels	Australia v India	1984-85
	105	S.V.Manjrekar	India v South Africa	1991-92
	102	R.L.Dias	Sri Lanka v India	1982-83
Best Bowling	6-41	I.V.A.Richards	West Indies v India	1989-90

GWALIOR (Roop Singh Stadium)

Wednesday 21 February – India v West Indies (Group B)

5 Limited-Overs Internationals

Highest Total	278-6	(50 overs)	West Indies v India	1987-88
Lowest Total	185-8	(45 overs)	South Africa v India	1991-92
Hundreds (5)	138*	D.L.Haynes	West Indies v England	1989-90
	134*	N.S.Sidhu	India v England	1992-93
	129	R.A.Smith	England v India	1992-93
	113*	C.L.Hooper	West Indies v India	1987-88
	105*	G.A.Hick	England v India	1992-93
Best Bowling	4-29	B.P.Patterson	West Indies v India	1987-88

HYDERABAD (Lal Bahadur Shastri Stadium, Fateh Maidan)

Friday 16 February – West Indies v Zimbabwe (Group B)

7 Limited-Overs Internationals

Highest Total	243-3	(50 overs)	England v Australia	1989-90
Lowest Total	99	(36.3 overs)	Zimbabwe v West Indies	1993-94
Hundreds (2)	142	D.L.Houghton	Zimbabwe v New Zealand	1987-88
	124	W.Larkins	England v Australia	1989-90
Best Bowling	5-35	M.Prabhakar	India v Sri Lanka	1993-94

JAIPUR (Sawai Mansingh Stadium)

Monday 4 March – Australia v West Indies (Group B)

5 Limited-Overs Internationals

Highest Total	269-5	(50 overs)	England v West Indies	1987-88
Lowest Total	166-9	(46 overs)	Pakistan v India	1983-84
Hundreds (5)	111	D.C.Boon	Australia v India	1986-87
	105	S.R.Tendulkar	India v West Indies	1994-95
	104	G.R.Marsh	Australia v India	1986-87
	102	K.Srikkanth	India v Australia	1986-87
	100*	V.G.Kambli	India v England	1992-93
Best Bowling	4-46	S.L.V.Raju	India v West Indies	1994-95

KANPUR (Green Park Stadium)

Wednesday 6 March – India v Zimbabwe (Group B)

5 Limited-Overs Internationals

Highest Total	259-4	(48.1 overs)	India v England	1989-90
Lowest Total	78	(24.1 overs)	India v Sri Lanka	1986-87
Hundreds (2)	102*	M.Prabhakar	India v West Indies	1994-95
	101*	C.Sharma	India v England	1989-90
Best Bowling	5-24	J.Srinath	India v Sri Lanka	1993-94

MADRAS (M.A.Chidambaram Stadium, Chepauk)

Monday 11 March – Fourth Quarter-Final (3rd in Group B v 2nd in Group A)

4 Limited-Overs Internationals

Highest Total	270-6	(50 overs)	Australia v India	1987-88
Lowest Total	139	(42.4 overs)	Zimbabwe v Australia	1987-88
Hundreds (1)	110	G.R.Marsh	Australia v India	1987-88
Best Bowling	4-39	S.P.O'Donnell	Australia v Zimbabwe	1987-88

NAGPUR (Vidarbha Cricket Association Ground)

Friday 1 March – Australia v Zimbabwe (Group B)

6 Limited-Overs Internationals

Highest Total	286-6	(44 overs)	Pakistan v India	1986-87
Lowest Total	193	(44.4 overs)	India v West Indies	1987-88
Hundreds (3)	104	P.A.de Silva	Sri Lanka v India	1990-91
	103*	S.M.Gavaskar	India v New Zealand	1987-88
	101*	R.J.Shastri	India v Sri Lanka	1990-91
Best Bowling	6-29	B.P.Patterson	West Indies v India	1987-88

PATNA (Moin-ul-Haq Stadium)

Monday 26 February – Zimbabwe v Kenya (Group B)

1 Limited-Overs International

Highest Total	263-6	(50 overs)	Sri Lanka v Zimbabwe	1993-94
Lowest Total	208	(49 overs)	Zimbabwe v Sri Lanka	1993-94
Highest Score	68	P.A.de Silva	Sri Lanka v Zimbabwe	1993-94
Best Bowling	4-19	S.T.Jayasuriya	Sri Lanka v Zimbabwe	1993-94

POONA (PUNE) (Nehru Stadium)

Thursday 29 February – West Indies v Kenya (Group B)

5 Limited-Overs Internationals

Highest Total	238-2	(45.3 overs)	India v Zimbabwe	1992-93
Lowest Total	120-9	(42 overs)	India v Pakistan	1986-87
Hundreds (2)	115*	M.W.Gatting	England v India	1984-85
	105	D.B.Vengsarkar	India v England	1984-85
Best Bowling	3-25	Salim Jaffer	Pakistan v India	1986-87

VISHAKHAPATNAM (Indira Priyadarshani Municipal Corporation Stadium)

Friday 23 February – Australia v Kenya (Group A)

2 Limited-Overs Internationals

Highest Total	260-4	(44 overs)	India v West Indies	1994-95
Lowest Total	196-9	(50 overs)	New Zealand v India	1988-89
Hundreds (1)	114*	N.S.Sidhu	India v West Indies	1994-95
Best Bowling	5-27	K.Srikkanth	India v New Zealand	1988-89

PAKISTAN

FAISALABAD (Iqbal Stadium)

Tuesday 20 February – South Africa v New Zealand (Group A)
Tuesday 27 February – New Zealand v UAE (Group A)
Saturday 9 March   – First Quarter-Final (1st in Group A v 4th in Group B)

6 Limited-Overs Internationals

Highest Total	297-7	(50 overs)	Pakistan v Sri Lanka	1987-88
Lowest Total	184-8	(50 overs)	Sri Lanka v Pakistan	1987-88
Hundreds (1)	100	Salim Malik	Pakistan v Sri Lanka	1987-88
Best Bowling	4-27	Mudassar Nazar	Pakistan v New Zealand	1984-85

GUJRANWALA (Municipal Stadium)

Saturday 24 February – Pakistan v UAE (Group A)

6 Limited-Overs Internationals

Highest Total	246-8	(49.3 overs)	England v West Indies	1987-88
Lowest Total	196-7	(50 overs)	West Indies v Pakistan	1986-87
Hundreds (1)	106*	Javed Miandad	Pakistan v India	1992-93
Best Bowling	3-18	Imran Khan	Pakistan v India	1989-90

KARACHI (National Stadium)

Thursday 29 February – Pakistan v South Africa (Group A)
Sunday   3 March   – Pakistan v England (Group A)
Monday 11 March   – Third Quarter-Final (1st in Group B v 4th in Group A)

17 Limited-Overs Internationals

Highest Total	360-4	(50 overs)	West Indies v Sri Lanka	1987-88
Lowest Total	127-9	(40 overs)	Pakistan v West Indies	1980-81
Hundreds (6)	181	I.V.A.Richards	West Indies v Sri Lanka	1987-88
	142	G.A.Gooch	England v Pakistan	1987-88
	113	Zaheer Abbas	Pakistan v India	1982-83
	113	Ramiz Raja	Pakistan v England	1987-88
	110	R.B.Richardson	West Indies v Pakistan	1987-88
	105	D.L.Haynes	West Indies v Sri Lanka	1987-88
Best Bowling	5-15	●Wasim Akram	Pakistan v Zimbabwe	1993-94
	5-52	Waqar Younis	Pakistan v West Indies	1990-91

LAHORE (Gaddafi Stadium)

Monday 26 February – Pakistan v Holland (Group A)
Friday   1 March   – Holland v UAE (Group A)
Sunday 17 March   – Final

19 Limited-Overs Internationals

Highest Total	269-5	(50 overs)	Australia v Pakistan	1994-95
Lowest Total	112	(30.2 overs)	India v Pakistan	1989-90
Hundreds (5)	123	Zaheer Abbas	Pakistan v Sri Lanka	1981-82
	119*	Javed Miandad	Pakistan v India	1982-83
	109	Zaheer Abbas	Pakistan v Australia	1982-83
	105	Zaheer Abbas	Pakistan v India	1982-83
	101	Saeed Anwar	Pakistan v New Zealand	1990-91
Best Bowling	5-35	Salim Malik	Pakistan v New Zealand	1990-91
	5-44	C.J.McDermott	Australia v Pakistan	1987-88
	5-52	G.D.McGrath	Australia v Pakistan	1994-95

PESHAWAR (Shahi Bagh Stadium)

Sunday   18 February – England v UAE (Group A)
Thursday 22 February – England v Holland (Group A)

8 Limited-Overs Internationals

Highest Total	296-4	(50 overs)	England v Sri Lanka	1987-88
Lowest Total	127	(37.4 overs)	New Zealand v Pakistan	1990-91
Hundreds (1)	100*	W.J.Cronje	South Africa v Australia	1994-95
Best Bowling	5-11	Waqar Younis	Pakistan v New Zealand	1990-91

RAWALPINDI (Cricket Stadium)

Thursday 15 February – South Africa v UAE (Group A)
Sunday   25 February – England v South Africa (Group A)
Thursday 5 March   – South Africa v Holland (Group A)

7 Limited-Overs Internationals

Highest Total	271-4	(40 overs)	Pakistan v Sri Lanka	1991-92
Lowest Total	154	(38.4 overs)	Sri Lanka v Pakistan	1991-92
Hundreds (5)	121*	M.E.Waugh	Australia v Pakistan	1994-95
	117	Inzamam-ul-Haq	Pakistan v Sri Lanka	1991-92
	110	Ijaz Ahmed, sr	Pakistan v South Africa	1994-95
	104*	Saeed Anwar	Pakistan v Australia	1994-95
	102	Salim Malik	Pakistan v Sri Lanka	1991-92
Best Bowling	4-31	Abdul Qadir	Pakistan v England	1987-88

SRI LANKA

COLOMBO (R.Premadasa Stadium, Khettarama)

Saturday 17 February – Sri Lanka v Australia (Group B)
Sunday 25 February – Sri Lanka v West Indies (Group B)

16 Limited-Overs Internationals

Highest Total	262-6	(49 overs)	Sri Lanka v New Zealand	1992-93
Lowest Total	98	(34 overs)	Sri Lanka v South Africa	1993-94
Hundreds (2)	110	S.R.Tendulkar	India v Australia	1994-95
	107	R.S.Mahanama	Sri Lanka v New Zealand	1994-95
Best Bowling	4-17	C.P.H.Ramanayake	Sri Lanka v South Africa	1993-94

COLOMBO (Sinhalese Sports Club)

Wednesday 21 February – Sri Lanka v Zimbabwe (Group B)

15 Limited-Overs Internationals

Highest Total	242-8	(44.3 overs)	India v Sri Lanka	1985-86
Lowest Total	130	(37.3 overs)	Sri Lanka v New Zealand	1983-84
Highest Score	93*	Salim Malik	Pakistan v Sri Lanka	1994-95
Best Bowling	4-28	Wasim Akram	Pakistan v Sri Lanka	1985-86

KANDY (Asgiriya Stadium)

Wednesday 6 March – Sri Lanka v Kenya (Group B)

3 Limited-Overs Internationals

Highest Total	179-5	(41.3 overs)	Sri Lanka v South Africa	1993-94
Lowest Total	131-8	(45 overs)	Bangladesh v Sri Lanka	1985-86
Highest Score	59	Mohsin Khan	Pakistan v Sri Lanka	1985-86
Best Bowling	3-23	Abdul Qadir	Pakistan v Sri Lanka	1985-86

PLAYING CONDITIONS

At its annual meeting at Lord's in July 1995 the International Cricket Council agreed a code of playing conditions for all Limited-Overs Internationals outside England.

LIMITED-OVERS INTERNATIONAL MATCH
PLAYING CONDITIONS
(excluding matches in England)

The Test Match Playing Conditions shall apply except where varied below.

1. Duration of Matches

Limited-Overs International Matches shall be of one day's scheduled duration. The participating countries in a series may provide for, and in the World Cup there shall be, a reserve day on which an incomplete match may be replayed (but not continued from the scheduled day). The matches will consist of one innings per side and each innings will be limited to 50 six-ball overs. A minimum of 25 overs per team shall constitute a match.

2. Hours of Play, Intervals and Minimum Overs in the Day

2.1 Start and Cessation Times: [To be determined by the Home Board], subject to:

– there will be 2 sessions of 3½ hours each separated by a 45 minutes break.

2.2 Interval Between Innings: The innings of the team batting second shall not commence before the scheduled time for commencement of the second session unless the team batting first has completed its innings at least 30 minutes prior to the scheduled interval, in which case a ten minute break will occur and the team batting second will commence its innings and the interval will occur as scheduled.

Where play is delayed or interrupted the Umpires will reduce the length of the interval as follows:-

Time Lost	Interval
Up to 60 Minutes	30 Minutes
Between 60 and 120 Minutes	20 Minutes
More than 120 Minutes	10 Minutes

Note: Refer also to the provisions of Clause 4.2.

2.3 Intervals for Drinks: Two drinks breaks per session shall be permitted, each 1 hour 10 minutes apart. The provisions of Law 16.6 shall be strictly observed except that under conditions of extreme heat the Umpires may permit extra intervals for drinks.

An individual player may be given a drink either on the boundary edge or at the fall of a wicket, on the field, provided that no playing time is wasted. No other drinks shall be taken onto the field without the permission of the Umpires. Any player taking drinks onto the field shall be dressed in proper cricket attire.

2.4 Extra Time: The participating countries may agree to provide for extra time.

3. Appointment of Umpires

The Home Board shall appoint all Umpires from its own panel of first-class Umpires.

4. Length of Innings

4.1 Uninterrupted matches

(a) Each team shall bat for 50 (six ball) overs unless all out earlier. A team shall not be permitted to declare its innings closed.

(b) If the team fielding first fails to bowl the required number of overs by the scheduled time for cessation of the first session, play shall continue until the required number of overs has been bowled.

Unless otherwise determined by the Referee, the innings of the team batting second shall be limited to the same number of overs bowled by it, at the scheduled time for cessation of the first session. The over in progress at the scheduled cessation time shall count as a completed over.

The interval shall not be extended and the second session shall commence at the scheduled time.

The Referee may increase the number of overs to be bowled by the team bowling second if, after consultation with the Umpires he is of the opinion that events beyond the control of the bowling team prevented that team from bowling the required number of overs by the scheduled time for the cessation of the innings of the team batting first.

(c) If the team batting first is all out and the last wicket falls at or after the scheduled time for the interval, the innings of the team batting second shall be limited to the same number of overs bowled to the team batting first at the scheduled time for the interval (the over in which the last wicket falls to count as a complete over).

(d) If the team batting first is dismissed in less than 50 overs, the team batting second shall be entitled to bat for 50 overs except as provided in (c) above.

(e) If the team fielding second fails to bowl 50 overs or the number of overs as provided in 4.1(b), (c) or (d) by the scheduled cessation time, the hours of play shall be extended until the required number of overs has been bowled or a result achieved.

(f) Penalties shall apply for slow over-rates (refer ICC Code of Conduct).

4.2 Delayed or Interrupted Matches

4.2.1 General

(a) The object shall always be to rearrange the number of overs so that both teams have the opportunity of batting for the same number of overs.

A minimum 25 overs have to be bowled to the side batting second to constitute a match.

The calculation of the number of overs to be bowled shall be based on an average rate of 15 overs per hour in the total time available for play. If a reduction of the number of overs is required, any recalculation must not cause the match to be rescheduled to finish earlier than the original cessation time. This time may be extended to allow for one extra over for both teams to be added if required.

(b) If the team fielding second fails to bowl the required number of overs by the scheduled cessation time, the hours of play shall be extended until the overs have been bowled or a result achieved.

(c) The team batting second shall not bat for a greater number of overs than the first team unless the latter has been all out in less than the agreed number of overs.

(d) Fractions are to be ignored in all calculations re the number of overs.

4.2.2 Delay or Interruption to the Innings of the Team Batting First

(a) If the number of overs of the team batting first is reduced, a fixed time will be specified for the completion of the first session, as calculated by applying the provisions of Clauses 2.2 and 4.2.1(a).

(b) If the team fielding first fails to bowl the required number of overs by the scheduled time for cessation of the first session, play shall continue until the required number of overs has been bowled, and 4.1(b) shall apply.

(c) If the team batting first is all out and the last wicket falls at or after the scheduled time for the interval, 4.1(c) shall apply.

4.2.3 Delay or Interruption to the Innings of the Team Batting Second

If it is not possible for the team batting second to have the opportunity of batting for the same number of overs as the team batting first, the overs to be bowled shall be reduced at the rate of 15 overs per hour, for time lost.

5. Restrictions on the Placement of Fieldsmen

Two semi circles shall be drawn on the field of play. The semi circles have as their centre the middle stump at either end of the pitch. The radius of each of the semi circles is 30 yards (27.5m). The ends of each semi circle are joined to the other by a straight line drawn on the field on the same side of the pitch.

The field restriction area should be marked by continuous painted white lines or 'dots' at five yard (4.5m) intervals, each 'dot' to be covered by a white plastic or rubber (but not metal) disc measuring seven inches (18cm) in diameter.

At the instant of delivery, there may not be more than five fieldsmen on the leg side.

For the first 15 overs only two fieldsmen are permitted to be outside the field restriction marking at the instant of delivery. For the remaining overs only five fieldsmen are permitted to be outside the field restriction marking at the instant of delivery.

In the first 15 overs there must be a minimum of two stationary fieldsmen within 15 yards of the striker at the instant of delivery.

Where play is delayed or interrupted affecting the innings of the team batting first and the total number of overs available is reduced, the number of overs in regard to field restrictions shall be reduced proportionately. Fractions are to be ignored.

In the event of an infringement, the square leg Umpire shall call and signal no ball.

6. Number of Overs per Bowler

No bowler shall bowl more than 10 (six ball) overs in an innings.

In a delayed or interrupted match where the overs are reduced for both teams or for the team bowling second, no bowler may bowl more than one-fifth of the total overs allowed.

Where the total overs is not divisible by 5, one additional over shall be allowed to the maximum number per bowler necessary to make up the balance.

In the event of a bowler breaking down and being unable to complete an over, the remaining balls will be bowled by another bowler. Such part of an over will count as a full over only in so far as each bowler's limit is concerned.

The scoreboard shall show the total number of overs bowled and the number of overs bowled by each bowler.

7. No Ball

Short Pitched Bowling - if the ball passes or would have passed above the shoulder height of the striker standing upright at the crease, either Umpire shall call and signal no ball.

8. Wide Bowling - Judging a Wide

Umpires are instructed to apply a very strict and consistent interpretation in regard to this Law in order to prevent negative bowling wide of the wicket.

Any offside or legside delivery which in the opinion of the Umpire does not give the batsman a reasonable opportunity to score shall be called a wide. As a guide, on the leg side a ball landing clearly outside the leg stump going further away shall be called wide.

9. The Ball

The Home Board shall provide cricket balls of an approved standard for Limited-Overs International cricket.

Where day/night matches are scheduled, white balls will be used in all matches (including day matches) in a series.

Each fielding team shall have one new ball for its innings.

In the event of a ball becoming wet and soggy as a result of play continuing in inclement weather or it being affected by dew, or a white ball becoming significantly discoloured and in the opinion of the Umpires being unfit for play, the ball may be replaced for a ball that has had a similar amount of wear, even though it has not gone out of shape.

Either bowler or batsman may raise the matter with the Umpires and the Umpires' decision as to a replacement or otherwise will be final.

10. The Result

10.1 A result can be achieved only if both teams have had the opportunity of batting for at least 25 overs, unless one team has been all out in less than 25 overs or unless the team batting second scores enough runs to win in less than 25 overs.

All matches in which both teams have not had an opportunity of batting for a minimum of 25 overs, shall be declared no result.

10.2 Tie

In matches in which both teams have had the opportunity of batting for the agreed number of overs, the team scoring the higher number of runs shall be the winner. If the scores are equal, the result shall be a tie and no account shall be taken of the number of wickets which have fallen.

10.3 Delayed or Interrupted Matches - Calculation of the Target Score

If the innings of the team batting second is delayed or interrupted and it is not able to receive its full quota of overs, the target score shall be calculated as follows: the score of the team batting first shall be multiplied by the percentage factor for the number of overs to be bowled to the team batting second, as set out on the Target Score Calculation Chart (Appendix A). Fractions shall be rounded to the next higher whole number

The percentage factors have been derived from a detailed mathematical analysis of a database of one day matches with the object of establishing "normal" performance.

APPENDIX A

TARGET SCORE CALCULATION CHART

Team A's Score _____

OVERS	% FACTOR	TARGET SCORE
25	66.7	
26	68.4	
27	70.2	
28	72.4	
29	74.2	
30	76.0	
31	77.8	
32	79.1	
33	80.9	
34	82.2	
35	84.0	
36	85.3	
37	86.7	
38	88.0	
39	89.3	
40	90.7	
41	92.0	
42	92.9	
43	94.2	
44	95.1	
45	96.0	
46	96.7	
47	97.8	
48	98.7	
49	99.6	
50	100.00	

e.g. Team batting first score 188. The innings of the team batting second is limited to 37 overs:

$188 \times 86.7\% = 162.996$

Target score = 163 runs

11. Points

11.1 Preliminary Matches

The points system shall be as follows:

Win	2
Tie or No Result	1
Loss	0

In the event of the teams finishing on equal points, the right to play in the final match or series will be decided by the most wins in the preliminary matches or, when teams have both equal wins and equal points, the team which was the winner of all of the preliminary match[es] (played between them) will be placed in the higher position or, if still equal, the higher net run rate in the preliminary matches. In a match declared no result, run rate is not applicable.

A team's net run rate is calculated by deducting from the average runs per over scored by that team throughout the competition, the average runs per over scored against that team throughout the competition.

In the event of a team being all out in less than its full quota of overs, the calculation of its net run rate shall be based on the full quota of overs to which it would have been entitled and not on the number of overs in which the team was dismissed.

11.2 Final Matches

If no result is achieved in a final on the scheduled day of play, the match shall be replayed on the scheduled reserve day. If no result is achieved in the replay on the reserve day, the match shall be declared drawn.

12. Day/Night Matches

(a) Pads and players' and umpires' clothing shall be coloured.

(b) Sight screens will be black.

(c) If during a day/night match, or a day match played with black sightscreens and white balls, in the opinion of the Umpires, natural light is deteriorating to an unfit level, they may authorise the Ground Authority to use the available artificial lighting so that the match can continue in acceptable conditions.

PRIZE MONEY AND AWARDS

PILCOM, the joint Pakistan, India and Sri Lanka committee hosting the Wills World Cup, has allocated a total of £200,000 in prize money and match awards for the 37-match tournament.

Distribution will be as follows:

TEAM PRIZE MONEY (£150,000)

Winner	£30,000
Runner-up	£20,000
Semi-final losers	£10,000 each
Quarter-final losers	£5000 each
Group match winners	£2000 each

MAN OF THE MATCH AWARDS (£50,000)

Final	£5000
Semi-finals	£3500 each
Quarter-finals	£2000 each
Group matches	£1000 each

WORLD CUP RADIO/TV COVERAGE

At the time of going to press (early December) only BBC Radio had confirmed its broadcasting schedule for the entire Wills World Cup. British Sky Broadcasting had completed its provisional scheduling up to 4 March and its coverage of the remaining matches was expected to follow similar lines, with the majority of the 37 matches, including all of those involving England, being broadcast in full to give a total of more than 200 hours' total coverage of the tournament. The schedule for Star TV had not been approved at that stage.

Key to radio coverage: **4** = Radio 4 LW (198kHz). **5** = Radio 5 Live (MW: 693, 909kHz). All times in GMT.

Key to BSkyB coverage: **1** = Sky Sports. **2** = Sky Sports 2. **L** = Live. **H** = Highlights.

FEBRUARY				BBC RADIO		SKY SPORTS TV	
Sun	11	Calcutta	Opening			1L	17.30–19.30
Wed	14	Ahmedabad	E v NZ	4	04.00–07.30	1L	03.00–11.30
				4	08.15–10.00	1H	19.00–22.00
				4	10.15–11.45		
Thu	15	Rawalpindi	SA v UAE			1L	03.45–12.00
						1H	20.00–22.00
Fri	16	Hyderabad	WI v Z			1L	08.55–17.00
						1H	21.00–23.00
Sat	17	Baroda	NZ v H			1L	03.45–12.00
		Colombo	SL v A			1L	08.55–17.00
						1H	20.00–23.00
Sun	18	Peshawar	E v UAE	5	04.30–08.00	1L	03.30–12.00
				5	08.45–12.15	1H	15.00–17.30
		Cuttack	I v K			1H	15.00–17.30
Tue	20	Faisalabad	SA v NZ			1L	03.45–12.00
						1H	22.00–23.30
Wed	21	Gwalior	I v WI			1L	08.55–17.00
						1H	22.00–23.59
		Colombo	SL v Z			1L	22.00–23.59
Thu	22	Peshawar	E v H	4	04.30–08.00	1L	03.45–12.00
				4	08.45–10.00	1H	19.00–20.55
				4	10.15–12.15		
Fri	23	Vishakhapatnam	A v K			1L	03.15–11.30
						1H	22.30–23.59
Sat	24	Gujranwala	P v UAE			1L	03.45–12.00
						1H	21.30–23.30
Sun	25	Rawalpindi	E v SA	5	04.30–08.00	1L	03.30–12.00
				5	08.45–12.15	1H	20.00–22.00
		Colombo	SL v WI			2L	12.00–17.00
						1H	20.00–22.00
Mon	26	Lahore	P v H			1L	09.25–17.30
						1H	22.45–00.30
		Patna	Z v K			1H	22.45–00.30
Tue	27	Bombay	I v A			1L	08.55–17.00
						1H	19.00–22.00
		Faisalabad	NZ v UAE			1H	19.00–22.00
Thu	29	Karachi	P v SA			1L	03.45–12.00
						1H	19.00–22.00
		Poona	WI v K			1H	19.00–22.00

MARCH			BBC RADIO		SKY SPORTS TV	
Fri 1	Nagpur	A v Z			1L	03.15–11.30
					1H	19.00–20.55
	Lahore	H v UAE				
Sat 2	Delhi	I v SL			1L	03.15–11.30
					1H	18.30–20.30
Sun 3	Karachi	P v E	5	04.30–08.00	1L	03.30–12.00
			5	08.45–12.15	1H	19.00–21.00
Mon 4	Jaipur	A v WI				
Tue 5	Rawalpindi	SA v H				
Wed 6	Kanpur	I v Z				
	Lahore	P v NZ				
	Kandy	SL v K				
Sat 9	Q-F Faisalabad	A1 v B4	*5	04.30–08.00		
			*5	08.45–12.15		
	Q-F Bangalore	A3 v B2	*4	09.00–12.25		
			*4	03.10–16.45		
Mon 11	Q-F Karachi	B1 v A4	*4	04.30–08.00		
			*4	08.45–10.00		
			*4	10.15–12.15		
	Q-F Madras	B3 v A2	*4	09.00–10.00		
			*4	10.15–12.25		
			*4	13.07–16.45		
Wed 13	S-F Calcutta		4	09.00–10.00		
			4	10.15–12.25		
			4	13.07–16.45		
Thu 14	S-F Mohali		4	09.00–10.00		
			4	10.15–12.25		
			4	13.07–16.45		
Sun 17	FINAL Lahore		4	09.30–13.00		
			4	13.45–17.15		

Only the Quarter-Final involving England will be broadcast on BBC Radio.

THE UMPIRES

THE WORLD CUP PANEL

Twelve umpires have been selected from the National Grid International Panel to officiate in the 37-match World Cup tournament. The three host countries (India, Pakistan and Sri Lanka) each provide BOTH their NGIP members, while the remaining six Test-playing countries supply one umpire apiece.

Numbers of Test and Limited-Overs International matches in which the panel members have officiated are to the end of the 1995 English season (18 September).

Abbreviations:

*	not out	f-c	first-class
BB	best innings bowling analysis	HS	highest score
ct	catches	st	stumpings

INDIA

RAMASWAMY, Virinchirpuram Krishnamoorthi (**'Ram'**)
Born Madras 26 Apr 1945. 5' 10". Confidential assistant to Hyderabad Indian Railways executive. Right-handed all-rounder for Moulali. Debut as first-class umpire 1973. Appointed to International Panel 1994. Has umpired 18 Tests (1984-85 to 1995) and 29 Limited-Overs Internationals (1983-84 to 1994-95), including the 1987-88 World Cup.

VENKATARAGHAVAN, Srinivasaraghavan
Born Madras 21 Apr 1946. 5' 11½". Right-hand batsman, off-break bowler. Madras/Tamil Nadu 1963-64 to 1984-85. Derbyshire 1973 to 1975 (cap 1973). **TESTS:** 57 (1964-65 to 1983-84, 5 as captain (lost 2, drew 3)). HS 64 v New Zealand (Madras) 1976-77. BB 8-72 (12-152 match) v New Zealand (Delhi) 1964-65. **TOURS** (f-c matches only): England 1967, 1971, 1974, 1979 (captain); Australia 1977-78; West Indies 1970-71, 1975-76, 1982-83; New Zealand 1975-76; Pakistan 1978-79; Ceylon 1973-74. Also represented Madras in Ceylon 1965-66, 1967-68, 1969-70, 1971-72. **F-C CAREER:** 6617 runs (av 17.73), 1 hundred; 1390 wkts (av 24.14), 5 wkts/inns (85), 10 wkts/match (21); 317 ct. HS 137 Tamil Nadu v Kerala (Tellicherry) 1970-71. BB 9-93 Indians v Hampshire (Bournemouth) 1971. Debut as first-class umpire 1991-92. Appointed to International Panel 1994. Has umpired 11 Tests (1992-93 to 1995) and 3 Limited-Overs Internationals (1992-93 to 1994-95).

PAKISTAN

KHIZER HAYAT (then India) Jan 1939. 5' 8½". Right-hand batsman, wicket-keeper. Played for Universal (Lahore), Punjab and Pakistan Railways. Toured England with Pakistan Eaglets 1957. Employed by Sports Office Apprentice Training Centre. Debut as first-class umpire 1974. Attached to English first-class list 1982. Appointed to International Panel 1994. Has umpired 31 Tests (1979-80 to 1994-95) and 46 Limited-Overs Internationals (1978-79 to 1994-95), including the 1987-88 and 1991-92 World Cups.

MAHBOOB SHAH (Syed Mahboob Ali Shah)
Born Delhi, India 13 Oct 1938. 5' 10". Right-handed batsman, right-arm medium pace bowler. Played for Karachi clubs City Gymkhana, Baluchista and University. Deputy manager (Marketing) for Pakistan Steel Mills Corporation in Lahore. Debut as first-class umpire 1970. Appointed to International Panel 1994. Has umpired 24 Tests (1974-75 to 1994-95) and 24 Limited-Overs Internationals (1976-77 to 1994-95), including the 1987-88 World Cup final.

SRI LANKA

COORAY, Bulathasinghalage **Cyril**
Born Colombo 15 May 1941. 5' 5". Sri Lanka Insurance Corporation executive. Right-hand opening batsman and wicket-keeper for Saracens and Nationalised Services Cricket Association. Debut as first-class umpire 1983. Appointed to International Panel 1994. Has umpired 5 Tests (1992-93 to 1994-95) and 15 Limited-Overs Internationals (1985-86 to 1994-95).

FRANCIS, Kandiah Thirugnanasampandapillai **('KT')**
Born Kegalle 15 Oct 1939. 5' 7". Retired Sri Lanka Railway employee. Right-handed all-rounder for Railway Sports Club. Debut as first-class umpire 1975. Appointed to International Panel 1994. Has umpired 14 Tests (Inaugural Test 1981-82 to 1994-95) and 21 Limited-Overs Internationals (1981-82 to 1994-95).

ENGLAND

SHEPHERD, David Robert
Born Bideford, Devon 27 Dec 1940. Height 5' 10". Educated at Barnstaple Grammar School; St Luke's College, Exeter. Right-hand batsman, right-arm medium pace bowler. Gloucestershire 1965 to 1979 (cap 1969; joint benefit with Jack Davey 1978). Scored 108 on debut (v Oxford U). Devon 1959 to 1964. **F-C CAREER:** 10,672 runs (av 24.47), 12 hundreds, 1000 runs in a season (2); most – 1079 (1970); 2 wkts (av 53.00); 95 ct. HS 153 Glos v Middx (Bristol) 1968. BB 1-1. Appointed to first-class list 1981. Appointed to International Panel 1994. Has umpired 27 Tests (1985 to 1995) and 55 Limited-Overs Internationals (1983 to 1995), including the 1983, 1987-88 and 1991-92 World Cups.

AUSTRALIA

RANDELL, Stephen Grant
Born Hobart, Tasmania 19 Feb 1956. 6' 1". Advanced skills teacher with education Department of Tasmania. Left-hand opening batsman for South Hobart. Debut as first-class umpire 1980. Appointed to International Panel 1994. Only Tasmanian to umpire Test cricket. Has umpired 21 Tests (1984-85 to 1994-95) and 61 Limited-Overs Internationals (1983-84 to 1994-95), including the 1991-92 World Cup.

SOUTH AFRICA

MITCHLEY, Cyril John
Born Johannesburg 4 Jul 1938. Height 5' 10". Educated at Troyville High School. Right-hand batsman, wicket-keeper. Transvaal B 1967-68 and 1968-69. **F-C CAREER:** 224 runs (av 20.36); 20 ct, 9 st. HS 66 Transvaal B v Rhodesia (Salisbury) 1967-68 – on debut. South African Umpires' Association chief training officer (development). Former professional footballer. Debut as first-class umpire 1981-82. Appointed to International Panel 1994. Has umpired 9 Tests (1992-93 to 1995) and 21 Limited-Overs Internationals (1992-93 to 1994-95).

WEST INDIES

BUCKNOR, Stephen Anthony
Born Montego Bay 31 May 1946. 6' 3". Sports consultant for Samuel Hart & Son. Sports columnist. International football referee 1985-92; officiated in the El Salvador v Netherlands World Cup match. Debut as first-class umpire 1987. Appointed to International Panel 1994. Has umpired 18 Tests (1988-89 to 1994-95) and 24 Limited-Overs Internationals (1988-89 to 1994-95), including the 1991-92 World Cup final.

NEW ZEALAND

DUNNE, Robert Stephen
Born Dunedin 22 Apr 1943. 5' 10". Right-hand batsman, left-arm medium pace bowler. Otago 1968-69 (5 matches). New Zealand U-23 1965-66 (1 match v Wellington). **F-C CAREER:** 30 runs (av 4.28); 10 wkts (av 41.10); 4 ct. HS 7. BB 3-47 Otago v Wellington (Dunedin) 1968-69. Breeds English bulldogs. Debut as first-class umpire 1986-87. Appointed to International Panel 1994. Has umpired 17 Tests (1988-89 to 1994-95) and 22 Limited-Overs Internationals (1988-89 to 1994-95).

ZIMBABWE

ROBINSON, Ian David
Born Oxford, England 11 Mar 1947. 6' 2". Regional training co-ordinator with BP Africa Ltd (30 years' employment within BP and Shell Marketing Services group). Right-hand opening batsman and wicket-keeper for Hatfield Sports Club, Harare. Debut as first-class umpire 1978. Appointed to International Panel 1994. Has umpired 12 Tests (1992-93 to 1995) and 23 Limited-Overs Internationals (1991-92 to 1994-95, including the 1991-92 World Cup).

VIDEO REPLAY (THIRD) UMPIRES

Video replay umpires will be selected from:
1. Any members of the World Cup Panel not officiating on that day.
2. The Test panels of the three host nations.
3. One umpire from each of the competing Associate Member countries (Holland, Kenya and the United Arab Emirates).

THE REFEREES

Six referees have been selected to officiate in the 37-match World Cup tournament, one each from the three host countries and the remaining three from England, West Indies and New Zealand.

Abbreviations:

*	not out	f-c	first-class
BB	best innings bowling analysis	HS	highest score
ct	catches	st	stumpings

LLOYD, Clive Hubert, OBE (West Indies)
Born Queenstown, Georgetown, British Guiana 31 Aug 1944. Left-hand batsman, right-arm medium pace bowler. British Guiana/Guyana 1963-64 to 1982-83. Lancashire 1968 to 1986. **TESTS:** 110 (1966-67 to 1984-85, 74 as captain). 7515 runs (av 46.67), 19 hundreds, HS 242*; 10 wkts (av 62.20), BB 2-13; 90 ct. **L-O INTERNATIONALS:** 87 (1973 to 1984-85). 1977 runs (av 39.54), 1 hundred, HS 102; 8 wkts (av 26.25); 39 ct. **F-C CAREER:** 31,232 runs (av 49.26), 79 hundreds, HS 242*; 114 wkts (av 36.00), BB 4-48; 377 ct.

MADUGALLE, Ranjan Senerath (Sri Lanka)
Born Kandy 22 Apr 1959. Right-hand batsman, off-break bowler. Nondescripts CC 1988-89. **TESTS:** 21 (1981-82 to 1988, 2 as captain). 1029 runs (av 29.40), 1 hundred, HS 103; 0 wkts; 9 ct. **L-O INTERNATIONALS:** 63 (1979 to 1988-89). 950 runs (av 18.62), HS 73; 0 wkts; 18 ct. **F-C CAREER:** 3301 runs (av 32.04), 2 hundreds, HS 142*; 2 wkts (av 79.50), BB 1-18; 42 ct.

NASIM-UL-GHANI (Pakistan)
Born Delhi, India 14 May 1941. Left-hand batsman, left-arm medium or orthodox slow bowler. Karachi 1956-57 to 1972-73. Universities 1958-59. Dacca 1965-66. East Pakistan 1966-67 and 1967-68. PWD 1966-67 to 1971-72. National Bank 1973-74 and 1974-75. **TESTS:** 29 (1957-58 to 1972-73). 747 runs (av 16.60), 1 hundred, HS 101; 52 wkts (av 37.67), BB 6-67, 5 wkts/inns (2); 11 ct. **L-O INTERNATIONALS:** 1 (1972-73). 1 run (av 1.00); 0 ct. **F-C CAREER:** 4490 runs (av 28.41), 7 hundreds, HS 139; 343 wkts (av 25.15), BB 6-24, 5 wkts/inns (23), 10 wkts/match (3); 104 ct.

PATAUDI, Mansur Ali Khan 'Tiger' (formerly Nawab of Pataudi) (India)
Born Bhopal 5 Jan 1941. Right-hand batsman, right-arm medium pace bowler. Sussex 1957 to 1970. Oxford U 1960 to 1963. Delhi 1960-61 to 1964-65. Hyderabad 1965-66 to 1975-76. **TESTS:** 46 (1961-62 to 1974-75, 40 as captain). 2793 runs (av 34.91), 6 hundreds, HS 203*; 1 wkt (av 88.00), BB 1-10; 27 ct. **F-C CAREER:** 15,425 runs (av 33.67), 33 hundreds, HS 203*; 10 wkts (av 77.60), BB 1-0; 208 ct.

REID, John Richard, OBE (New Zealand)
Born Auckland 3 Jun 1928. Right-hand batsman, right-arm fast-medium/ off-break bowler, occasional wicket-keeper. Wellington 1947-48 to 1964-65. Otago 1956-57 and 1957-58. **TESTS:** 58 (1949 to 1965, 34 as captain). 3428 runs (av 33.28), 6 hundreds, HS 142; 85 wkts (av 33.35), BB 6-60, 5 wkts/inns (1); 43 ct, 1 st. **F-C CAREER:** 16,128 runs (av 41.35), 39 hundreds, HS 296; 466 wkts (av 22.60), BB 7-20, 5 wkts/inns (15), 10 wkts/match (1); 240 ct, 7 st.

SUBBA ROW, Raman, CBE (England)
Born Streatham, Surrey 29 Jan 1932. Left-hand batsman, right-arm leg-break/googly bowler. Cambridge U 1951 to 1953. Surrey 1953 and 1954. Northamptonshire 1955 to 1961. **TESTS:** 13 (1958 to 1961). 984 runs (av 46.85), 3 hundreds, HS 137; 0 wkts; 5 ct. **F-C CAREER:** 14,182 runs (av 41.46), 30 hundreds, HS 300; 87 wkts (av 38.65), BB 5-21; 5 wkts/inns (2).

THE TEAMS

ASSESSMENT AND KEY PLAYERS

If the outcome of Test cricket is difficult to predict, except when there is a gross imbalance of ability between the two teams, then the instant variation of the game is quite impossible to forecast. Pakistan looked totally outclassed for the first half of the last World Cup and yet scraped into the final and triumphed convincingly on the day. Despite their usual shambles behind the scenes, they might well do so again. They have the vital, overwhelming advantage of playing at home on low, slow, turning pitches which suit them best. It was no coincidence that after two massively demoralising defeats in Australia last November, they took full advantage of a typically Pakistani pitch at Sydney to win the third Test.

Pakistan has three outstanding players in Wasim Akram, Waqar Younis and Mushtaq Ahmed. Wasim, in his second term as captain, was an outstanding success on and off the field in Australia. To have led his team into the backyard of the players who had instituted the bribery allegations against Salim Malik, to have been saddled with that player at the eleventh hour and to have completed the three-match rubber with the teams respecting each other to such an extent that Mark Taylor led his players on to the field to congratulate Wasim's team after their splendid victory, was a supreme achievement. David Lloyd, Wasim's coach at Old Trafford, had no hesitation in appointing Wasim deputy captain when the two Mikes, Watkinson and Atherton, were on Test duty. He responded by leading Lancashire to a thrilling victory at Leicester, contributing twelve wickets and a match-winning unbeaten second innings fifty. Along with Allan Donald he is probably the most dangerous new ball bowler in world cricket, harnessing exceptional control with astute changes of pace and the ability to swing a ball, whatever its age. Waqar is more of an enigma but if he can regain his fitness and overcome the psychological stress of a severe back injury, he can be a lethal prospect. The tireless legspinner, Mushtaq, is, according to his own assessment, probably at the peak of his powers. At Sydney he matched the genius Warne in his range of flight, turn and mystery. Doubtless his long, hot summer at Taunton, where he seemed to bowl 40 overs every day, helped him to recapture his confidence and skills. The other Mushtaq is one to watch too, Saqlain, the young offspinner. So is the colt opening batsman, Salim Elahi, who went straight from school cricket to be tossed into the Pakistan team as a stand-in opener and become only the fourth player to score a hundred in his first limited-overs international. Pakistan's main problems lie in their administration which is government controlled and has conspired to have five changes of captain in two years, and in their fielding. The latter, such a key factor in the contracted version of the game, was absolutely abysmal in Australia. Perhaps it will recover on the lower-bouncing grounds at home.

On a 'horses for courses' basis, one must also fancy India to make the semi-finals. In Mohammed Azharuddin they have the most experienced captain in limited-overs internationl cricket now that Allan Border has stepped down. He led India for the hundredth time in these games during the recent visit by New Zealand. Under his command, he has a batting genius in Sachin Tendulkar, alone in scoring three Test hundreds before his 19th birthday, five before his 20th and seven before his 21st. Also at his disposal is the outstanding talent of Anil Kumble who last season became the first bowler to take a hundred wickets in the four-day County Championship. His top-spinners and drifters will pose greater dangers on the helpful surfaces of his home grounds.

Sri Lanka, the third host country, could easily join their colleagues in the semi-finals and go on to greater heights. They have already defeated Pakistan in both forms of international cricket this season and have the added bonus of playing four of their five preliminary matches at home. Arjuna Ranatunga is also approaching his century of appearances as captain in these internationals and he has the vastly experienced and talented Aravinda de Silva to tear apart attacks as he did Lancashire's during his magnificent hundred in last season's Benson and Hedges final. Roshan Mahanama has matured as an opening batsman and Ranatunga's attack includes the aggressive off-spinner Muthiah Muralitharan. You will see his first name spelt in various ways but that is the version he printed clearly on his biographical questionnaire. Although his action has inspired much criticism, it has passed inspection by every umpire he has bowled in front of and he will pose a major threat to opposing batsmen in this tournament. So too will the overnamed Warnakulasooriya Patabendige Ushantha Chaminda Joseph Vaas. Again that is the correct batting order for his names although the one he uses, Chaminda, is usually listed last. A left-hander, he moves the ball both ways at a lively medium pace and creates unusual problems with his different angle of delivery; definitely a player to watch.

Australia or England would be my tip to join the host countries in the semi-finals. At Test level, Australia can justifiably claim to be the current world champions, having convincingly beaten England, West Indies (on their own patch) and Pakistan within twelve months. They have a quite remarkable team spirit and will attack the opposition like a marauding horde of street fighters. Their fielding is outstanding, the batting line-up probably the strongest in world cricket and they have a superb wicket-keeping shop steward in Ian Healy. All that and Shane Warne too! In one-day cricket he is not quite the force that he is in the five-day game, particularly because of the field placing restrictions. Yet he averages nearly two wickets a match and concedes fewer than four runs an over, highly creditable figures for a 'leggie' in this type of cricket. He is a flamboyant character who tends to unsettle and dominate batsmen, a tremendous crowd-puller and entertainer. One only hopes that the Salim Malik saga will not cause crowd disruptions if Australia play any of their later matches in Pakistan – their five group games are in Sri Lanka and India.

Simply because they play more limited-overs domestic cricket than any other nation, England should start any World Cup tournament as favourites. Had the competition been staged in England (as its successor will be), that would definitely be the case. Recent England teams have not travelled well and memories of their batting and out-cricket on the 1992-93 tour of India and Sri Lanka, in which they lost all four Tests and won only three of their eight one-day games, give little cause for optimism. Under Michael Atherton they are a vastly improved side but their bowling, Dominic Cork apart, is suspect and their fielding inconsistent. Atherton and his guru, Raymond Illingworth, have achieved a formidable fighting spirit by example and careful selections. Can any international captain have been held in greater esteem by his players than Atherton is now? His innings at Johannesburg was the most remarkable I have witnessed in terms of commitment, concentration and endurance for nearly eleven hours. 'Jack' Russell's return to the side has been a major factor, a transformed player after his season as Gloucestershire's captain. At The Wanderers he inspired his captain to stay the course as they climbed their cricketing Everest, rather like Tensing had motivated Edmund Hilary in the same month that Watson and Bailey foiled Australia at Lord's. Instant cricket is a fickle game and all things are possible. Unless there are outside influences like crucial injuries or gross umpiring errors, the team that plays better on the day invariably wins. It would be extremely arrogant to write off any of the remaining seven sides. Although home advantage is often crucial, neither host country reached the Calcutta final nine years ago.

Since the anti-bouncer lobby gained power West Indies have struggled to dominate the one-day game. Anything above shoulder height is an expensive no-ball. Moreover the pitches in India, where Richie Richardson's team will play four of their group matches, are unlikely to help their pace battery. Their team is currently in a state of transition with several highly promising players on an upward learning curve. Their dressing room was a disaster area in terms of *esprit de corps* during last summer's tour of England. Currently in Australia to play against their hosts and Sri Lanka for the 'World Series', they may well gain by not being able to rely on Brian Lara scoring most of their runs. They have some outstanding fielders, potentially devastating batting and a lethal attack in certain conditions. The absence of a front-line spinner will tell against them and much will depend on whether Lara is selected for the World Cup and in what frame of mind he is, if he condescends to go. Undoubtedly his absence would greatly devalue the competition.

The lack of a class spin bowler will probably also prove crucial to South Africa's chances, although the inclusion of Paul Adams in their provisional squad is a thrilling selection. A diminutive 18-year-old left-arm unorthodox spinner, he has a uniquely contorted action in which he delivers the ball while looking at mid-off's feet. He gives the ball a real 'rip' and is astonishingly accurate. Devon Malcolm apart, England's batsmen had no idea what to make of him when he played for South Africa A against them last November. Playing in only his third first-class contest, he returned match figures of 67.1 overs, 16 maidens, 181 runs and 9 wickets. Atherton's side was relieved when the home selectors declined to gamble and include him in the first Test soon afterwards. 'Hansie' Cronje has proved a worthy successor to Kepler Wessels and in the short time since the Proteas' return to the international arena, they have shown themselves to be a well-drilled and hugely combative team. In Allan Donald they have the world's outstanding fast bowler and in 'Jonty' Rhodes one of the greatest outfielders of all time. The latter's balance, fleetness of foot and reaction speed are truly remarkable. And now they have Shaun Pollock, possibly a great all-rounder in the making. He is already a dangerous fast-medium bowler who will gain in pace as he fills out and he looks extremely useful with the bat. The presence of Malcolm Marshall as his captain for Natal hints that his development in the last two seasons has not come by accident.

With Glenn Turner as their 'Illingworth', New Zealand should soon recover their form and spirit. They were always going to struggle once the likes of Geoff Howarth, Jeremy Coney, John Wright and Richard Hadlee retired in a cluster. They have some useful players but this World Cup has probably been scheduled at least a season too early for the Kiwis to make much impact.

Zimbabwe could prove to be the dark horses. They will be sorry that England are not in their group, having beaten them in two of their three encounters, before narrowly losing the third. The Flower brothers, Andy and Grant, are staunch competitors, and in Dave Houghton they have a veteran with the invaluable experience of 20 World Cup appearances and compiler of the record score both for Zimbabwe and in all first-class matches in that country (266). Hampshire followers will not need reminding of Heath Streak's ability; a lively opening bowler with boundless enthusiasm and stamina, he has already made his mark at international level.

The three Associate members will attract plenty of interest and much is expected of the Emirates team, winners of the 1994 ICC Trophy competition in Kenya which produced the three qualifiers to join the nine Test-playing countries. With the exception of their captain, Sultan Zarawani, their entire squad hails from one or other of the three host countries. Their preparation for this tournament has been highly professional. Since mid-November 1995 they have played six one-day and two two-day matches against Indian State teams on a 17-day tour and competed with 'A' teams from India, Pakistan and Sri Lanka in Sharjah for the Interface Cup. Shortly before this guide is published they will be in Pakistan participating in that Board's domestic limited-overs tournament for the Wills Trophy, all providing excellent familiarisation for the World Cup itself.

Unlike the UAE team which has already appeared in two full internationals (v India and Pakistan in Sharjah during the Australasian Cup in April 1994), both Holland and Kenya will be making their debuts at this level. Their two cricketing cultures could hardly be more contrasting, with Holland playing in a relatively cool climate on artificial pitches, while Kenya's cricketers operate in extreme heat and humidity reminiscent of Sri Lanka, some of their grounds, particularly the Nairobi Gymkhana (the 'Lord's of Africa'), boasting locations as exotic as that surrounding the Asgiriya Stadium in Kandy. Although the Dutch team includes a number of imported cricketers, notably the former Barbados opener Nolan Clarke, who, at 47, will be the tournament's oldest player by some distance, their cricket has been kept alive by native-born players for more than a century. Holland's first known cricket club was formed at Northey as long ago as 1857 and they now have a thriving infrastructure and many delightful grounds. Their major problem lies in the soil, the Dutch variety being too soft to hold grass of any hard texture. However, they are starting to create turf pitches and their introduction to the NatWest Trophy last season can only help the game gain publicity in the Netherlands and so attract more Dutch youngsters to take it up. Kenya's cricket has been kept alive by the Asians living there but now some impressive African players are coming to the front, the Tikolo and Odumbe brethren providing a quarter of their provisional squad of 20. Both countries' participation in this World Cup can only provide a tremendous impetus for their prospective young cricketers.

The Wills World Cup will undoubtedly dominate the first quarter of 1996 and it will provide some spectacular action for those fortunate enough to witness the play and sample the unique atmosphere of the subcontinent. However, although it will create much needed funds for the impoverished cricket infrastructures of India and Pakistan, it will prove very little in cricketing terms. At the end of this event we shall have discovered which of the dozen teams is the most efficient at limited-overs cricket in certain conditions. Only a tournament featuring five-day Test matches could determine a true world champion.

WILLS WORLD CUP

REGISTER

Although each of the twelve competing nations was required to submit to PILCOM, the tournament's organising committee, the names of 20 selected players by 30 November 1995, only in the cases of England, Pakistan, South Africa, Holland and Kenya had these been made public at the time of our going to press (8 December).

Each Board was further required to reduce their selected lists of 20 to 14 players plus four reserves by 31 December 1995 and to a final squad of 14 by 22 January 1996. However, such was the ambiguity of the wording of the rules covering this selection process, that it was unclear as to whether or not the final 14 players had to be chosen from the original list of 20. England, believing that the supplying of 20 names more than three months before the competition was due to start, was merely to assist the organisers in their preparation of programmes and promotional material, for simplicity's sake just named the touring team of 16 currently in South Africa, adding the three limited-overs specialists nominated in September (Neil Fairbrother, Dermot Reeve and Neil Smith), plus a reserve wicket-keeper (Steve Rhodes). They assumed that they could introduce any other players, particularly the more successful members of the England A expedition then touring Pakistan (Dean Headley and Nasser Hussain), before the final deadline. South Africa's convenor of selectors, Peter Pollock, supported England's interpretation of the PILCOM regulations.

With the exception of the four teams listed above, this register includes 20 (or more) most probable players for each country, with apologies to any eventually selected player who has been inadvertently omitted.

All career statistics, except tours, are up to the end of the 1995 season (18 September).

Key to abbreviations:

*	not out/unbroken partnership	A	Australia
BB	best innings bowling analysis	E	England
Cap	awarded 1st XI County Cap	I	India
ct	catches	NZ	New Zealand
f-c	first-class	P	Pakistan
HS	highest score	SA	South Africa
st	stumpings	SL	Sri Lanka
Tests	official Test matches	WI	West Indies
		Z	Zimbabwe

WORLD CUP REGISTER

ENGLAND

All career statistics are up to the end of the 1995 season (18 September). Key to abbreviations on page 32. England's provisionally selected 20 players for the Wills World Cup are:

ATHERTON, Michael Andrew **(CAPTAIN) (Lancashire)**
Born Failsworth, Manchester 23 Mar 1968. 5' 11". Educated at Manchester Grammar School; Downing College, Cambridge U – BA (Hons). Right-hand opening batsman, occasional leg-break bowler. First captained England YC (U19) when aged 16 and led their tours to Sri Lanka 1986-87 and to Australia 1987-88. Cambridge U 1987-89 (blue 1987-88-89; captain 1988-89). Lancashire debut 1987. Cap 1989. Cricket Writers' Club Young Cricketer of 1990. One of *Wisden's* Five Cricketers of 1990. Appointed England captain 1993. **TESTS:** 51 (1989 to 1995, 24 as captain – 7 won, 10 lost, 7 drawn). 3812 runs (av 40.12), 8 hundreds; 1 wkt (av 282.00); 37 ct. HS 151 v NZ (Nottingham) 1990 – youngest Lancastrian to score a Test hundred. BB 1-60. **L-O INTERNATIONALS:** 25 (1990 to 1995, 15 as captain – won 9, lost 6). 1068 runs (av 46.43), 1 hundred; 9 ct. HS 127 v WI (Lord's) 1995. **TOURS** (f-c matches only; C = captain): A 1990-91, 1994-95C; SA 1995-96C; WI 1993-94C; I/SL 1992-93; Z 1989-90 (Eng A). **F-C CAREER:** 13,722 runs (av 44.12), 38 hundreds, 1000 runs in a season (6); most – 1924 (1990); 107 wkts (av 43.84), 5 wkts/inns (3); 167 ct. Scored 1193 in season of f-c debut (first instance since 1976). HS 199 v Durham (Gateshead) 1992. BB 6-78 v Notts (Nottingham) 1990. **1995 SEASON** (f-c): 1323 runs (av 44.10); 4 hundreds; 0 wkts.

CORK, Dominic Gerald **(Derbyshire)**
Born Newcastle-under-Lyme, Staffordshire 7 Aug 1971. 6' 2". Educated at St Joseph's College, Stoke-on-Trent; Newcastle College. Right-hand batsman, right-arm medium-fast bowler. Staffordshire 1989-90. Derbyshire debut 1990. Cap 1993. **TESTS:** 5 (1995). 197 runs (av 28.14); 26 wkts (av 25.42), 5 wkts/inns (1); 1 ct. HS 56* v WI (Manchester) 1995. BB 7-43 v WI (Lord's) 1995 – on debut (record England analysis by Test match debutant). Hat-trick v WI (Manchester) 1995 – the first in Test history to occur in the opening over of a day's play. **L-O INTERNATIONALS:** 8 (1992 to 1995). 25 runs (av 8.33); 11 wkts (av 31.27); 1 ct. HS 14 v WI (Nottingham) 1995. BB 3-27 v WI (Lord's) 1995. **TOURS** (f-c matches only): A 1992-93 (Eng A); SA 1993-94 (Eng A), 1995-96; WI 1991-92 (Eng A); I 1994-95 (Eng A). **F-C CAREER:** 2938 runs (av 22.60), 1 hundred; 318 wkts (av 25.32), 5 wkts/inns (9), 10 wkts/match (2), 50 wkts in a season (2); most – 90 (1995); 64 ct. HS 104 v Glos (Cheltenham) 1993. BB 9-43 (13-93 match) v Northants (Derby) 1995. Took 8-53 before lunch on his 20th birthday v Essex (Derby) 1991. 2 hat-tricks: v Kent (Derby) 1994 and England v WI (Manchester) 1995. **1995 SEASON** (f-c): 589 runs (av 21.81); 90 wkts (av 20.00), 5 wkts/inns (4), 10 wkts/match (1). Took a hat-trick for England v WI (Manchester).

CRAWLEY, John Paul **(Lancashire)**
Born Maldon, Essex 21 Sep 1971. Brother of M.A. (Oxford U 1987-90, Lancashire 1990, and Nottinghamshire 1991-94) and P.M. (Cambridge U 1992). 6' 1". Educated at Manchester Grammar School; Trinity College, Cambridge U – BA. Right-hand batsman, occasional right-arm medium-pace bowler/wicket-keeper. Captained England YC (U19) to New Zealand 1990-91 and in home series v Australia 1991. Lancashire debut 1990. Cap 1994. Cambridge U 1991-93 (blue 1991-92-93; captain 1992-93). Cricket Writers' Club Young Cricketer of 1994. **TESTS:** 9 (1994 to 1995). 330 runs (av 22.00); 9 ct. HS 72 v A (Sydney) 1994-95. **L-O INTERNATIONALS:** 3 (1994-95). 34 runs (av 11.33); 0 ct. HS 18 v Z (Sydney) 1994-95. **TOURS** (f-c matches only): A 1994-95; SA 1993-94 (Eng A), 1995-96. **F-C CAREER:** 7890 runs (av 48.70), 14 hundreds (inc 3 doubles), 1000 runs in a season (4); most – 1570 (1994); 1 wkt (av 108.00); 90 ct. HS 286 England A v Eastern Province (Port

CRAWLEY – continued:
Elizabeth) 1993-94. Lancs HS 281* v Somerset (Southport) 1994. BB 1-90. Made his maiden f-c hundred (for Cambridge U) on same day as his brother Mark made his (for Nottinghamshire). **1995 SEASON** (f-c): 1377 runs (av 47.48), 3 hundreds; did not bowl.

FAIRBROTHER, Neil Harvey (Lancashire)
Born Warrington, Lancashire 9 Sep 1963. 5′ 8″. Educated at Lymm Grammar School. Left-hand batsman, occasional left-arm medium bowler. Debut 1982. Cap 1985. Captain 1992-93. Benefit 1995. **TESTS:** 10 (1987 to 1992-93). 219 runs (av 15.64); 0 wkt; 1 ct. HS 83 v I (Madras) 1992-93. **L-O INTERNATIONALS:** 46 (1987 to 1995). 1341 runs (av 39.44), 1 hundred; 0 wkt; 19 ct. HS 113 v WI (Lord's) 1991. **TOURS** (f-c matches only): NZ 1987-88, 1991-92; I/SL 1992-93; P 1987-88, 1990-91 (Eng A); SL 1990-91 (Eng A). **F-C CAREER:** 15,227 runs (av 40.82), 33 hundreds (inc 2 doubles and 1 treble), 1000 runs in a season (9); most – 1740 (1990); 5 wkts (av 88.00); 191 ct. HS 366 v Surrey (Oval) 1990 (ground record), including 311 in a day and 100 or more in each session. BB 2-91 v Notts (Manchester) 1987. **1995 SEASON** (f-c): 602 runs (av 30.10), 2 hundreds; 0 wkts; 17 ct.

FRASER, Angus Robert Charles (Middlesex)
Born Billinge, Lancashire 8 Aug 1965. Brother of A.G.J. (Middlesex and Essex 1986-92). 6′ 5″. Educated at Gayton High School, Harrow; Orange Senior High School, Edgware. Right-hand batsman, right-arm fast-medium bowler. Middlesex debut 1984. Cap 1988. **TESTS:** 29 (1989 to 1995). 255 runs (av 7.50); 115 wkts (av 28.88), 5 wkts/inns (8); 7 ct. HS 29 v A (Nottingham) 1989. BB 8-75 v WI (Bridgetown) 1993-94 – record England analysis v WI. **L-O INTERNATIONALS:** 33 (1989-90 to 1995). 80 runs (av 10.00); 38 wkts (av 29.78), 4 wkts (1); 1 ct. HS 38* v A (Melbourne) 1990-91. BB 4-22 v A (Melbourne) 1994-95. **TOURS** (f-c matches only): A 1990-91, 1994-95 (part); SA 1995-96; WI 1989-90, 1993-94. **F-C CAREER:** 1657 runs (av 10.97); 556 wkts (av 26.58), 5 wkts/inns (22), 10 wkts/match (2), 50 wkts in a season (6); most – 92 (1989); 34 ct. HS 92 v Surrey (Oval) 1990. BB 8-75 (*see* TESTS). Middlesex BB 7-40 v Leics (Lord's) 1993. **1995 SEASON** (f-c): 95 runs (av 7.30); 56 wkts (av 29.14), 5 wkts/inns (2).

GOUGH, Darren (Yorkshire)
Born Barnsley, Yorkshire 18 Sep 1970. 5′ 11″. Educated at Priory Comprehensive School, Lundwood. Right-hand batsman, right-arm fast bowler. Yorkshire debut 1989. Cap 1993. **TESTS:** 10 (1994 to 1995). 317 runs (av 24.38); 43 wkts (av 28.97), 5wkts/inns (1); 6 ct. HS 65 v NZ (Manchester) 1994 – on debut. BB 6-49 v A (Sydney) 1994-95. Took wicket with sixth ball in Tests. **L-O INTERNATIONALS:** 10 (1994 to 1995). 78 runs (av 15.60); 17 wkts (av 20.58), 4 wkts (1); 2 ct. HS 45 v A (Melbourne) 1994-95. BB 5-44 v Z (Sydney) 1994-95. Took wicket with sixth ball in LOIs. **TOURS** (f-c matches only): A 1994-95; SA 1991-92 (Yorks), 1992-93 (Yorks), 1993-94 (Eng A), 1995-96. **F-C CAREER:** 1674 runs (av 16.90); 300 wkts (av 29.52), 5 wkts/inns (11), 10 wkts/match (2), 50 wkts in a season (3) – most 62 (1994); 24 ct. HS 72 v Northants (Northampton) 1991. BB 7-28 (10-80 match) v Lancs (Leeds) 1995 (friendly). Championship BB 7-42 (10-96 match) v Somerset (Taunton) 1993. Hat-trick and four wickets in 5 balls v Kent (Leeds) 1995. **1995 SEASON** (f-c): 332 runs (av 18.44); 51 wkts (av 26.76), 5 wkts/inns (1), 10 wkts/match (1).

HEADLEY, Dean Warren (Kent)
Born Norton, Stourbridge, Worcestershire 27 Jan 1970. 6′ 4″. Son of Ron G.A. Headley (Worcestershire, Jamaica and West Indies 1958 to 1974); grandson of George A. Headley, MBE (Jamaica and West Indies 1927-28 to 1953-54). Educated at Oldswinford Hospital School; Worcester Royal Grammar School. Right-hand batsman, right-arm fast-medium bowler. Debut Middlesex v MCC (Lord's) 1991. Took 5-46 on Championship debut v Yorks (Lord's) 1991, including the wicket of A.A.Metcalfe with his first ball. Middlesex 1991, 1992 (uncapped). Kent debut v Zimbabwe B (Harare) 1992-93. Kent cap 1993. **TESTS:** 0. **L-O INTERNATIONALS:** 0. **TOURS** (f-c matches): P 1995-96 (Eng A); Z 1992-93 (Kent). **F-C CAREER:** 1140 runs (av 17.81); 182 wkts (av 32.96), 5 wkts/inns (9), 10 wkts/match (0), 50 wkts in a season (0); 31 ct. HS 91 Middx v Leics (Leicester) 1992. Kent

HEADLEY – continued:
HS 54 v Worcs (Worcester) 1995. BB 7-58 (9-127 match) Kent v Sussex (Hove) 1995. **1995 SEASON** (f-c): 253 runs (av 14.05); 44 wkts (av 29.00), 5 wkts/inns (3).

HICK, Graeme Ashley (Worcestershire)
Born Salisbury, Rhodesia (now Harare, Zimbabwe) 23 May 1966. 6' 3". Educated at Prince Edward Boys' High School, Salisbury. Right-hand batsman, off-break bowler. Outstanding slip fielder. Zimbabwe 1983-84 to 1985-86. Worcestershire debut 1984. Cap 1986. N Districts 1987-88 to 1988-89. Queensland 1990-91. One of *Wisden's* Five Cricketers of 1986. Scored his first hundred when aged six (for Banket Primary School). At 17 was youngest player to appear in 1983 World Cup and youngest to represent Zimbabwe. **TESTS:** 37 (1991 to 1995). 2336 runs (av 37.67), 3 hundreds; 20 wkts (av 51.85); 55 ct. HS 178 v I (Bombay) 1992-93. BB 4-126 v NZ (Wellington) 1991-92. **L-O INTERNATIONALS:** 47 (1991 to 1995). 1571 runs (av 39.27), 1 hundred; 13 wkts (av 37.07); 25 ct. HS 105* v I (Gwalior) 1992-93. BB 3-41 v A (Melbourne) 1994-95. **TOURS** (f-c matches only): E 1985 (Z); A 1994-95; SA 1995-96; WI 1993-94; NZ 1991-92; I 1992-93; SL 1983-84 (Z), 1992-93; Z 1990-91 (Worcs). **F-C CAREER:** 25,194 runs (av 57.00), 84 hundreds (inc 8 doubles and one quadruple), 1000 runs in a season (11+1) inc 2000 (3); most – 2713 (1988); youngest to score 2000 (1986); scored 1019 runs before June 1988, including a record 410 runs in April; 187 wkts (av 42.86), 5 wkts/inns (5), 10 wkts/match (1); 369 ct. HS 405* (Worcs record and then the second highest in UK f-c matches) v Somerset (Taunton) 1988. BB 5-18 v Leics (Worcester) 1995. Fewest innings for 10,000 runs in county cricket (179). Youngest (24) to score 50 first-class hundreds. Scored 645 runs without being dismissed (UK record) in 1990. **1995 SEASON** (f-c): 1193 runs (av 49.70), 4 hundreds; 9 wkts (av 58.44), 5 wkts/inns (1).

HUSSAIN, Nasser (Essex)
Born Madras, India 28 Mar 1968. 5' 11". Son of Javaid ('Joe') Hussain (Madras 1966-67). Brother of Mehriyar ('Mel') Hussain (Worcestershire 1985 – 1 match). Educated at Forest School, Snaresbrook; Durham University (BSc Hons – Geology). Right-hand batsman, occasional leg-break bowler, outstanding close fielder. Debut 1987. Cap 1989. Cricket Writers' Club Young Cricketer of 1989. **TESTS:** 7 (1989-90 to 1993). 284 runs (av 25.81); 3 ct. HS 71 v A (Nottingham) 1993. **L-O INTERNATIONALS:** 4 (1989-90 to 1993-94). 43 runs (av 14.33); 2 ct. HS 16 v WI (St Vincent) 1993-94. **TOURS** (f-c matches): WI 1989-90, 1991-92 (Eng A), 1993-94; P 1990-91 (Eng A), 1995-96 (Eng A – captain); SL 1990-91 (Eng A). **F-C CAREER:** 9687 runs (av 44.84), 26 hundreds, 1000 runs in a season (3); most – 1854 (1995); 2 wkts (av 153.50); 208 ct. HS 197 v Surrey (Oval) 1990. BB 1-38 v Worcs (Kidderminster) 1992. **1995 SEASON** (f-c): 1854 runs (av 54.52), 6 hundreds; did not bowl; 34 ct.

ILLINGWORTH, Richard Keith (Worcestershire)
Born Bradford, Yorkshire 23 Aug 1963. 5' 11". Educated at Salts Grammar School, Saltaire, Bradford (*old boys include J.C.Laker*). Right-hand batsman, orthodox left-arm slow bowler. Worcestershire debut 1982. Cap 1986. Natal 1988-89. **TESTS:** 6 (all v WI – 1991 to 1995) 100 runs (av 20.00); 10 wkts (av 42.80); 3 ct. HS 17* v WI (Leeds) 1995. BB 4-96 v WI (Nottingham) 1995. Took wicket of P.V.Simmons (WI) with his first ball in Test cricket (Nottingham 1991) – 11th instance in Tests, sixth for England. Despite a fractured finger, batted 91 minutes to share an unbroken match-saving tenth-wicket stand of 80 with M.Watkinson v WI (Nottingham) 1995. **L-O INTERNATIONALS:** 18 (1991 to 1993). 61 runs (av 12.20); 24 wkts (av 31.66); 8 ct. HS 14 v P (Melbourne) 1991-92. BB 3-33 v Z (Albury) 1991-92. **TOURS** (f-c matches only): SA 1995-96; NZ 1991-92; P 1990-91 (Eng A); SL 1990-91 (Eng A); Z 1989-90 (Eng A), 1990-91 (Worcs), 1993-94 (Worcs). **F-C CAREER:** 5101 runs (av 21.25), 3 hundreds; 686 wkts (av 30.67), 5 wkts/inns (22), 10 wkts/match (5), 50 wkts in a season (4); most – 75 (1990); 127 ct. HS 120* v Warwks (Worcester) 1987 – as night-watchman. Scored 106 for England A v Z (Harare) 1989-90 – again as night-watchman. BB 7-50 v Oxford U (Oxford) 1985. Championship BB 6-28 v Glos (Gloucester) 1993. **1995 SEASON** (f-c): 160 runs (av 16.00); 45 wkts (av 26.93).

ILOTT, Mark Christopher **(Essex)**
Born Watford, Hertfordshire 27 Aug 1970. 6' 1". Educated at Francis Combe School, Garston, Watford. Left-hand batsman, left-arm fast-medium bowler. Essex debut 1988. Cap 1993. Hertfordshire 1987-88 (at 16, youngest to represent that county). **TESTS:** 3 (1993). 28 runs (av 7.00); 8 wkts (av 51.50); 0 ct. HS 15 v A (Birmingham) 1993. BB 3-108 v A (Nottingham) 1993 – on debut. **L-O INTERNATIONALS:** 0. **TOURS** (f-c matches): A 1992-93 (Eng A); SA 1993-94 (Eng A), 1995-96; I 1994-95 (part)(Eng A); SL 1990-91 (Eng A). **F-C CAREER:** 1235 runs (av 13.72); 353 wkts (av 28.24), 5 wkts/inns (18), 10 wkts/match (3), 50 wkts in a season (4); most – 78 (1995); 27 ct. HS 60 England A v Warwicks (Birmingham) 1995. Essex HS 51 v Sussex (Hove) 1993. BB 9-19 (14-105 match) v Northants (Luton) 1995. Missed entire 1991 season because of stress fracture of spine. **1995 SEASON** (f-c): 350 runs (av 14.00); 78 wkts (av 24.32), 5 wkts/inns (6), 10 wkts/match (2).

MALCOLM, Devon Eugene **(Derbyshire)**
Born Kingston, Jamaica 22 Feb 1963. 6' 2". Educated at St Elizabeth Technical High School; Richmond College, Sheffield; Derby College of Higher Education. Qualified for England 1987. Right-hand batsman, right-arm fast bowler. Derbyshire debut 1984. Cap 1989. Benefit 1997. **TESTS:** 34 (1989 to 1995). 223 runs (av 6.55); 116 wkts (av 36.60), 5wkts/inns (5), 10wkts/match (2); 5 ct. HS 29 v A (Sydney) 1994-95. BB 9-57 v SA (Oval) 1994 – sixth best analysis in Test cricket. **L-O INTERNATIONALS:** 10 (1990 to 1993-94). 9 runs (av 3.00); 16 wkts (av 25.25); 1 ct. HS 4, BB 3-40 v I (Gwalior) 1992-93. **TOURS** (f-c matches only): A 1990-91, 1994-95; SA 1995-96; WI 1989-90, 1991-92 (Eng A), 1993-94; I 1992-93; SL 1992-93. **F-C CAREER:** 1251 runs (av 7.91); 627 wkts (av 31.00), 5 wkts/inns (20), 10 wkts/match (3), 50 wkts in a season (4); most – 69 (1994); 30 ct. HS 51 v Surrey (Derby) 1989. BB 9-57 (see TESTS). Derbyshire BB 6-57 v Sussex (Derby) 1993. **1995 SEASON** (f-c): 125 runs (av 7.35); 65 wkts (av 26.03), 5 wkts/inns (3), 10 wkts/match (1).

MARTIN, Peter James **(Lancashire)**
Born Accrington, Lancashire 15 Nov 1968. 6' 4". Educated at Danum School, Doncaster. Right-hand batsman, right-arm fast-medium bowler. Lancashire debut 1989. Cap 1994. **TESTS:** 3 (1995). 52 runs (av 8.66); 5 wkts (av 48.20); 4 ct. HS 29 and BB 2-65 v WI (Lord's) 1995. **L-O INTERNATIONALS:** 2 (1995). 4 runs (av –); 6 wkts (av 13.33), 4 wkts (1); 0 ct. HS 4* v WI (Lord's) 1995. BB 4-44 v WI (Oval) 1995 – on debut. **TOUR** (f-c matches only): SA 1995-96. **F-C CAREER:** 1723 runs (av 21.01), 1 hundred; 223 wkts (av 33.65), 5 wkts/inns (3), 10 wkts/match (0), 50 wkts in a season (1): 54 (1994); 28 ct. HS 133 v Durham (Gateshead) 1992. BB 5-35 v Yorks (Leeds) 1993 (friendly). Championship BB 5-61 v Northants (Northampton) 1994. **1995 SEASON** (f-c): 300 runs (av 20.00); 35 wkts (av 26.34).

RAMPRAKASH, Mark Ravin **(Middlesex)**
Born Bushey, Hertfordshire 5 Sep 1969. 5' 9". Son of Guyanese father and English (Essex-born) mother. Educated at Gayton High School; Harrow Weald Sixth Form College. Right-hand batsman, off-break bowler (formerly medium-pace). Outstanding cover fielder. Middlesex debut 1987. Cap 1990. Cricket Writers' Club Young Cricketer of 1991. **TESTS:** 17 (inc 11 v WI)(1991 to 1995). 520 runs (av 17.93); 0 wkts; 12 ct. HS 72 v A (Perth) 1994-95 having been drafted from England A tour of India as emergency replacement. **L-O INTERNATIONALS:** 7 (1991 to 1995 – all v WI). 124 runs (av 31.00); has not bowled; 4 ct. HS 32 v WI (Nottingham) 1995. **TOURS** (f-c matches only): A 1994-95 (part); SA 1995-96; WI 1991-92 (Eng A), 1993-94; NZ 1991-92; I 1994-95 (Eng A); P 1990-91 (Eng A); SL 1990-91 (Eng A). **F-C CAREER:** 11,519 runs (av 45.35), 29 hundreds (inc 4 doubles), 1000 runs in a season (6) including 2000 (1): 2258 (1995); 12 wkts (av 71.66); 103 ct. HS 233 v Surrey (Lord's) 1992. BB 3-91 v Somerset (Taunton) 1995. **1995 SEASON** (f-c): 2258 runs (av 77.86), 10 hundreds; 4 wkts (av 27.00). Only batsman to score 2000 runs, reaching target on 11 September. Scored hundreds in three successive innings.

REEVE, Dermot Alexander **(Warwickshire)**
Born Kowloon, Hong Kong 2 Apr 1963. 6' 0". Educated at King George V School, Kowloon. Right-hand batsman, right-arm medium fast bowler. Sussex 1983-87 (cap 1986). Warwickshire debut 1988. Cap 1989. Captain 1993-96. Benefit 1996. Hong Kong 1982 (ICC Trophy). MCC Young Cricketer. **TESTS:** 3 (1991-92). 124 runs (av 24.80); 2 wkts (av 30.00); 1 ct. HS 59 v NZ (Christchurch) 1991-92 (on debut); BB 1-4. **L-O INTERNATIONALS:** 25 (1991 to 1994). 241 runs (av 30.12); 18 wkts (av 38.11); 11 ct. HS 33* v I (Chandigarh) 1992-93. BB 3-20 v NZ (Auckland) 1991-92. **TOURS** (f-c matches only; C = captain): SA 1992-93C (Warwks); NZ 1991-92; I 1992-93; Z 1993-94C (Warwks). **F-C CAREER:** 8190 runs (av 34.41), 6 hundreds (inc 1 double), 1000 runs in a season 2); most – 1412 (1990); 447 wkts (av 26.92), 5 wkts/inns (7), 10 wkts/match (0), 50 wkts in a season; most – 55 (1984); 193 ct. HS 202* Warwks v Northants (Northampton) 1990. BB 7-37 Sussex v Lancs (Lytham) 1987. Warwks BB 6-73 v Kent (Tunbridge Wells) 1991. **1995 SEASON** (f-c): 652 runs (av 36.22); 38 wkts (av 17.39), 5 wkts/inns (1); 17 ct.

RHODES, Steven John (Worcestershire)
Born Bradford, Yorkshire 17 Jun 1964. Son of W.E. (Nottinghamshire 1961-64). 5' 7". Educated in Bradford at Lapage Middle School and Carlton-Bolling School. Right-hand batsman, wicket-keeper. Yorkshire 1981-84. Worcestershire debut 1985. Cap 1986. One of *Wisden's* Five Cricketers of 1994. **TESTS:** 11 (1994 to 1994-95). 294 runs (av 24.50); 46 ct, 3 st. HS 65* v SA (Leeds) 1994. **L-O INTERNATIONALS:** 9 (1989 to 1994-95). 107 runs (av 17.83); 9 ct, 2 st. HS 56 v SA (Manchester) 1994. **TOURS** (f-c matches only): A 1994-95; SA 1993-94 (Eng A); WI 1991-92 (Eng A); SL 1985-86 (Eng B), 1990-91 (Eng A); Z 1989-90 (Eng A), 1990-91 (Wo), 1993-94 (Wo). **F-C CAREER:** 9246 runs (av 32.90), 8 hundreds, 1000 runs in a season (1): 1018 (1995); 0 wkts; 734 ct, 95 st. HS 122* v Young Australia (Worcester) 1995. Championship HS 116* v Warwks (Worcester) 1992. **1995 SEASON** (f-c): 1018 runs (av 40.72), 1 hundred; 51 ct, 7 st.

RUSSELL, Robert Charles ('Jack') (Gloucestershire)
Born Stroud, Gloucestershire 15 Aug 1963. 5' 8½". Educated at Archway Comprehensive School. Left-hand batsman, wicket-keeper, very occasional off-break bowler. Gloucestershire debut 1981. Cap 1985. Benefit 1994. Captain 1995. Youngest Gloucestershire wicket-keeper (17 years 307 days) and set record for most dismissals in a match on first-class debut: 8 (7 ct, 1 st) v Sri Lankans (Bristol) 1981. One of *Wisden's* Five Cricketers of 1989. **TESTS:** 39 (1988 to 1995). 1454 runs (av 28.50), 1 hundred; 108 dismissals (99 ct, 9 st). HS 128* v A (Manchester) 1989. Held 6ct/inns v A (Melbourne) 1990-91 and 5 ct/inns v WI (Bridgetown) 1989-90. Scored 94 (then his HS in first-class cricket) as night-watchman on his Test debut (v SL at Lord's). **L-O INTERNATIONALS:** 26 (1987-88 to 1991). 261 runs (av 20.07); 31 dismissals (26 ct, 5 st). HS 50 v I (Nottingham) 1990. **TOURS** (f-c matches only): A 1990-91, 1992-93 (Eng A); SA 1995-96; WI 1989-90, 1993-94; NZ 1991-92; P 1987-88; SL 1986-87 (Glos). *Stood by for injured Alec Stewart for final phase of 1994-95 tour of Australia but played in no first-class matches.* F-C CAREER: 10,446 runs (av 29.01), 4 hundreds; 1 wkt (av 53.00); 847 dismissals (751 ct, 96 st). HS 128* *(see TESTS)*. Glos HS 120 v Somerset (Bristol) 1990. BB 1-4 v WI (Bristol) 1991. Held 2 catches off successive balls v Surrey (Oval) 1986 (the first off C.A.Walsh, followed by two off D.V.Lawrence) to equal the world first-class record set by G.O.Dawkes in 1958. **1995 SEASON** (f-c): 977 runs (av 44.40); 52 dismissals (50 ct, 2 st). Scored 8 fifties in 26 innings (HS 91). Captained Gloucestershire in 14 matches (7 wins, 3 defeats, 4 draws).

SMITH, Neil Michael Knight **(Warwickshire)**
Born Birmingham 27 Jul 1967. Son of M.J.K. (Leicestershire, Warwickshire and England 1951-75). 6' 0". Educated at Warwick School. Right-hand batsman, off-break bowler. Debut 1987. Cap 1993. MCC Young Cricketer. **TESTS:** 0. **L-0 INTERNATIONALS:** 0. **TOURS** (f-c matches only) (Warwks): SA 1991-92; Z 1993-94. **F-C CAREER:** 2816 runs (av 24.48), 1 hundred; 199 wkts (av 38.27), 5 wkts/inns (12), 10 wkts/match (0), 50 wkts in a season (0); 26 ct. HS 161 v Yorks (Leeds) 1989. BB 7-42 v Lancs (Birmingham) 1994. **1995 SEASON** (f-c): 486 runs (av 23.14); 39 wkts (av 35.25), 5 wkts/inns (3).

SMITH, Robin Arnold **(Hampshire)**
Born Durban, South Africa 13 Sep 1963. Brother of C.L. (Natal, Glamorgan, Hampshire and England 1977-78 to 1992) and grandson of Dr V.L.Shearer (Natal). 5' 11". Educated at Northlands Boys' High School, Durban. Right-hand batsman, occasional leg-break bowler. Natal 1980-81 to 1984-85. Hampshire debut 1982. Cap 1985. Benefit 1996. One of *Wisden*'s Five Cricketers of 1989. **TESTS:** 57 (1988 to 1995). 3982 runs (av 44.24); 9 hundreds; 0 wkts; 35 ct. HS 175 v WI (St John's) 1993-94. Top-scorer in 4 successive innings v WI in 1995: 61 and 90 at Lord's and 46 and 41 at Birmingham. Scored hundreds in his first Tests against India and Pakistan. **L-O INTERNATIONALS:** 64 (1988 to 1994). 2218 runs (av 40.32), 4 hundreds; 23 ct. HS 167* v A (Birmingham) 1993 – record England score in LOIs. **TOURS** (f-c matches only): A 1990-91; SA 1995-96; WI 1989-90, 1993-94; NZ 1991-92; I/SL 1992-93. **F-C CAREER:** 18,930 runs (av 44.75), 48 hundreds (inc 1 double), 1000 runs in a season (9); most – 1577 (1989); 12 wkts (av 57.75); 177 ct. HS 209* v Essex (Southend) 1987. BB 2-11 v Surrey (Southampton) 1985. **1995 SEASON** (f-c): 1117 runs (av 53.19), 3 hundreds. Suffered depressed fracture of cheek bone during Fourth Test at Manchester and missed remainder of season.

STEWART, Alec James **(VICE-CAPTAIN) (Surrey)**
Born Merton, Surrey 8 Apr 1963. Son of M.J. (Surrey and England 1954-72). 5' 11". Educated at Tiffin Boys' School, Kingston-upon-Thames. Right-hand opening batsman, wicket-keeper, occasional right-arm medium pace bowler. Surrey debut 1981. Cap 1985. Captain 1992 to date. Benefit 1994. One of *Wisden*'s Five Cricketers of 1992. **TESTS:** 48 (1989-90 to 1995, 2 as captain – 2 lost). 3168 runs (av 39.11), 7 hundreds; 64 ct, 4 st. HS 190 v P (Birmingham) 1992. Scored hundreds in his first Tests against Sri Lanka and Pakistan. Carried his bat through the innings v P (Lord's) 1992. Only England batsman to score hundred in each innings v WI (118 and 143 at Bridgetown 1993-94). **L-O INTERNATIONALS:** 64 (1989-90 to 1995, 6 as captain – won 2, lost 4). 1665 runs (av 30.27), 1 hundred; 50 ct, 4 st. HS 103 v P (Oval) 1992. **TOURS** (f-c matches only): A 1990-91, 1994-95; SA 1995-96; WI 1989-90, 1993-94; NZ 1991-92; I 1992-93; SL 1992-93 (captain). **F-C CAREER:** 16,462 runs (av 39.57), 33 hundreds (inc 1 double), 1000 runs in a season (8); most – 1665 (1986); 3 wkts (av 131.00); 367 ct, 13 st. HS 206* v Essex (Oval) 1989. BB 1-7 v Lancs (Manchester) 1989. Held 11 catches (equalling world f-c match record) v Leics (Leicester) 1989. **1995 SEASON** (f-c): 647 runs (av 38.05), 2 hundreds; 0 wkts; 23 ct. Because of finger injury he played only 10 matches.

THORPE, Graham Paul **(Surrey)**
Born Farnham, Surrey 1 Aug 1969. 5' 11". Educated at Weydon Comprehensive School; Farnham Sixth Form College. Left-hand batsman, occasional right-arm medium-pace bowler, specialist slip fielder. Surrey debut 1988. Cap 1991. **TESTS:** 21 (1993 to 1995). 1658 runs (av 43.63), 2 hundreds; 21 ct. HS 123 v A (Perth) 1994-95. Scored 114* v A (Nottingham) 1993 on debut. **L-O INTERNATIONALS:** 13 (1993 to 1995). 353 runs (av 27.15); 6 ct. HS 89 v Z (Brisbane) 1994-95. **TOURS** (f-c matches only): A 1992-93 (Eng A), 1994-95; SA 1995-96; WI 1991-92 (Eng A), 1993-94; P 1990-91 (Eng A); SL 1990-91 (Eng A); Z 1989-90 (Eng A). **F-C CAREER:** 10,393 runs (av 42.24), 18 hundreds (inc 1 double), 1000 runs in a season (6); most – 1895 (1992); 22 wkts (av 50.36); 121 ct. HS 216 v Somerset (Oval) 1992. BB 4-40 v Australians (Oval) 1993. Championship BB 2-31 v Essex (Oval) 1989. **1995 SEASON** (f-c): 1223 runs (av 40.76), 2 hundreds; 2 wkts (av 29.50).

ROBIN SMITH'S 167 NOT OUT

RECORD ENGLAND SCORE IN LIMITED–OVERS INTERNATIONALS

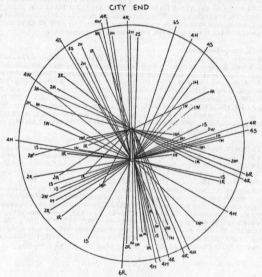

CITY END

PAVILION END

BOWLER	SYMBOL	BALLS	R U N S					TOTAL	PER 100 BALLS
			1	2	3	4	6		
McDERMOTT	Mc	20	6	2	·	·	·	10	50·0
HUGHES	H	31	6	5	·	5	·	36	116·1
REIFFEL	R	45	7	4	·	6	2	51	113·3
MAY	M	32	9	2	2	1	·	23	71·8
S.R.WAUGH	S	24	7	1	1	3	1	30	125·0
M.E.WAUGH	W	11	5	2	·	2	·	17	154·5
TOTALS		163	40	16	3	17	3	167	102·4

ENGLAND v AUSTRALIA
2ND TEXACO TROPHY INTERNATIONAL
AT EDGBASTON, BIRMINGHAM
ON FRIDAY, 21 MAY 1993

© BILL FRINDALL 1993

UDAL, Shaun David **(Hampshire)**
Born Cove, Farnborough, Hampshire 18 Mar 1969. 6' 2". Grandson of G.F.U. (Middlesex 1932 and Leicestershire 1946). Great-grandson of J.S. (MCC 1871-75; former Attorney-General of Fiji and Chief Justice of Leeward Islands). Educated at Cove Comprehensive School. Right-hand batsman, off-break bowler. Debut 1989. Cap 1992. **TESTS:** 0. **L-O INTERNATIONALS:** 10 (1994 to 1995). 35 runs (av 17.50); 8 wkts (av 46.50.); 1 ct. HS 11* v Z (Brisbane) 1994-95. BB 2-37 v A (Sydney) 1994-95. **TOURS** (f-c matches): A 1994-95; P 1995-96 (Eng A). **F-C CAREER:** 2214 runs (av 21.28); 285 wkts (av 32.85), 5 wkts/inns (19), 10 wkts/match (4), 50 wkts in a season (4); most 74 – (1993); 43 ct. HS 94 v Glam (Southampton) 1994. BB 8-50 v Sussex (Southampton) 1992. **1995 SEASON** (f-c): 512 runs (av 20.48); 55 wkts (av 33.89), 5 wkts/inns (5), 10 wkts/match (1).

WHITE, Craig (Yorkshire)
Born Morley, Yorkshire 16 Dec 1969. 6' 0". Educated in Victoria, Australia at Flora Hill High School, Bendigo and Bendigo High School. Right-hand batsman, right-arm fast-medium bowler. Debut 1990. Cap 1993. Victoria 1990-91 (2 matches). **TESTS:** 6 (1994 to 1995). 157 runs (av 15.70); 8 wkts (av 41.75), 3 ct. HS 51 v NZ (Lord's) 1994. BB 3-18 v NZ (Manchester) 1994. **L-O INTERNATIONALS:** 1 (v A, Sydney, 1994-95). 0 runs; 0 wkts; 0 ct. **TOURS** (f-c matches): A 1991-92 (Yorks); SA 1991-92 (Yorks); P 1995-96 (Eng A). **F-C CAREER:** 3616 runs (av 32.87), 5 hundreds, 1000 runs in a season (0); 95 wkts (av 30.52), 5 wkts/inns (3), 10 wkts/match (0), 50 wkts in a season (0); 52 ct. HS 146 Yorks v Durham (Leeds) 1993. BB 5-40 Yorks v Essex (Leeds) 1994. **1995 SEASON** (f-c): 874 runs (av 31.21), 3 hundreds; 25 wkts (av 37.36).

WATKINSON, Michael (Lancashire)
Born Westhoughton, Lancashire 1 Aug 1961. 6' 1". Educated at Rivington and Blackrod HS, Horwich. Qualified draughtsman (HTC Civil Engineering). Right-hand batsman, right-arm medium-fast or off-break bowler. Lancashire debut 1982. Cap 1987. Captain 1994 to date. Cheshire 1982. **TESTS:** 3 (1995). 156 runs (av 52.00); 8 wkts (av 36.12); 1 ct. HS 82* v WI (Nottingham) 1995, sharing unbroken match-saving tenth-wicket stand of 80 with Richard Illingworth. BB 3-64 v WI (Manchester) 1995 – on debut. **L-O INTERNATIONALS:** 0. **TOUR** (f-c matches only): SA 1995-96. **F-C CAREER:** 8984 runs (av 26.89), 9 hundreds, 1000 runs in a season (1): 1016 (1993); 639 wkts (av 33.12), 5 wkts/inns (25), 10 wkts/match (3), 50 wkts in a season (7); most – 66 (1992); 125 ct. HS 161 v Essex (Manchester) 1995. BB 8-30 (11-87 match) v Hants (Manchester) 1994 – completing match 'double' by scoring 128 runs. Hat-trick v Warwicks (Birmingham) 1992. **1995 SEASON** (f-c): 887 runs (av 34.11), 2 hundreds; 65 wkts (av 29.38), 5 wkts/inns (2), 10 wkts/match (1).

WORLD CUP CAREER RECORDS

ENGLAND – BATTING AND FIELDING

	M	I	NO	HS	Runs	Avge	100	50	Ct/St
Allott, P.J.W.	7	3	1	8	8	4.00	–	–	1
Amiss, D.L.	4	4	–	137	243	60.75	1	1	1
Arnold, G.G.	3	1	1	18*	18	–	–	–	1
Athey, C.W.J.	6	6	2	86	211	52.75	–	2	4
Botham, I.T.	22	18	2	53	297	18.56	–	1	10
Boycott, G.	5	5	1	57	92	23.00	–	1	1
Brearley, J.M.	5	5	–	64	161	32.20	–	2	4
Broad, B.C.	3	3	–	36	67	22.33	–	–	1
Cowans, N.G.	1	–	–	–	–	–	–	–	1
DeFreitas, P.A.J.	18	11	3	23	95	11.87	–	–	5
Denness, M.H.	4	4	2	37*	113	56.50	–	–	1
Dilley, G.R.	6	4	2	31*	90	45.00	–	–	1
Downton, P.R.	8	5	1	9	19	4.75	–	–	8/1
Edmonds, P.H.	3	2	1	5*	7	7.00	–	–	–
Emburey, J.E.	8	7	2	30*	96	19.20	–	–	3
Fairbrother, N.H.	9	7	2	75*	285	57.00	–	3	6
Fletcher, K.W.R.	4	3	–	131	207	69.00	1	1	1
Foster, N.A.	7	4	3	20*	42	42.00	–	–	1
Fowler, G.	7	7	2	81*	360	72.00	–	4	–
Gatting, M.W.	15	13	2	60	437	39.72	–	3	3
Gooch, G.A.	21	21	1	115	897	44.85	1	8	3
Gould, I.J.	7	4	1	35	66	22.00	–	–	11/1
Gower, D.I.	12	11	3	130	434	54.25	1	1	2
Greig, A.W.	4	4	–	9	29	7.25	–	–	–
Hayes, F.C.	3	3	–	52	90	30.00	–	1	–
Hemmings, E.E.	6	1	1	4*	4	–	–	–	2
Hendrick, M.	5	2	1	1*	1	1.00	–	–	3
Hick, G.A.	10	9	1	83	264	33.00	–	3	5
Illingworth, R.K.	6	3	1	14	27	13.50	–	–	3
Jameson, J.A.	2	2	–	21	32	16.00	–	–	–
Knott, A.P.E.	4	2	1	18*	18	18.00	–	–	1
Lamb, A.J.	19	17	4	102	656	50.46	1	3	9
Larkins, W.	2	2	–	7	7	3.50	–	–	–
Lever, P.	4	1	–	5	5	5.00	–	–	1
Lewis, C.C.	9	6	2	33	81	20.25	–	–	4
Marks, V.J.	7	3	–	8	18	6.00	–	–	2
Miller, G.	1	–	–	–	–	–	–	–	–
Old, C.M.	9	7	2	51*	91	18.20	–	1	2
Pringle, D.R.	11	7	2	18*	50	10.00	–	–	2
Randall, D.W.	5	5	1	42*	64	16.00	–	–	1
Reeve, D.A.	9	5	3	25*	79	9.50	–	–	5
Robinson, R.T.	7	7	–	55	142	20.28	–	1	1
Small, G.C.	13	4	1	5	8	2.66	–	–	4
Smith, R.A.	8	8	2	91	193	32.16	–	1	3
Snow, J.A.	3	1	–	2	2	2.00	–	–	–
Stewart, A.J.	10	8	1	77	259	37.00	–	2	8/1
Tavaré, C.J.	7	7	–	58	212	30.28	–	1	2
Taylor, R.W.	5	3	1	20*	32	16.00	–	–	4
Tufnell, P.C.R.	4	2	2	3*	3	–	–	–	–
Underwood, D.L.	2	–	–	–	–	–	–	–	–
Willis, R.G.D.	11	4	1	24	25	8.33	–	–	4
Wood, B.	3	2	–	77	83	41.50	–	1	–

ENGLAND – BOWLING

	O	M	R	W	Avge	Best	4w	R/O
Allott, P.J.W.	80.3	10	335	8	41.87	3-41	–	4.16
Arnold, G.G.	29.4	7	70	3	23.33	1-15	–	2.35
Athey, C.W.J.	1	0	10	0	–	–	–	10.00
Botham, I.T.	222	33	762	30	25.40	4-31	1	3.43
Boycott, G.	27	1	94	5	18.80	2-14	–	3.48
Broad, B.C.	1	0	6	0	–	–	–	6.00
Cowans, N.G.	12	3	31	2	15.50	2-31	–	2.58
DeFreitas, P.A.J.	154.4	24	602	23	26.17	3-28	–	3.89
Dilley, G.R.	66	4	243	7	34.71	4-45	1	3.68
Edmonds, P.H.	26	3	73	3	24.33	2-40	–	2.80
Emburey, J.E.	79	4	295	6	49.16	2-26	–	3.73
Foster, N.A.	70	1	313	9	34.77	3-47	–	4.47
Gatting, M.W.	12	3	48	1	48.00	1-35	–	4.00
Gooch, G.A.	23	2	115	1	115.00	1-42	–	5.00
Greig, A.W.	31	2	89	6	14.83	4-45	1	2.87
Hemmings, E.E.	59.3	4	274	13	21.07	4-52	1	4.60
Hendrick, M.	56	14	149	10	14.90	4-15	1	2.66
Hick, G.A.	14.2	0	70	2	35.00	2-44	–	4.88
Illingworth, R.K.	58.1	2	250	8	31.25	3-33	–	4.29
Jameson, J.A.	2	1	3	0	–	–	–	1.50
Lamb, A.J.	1	0	3	0	–	–	–	3.00
Larkins, W.	2	0	21	0	–	–	–	10.50
Lever, P.	36	3	92	5	18.40	3-32	–	2.55
Lewis, C.C.	50.4	5	214	7	30.57	4-30	1	4.22
Marks, V.J.	78	9	246	13	18.92	5-39	1	3.15
Miller, G.	2	1	1	0	–	–	–	0.50
Old, C.M.	90.3	18	243	16	15.18	4- 8	1	2.68
Pringle, D.R.	90.4	15	366	8	45.75	3- 8	–	4.03
Reeve, D.A.	34.4	4	126	8	15.75	3-38	–	3.63
Small, G.C.	103	5	458	11	41.63	2-29	–	4.44
Snow, J.A.	36	8	65	6	10.83	4-11	1	1.80
Tufnell, P.C.R.	28	2	133	3	44.33	2-36	–	4.75
Underwood, D.L.	22	7	41	2	20.50	2-30	–	1.86
Willis, R.G.D.	118.1	27	315	18	17.50	4-11	2	2.66
Wood, B.	12	5	14	0	–	–	–	1.16

WORLD CUP REGISTER

AUSTRALIA

The Australian World Cup selections had not been released at the time of going to press. All career statistics are up to the end of the 1995 season (18 September). Key to abbreviations on page 32.

BEVAN, Michael Gwyl **(New South Wales)**
Born Belconnen, ACT 8 May 1970. Left-hand batsman, left-arm slow bowler (Chinamen/googlies). South Australia 1989-90. NSW debut 1990-91. Yorkshire debut/cap 1995. **TESTS:** 6 (1994-95). 324 runs (av 32.40); 1 wkt (av 67.00), 3 ct. HS 91 and BB 1-21 v P (Lahore) 1994-95. **L-O INTERNATIONALS:** 15 (1993-94 to 1994-95). 432 runs (av 54.00); 0 wkts; 6 ct. HS 53* v P (Lahore) 1994-95. **F-C CAREER:** 6486 runs (av 51.07), 22 hundreds; 16 wkts (av 74.87), 52 ct. HS 203* v WA (Sydney) 1993-94. BB 3-6 v Wellington (Sydney) 1990-91.

BLEWETT, Gregory Scott **(South Australia)**
Born North Adelaide 29 Oct 1971. Right-hand batsman, right-arm medium pace bowler. South Australia debut 1991-92. **TESTS:** 6 (1994-95). 381 runs (av 42.33), 2 hundreds; 0 wkts; 8 ct. HS 115 v E (Perth) 1994-95. Scored 102* v E (Adelaide) on debut. **L-O INTERNATIONALS:** 8 (1994-95). 111 runs (av 13.87); 4 wkts (av 62.25); 1 ct. HS 46 v I (Dunedin) 1994-95. BB 1-30. **F-C CAREER:** 3579 runs (av 45.88), 9 hundreds; 31 wkts (av 38.12); 25 ct. HS 268 v Victoria (Melbourne) 1993-94. BB 4-39 v NSW (Adelaide) 1994-95.

BOON, David Clarence, MBE **(Tasmania)**
Born Launceston 29 Dec 1960. 5′ 7½″. Educated Launceston Grammar School. Right-hand batsman, off-break bowler. Tasmania debut 1978-79. **TESTS:** 101 (1984-85 to 1994-95). 7111 runs (av 44.16), 20 hundreds; 0 wkts; 94 ct. HS 200 v NZ (Perth) 1989-90. **L-O INTERNATIONALS:** 181 (1983-84 to 1994-95). 5964 runs (av 37.04), 5 hundreds; 0 wkts; 45 ct. HS 122 v SL (Adelaide) 1987-88. **F-C CAREER:** 17,547 runs (av 46.29), 55 hundreds; 7 wkts (av 55.57); 208 ct. HS 227 v Victoria (Melbourne) 1983-84. BB 1-12.

FLEMING, Damien William **(Victoria)**
Born Bentley, WA 24 Apr 1970. Right-hand batsman, right-arm fast-medium bowler. Victoria debut 1989-90. **TESTS:** 4 (1994-95). 40 runs (av 10.00); 17 wkts (av 25.58), 1 hat-trick; 2 ct. HS 24 v E (Adelaide) 1994-95. BB 4-75 v P (Rawalpindi) 1994-95. **L-O INTERNATIONALS:** 14 (1993-94 to 1994-95). 13 runs (av 13.00); 20 wkts (av 25.85); 3 ct. HS 5*. BB 4-39 v NZ (Sharjah) 1993-94. **F-C CAREER:** 515 runs (av 15.14); 170 wkts (av 28.50), 5 wkts/inns (6); 26 ct. HS 63* Victoria v SL (Sale) 1989-90. BB 7-90 v S Aus (Adelaide) 1992-93.

HAYDEN Matthew Lawrence **(Queensland)**
Born Kingaroy, Queensland 29 Oct 1971. 6′ 2″. Educated at Marist College, Ashgrove; Queensland University of Technology. Left-hand batsman, right-arm medium pace bowler. Queensland debut 1991-92. **TESTS:** 1 (1993-94). 20 runs (av 10.00); 1 ct. HS 15 v SA (Johannesburg) 1993-94. **L-O INTERNATIONALS:** 13 (1993 to 1993-94). 286 runs (av 26.00); 4 ct. HS 67 v NZ (Sharjah) 1993-94. **F-C CAREER:** 6219 runs (av 57.05), 19 hundreds; 1 wkt (av 116.00); 59 ct. HS 201* v Victoria (Brisbane) 1994-95. BB 1-24.

HEALY, Ian Andrew **(Queensland)**
Born Spring Hill, Brisbane 30 Apr 1964. 5' 9". Educated at Brisbane State High School. Right-hand batsman, wicket-keeper. Queensland debut 1986-87. **TESTS:** 73 (1988-89 to 1994-95). 2557 runs (av 26.91), 2 hundreds; 231 ct, 17 st. HS 113* v NZ (Perth) 1993-94. **L-O INTERNATIONALS:** 129 (1988-89 to 1994-95). 1341 runs (av 21.98); 155 ct, 27 st. HS 56 v E (Melbourne) 1994-95. **F-C CAREER:** 5278 runs (av 31.23), 2 hundreds; 0 wkts; 449 ct, 41 st. HS 113* A v NZ (Perth) 1993-94.

JULIAN, Brendon Paul **(Western Australia)**
Born Hamilton, New Zealand 10 Aug 1970. 6' 5". Educated at Guildford Grammar School, WA. Right-hand batsman, left-arm fast-medium bowler. WA debut 1989-90. **TESTS:** 6 (1993 to 1994-95). 128 runs (av 16.00); 14 wkts (av 37.64), 3 ct. HS 56* v E (Nottingham) 1993. BB 4-36 v WI (Bridgetown) 1994-95. **L-O INTERNATIONALS:** 2 (1993 to 1994-95). 11 runs (av 11.00); 3 wkts (av 38.66); 0 ct. HS 11 v WI (Georgetown) 1994-95. BB 3-50 v E (Lord's) 1993. **F-C CAREER:** 1403 runs (av 20.04); 179 wkts (av 31.44), 5 wkts/inns (10), 10 wkts/match (1); 31 ct. HS 87 v Tasmania (Hobart) 1992-93. BB 5-26 v Tasmania (Hobart) 1991-92.

LANGER, Justin Lee **(Western Australia)**
Born Perth 21 Nov 1970. 5' 8". Educated at Aquinas College, University of West Australia. Left-hand batsman, right-arm medium pace bowler. WA debut 1991-92. **TESTS:** 6 (1992-93 to 1994-95). 241 runs (av 26.77); 2 ct. HS 69 v P (Lahore) 1994-95. **L-O INTERNATIONALS:** 7 (1993-94 to 1994-95). 131 runs (av 32.75); 1 ct, 1 st. HS 36 v I (Sharjah) 1993-94. **F-C CAREER:** 3821 runs (av 50.27), 9 hundreds; 0 wkts; 39 ct. HS 241* v NSW (Perth) 1994-95.

LAW, Stuart Grant **(Queensland)**
Born Herston, Brisbane 18 Oct 1968. 6' 2". Educated at Craigslea State High School. Right-hand batsman, right-arm medium-pace/leg-break bowler. Queensland debut 1988-89. **TESTS:** 0. **L-O INTERNATIONALS:** 4 (1994-95). 134 runs (av 44.66), 1 hundred; 3 wkts (av 45.33); 1 ct. HS 110 v Z (Hobart) 1994-95. **F-C CAREER:** 5313 runs (av 42.16), 14 hundreds; 30 wkts (av 42.06); 69 ct. HS 179 v Tasmania (Brisbane) 1988-89. BB 3-25 v Victoria (Brisbane) 1992-93.

McDERMOTT, Craig John **(Queensland)**
Born Ipswich, Queensland 14 Apr 1965. 6' 3½". Educated at Ipswich Grammar School. Right-hand batsman, right-arm fast bowler. Queensland debut 1983-84. **TESTS:** 65 (1984-85 to 1994-95). 897 runs (av 12.45); 270 wkts (av 28.50), 5 wkts/inns (13), 10 wkts/match (2); 15 ct. HS 42* v E (Adelaide) 1990-91. BB 8-97 v E (Perth) 1990-91. **L-O INTERNATIONALS:** 129 (1984-85 to 1994-95). 431 runs (av 7.18); 190 wkts (av 24.91); 26 ct. HS 37 v NZ (Christchurch) 1985-86. BB 5-44 v P (Lahore) 1987-88. **F-C CAREER:** 2797 runs (av 16.64); 643 wkts (av 27.90), 5 wkts/inns (35), 10 wkts/match (4); 46 ct. HS 74 v WA (Perth) 1990-91. BB 8-44 v Tasmania (Brisbane) 1989-90.

McGRATH, Glenn Donald **(New South Wales)**
Born Dubbo, NSW 9 Feb 1970. 6' 6". Educated at Narromine High School. Right-hand batsman, right-arm fast-medium bowler. NSW debut 1992-93. **TESTS:** 13 (1993-94 to 1994-95). 22 runs (av 2.00); 42 wkts (av 31.59), 5 wkts/inns (2); 0 ct. HS 9 v SA (Sydney) 1993-94. BB 6-47 v WI (Port-of-Spain) 1994-95. **L-O INTERNATIONALS:** 36 (1993-94 to 1994-95). 25 runs (av 3.57); 49 wkts (av 24.91); 3 ct. HS 10 v E (Melbourne) 1994-95. BB 5-52 v P (Lahore) 1994-95. **F-C CAREER:** 50 runs (av 2.38); 126 wkts (av 24.69), 5 wkts/inns (7), 10 wkts/match (1); 2 ct. HS 9. BB 6-47 A v WI (Port-of-Spain) 1994-95.

MARTYN, Damian Richard **(Western Australia)**
Born Darwin 21 Oct 1971. 5′ 10″. Educated at Girrawheen High School. Right-hand batsman, right-arm medium pace/off-break bowler. WA debut 1990-91. **TESTS**: 7 (1992-93 to 1993-94). 317 runs (av 28.81); 0 wkts; 1 ct. HS 74 v NZ (Auckland) 1992-93. **L-O INTERNATIONALS**: 11 (1992-93 to 1993-94). 166 runs (av 18.44); 6 ct. HS 51* v E (Lord's) 1993. **F-C CAREER**: 4501 runs (av 47.88), 14 hundreds; 9 wkts (av 55.11); 46 ct, 2 st. HS 197 v NSW (Perth) 1993-94. BB 3-29 v S Aus (Perth) 1993-94.

MAY, Timothy Brian Alexander **(South Australia)**
Born North Adelaide 26 Jan 1962. 5′ 11½″. Educated at Prince Alfred College; Adelaide University. Right-hand batsman, off-break bowler. SA debut 1984-85. **TESTS**: 24 (1987-88 to 1994-95). 225 runs (av 14.06); 75 wkts (av 34.74), 5 wkts/inns (3); 6 ct. HS 42* and BB 5-9 v WI (Adelaide) 1992-93. **L-O INTERNATIONALS**: 47 (1987-88 to 1994-95). 39 runs (av 9.75); 39 wkts (av 45.41); 3 ct. HS 15 v NZ (Chandigarh) 1987-88. BB 3-19 v NZ (Auckland) 1994-95. **F-C CAREER**: 1661 runs (av 15.37), 1 hundred; 395 wkts (av 35.90), 5 wkts/inns (16), 10 wkts/match (1); 38 ct. HS 128 v Tasmania (Adelaide) 1990-91. BB 7-93 v Vic (Melbourne) 1988-89.

PONTING, Ricky Thomas **(Tasmania)**
Born Launceston 19 Dec 1974. 5′ 10″. Educated at Brooks High School. Right-hand batsman, off-break bowler. Tasmania debut 1992-93. **TESTS**: 0. **L-O INTERNATIONALS**: 6 (1994-95). 123 runs (av 30.75); 0 ct. HS 62 v 1 (Dunedin) 1994-95. **F-C CAREER**: 2998 runs (av 49.96), 10 hundreds; 2 wkts (av 95.00); 31 ct. HS 211 v WA (Hobart) 1994-95. BB 1-7.

REIFFEL, Paul Ronald **(Victoria)**
Born Box Hill, Victoria 19 Apr 1966. 6′ 2″. Educated at Jordan Ville Technical School. Right-hand batsman, right-arm fast-medium bowler. Victoria debut 1987-88. **TESTS**: 16 (1991-92 to 1994-95). 303 runs (av 21.64); 46 wkts (av 28.54), 5 wkts/inns (2); 8 ct. HS 51 v NZ (Perth) 1993-94. BB 6-71 v E (Birmingham) 1993. **L-O INTERNATIONALS**: 48 (1991-92 to 1994-95). 302 runs (av 17.76); 64 wkts (av 24.39); 17 ct. HS 58 v SA (Pt Elizabeth) 1993-94. BB 4-13 v SA (Sydney) 1993-94. **F-C CAREER**: 1559 runs (av 22.59); 286 wkts (av 28.88), 5 wkts/inns (10), 10 wkts/match (2); 47 ct. HS 86 and BB 6-57 v Tasmania (St Kilda, Melbourne) 1990-91.

SLATER, Michael Jonathon **(New South Wales)**
Born Wagga Wagga, NSW 21 Feb 1970. 5′ 9″. Educated at Wagga Wagga High School. Right-hand opening batsman, occasional right-arm medium pace bowler. NSW debut 1991-92. **TESTS**: 27 (1993 to 1994-95). 2163 runs (av 48.06), 6 hundreds; 1 wkt (av 4.00); 7 ct. HS 176 v E (Brisbane) 1994-95. BB 1-4. **L-O INTERNATIONALS**: 27 (1993-94 to 1994-95). 714 runs (av 26.44); 0 wkts; 7 ct. HS 73 v SA (Melbourne) 1993-94 – on debut. **F-C CAREER**: 5285 runs (av 48.93), 14 hundreds; 1 wkt (av 24.00); 33 ct. HS 176 A v E (Brisbane) 1994-95. BB 1-4.

SYMONDS, Andrew (Queensland)
Born Birmingham 9 Jun 1975. Emigrated to Australia when 18 months old. 6′ 1½″. Educated at All Saints Anglican School, Mudgeeraba, Queensland. Right-hand batsman, off-break bowler. Queensland debut/cap 1995. Gloucestershire debut/cap 1995. **TESTS**: 0. **L-O INTERNATIONALS**: 0. **F-C CAREER**: 1762 runs (av 53.39), 6 hundreds; 5 wkts (av 59.60); 10 ct. HS 254* Glos v Glamorgan (Abergavenny) 1995 (a match in which he recorded world records for most sixes in an innings (16) and match (20)). BB 3-77 v NSW (Sydney) 1994-95.

TAYLOR, Mark Anthony **(New South Wales)**
Born Leeton, NSW 27 Oct 1964. 5' 10". Educated at Mt Austin High School, Wagga Wagga; Chatswood High School, Stoney; University of NSW. Left-hand opening batsman, occasional right-arm medium pace bowler. NSW debut 1985-86. **TESTS:** 66 (1988-89 to 1994-95, 12 as captain). 5005 runs (av 45.09), 13 hundreds; 1 wkt (av 26.00); 93 ct. HS 219 v E (Nottingham) 1989. BB 1-11. **L-O INTERNATIONALS:** 79 (1989-90 to 1994-95, 33 as captain). 2411 runs (av 32.14); 42 ct. HS 97 v NZ (Auckland) 1994-95. **F-C CAREER:** 13,018 runs (av 43.83), 32 hundreds; 2 wkts (av 34.00); 249 ct. HS 219 A v E (Nottingham) 1989. BB 1-4.

WARNE, Shane Keith **(Victoria)**
Born Ferntree Gully, Melbourne 13 Sep 1969. 6' 0". Educated at Hampton High School; Mentone Grammar School. Right-hand batsman, right-arm leg-break/googly bowler. Victoria debut 1990-91. **TESTS:** 38 (1991-92 to 1994-95). 597 runs (av 13.26); 176 wkts (av 24.08), 5 wkts/inns (9), 10 wkts/match (2), 1 hat-trick; 25 ct. HS 74* v NZ (Brisbane) 1993-94. BB 8-71 v E (Brisbane) 1994-95. **L-O INTERNATIONALS:** 43 (1992-93 to 1994-95). 234 runs (av 14.62); 72 wkts (av 21.56); 14 ct. HS 55 v SA (Pt Elizabeth) 1993-94. BB 4-19 v NZ (Melbourne) 1993-94. **F-C CAREER:** 1189 runs (av 14.86); 329 wkts (av 24.65), 5 wkts/inns (15), 10 wkts/match (2); 41 ct. HS 74* A v NZ (Brisbane) 1993-94. BB 8-71 A v E (Brisbane) 1994-95.

WAUGH, Mark Edward **(New South Wales)**
Born Canterbury, Sydney 2 Jun 1965. Younger twin of Steve. 6' 1". Educated East Hills High School. Right-hand batsman, right-arm medium-fast/off-break bowler. NSW debut 1985-86. Essex 1988-90 (cap 1989), 1992 and 1995. One of *Wisden's* Five Cricketers of 1990. **TESTS:** 48 (1990-91 to 1994-95). 3072 runs (av 42.08), 8 hundreds; 34 wkts (av 34.47), 5 wkts/inns (1); 62 ct. HS 140 v E (Brisbane) 1994-95; BB 5-40 v E (Adelaide) 1994-95. **L-O INTERNATIONALS:** 96 (1988-89 to 1994-95). 2887 runs (av 34.36), 4 hundreds; 52 wkts (av 26.26); 39 ct. HS 121* v P (Rawalpindi) 1994-95. BB 5-24 v WI (Melbourne) 1992-93. **F-C CAREER:** 17,260 runs (av 55.67), 57 hundreds; 163 wkts (av 38.75), 5 wkts/inns (2); 262 ct. HS 229* v WA (Perth) 1990-91, sharing world record 5th wkt stand of 464* with S.R.Waugh. BB 5-37 Essex v Northants (Chelmsford) 1990.

WAUGH, Stephen Rodger **(New South Wales)**
Born Canterbury, Sydney 2 Jun 1965. Elder twin of Mark. 5' 11". Educated East Hills High School. Right-hand batsman, right-arm medium-fast bowler. NSW debut 1984-85. Somerset 1987 and 1988. **TESTS:** 76 (1985-86 to 1994-95). 4440 runs (av 47.23), 8 hundreds; 72 wkts (av 36.61), 5 wkts/inns (3); 59 ct. HS 200 v WI (Kingston) 1994-95. BB 5-28 v SA (Cape Town) 1993-94. **L-O INTERNATIONALS:** 185 (1985-86 to 1994-95). 3852 runs (av 30.57); 162 wkts (av 33.42); 62 ct. HS 86 v SA (Verwoerdburg) 1993-94. BB 4-33 v SL (Sydney) 1987-88. **F-C CAREER:** 12,585 runs (av 50.54), 34 hundreds; 219 wkts (av 31.38), 5 wkts/inns (5); 175 ct. HS 216* v WA (Perth) 1990-91, sharing world record 5th wkt stand of 464* with M.E.Waugh. BB 6-51 v Queensland (Sydney) 1988-89.

46

WORLD CUP CAREER RECORDS

AUSTRALIA – BATTING AND FIELDING

	M	I	NO	HS	Runs	Avge	100	50	Ct/St
Boon, D.C.	16	16	1	100	815	54.33	2	5	2
Border, A.R.	25	24	–	67	452	18.83	–	1	10
Chappell, G.S.	5	5	–	50	129	25.80	–	1	3
Chappell, I.M.	5	5	–	62	121	24.20	–	1	–
Chappell, T.M.	4	4	–	110	139	34.75	1	–	1
Cosier, G.J.	3	2	–	6	6	3.00	–	–	1
Darling, W.M.	3	3	–	25	51	17.00	–	–	–
Dyer, G.C.	8	4	–	27	50	12.50	–	–	9/2
Dymock, G.	3	2	1	10	14	14.00	–	–	–
Edwards, R.	5	4	1	80*	166	55.33	–	2	–
Gilmour, G.J.	2	2	1	28*	42	42.00	–	–	1
Healy, I.A.	7	6	2	16	51	12.75	–	–	9
Hilditch, A.M.J.	3	3	–	72	143	47.66	–	1	1
Hogan, T.G.	4	4	2	11	24	12.00	–	–	2
Hogg, R.M.	8	5	4	19*	29	29.00	–	–	1
Hookes, D.W.	6	6	–	56	133	22.16	–	1	3
Hughes, K.J.	8	8	1	69	218	31.14	–	2	3
Hughes, M.G.	1	1	–	0*	0	–	–	–	–
Hurst, A.G.	3	2	2	3*	6	–	–	–	–
Jones, D.M.	16	16	2	90	590	42.14	–	5	6
Laughlin, T.J.	1	1	–	8	8	8.00	–	–	–
Lawson, G.F.	4	4	–	16	24	6.00	–	–	–
Lillee, D.K.	9	3	1	16*	19	9.50	–	–	–
McCosker, R.B.	5	5	–	73	120	24.00	–	1	–
McDermott, C.J.	16	11	–	14	43	3.90	–	–	4
Macleay, K.H.	4	4	–	9	19	4.75	–	–	1
Mallett, A.A.	3	1	–	0	0	0.00	–	–	1
Marsh, G.R.	13	13	1	126*	579	48.25	2	2	2
Marsh, R.W.	11	11	4	52*	220	31.42	–	2	17/1
May, T.B.A.	6	3	1	15	16	8.00	–	–	1
Moody, T.M.	11	11	1	57	212	21.20	–	2	3
Moss, J.K.	1	1	–	7	7	7.00	–	–	2
O'Donnell, S.P.	7	4	–	7	15	3.75	–	–	4
Porter, G.D.	2	1	–	3	3	3.00	–	–	1
Reid, B.A.	14	5	2	5*	10	3.33	–	–	4
Taylor, M.A.	2	2	–	13	13	6.50	–	–	–
Taylor, P.L.	9	7	3	17*	34	8.50	–	–	1
Thomson, J.R.	8	5	2	21	51	17.00	–	–	1
Turner, A.	5	5	–	101	201	40.20	1	–	3
Veletta, M.R.J.	4	4	–	48	136	45.33	–	–	–
Walker, M.H.N.	5	3	–	18	33	11.00	–	–	1
Walters, K.D.	5	5	1	59	123	30.75	–	1	–
Waugh, M.E.	5	5	1	66*	145	36.25	–	1	4
Waugh, S.R.	16	15	5	55	354	35.40	–	1	5
Wessels, K.C.	3	3	–	76	92	30.66	–	1	1
Whitney, M.R.	7	3	2	9*	22	22.00	–	–	1
Wood, G.M.	5	5	1	73	144	36.00	–	1	1
Wright, K.J.	3	2	–	23	29	14.50	–	–	5
Yallop, G.N.	9	9	3	66*	247	41.16	–	2	1
Zesers, A.K.	2	2	2	8*	10	–	–	–	1
Record in all World Cup matches:									
Wessels, K.C. (A/SA)	12	12	2	85	405	40.50	–	4	8

	O	M	R	W	Avge	Best	4w	R/O
Boon, D.C.	1	0	17	0	–	–	–	17.00
Border, A.R.	73	1	342	9	38.00	2-27	–	4.68
Chappell, G.S.	18	0	88	0	–	–	–	4.88
Chappell, I.M.	7	1	23	2	11.50	2-14	–	3.28
Chappell, T.M.	19.4	0	98	4	24.50	3-47	–	4.98
Cosier, G.J.	27.2	4	95	5	19.00	3-54	–	3.47
Dymock, G.	31	7	64	2	32.00	1-17	–	2.06
Gilmour, G.J.	24	8	62	11	5.63	6-14	2	2.58
Hogan, T.G.	47	2	172	6	28.66	2-33	–	3.65
Hogg, R.M.	78	9	271	10	27.10	3-40	–	3.47
Hughes, M.G.	9	1	49	1	49.00	1-49	–	5.44
Hurst, A.G.	32	6	119	7	17.00	5-21	1	3.71
Jones, D.M.	1	0	5	0	–	–	–	5.00
Laughlin, T.J.	9.1	0	38	2	19.00	2-38	–	4.14
Lawson, G.F.	38	7	127	5	25.40	3-29	–	3.34
Lillee, D.K.	98	8	400	12	33.33	5-34	1	4.08
McDermott, C.J.	146	8	587	26	22.57	5-44	2	4.02
Macleay, K.H.	44.5	6	163	8	20.37	6-39	1	3.63
Mallett, A.A.	35	3	156	3	52.00	1-35	–	4.45
May, T.B.A.	44	1	213	4	53.25	2-29	–	4.84
Moody, T.M.	51	2	240	7	34.28	3-56	–	4.70
O'Donnell, S.P.	60.4	6	261	9	29.00	4-39	1	4.30
Porter, G.D.	18	5	33	3	11.00	2-13	–	1.83
Reid, B.A.	122.4	10	512	9	56.88	2-38	–	4.17
Taylor, P.L.	47.4	1	218	6	36.33	2-14	–	4.57
Thomson, J.R.	76.5	10	290	7	41.42	3-51	–	3.77
Walker, M.H.N.	57.2	10	210	6	35.00	3-22	–	3.66
Walters, K.D.	17	1	85	1	85.00	1-29	–	5.00
Waugh, M.E.	5	0	40	0	–	–	–	8.00
Waugh, S.R.	124.1	5	565	19	29.73	3-36	–	4.55
Whitney, M.R.	66	12	215	9	23.88	4-34	1	3.25
Yallop, G.N.	22	0	110	3	36.66	2-28	–	5.00
Zesers, A.K.	15	1	74	1	74.00	1-37	–	4.93

WORLD CUP REGISTER

SOUTH AFRICA

All career statistics are up to the end of the 1995 season (18 September). Key to abbreviations on page 32. South Africa's provisionally selected 20 players for the Wills World Cup are:

ADAMS, Paul Regan **(Western Province)**
Born Cape Town 20 Jan 1977. Educated at Plumstead High School. Right-hand batsman, left-arm unorthodox slow bowler. First-class debut 1995-96. **TESTS:** 0. **L-O INTERNATIONALS:** 0.

BOJE, Nicky (Orange Free State)
Born Bloemfontein 20 Mar 1973. Educated at Grey College. Left-hand batsman, left-arm orthodox slow bowler. OFS debut 1990-91. **TESTS:** 0. **L-O INTERNATIONALS:** 0. **F-C CAREER:** 814 runs (av 29.07), 1 hundred; 85 wkts (av 34.45), 5 wkts/inns (4); 10 ct. HS 102 South Africa A v Mashonaland (Harare) 1994-95. BB 6-100 OFS B v Natal B (Pietermaritzburg) 1990-91.

CRONJE, Wessel Johannes ('Hansie') (Orange Free State)
Born Bloemfontein 25 Sep 1969. 6' 4". Educated at Grey College, Bloemfontein; OFS University. Right-hand batsman, right-arm medium pace bowler. OFS debut 1987-88. (captain 1990-91 to date). Leicestershire 1995 (cap 1995). **TESTS:** 21 (1991-92 to 1994-95, 6 as captain). 1342 runs (av 39.47), 5 hundreds; 8 wkts (av 61.62); 9 ct. HS 135* v I (Port Elizabeth) 1992-93; BB 2-17 v I (Cape Town) 1992-93. **L-O INTERNATIONALS:** 68 (1991-92 to 1994-95, 18 as captain). 1975 runs (av 36.57), 2 hundreds; 45 wkts (av 35.57); 25 ct. HS 112 v A (Johannesburg) 1993-94. BB 5-32 v I (Cape Town) 1992-93. **F-C CAREER:** 6931 runs (av 42.26), 20 hundreds; 51 wkts (av 42.07); 70 ct. HS 251 OFS v A (Bloemfontein) 1993-94. BB 4-47 SA v Kent (Canterbury) 1994.

CROOKES, Derek Norman **(Natal)**
Born Kloof 5 Mar 1969. Educated at Hilton College. Right-hand batsman, off-break bowler. Natal debut 1989-90. **TESTS:** 0. **L-O INTERNATIONALS:** 3 (1994-95). 30 runs (av 10.00); 0 wkts; 0 ct. HS 20 v A (Faisalabad) 1994-95. **F-C CAREER:** 1245 runs (av 31.93), 2 hundreds; 75 wkts (av 32.19), 5 wkts/inns (2); 23 ct. HS 123* v E Province (Port Elizabeth) 1994-95. BB 5-84 v N Transvaal (Durban) 1993-94.

CULLINAN, Daryll John (Transvaal)
Born Kimberley 4 Mar 1967. 5' 10". Educated at Queens College, Queenstown; Stellenbosch University. Right-hand batsman, off-break bowler. Border 1983-84 and 1984-85, making debut while at school. W Province 1985-86 to 1990-91. Transvaal debut 1991-92. Derbyshire 1995 (uncapped). **TESTS:** 13 (1992-93 to 1994-95). 777 runs (av 35.31), 1 hundred; 8 ct. HS 102 v SL (Colombo) 1993-94. **L-O INTERNATIONALS:** 38 (1992-93 to 1994-95). 860 runs (av 25.29); 13 ct. HS 70* v WI (Bombay) 1993-94. **F-C CAREER:** 7404 runs (av 40.68), 17 hundreds; 3 wkts (av 23.33); 106 ct. HS 337* v N Transvaal (Johannesburg) 1993-94 (SA f-c record). BB 2-27 Border v Natal B (E London) 1983-84. Youngest player (16 years 304 days) to score f-c hundred in SA.

DONALD, Allan Anthony **(Orange Free State)**
Born Bloemfontein 20 Oct 1966. 6' 2". Grey College High School. Right-hand batsman, right-arm fast bowler. OFS debut 1985-86. Warwickshire 1987 to 1993, 1995 (cap 1989). One of *Wisden*'s Five Cricketers of 1991. **TESTS:** 19 (1991-92 to 1994-95). 132 runs (av 12.00); 84 wkts (av 26.50), 5 wkts/inns (4), 10 wkts/match (1); 5 ct. HS 27 v E (Leeds) 1994;

49

DONALD – continued:
BB 7-84 (12-139 match) v I (Port Elizabeth) 1992-93. **L-O INTERNATIONALS:** 50 (1991-92 to 1994-95). 29 runs (av 3.62); 67 wkts (av 26.44); 5 ct. HS 7*. BB 5-29 v I (Calcutta) 1991-92 – on debut. **F-C CAREER:** 1744 runs (av 11.86); 792 wkts (av 23.27), 5 wkts/inns (43), 10 wkts/match (6); 84 ct. HS 46* v W Province (Cape Town) 1990-91. BB 8-37 v Transvaal (Johannesburg) 1986-87.

HUDSON, Andrew Charles (Natal)
Born Eshowe, Zululand 17 Mar 1965. 5′ 11″. Educated at Kearsney College; Natal University. Right-hand batsman, occasional right-arm medium pace bowler. Natal debut 1984-85. **TESTS:** 19 (1991-92 to 1994-95). 1181 runs (av 34.73), 2 hundreds; 15 ct. HS 163 v WI (Bridgetown) 1991-92 – on debut (first instance for South Africa). **L-O INTERNATIONALS:** 54 (1991-92 to 1994-95). 1476 runs (av 27.84), 1 hundred; 7 ct. HS 108 v I (Bloemfontein) 1992-93. **F-C CAREER:** 6062 runs (av 35.04), 11 hundreds; 0 wkts; 94 ct. HS 184* v Transvaal (Durban) 1990-91.

KALLIS, Jacques Henry (Western Province)
Born Pinelands 16 Oct 1975. Educated at Wynberg High School. Right-hand batsman, right-arm medium pace bowler. W Province debut 1993-94. **TESTS:** 0. **L-O INTERNATIONALS:** 0. **F-C CAREER:** 623 runs (av 38.94); 4 wkts (av 74.25); 9 ct. HS 77 v E Province (Port Elizabeth) 1994-95. BB 1-6.

KIRSTEN, Gary (Western Province)
Born Cape Town 23 Nov 1967. 5′ 9″. Brother of Peter N. Educated at Rondebosch High School; Cape Town University. Left-hand batsman, off-break bowler. W Province debut 1987-88. **TESTS:** 14 (1993-94 to 1994-95). 948 runs (av 37.92); 2 wkts (av 66.50); 15 ct. HS 76 v NZ (Auckland) 1994-95. BB 1-0. **L-O INTERNATIONALS:** 27 (1993-94 to 1994-95). 909 runs (av 36.36), 1 hundred; 0 wkts; 8 ct. HS 112* v A (Melbourne) 1993-94. **F-C CAREER:** 5887 runs (av 44.26), 13 hundreds; 17 wkts (av 37.65), 5 wkts/inns (1); 66 ct. HS 201* SA v N Transvaal (Chester-le-Street) 1994. BB 6-68 v N Transvaal (Verwoerdburg) 1993-94.

KLUSENER, Lance (Natal)
Born Durban 4 Sep 1971. Educated at Durban High School. Right-hand batsman, right-arm fast-medium bowler. Natal debut 1993-94. **TESTS:** 0. **L-O INTERNATIONALS:** 0. **F-C CAREER:** 686 runs (av 40.35), 1 hundred; 48 wkts (av 22.27), 5 wkts/inns (1); 7 ct. HS 105 and BB 5-46 Natal B v W Province B (Durban) 1994-95.

KUIPER, Adrian Paul (Western Province)
Born Johannesburg 24 Aug 1959. 5′ 11″. Educated at Diocesan College; Stellenbosch University. Right-hand batsman, right-arm medium-fast bowler. W Province debut 1977-78. Derbyshire 1990. **TESTS:** 1 (1991-92). 34 runs (av 17.00); 1 ct. HS 34 v WI (Bridgetown) 1991-92. **L-O INTERNATIONALS:** 22 (1991-92 to 1993-94). 414 runs (av 27.60); 18 wkts (av 28.77); 3 ct. HS 63* v I (Delhi) 1991-92. BB 3-33 v WI (Kingston) 1991-92. **F-C CAREER:** 6613 runs (av 32.73), 7 hundreds; 183 wkts (av 28.73), 5 wkts/inns (4); 96 ct. HS 161* v Natal (Durban) 1989-90. BB 6-55 v N Transvaal (Pretoria) 1983-84.

McMILLAN, Brian Mervin (Western Province)
Born Welkom, OFS 22 Dec 1963. 6′ 4″. Educated at Carleton Jones High School; Witwatersrand University. Right-hand batsman, right-arm fast-medium bowler. Transvaal 1984-85 to 1988-89. Warwickshire 1986. W Province debut 1989-90. **TESTS:** 17 (1992-93 to 1994-95). 879 runs (av 36.62), 1 hundred; 51 wkts (av 28.94); 21 ct. HS 113 v P (Johannesburg) 1994-95. BB 4-65 v NZ (Cape Town) 1994-95. **L-O INTERNATIONALS:** 41 (1991-92 to 1994-95). 326 runs (av 20.37); 37 wkts (av 39.83); 24 ct. HS 48* v I (Calcutta) 1993-94. BB 4-32 v I (Port Elizabeth) 1992-93. **F-C CAREER:** 5279 runs (av 38.82), 9 hundreds; 254 wkts (av 27.06), 5 wkts/inns (4); 103 ct. HS 140 W Province v Boland (Cape Town) 1994-95. BB 5-35 W Province v Natal (Cape Town) 1993-94.

MATTHEWS, Craig Russell (Western Province)
Born Cape Town 15 Feb 1965. 6' 3". Educated at Pinelands High School; Cape Town University. Right-hand batsman, right-arm fast-medium bowler. W Province debut 1986-87. **TESTS:** 14 (1992-93 to 1994-95). 318 runs (av 21.20); 46 wkts (av 27.28), 5 wkts/inns (2); 1 ct. HS 62* v E (Leeds) 1993. BB 5-42 v NZ (Johannesburg) 1994-95. **L-O INTERNATIONALS:** 37 (1991-92 to 1994-95). 108 runs (av 9.81); 58 wkts (av 23.08); 4 ct. HS 26 v E (Manchester) 1994. BB 4-10 v A (Durban) 1993-94. **F-C CAREER:** 1149 runs (av 19.15), 1 hundred; 214 wkts (av 23.26), 5 wkts/inns (8); 36 ct. HS 105 v N Transvaal (Verwoerdburg) 1990-91. BB 6-22 W Province v Yorkshire (Cape Town) 1991-92.

PALFRAMAN, Steven John (Border)
Born East London 12 May 1970. Educated at Dale College; Rhodes University. Right-hand batsman, wicket-keeper. E Province 1990-91. Border debut 1991-92. **TESTS:** 0. **L-O INTERNATIONALS:** 0. **F-C CAREER:** 1230 runs (av 23.21), 1 hundred; 112 ct, 13 st. HS 123 Border v Natal (East London) 1993-94.

POLLOCK, Shaun Maclean (Natal)
Born Port Elizabeth 16 Jul 1973. Son of Peter M.; nephew of R. Graeme. Educated at Northwood High School; Durban University. Right-hand batsman, right-arm fast-medium bowler. Natal debut 1991-92. **TESTS:** 0. **L-O INTERNATIONALS:** 0. **F-C CAREER:** 385 runs (av 22.65); 49 wkts (av 22.51); 7 ct. HS 56 v Border (East London) 1993-94. BB 4-24 v OFS (Durban) 1994-95.

RHODES, Jonathan Neil ('Jonty') (Natal)
Born Pietermaritzburg 27 Jul 1969. 5' 8". Educated at Maritzburg College; Natal University. Right-hand batsman, right-arm medium pace bowler. Natal debut 1988-89 scoring 108 v W Province (Durban). **TESTS:** 21 (1992-93 to 1994-95). 1037 runs (av 34.56), 1 hundred; 0 wkts; 11 ct. HS 101* v SL (Moratuwa) 1993-94. **L-O INTERNATIONALS:** 68 (1991-92 to 1994-95). 1581 runs (av 28.23); 25 ct – including 5 v WI (Bombay) 1993-94 (*world record*). HS 66 v A (Port Elizabeth) 1993-94. **F-C CAREER:** 3792 runs (av 34.47), 5 hundreds; 1 wkt (av 49.00); 50 ct. HS 135* v Border (Pietermaritzburg) 1992-93. BB 1-13.

RICHARDSON, David John (Eastern Province)
Born Johannesburg 16 Sep 1959. 5' 11". Educated at Marist Brothers College; Port Elizabeth University. Right-hand batsman, wicket-keeper. E Province debut 1977-78. **TESTS:** 22 (1991-92 to 1994-95). 825 runs (av 26.61), 1 hundred; 93 ct, 0 st. HS 109 v NZ (Cape Town) 1994-95. **L-O INTERNATIONALS:** 69 (1991-92 to 1994-95). 631 runs (av 21.75); 83 ct, 12 st. HS 53 v P (Durban) 1994-95. **F-C CAREER:** 6007 runs (av 27.43), 5 hundreds; 481 ct, 33 st. HS 134 E Province v SL (Port Elizabeth) 1982-83.

SNELL, Richard Peter (Transvaal)
Born Durban 12 Sep 1968. 6' 1". Educated at Durban High School; Witwatersrand University. Right-hand batsman, right-arm medium-fast bowler. Transvaal debut 1987-88. Somerset 1992. **TESTS:** 5 (1991-92 to 1994-95). 95 runs (av 13.57); 19 wkts (av 28.31); 1 ct. HS 48 v SL (SSC, Colombo) 1993-94. BB 4-74 v WI (Bridgetown) 1991-92 – on debut. **L-O INTERNATIONALS:** 39 (1991-92 to 1994-95). 243 runs (av 14.29); 41 wkts (av 36.19); 7 ct. HS 51 v SL (RPS, Colombo) 1993-94. BB 5-40 v A (Melbourne) 1993-94. **F-C CAREER:** 1442 runs (av 18.73); 216 wkts (av 29.22), 5 wkts/inns (7), 10 wkts/match (1); 19 ct. HS 94 SA v Glamorgan (Pontypridd) 1994. BB 6-33 v Border (Johannesburg) 1992-93.

STEYN, Philippus Jeremia Rudolf (Orange Free State)
Born Kimberley 30 Jun 1967. Educated at Diamantveld High School. Right-hand batsman, right-arm medium pace bowler, occasional wicket-keeper. Griqualand West 1985-86. OFS debut 1986-87. **TESTS:** 3 (1994-95). 127 runs (av 21.16); 0 ct. HS 46 v NZ (Auckland) 1994-95. **L-O INTERNATIONALS:** 0. **F-C CAREER:** 4163 runs (av 28.51), 4 hundreds; 1 wkt (av 24.00); 38 ct, 1 st. HS 178 OFS v W Province (Cape Town) 1988-89. BB 1-22.

SYMCOX, Patrick Leonard **(Natal)**
Born Kimberley 14 Apr 1960. 6′ 3″. Educated at Damelin College. Right-hand batsman, off-break bowler. Griqualand West 1977-78 to 1982-83, 1988-89 and 1989-90. N Transvaal 1983-84 to 1987-88. Natal debut 1990-91. **TESTS:** 5 (1993-94). 160 runs (av 26.66); 8 wkts (av 47.87); 0 ct. HS 50 v SL (SSC, Colombo) 1993-94. BB 3-75 v SL (Moratuwa) 1993-94 – on debut. **L-O INTERNATIONALS:** 16 (1993-94 to 1994-95). 71 runs (av 6.45); 13 wkts (av 32.84); 3 ct. HS 12 (twice). BB 3-20 v WI (Bombay) 1993-94. **F-C CAREER:** 2808 runs (av 25.07), 1 hundred; 155 wkts (av 30.95), 5 wkts/inns (4); 47 ct. HS 107 N Transvaal B v Transvaal B (Pietersburg) 1985-86. BB 7-93 N Transvaal B v Transvaal B (Verwoerdburg) 1987-88.

WORLD CUP CAREER RECORDS

SOUTH AFRICA – BATTING AND FIELDING

	M	I	NO	HS	Runs	Avge	100	50	Ct/St
Bosch, T.	1	–	–	–	–	–	–	–	–
Cronje, W.J.	8	6	3	47*	102	34.00	–	–	3
Donald, A.A.	9	1	–	3	3	3.00	–	–	1
Henry, O.	1	1	–	11	11	11.00	–	–	–
Hudson, A.C.	8	8	–	79	296	37.00	–	3	–
Kirsten, P.N.	8	8	2	90	410	68.33	–	4	2
Kuiper, A.P.	9	8	1	36	113	16.14	–	–	3
McMillan, B.M.	9	5	3	33*	125	62.50	–	–	4
Pringle, M.W.	7	1	1	5*	5	5.00	–	–	1
Rhodes, J.N.	9	8	1	43	132	18.85	–	–	4
Richardson, D.J.	9	5	2	28	66	22.00	–	–	14/1
Rushmere, M.W.	3	3	–	35	49	16.33	–	–	1
Snell, R.P.	9	4	2	11*	24	12.00	–	–	1
Wessels, K.C.	9	9	2	85	313	44.71	–	3	7

Record in all World Cup matches:

	M	I	NO	HS	Runs	Avge	100	50	Ct/St
Wessels, K.C. (A/SA)	12	12	2	85	405	40.50	–	4	8

SOUTH AFRICA – BOWLING

	O	M	R	W	Avge	Best	4w	R/O
Bosch, T.	2.3	0	19	0	–	–	–	7.60
Cronje, W.J.	20	1	85	2	42.50	2-17	–	4.25
Donald, A.A.	78	5	329	13	25.30	3-34	–	4.21
Henry, O.	10	0	31	1	31.00	1-31	–	3.10
Kirsten, P.N.	18	1	87	5	17.40	3-31	–	4.83
Kuiper, A.P.	41	0	235	9	26.11	3-40	–	5.73
McMillan, B.M.	73	7	306	11	27.81	3-30	–	4.19
Pringle, M.W.	57	6	236	8	29.50	4-11	1	4.14
Snell, R.P.	72.5	10	310	8	38.75	3-42	–	4.25

52

WORLD CUP REGISTER

WEST INDIES

The West Indies World Cup selections had not been released at the time of going to press. All career statistics are up to the end of the 1995 season (18 September). Key to abbreviations on page 32.

ADAMS, James Clive **(Jamaica)**
Born Port Maria, Jamaica 9 Jan 1968. 5′ 11". Educated at Jamaica College, Kingston. Left-hand batsman, left-arm orthodox slow bowler, wicket-keeper. Jamaica debut 1984-85. Nottinghamshire 1994. **TESTS:** 22 (1991-92 to 1995). 1616 runs (av 62.15), 4 hundreds; 9 wkts (av 53.44); 24 ct. HS 174* v I (Chandigarh) 1994-95; BB 4-43 v SA (Bridgetown) 1991-92 – on debut. **L-O INTERNATIONALS:** 47 (1992-93 to 1995). 661 runs (av 30.04); 2 wkts (av 29.50); 26 ct, 4 st. HS 81* v P (Sharjah) 1993-94. BB 1-2. **F-C CAREER:** 6200 runs (av 43.35), 14 hundreds, HS 174*; 50 wkts (av 38.04), BB 4-43; 101 ct.

AMBROSE, Curtly Elconn Lynall **(Leeward Islands)**
Born Swetes Village, Antigua 21 Sep 1963. 6′ 7". Educated at All Saints Village Secondary School. Left-hand batsman, right-arm fast bowler. Leeward Islands debut 1985-86. Northamptonshire 1989 to 1994 (cap 1990). One of *Wisden*'s Five Cricketers of 1991. **TESTS:** 59 (1987-88 to 1995). 815 runs (av 12.34); 258 wkts (av 21.29), 5 wkts/inns (13), 10 wkts/match (3); 13ct. HS 53 v A (Port-of-Spain) 1990-91. BB 8-45 v E (Bridgetown) 1989-90. **L-O INTERNATIONALS:** 114 (1987-88 to 1995). 391 runs (av 11.84); 154 wkts (av 23.18); 31 ct. HS 26* v P (Sharjah) 1989-90. BB 5-17 v A (Melbourne) 1988-89. **F-C CAREER:** 2506 runs (av 15.09), 60 ct; 694 wkts (av 20.73), 5 wkts/inns (34), 10 wkts/match (7), 50 wkts in a season (6), BB 8-45; 60 ct.

ARTHURTON, Keith Lloyd Thomas **(Leeward Islands)**
Born Charlestown, Nevis 21 Feb 1965. 5′ 8". Educated at Charlestown Secondary School. Left-hand batsman, left-arm orthodox slow bowler. Leeward Islands debut 1985-86. **TESTS:** 33 (1988 to 1995). 1382 runs (av 30.71), 2 hundreds; 1 wkt (av 183.00); 22 ct. HS 157* v A (Brisbane) 1992-93. BB 1-17. **L-O INTERNATIONALS:** 81 (1988-89 to 1995). 1650 runs (av 29.46); 21 wkts (av 26.57); 20 ct. HS 84 v P (Sharjah) 1993-94. BB 3-31 v NZ (Christchurch) 1994-95. **F-C CAREER:** 6401 runs (av 45.72), 18 hundreds, 1000 runs in a season (1), HS 157*; 22 wkts (av 35.31), BB 3-14; 55 ct.

BENJAMIN, Kenneth Charlie Griffith **(Leeward Islands)**
Born St John's, Antigua 8 Apr 1967. 6′ 2". Educated at All Saints Village Secondary School. Right-hand batsman, right-arm fast bowler. Leeward Islands debut 1988-89. Worcestershire 1993. **TESTS:** 21 (1991-92 to 1995). 184 runs (av 9.20); 80 wkts (av 28.21), 5 wkts/inns (4), 10 wkts/match (1); 1 ct. HS 43* v E (Bridgetown) 1993-94. BB 6-66 v E (Kingston) 1993-94. **L-O INTERNATIONALS:** 23 (1988-89 to 1995). 54 runs (av 13.50); 31 wkts (av 25.80); 4 ct. HS 17 v A (Brisbane) 1992-93. BB 3-34 v I (Sharjah) 1993-94. **F-C CAREER:** 773 runs (av 12.67), HS 52*; 253 wkts (av 25.16), 5 wkts/inns (11), 10 wkts/match (1); 11 ct.

BISHOP, Ian Raphael **(Trinidad)**
Born Port-of-Spain, Trinidad 24 Oct 1967 6′ 5″. Educated at Belmont Boys Secondary School. Right-hand batsman, right-arm fast bowler. Trinidad debut 1986-87. Derbyshire 1989 to 1992. **TESTS:** 24 (1988-89 to 1995). 302 runs (av 11.18); 110 wkts (av 21.33), 5 wkt/inns (6); 3 ct. HS 30* v I (Port-of-Spain) 1988-89. BB 6-40 v A (Perth) 1992-93. **L-O INTERNATIONALS:** 56 (1988 to 1995). 242 runs (av 16.13); 91 wkts (av 22.16); 10 ct. HS 33* v A (Melbourne) 1988-89. BB 5-25 v P (Brisbane) 1992-93. **F-C CAREER:** 1644 runs (av 14.94), 1 hundred, HS 103*; 413 wkts (av 21.14), 5 wkts/inns (21), 10 wkts/match (1), 50 wkts in a season (2), BB 7-34; 31 ct.

BROWNE, Courtney Oswald **(Barbados)**
Born Lambeth, London, England 7 Dec 1970. 6′ 1″. Educated at Coleridge & Parry Secondary School; Barbados Community College. Right-hand batsman, wicket-keeper. Barbados debut 1990-91. **TESTS:** 3 (1994-95 to 1995). 94 runs (av 47.00); 14 ct. HS 34 v E (Nottingham) 1995. **L-O INTERNATIONALS:** 0. **F-C CAREER:** 1540 runs (av 30.80), 2 hundreds, HS 102*; 0 wkts; 141 ct, 16 st.

CAMPBELL, Sherwin Legay **(Barbados)**
Born Bridgetown, Barbados 1 Nov 1970. 5′ 4″. Educated at Ellerslie Secondary School. Right-hand batsman. Barbados debut 1990-91. **TESTS:** 9 (1994-95 to 1995). 599 runs (av 42.78); 11 ct. HS 93 v E (Lord's) 1995. **L-O INTERNATIONALS:** 9 (1994-95 to 1995). 192 runs (av 21.33); 2 ct. HS 80 v E (Nottingham) 1995. **F-C CAREER:** 2417 runs (av 41.67), 8 hundreds, 1000 runs in a season (1), HS 172; 0 wkts; 40 ct.

CHANDERPAUL, Shivnarine (**Guyana**)
Born Unity Village, Guyana 18 Aug 1974. Left-hand batsman, right-arm leg-break bowler. Guyana debut 1991-92. **TESTS:** 9 (1993-94 to 1995). 536 runs (av 59.55); 2 wkts (av 152.00); 4 ct. HS 80 v E (Oval) 1995. BB 1-63. **L-O INTERNATIONALS:** 6 (1994-95). 49 runs (av 12.25); 1 ct. HS 22 v I (Bombay) 1994-95. **F-C CAREER:** 2540 runs (av 50.80), 6 hundreds, 1000 runs in a season (1), HS 140*; 32 wkts (av 40.46), BB 4-48; 32ct.

CUMMINS, Anderson Cleophas **(Barbados)**
Born Packer's Valley, Barbados 7 May 1966. Educated at Foundation School; Combermere School; Bridgetown University. Right-hand batsman, right-arm fast-medium bowler. Barbados debut 1988-89. Durham 1993 to 1994 (cap 1993). **TESTS:** 5 (1992-93 to 1994-95). 98 runs (av 19.60); 8 wkts (av 42.75); 1 ct. HS 50 v I (Chandigarh) 1994-95. BB 4-54 v P (St John's) 1992-93. **L-O INTERNATIONALS:** 58 (1991-92 to 1994-95). 429 runs (av 15.32); 72 wkts (av 28.23); 10 ct. HS 44* v NZ (Wellington) 1994-95. BB 5-31 v I (Brisbane) 1991-92. **F-C CAREER:** 1593 runs (av 20.68), 1 hundred, HS 107; 188 wkts (av 30.87), 5 wkts/inns (8), 10 wkts/match (1), BB 6-64; 14 ct.

DRAKES, Vasbert Conneil **(Barbados)**
Born St James, Barbados 5 August 1969. 6′ 2″. Educated at St Lucy Secondary & College School. Right-hand batsman, right-arm fast-medium bowler. Barbados debut 1991-92. **TESTS:** 0. **L-O INTERNATIONALS:** 5 (1994-95). 25 runs (av 12.50); 3 wkts (av 68.00); 1 ct. HS 16 v A (Port-of-Spain) 1994-95. BB 1-36. **F-C CAREER:** 880 runs (av 29.33), 2 hundreds, HS 180*; 85 wkts (av 26.47), 5 wkts/inns (3), BB 7-47; 6 ct.

GIBSON, Ottis Delroy **(Barbados)**
Born Barbados, Barbados 16 Mar 1969. 6′ 2″. Educated at Ellerslie Secondary School. Right-hand batsman, right-arm fast-medium bowler. Barbados debut 1990-91. Border debut 1992-93. Glamorgan 1994 (cap 1994). **TESTS:** 1 (1995). 43 runs (av 21.50); 2 wkts (av 66.00); 0 ct. HS 29 and BB 2-81 v E (Lord's) 1995. **L-O INTERNATIONALS:** 1 (1995). 7 runs (av 7.00); 3 wkts (av 17.00); 0 ct. HS 7 and BB 3-51 v E (Lord's) 1995. **F-C CAREER:** 1811 runs (av 21.55), 1 hundred; 241 wkts (av 28.59), 5 wkts/inns (11), 10 wkts/match (3), 50 wkts in a season (1), BB 7-55; 23 ct.

HARPER, Roger Andrew **(Guyana)**
Born Georgetown, Guyana 17 Mar 1963. 6′ 5″. Queen's College High School, Georgetown. Right-hand batsman, off-break bowler. Debut (Demerara) 1979-80. Guyana debut 1979-80. Northamptonshire 1985 to 1987 (cap 1986). **TESTS:** 25 (1983-84 to 1993-94). 535 runs (av 18.44); 46 wkts (av 28.06), 5 wkts/inns (1); 36 ct. HS 74 v E (Manchester) 1988. BB 6-57 v E (Manchester) 1984. **L-O INTERNATIONALS:** 81 (1983-84 to 1993-94). 555 runs (av 15.00); 73 wkts (av 35.54); 38 ct. HS 45* v NZ (St John's) 1984-85. BB 4-40 v E (Port-of-Spain) 1993-94. **F-C CAREER:** 7207 runs (av 33.67), 9 hundreds, HS 234; 540 wkts (av 26.43), 5 wkts/inns (26), 10 wkts/match (3), 50 wkts in a season (1), BB 6-24; 253 ct.

HOLDER, Roland Irwin Christopher **(Barbados)**
Born Port-of-Spain, Trinidad 22 Dec 1967. Right-hand batsman. Barbados debut 1985-86. **TESTS:** 0. **L-O INTERNATIONALS:** 15 (1993-94 to 1994-95). 255 runs (av 25.50); 6 ct. HS 50 v Z (Hyderabad, India) 1993-94. **F-C CAREER:** 2768 runs (av 41.31), 10 hundreds, HS 162*; 20 ct.

HOOPER, Carl Llewellyn **(Guyana)**
Born Georgetown, Guyana 15 Dec 1966. 6′ 1″. Educated at Christchurch Secondary School, Georgetown. Right-hand batsman, off-break bowler. Debut (Demerara) 1983-84. Guyana debut 1984-85. Kent 1992 to 1994 (cap 1992). **TESTS:** 52 (1987-88 to 1995). 2548 runs (av 31.85), 5 hundreds; 51 wkts (av 52.39), 5 wkts/inns (2); 57 ct. HS 178* v P (St John's) 1992-93; BB 5-40 v P (P-o-S) 1992-93. **L-O INTERNATIONALS:** 133 (1986-87 to 1995). 3071 runs (av 33.74), 2 hundreds; 125 wkts (av 31.37); 65 ct. HS 113* v I (Gwalior) 1987-88. BB 4-34 v P (Karachi) 1991-92. **F-C CAREER:** 11,921 runs (av 44.64), 30 hundreds, 1000 runs in a season (5), HS 236*; 314 wkts (av 35.58), 5 wkts/inns (10), BB 5-33; 204 ct.

LARA, Brian Charles **(Trinidad)**
Born Santa Cruz, Trinidad 2 May 1969. 5′ 8″. Left-hand batsman, right-arm leg-break bowler. Trinidad debut 1987-88. Warwickshire 1994 (cap 1994). One of *Wisden*'s Five Cricketers of 1994. **TESTS:** 31 (1990-91 to 1995). 3048 runs (av 60.96), 7 hundreds; 0 wkts; 42 ct. HS 375 (world Test record) v E (St John's) 1993-94. **L-O INTERNATIONALS:** 87 (1990-91 to 1995, 2 as captain). 3433 runs (av 43.45), 5 hundreds; 2 wkts (av 11.00); 47 ct. HS 153 v P (Sharjah) 1993-94. BB 2-5 v E (Arnos Vale) 1993-94. **F-C CAREER:** 9171 runs (av 56.26), 26 hundreds, 1000 runs in a season (3) including 2000 (1): 2066 off 2262 balls in 1994. HS 501* (world f-c record) Warwks v Durham (Birmingham) 1994. Scored 6 hundreds in his first 7 innings for Warwks (147, 106, 120*, 136, 26, 140, 501*); 1 wkt (av 268.00), BB 1-22; 129 ct.

MURRAY, Junior Randalph **(Windward Islands)**
Born St George's, Grenada 20 Jan 1968. 6′ 0″. Educated at Grenada Secondary School. Right-hand batsman, wicket-keeper. Windward Islands debut 1986-87. **TESTS:** 24 (1992-93 to 1995). 712 runs (av 25.42), 1 hundred; 86 ct, 2 st. HS 101* v NZ (Wellington) 1994-95. **L-O INTERNATIONALS:** 38 (1992-93 to 1995). 213 runs (av 16.38); 35 ct, 5 st. HS 86 v E (Oval) 1995. **F-C CAREER:** 2808 runs (av 27.52), 4 hundreds, HS 141*; 179 ct, 12 st.

RICHARDSON, Richard Benjamin **('Richie') (Leeward Islands)**
Born Five Islands, Antigua 12 Jan 1962. 5′ 11½″. Right-hand batsman, right-arm medium pace bowler. Leeward Islands debut 1981-82. Yorkshire 1993 and 1994 (cap 1993). **TESTS:** 86 (1983-84 to 1995, 24 as captain). 5949 runs (av 44.39), 16 hundreds; 0 wkts; 90 ct. HS 194 v I (Georgetown) 1988-89. **L-O INTERNATIONALS:** 206 (1983-84 to 1995, 69 as captain). 5689 runs (av 33.07), 5 hundreds; 1 wkt (av 46.00); 70 ct. HS 122 v P (Sharjah) 1991-92. BB 1-4. **F-C CAREER:** 13,857 runs (av 42.37), 37 hundreds, 1000 runs in a season (3), HS 194; 6 wkts (av 39.66), BB 5-40 *(his first f-c wkts)*; 198 ct.

SIMMONS, Philip Verant **(Trinidad)**
Born Arima, Trinidad 18 Apr 1963. 6′ 3½". Educated at Holy Cross College, Arima. Right-hand batsman, right-arm medium pace bowler. Debut (N Trinidad) 1982-83. Trinidad debut 1982-83. Leicestershire 1994 (cap 1994). **TESTS:** 22 (1987-88 to 1994-95). 919 runs (av 23.56), 1 hundred; 2 wkts (av 79.00); 21 ct. HS 110 and BB 2-34 v A (Melbourne) 1992-93. **L-O INTERNATIONALS:** 98 (1987-88 to 1994-95). 2810 runs (av 31.22), 4 hundreds; 49 wkts (av 31.97); 35 ct. HS 122 v SA (Kingston) 1992-92. BB 4-3 v P (Sydney) 1992-93. **F-C CAREER:** 7876 runs (av 34.84), 15 hundreds, 1000 runs in a season (1), HS 262 v Northants (Leicester) 1994 – on Leics debut *(county record)*; 90 wkts (av 35.37), 5 wkts/inns (1), BB 5-24; 141 ct.

WALSH, Courtney Andrew **(Jamaica)**
Born Kingston, Jamaica 30 Oct 1962. 6′ 5½". Educated at Excelsior High School. Right-hand batsman, right-arm fast bowler. Jamaica debut 1981-82. Gloucestershire 1984 to 1994 (cap 1985; captain 1993-94; benefit 1992). One of *Wisden's* Five Cricketers of 1986. **TESTS:** 80 (1984-85 to 1995, 6 as captain). 683 runs (av 8.98); 301 wkts (av 25.02), 5 wkts/inns (11), 10wkts/match (2). HS 30* v A (Melbourne) 1988-89. BB 7-37 (13-55 match) v NZ (Wellington) 1994-95. **L-O INTERNATIONALS:** 142 (1984-85 to 1995, 15 as captain). 251 runs (av 8.65); 158 wkts (av 30.29); 20 ct. HS 30 v I (Calcutta) 1994-95. BB 5-1 v SL (Sharjah) 1986-87. **F-C CAREER:** 3837 runs (av 12.37), HS 66; 1305 wkts (av 22.37), 5 wkts/inns (75), 10 wkts/match (15); 50 wkts in a season (10) including 100 (1): 118 (1986); 1 hat-trick 1988-89, BB 9-72; 82 ct.

WILLIAMS, Stuart Clayton **(Leeward Islands)**
Born Charlestown, Nevis 12 Aug 1969. 5′ 7". Right-hand batsman. Leeward Islands debut 1988-89. **TESTS:** 12 (1993-94 to 1995). 386 runs (av 22.70); 14 ct. HS 62 v E (Nottingham) 1995. **L-O INTERNATIONALS:** 18 (1994-95 to 1995). 533 runs (av 33.31); 4 ct. HS 73* v NZ (Auckland) 1994-95. **F-C CAREER:** 2898 runs (av 32.93), 7 hundreds, HS 157; 37 ct.

WORLD CUP CAREER RECORDS

WEST INDIES – BATTING AND FIELDING

	M	I	NO	HS	Runs	Avge	100	50	Ct/St
Ambrose, C.E.L.	7	4	1	15*	33	11.00	–	–	1
Arthurton, K.L.T.	8	7	1	58*	233	38.83	–	2	1
Bacchus, S.F.A.F.	8	5	1	80*	157	39.25	–	1	–
Baptiste, E.A.E.	1	1	–	14	14	14.00	–	–	1
Benjamin, W.K.M.	13	10	5	24*	69	13.80	–	–	4
Best, C.A.	2	2	–	18	23	11.50	–	–	1
Boyce, K.D.	5	2	–	34	41	20.50	–	–	–
Croft, C.E.H.	4	1	1	0*	0	–	–	–	–
Cummins, A.C.	6	2	1	6	11	11.00	–	–	–
Daniel, W.W.	3	1	1	16*	′16	–	–	–	–
Davis, W.W.	5	1	1	0*	0	–	–	–	–
Dujon, P.J.L.	14	·9	1	46	112	14.00	–	–	19/1
Fredericks, R.C.	5	5	–	58	116	23.20	–	1	2

	M	I	NO	HS	Runs	Avge	100	50	Ct/St
Garner, J.	8	5	3	37	52	26.00	–	–	4
Gibbs, L.R.	1	–	–	–	–	–	–	–	–
Gomes, H.A.	8	7	3	78	258	64.50	–	3	3
Greenidge, C.G.	15	15	2	106*	591	45.46	2	4	1
Harper, R.A.	8	7	1	24	40	6.66	–	–	3
Haynes, D.L.	25	25	2	105	854	37.13	1	3	12
Holder, V.A.	5	2	1	16	22	22.00	–	–	2
Holding, M.A.	11	5	–	20	36	7.20	–	–	5
Hooper, C.L.	14	12	3	63	162	18.00	–	1	8
Julien, B.D.	5	3	2	26*	48	48.00	–	–	–
Kallicharran, A.I.	9	8	1	78	251	35.85	–	2	6
Kanhai, R.B.	5	4	2	55	109	54.50	–	1	3
King, C.L.	4	3	–	86	132	44.00	–	1	2
Lara, B.C.	8	8	1	88*	333	47.57	–	4	2
Lloyd, C.H.	17	11	2	102	393	43.66	1	2	12
Logie, A.L.	15	13	2	65*	282	25.63	–	2	4
Marshall, M.D.	11	7	–	18	40	5.71	–	–	–
Murray, D.L.	9	5	2	61*	122	40.66	–	1	16
Patterson, B.P.	7	2	2	4*	4	–	–	–	2
Richards, I.V.A.	23	21	5	181	1013	63.31	3	5	9
Richardson, R.B.	14	14	1	110	403	31.00	1	3	5
Roberts, A.M.E.	16	8	3	37*	85	17.00	–	–	1
Simmons, P.V.	8	8	–	110	323	40.37	1	2	1
Walsh, C.A.	6	3	1	9*	18	9.00	–	–	1
Williams, D.	8	6	2	32*	52	13.00	–	–	11/3

WEST INDIES – BOWLING

	O	M	R	W	Avge	Best	4w	R/O
Ambrose, C.E.L.	68	6	235	7	33.57	2-24	–	3.45
Arthurton, K.L.T.	15	0	70	2	35.00	2-40	–	4.66
Baptiste, E.A.E.	8	1	33	0	–	–	–	4.12
Benjamin, W.K.M.	123	10	515	14	36.78	3-27	–	4.18
Boyce, K.D.	52	3	185	10	18.50	4-50	1	3.55
Croft, C.E.H.	43	3	140	8	17.50	3-29	–	3.25
Cummins, A.C.	59	1	246	12	20.50	4-33	1	4.16
Daniel, W.W.	24	6	84	3	28.00	3-28	–	3.50
Davis, W.W.	54.3	6	206	8	25.75	7-51	1	3.77
Garner, J.	90	12	289	13	22.23	5-38	1	3.21
Gibbs, L.R.	4	0	17	0	–	–	–	4.25
Gomes, H.A.	74	4	304	9	33.77	2-46	–	4.10
Harper, R.A.	74	4	269	6	44.83	1-28	–	3.63
Holder, V.A.	43.2	4	184	5	36.80	3-30	–	4.24
Holding, M.A.	115.5	16	341	20	17.05	4-33	1	2.94
Hooper, C.L.	121	2	493	15	32.86	3-42	–	4.07
Julien, B.D.	60	11	177	10	17.70	4-20	2	2.95
King, C.L.	32	2	128	2	64.00	1-36	–	4.00
Lloyd, C.H.	36	4	125	3	41.66	1-31	–	3.47
Marshall, M.D.	113	13	349	14	24.92	3-28	–	3.08
Patterson, B.P.	66	2	278	15	18.53	3-31	–	4.21
Richards, I.V.A.	83	2	345	10	34.50	3-41	–	4.15
Richardson, R.B.	4	0	24	0	–	–	–	6.00
Roberts, A.M.E.	170.1	29	552	26	21.23	3-32	–	3.24
Simmons, P.V.	20	1	91	3	30.33	2-40	–	4.55
Walsh, C.A.	55.3	6	229	9	25.44	4-40	1	4.12

WORLD CUP REGISTER

NEW ZEALAND

New Zealand's World Cup selections had not been released at the time of going to press. All career statistics are up to the end of the 1995 season (18 September). Key to abbreviations on page 32.

ASTLE, Nathan John **(Canterbury)**
Born Christchurch 15 Sep 1971. Right-hand batsman, right-arm medium pace bowler. First-class debut (Canterbury) 1991-92. **TESTS:** 0. **L-O INTERNATIONALS:** 5 (1994-95). 175 runs (av 35.00); 1 wkt (av 119.00); 0 ct. HS 95 v SL (Hamilton) 1994-95. BB 1-46. **F-C CAREER:** 1051 runs (av 37.53), 2 hundreds, HS 191; 25 wkts (av 40.52), BB 3-45; 11 ct.

CAIRNS, Christopher Lance **(Canterbury)**
Born Picton 13 Jun 1970. 6' 2". Son of B.L.Cairns (C Districts, Otago, N Districts and NZ). 6' 2". Educated at Christchurch High School. Right-hand batsman, right-arm fast-medium bowler First-class debut (Nottinghamshire) 1988 (cap 1993). **TESTS:** 10 (1989-90 to 1993-94). 349 runs (av 20.52); 28 wkts (av 43.10), 5 wkts/inns (2); 2 ct. HS 78 v A (Perth) 1993-94; BB 6-52 v E (Auckland) 1991-92. **L-O INTERNATIONALS:** 29 (1990-91 to 1994-95). 586 runs (av 26.63); 27 wkts (av 33.03); 12 ct. HS 72 v SL (Christchurch) 1994-95. BB 4-55 v E (Auckland) 1990-91. **F-C CAREER:** 4813 runs (av 34.13), 5 hundreds, HS 115; 326 wkts (av 28.30), 5 wkts/inns (13), 10 wkts/match (3), 50 wkts/season (3), BB 8-47; 47 ct.

CROWE, Martin David **(Wellington)**
Born Henderson, Auckland 22 Sep 1962. 6' 1½". Educated at Auckland Grammar School. Right-hand batsman, right-arm medium pace bowler. First-class debut (Auckland) 1979-80. Somerset 1984 to 1988 (cap 1984). **TESTS:** 74 (1981-82 to 1994-95, 16 as captain). 5394 runs (av 46.10), 17 hundreds; 14 wkts (av 48.28); 18 ct. HS 299 v SL (Wellington) 1990-91. BB 2-25 v WI (Bridgetown) 1984-85. **L-O INTERNATIONALS:** 139 (1981-82 to 1994-95, 44 as captain). 4517 runs (av 37.95), 3 hundreds; 29 wkts (av 32.89); 64 ct. HS 105* v E (Auckland) 1983-84. BB 2-9 v A (Auckland) 1981-82 – on debut. **F-C CAREER:** 19,333 runs (av 56.03), 69 hundreds, 1000 runs/season (7), HS 299; 119 wkts (av 33.69), 5 wkts/inns (4), BB 5-18; 213 ct.

De Groen, Richard Paul **(Northern Districts)**
Born Otorohanga 5 Aug 1962. Right-hand batsman, right-arm fast-medium bowler. First-class debut (Auckland) 1987-88 **TESTS:** 5 (1993-94 to 1994-95). 45 runs (av 7.50); 11 wkts (av 45.90); 0 ct. HS 26 v SA (Johannesburg) 1994-95. BB 3-40 v P (Auckland) 1993-94. **L-O INTERNATIONALS:** 12 (1993-94 to 1994-95). 12 runs (av 2.40); 8 wkts (av 59.62); 2 ct. HS 7* and BB 2-34 v A (Sydney) 1993-94. **F-C CAREER:** 293 runs (av 7.91), HS 35; 188 wkts (av 25.60), 5 wkts/inns (9), 10 wkts/match (1), BB 7-50; 9 ct.

DOUGLAS, Mark William **(Wellington)**
Born Nelson 20 Oct 1968. Left-hand batsman. First-class debut (C Districts) 1987-88. **TESTS:** 0. **L-O INTERNATIONALS:** 6 (1993-94 to 1994-95). 55 runs (av 9.16); 2 ct. HS 30 v SL (Sharjah) 1993-94. **F-C CAREER:** 3386 runs (av 33.86), 6 hundreds, HS 144; 4 wkts (av 30.00), BB 2-29; 57 ct.

DOULL, Simon Blair **(Northern Districts)**
Born Pukekohe 6 Aug 1969. Right-hand batsman, right-arm medium pace bowler. First-class debut (N Districts) 1989-90. **TESTS:** 11 (1992-93 to 1994-95). 210 runs (av 13.12); 33 wkts (av 32.63), 5 wkts/inns (2); 8 ct. HS 31* v SA (Johannesburg) 1994-95. BB 5-66 v P (Auckland) 1993-94. **L-O INTERNATIONALS:** 8 (1992-93 to 1994-95). 61 runs (av 20.33); 6 wkts (av 67.50); 0 ct. HS 19* v SA (Cape Town) 1994-95. BB 2-42 v Z (Bulawayo) 1992-93. **F-C CAREER:** 754 runs (av 16.04), 1 hundred, HS 108; 138 wkts (av 26.72), 5 wkts/inns (8), 10 wkts/match (1), BB 6-37; 17 ct.

FLEMING, Stephen Paul **(Canterbury)**
Born Christchurch 1 Apr 1973. 6′ 3″. Educated at Cashmere High School; Christchurch College of Education. Left-hand batsman. First-class debut (Canterbury) 1991-92. **TESTS:** 12 (1993-94 to 1994-95). 786 runs (av 35.72); 6 ct. HS 92 v I (Hamilton) 1993-94 — on debut. **L-O INTERNATIONALS:** 25 (1993-94 to 1994-95). 551 runs (av 25.04); 0 wkts; 8 ct. HS 90 v I (Napier) 1993-94 — on debut. **F-C CAREER:** 2416 runs (av 37.16), 6 hundreds, HS 151; 0 wkts; 47 ct.

GERMON, Lee Kenneth **(Canterbury)**
Born Christchurch 4 Nov 1968. Right-hand batsman, wicket-keeper. First-class debut (Canterbury) 1987-88. Appointed New Zealand captain 1994-95. **TESTS:** 0. **L-O INTER-NATIONALS:** 1 (1994-95). Did not bat; 1 ct. **F-C CAREER:** 2307 runs (av 32.49), 4 hundreds, HS 160*; 1 wkt (av 12.00), BB 1-12; 201 ct, 23 st.

GREATBATCH, Mark John **(Central Districts)**
Born Auckland 11 Dec 1963. 6′ 2″. Auckland Grammar School. Left-hand batsman, right-arm medium pace bowler, occasional wicket-keeper. First-class debut (Auckland) 1982-83. **TESTS:** 36 (1987-88 to 1994-95). 1905 runs (av 32.28), 3 hundreds; 0 wkts; 25 ct. HS 146* v A (Perth) 1989-90. **L-O INTERNATIONALS:** 73 (1987-88 to 1994-95). 1998 runs (av 29.38), 2 hundreds; 0 wkts; 30 ct. HS 111 v E (Oval) 1990. **F-C CAREER:** 8067 runs (av 36.66), 16 hundreds, HS 202*; 1 wkt (av 88.00), BB 1-23; 116 ct.

HART, Matthew Norman **(Northern Districts)**
Born Hamilton 16 May 1972. 6′ 0″. Te Puke High School; Waikato Polytechnic. Left-hand batsman, left-arm orthodox slow bowler. First-class debut (N Districts) 1990-91. **TESTS:** 12 (1993-94 to 1994-95). 317 runs (av 17.61); 27 wkts (av 49.85), 5 wkts/inns (1); 7 ct. HS 45 v WI (Christchurch) 1994-95. BB 5-77 v SA (Johannesburg) 1994-95. **L-O INTER-NATIONALS:** 10 (1993-94 to 1994-95). 49 runs (av 8.16); 11 wkts (av 28.54); 7 ct. HS 16 v I (Delhi) 1994-95. BB 5-22 v WI (Margao) 1994-95. **F-C CAREER:** 1241 runs (av 17.47), HS 83: 139 wkts (av 34.96), 5 wkts/inns (5), BB 5-37; 59 ct.

LARSEN, Gavin Rolf **(Wellington)**
Born Wellington 27 Sep 1962. 5′ 11″. Educated at Onslow College. Right-hand batsman, right-arm medium pace bowler. First-class debut (Wellington) 1984-85. **TESTS:** 4 (1994 to 1994-95). 74 runs (av 14.80); 14 wkts (av 26.92); 5 ct. HS 26* and BB 3-57 v SA (Auckland) 1994-95. **L-O INTERNATIONALS:** 65 (1989-90 to 1994-95, 3 as captain). 371 runs (av 17.66); 48 wkts (av 44.77); 10 ct. HS 37 v P (Christchurch) 1991-92. BB 4-24 v P (Auckland) 1993-94. Appeared in 55 LOIs before making his Test debut. **F-C CAREER:** 3020 runs (av 29.60), 1 hundred, HS 161; 136 wkts (av 29.00), 5 wkts/inns (4), BB 6-37; 62 ct.

MORRISON, Daniel Kyle **(Auckland)**
Born Auckland 3 Feb 1966. 5′ 10″. Educated at Takapuna Grammar School. Right-hand batsman, right-arm fast-medium bowler. First-class debut (Auckland) 1985-86. **TESTS:** 41 (1987-88 to 1994-95). 318 runs (av 7.95); 143 wkts (av 33.53), 5 wkts/inns (9); 13 ct. HS 42 v P (Wellington) 1993-94. BB 7-89 v A (Wellington) 1992-93. **L-O INTERNATIONALS:** 74 (1987-88 to 1994-95). 139 runs (av 8.17); 94 wkts (av 28.39), 1 hat-trick; 17 ct. HS 20* v A (Dunedin) 1992-93. BB 4-33 v P (Hamilton) 1988-89. **F-C CAREER:** 856 runs (av 9.83), HS 46*; 373 wkts (av 30.21), 5 wkts/inns (16), BB 7-82; 41 ct.

NASH, Dion Joseph **(Otago)**
Born Auckland 20 Nov 1971. 6′ 1″. Educated at Dargaville High School; Auckland Grammar School; Otago University. Right-hand batsman, right-arm fast-medium bowler. First-class debut (N Districts) 1990-91. Middlesex debut 1995. **TESTS:** 10 (1992-93 to 1994-95). 176 runs (av 16.00); 32 wkts (av 31.68), 5 wkts/inns (2), 10 wkts/match (1); 7 ct. HS 56 and BB 6-76 (11-169 match) v E (Lord's) 1994. **L-O INTERNATIONALS:** 15 (1992-93 to 1994-95). 94 runs (av 11.75); 12 wkts (av 45.50); 4 ct. HS 40* v SL (PSS, Colombo) 1992-93. BB 3-43 v SL (Sharjah) 1993-94. **F-C CAREER:** 1163 runs (av 18.17), HS 67; 146 wkts (av 28.08), 5 wkts/inns (7), 10 wkts/match (1), 50 wkts/season (1), BB 6-30; 28 ct.

PARORE, Adam Craig **(Auckland)**
Born Auckland 23 Jan 1971. 5′ 9″. Educated at Auckland University. Right-hand batsman, wicket-keeper. First-class debut (Auckland) 1988-89. **TESTS:** 20 (1990 to 1994-95). 805 runs (av 25.96), 1 hundred; 56 ct, 2 st. HS 100* v WI (Christchurch) 1994-95. **L-O INTERNATIONALS:** 37 (1992-93 to 1994-95). 1004 runs (av 38.61), 1 hundred; 30 ct, 8 st. HS 108 v SA (Verwoerdburg) 1994-95. **F-C CAREER:** 3119 runs (av 34.65), 6 hundreds, HS 155*; 0 wkts; 164 ct, 13 st.

PATEL, Dipak Narshibhai **(Auckland)**
Born Nairobi, Kenya 25 Oct 1958. Right-hand batsman, off-break bowler. Worcestershire 1976 to 1986 (cap 1979). Auckland debut 1985-86. **TESTS:** 27 (1986-87 to 1994-95). 927 runs (av 21.06); 54 wkts (av 43.01), 5 wkts/inns (3); 11 ct. HS 99 v E (Christchurch) 1991-92. BB 6-50 v Z (Harare) 1992-93. **L-O INTERNATIONALS:** 50 (1986-87 to 1994-95). 427 runs (av 12.55); 32 wkts (av 43.12); 16 ct. HS 40 v I (Nagpur) 1987-88. BB 3-22 v SL (Sharjah) 1987-88. **F-C CAREER:** 14,889 runs (av 30.32), 26 hundreds, HS 204; 632 wkts (av 32.91), 5 wkts/inns (27), 10 wkts/match (2), BB 7-46; 188 ct.

PRINGLE, Christopher (Auckland)
Born Auckland 26 Jan 1968. 6′ 3″. Educated at Rosmini College. Right-hand batsman, right-arm medium-fast bowler. First-class debut (Auckland) 1989-90. **TESTS:** 14 (1990-91 to 1994-95). 175 runs (av 10.29); 30 wkts (av 46.30), 5 wkts/inns (1), 10 wkts/match (1); 3 ct. HS 30 v SA (Cape Town) 1994-95. BB 7-52 (11-152 match) v P (Faisalabad) 1990-91. **L-O INTERNATIONALS:** 64 (1990 to 1994-95). 193 runs (av 8.77); 103 wkts (av 23.83); 7 ct. HS 34* v WI (Gauhati) 1994-95. BB 5-45 v E (Birmingham) 1994. **F-C CAREER:** 658 runs (av 12.18); HS 45*; 169 wkts (av 29.65), 5 wkts/inns (6), 10 wkts/match (2), BB 7-52; 14 ct.

SU′A, Murphy Logo **(Auckland)**
Born Wanganui 7 Nov 1966. Left-hand batsman, left-arm fast-medium bowler. First-class debut (N Districts) 1988-89. **TESTS:** 13 (1991-92 to 1994-95). 165 runs (av 12.69); 36 wkts (av 38.25), 5 wkts/inns (2); 9 ct. HS 44 v A (Christchurch) 1992-93. BB 5-73 v P (Hamilton) 1992-93. **L-O INTERNATIONALS:** 12 (1991-92 to 1994-95). 24 runs (av 4.80); 9 wkts (av 40.77); 1 ct. HS 12* v E (Christchurch) 1991-92. BB 4-59 v SA (Verwoerdburg) 1994-95. **F-C CAREER:** 828 runs (av 18.40); HS 56; 141 wkts (av 34.00), 5 wkts/inns (7), BB 6-56; 12 ct.

THOMSON, Shane Alexander **(Northern Districts)**
Born Hamilton 27 Jan 1969. 6′ 0″. Educated at Hamilton High School. Right-hand batsman, off-break bowler. First-class debut (N Districts) 1987-88. **TESTS:** 17 (1989-90 to 1994-95). 935 runs (av 32.24), 1 hundred; 19 wkts (av 45.05); 7 ct. HS 120* v P (Christchurch) 1993-94. BB 3-63 v SL (Auckland) 1990-91. **L-O INTERNATIONALS:** 41 (1989-90 to 1994-95). 780 runs (av 22.94); 29 wkts (av 40.00); 11 ct. HS 83 v I (Napier) 1993-94. BB 3-14 v P (Auckland) 1993-94. **F-C CAREER:** 4014 runs (av 39.35), 6 hundreds, HS 167; 108 wkts (av 38.16), 5 wkts/inns (2), BB 5-49; 35 ct.

TWOSE, Roger Graham **(Wellington)**
Born Torquay, England 17 Apr 1968. 6' 0". Educated at Ling's College, Taunton. Nephew of R.W.Tolchard (Leicestershire and England). Left-hand batsman, right-arm medium pace bowler. Warwickshire 1989 to 1995 (cap 1992). N Districts 1989-90. C Districts 1991-92 to 1993-94. Wellington debut 1994-95. **TESTS:** 0. **L-O INTERNATIONALS:** 0. **F-C CAREER:** 7450 runs (av 39.62), 15 hundreds, 1000 runs/season (3), HS 277*; 117 wkts (av 32.32), 5 wkts/inns (2), BB 6-28; 67 ct.

WALMSLEY, Kerry P. **(Auckland)**
Right-hand batsman, right-arm fast-medium bowler. First-class debut 1994-95. **TESTS:** 2 (1994-95). 8 runs (av 2.66); 7 wkts (av 49.14); 0 ct. HS 4 and BB 3-70 v SL (Napier) 1994-95. **L-O INTERNATIONALS:** 0. **F-C CAREER:** 36 runs (av 6.00), HS 14*; 20 wkts (av 35.05), 5 wkts/inns (1), BB 5-73; 1 ct.

YOUNG, Bryan Alexander **(Northern Districts)**
Born Whangerei 3 Nov 1964. 5' 10". Right-hand batsman, wicket-keeper. First-class debut (N Districts) 1983-84. **TESTS:** 16 (1993-94 to 1994-95). 996 runs (av 32.12), 1 hundred; 25 ct. HS 120 v P (Christchurch) 1993-94. **L-O INTERNATIONALS:** 43 (1990-91 to 1994-95). 931 runs (av 24.50); 19 ct. HS 74 v SA (Hobart) 1993-94. **F-C CAREER:** 5312 runs (av 34.27), 6 hundreds, HS 138*; 1 wkt (av 76.00), BB 1-76; 230 ct, 11 st.

WORLD CUP CAREER RECORDS

NEW ZEALAND – BATTING AND FIELDING

	M	I	NO	HS	Runs	Avge	100	50	Ct/St
Boock, S.L.	4	3	2	12	19	19.00	–	–	2
Bracewell, J.G.	7	7	2	34	80	16.00	–	–	1
Burgess, M.G.	4	2	–	35	45	22.50	–	–	2
Cairns, B.L.	11	9	–	44	43	4.77	–	–	4
Cairns, C.L.	5	3	3	16*	21	–	–	–	5
Chatfield, E.J.	13	8	7	19*	45	45.00	–	–	2
Collinge, R.O.	4	2	–	6	8	4.00	–	–	1
Coney, J.V.	10	8	2	66*	244	40.66	–	2	4
Crowe, J.J.	8	8	1	88*	220	31.42	–	1	4
Crowe, M.D.	21	21	5	100*	880	55.00	1	8	8
Edgar, B.A.	8	8	1	84*	194	27.71	–	1	5
Greatbatch, M.J.	7	7	–	73	313	44.71	–	3	4
Hadlee, B.G.	1	1	–	19	19	19.00	–	–	–
Hadlee, D.R.	4	3	1	20	28	14.00	–	–	–
Hadlee, R.J.	13	10	1	42	149	16.55	–	–	3
Harris, C.Z.	9	6	1	14	44	8.80	–	–	4
Hastings, B.F.	4	4	1	34	76	25.33	–	–	3
Horne, P.A.	1	1	–	18	18	18.00	–	–	–
Howarth, G.P.	11	11	1	76	374	37.40	–	4	2
Howarth, H.J.	4	2	1	1*	1	1.00	–	–	2

	M	I	NO	HS	Runs	Avge	100	50	Ct/St
Jones, A.H.	13	13	2	78	416	37.81	–	4	3
Larsen, G.R.	9	2	1	37	45	45.00	–	–	5
Latham, R.T.	7	7	–	60	136	19.42	–	1	3
Lees, W.K.	8	6	1	26	88	17.60	–	–	10
McKechnie, B.J.	8	4	2	27	45	22.50	–	–	2
Morrison, D.K.	6	1	–	12	12	12.00	–	–	1
Morrison, J.F.M.	6	5	–	55	102	20.40	–	1	3
Parker, J.M.	4	4	–	66	71	17.75	–	1	–
Patel, D.N.	15	9	1	40	83	10.37	–	–	3
Rutherford, K.R.	14	12	2	75	416	41.60	–	4	5
Smith, I.D.S.	17	13	3	29	138	13.80	–	–	9
Snedden, M.C.	9	8	–	64	218	27.25	–	1	2
Stott, L.W.	1	–	–	–	–	–	–	–	1
Troup, G.B.	3	1	1	3*	3	–	–	–	–
Turner, G.M.	14	14	4	171*	612	61.20	2	2	3
Wadsworth, K.J.	4	4	–	25	68	17.00	–	–	3/1
Watson, W.	14	5	4	12*	29	29.00	–	–	2
Wright, J.G.	18	18	–	69	493	27.38	–	3	4

NEW ZEALAND – BOWLING

	O	M	R	W	Avge	Best	4w	R/O
Boock, S.L.	32.4	2	156	4	39.00	2-42	–	4.77
Bracewell, J.G.	59	2	310	1	310.00	1-66	–	5.25
Cairns, B.L.	115.2	16	436	14	31.14	3-36	–	3.78
Cairns, C.L.	25	1	161	2	80.50	2-43	–	6.44
Chatfield, E.J.	131.3	16	524	14	37.42	2-24	–	3.98
Collinge, R.O.	48	13	137	6	22.83	3-28	–	2.85
Coney, J.V.	89	7	303	12	25.25	3-28	–	3.40
Crowe, M.D.	18	2	116	1	116.00	1-15	–	6.44
Greatbatch, M.J.	1	0	5	0	–	–	–	5.00
Hadlee, D.R.	46	5	162	8	20.25	3-21	–	3.52
Hadlee, R.J.	146.1	38	421	22	19.13	5-25	1	2.88
Harris, C.Z.	72.1	4	342	16	21.37	3-15	–	4.73
Howarth, H.J.	40	5	148	4	29.60	3-29	–	3.70
Jones, A.H.	12	0	52	2	26.00	2-42	–	4.33
Larsen, G.R.	76	7	262	9	29.11	3-16	–	3.44
Latham, R.T.	23	0	136	1	136.00	1-35	–	5.91
McKechnie, B.J.	89.5	9	304	13	23.38	3-24	–	3.38
Morrison, D.K.	50	1	249	5	49.80	3-42	–	4.98
Morrison, J.F.M.	8	0	31	0	–	–	–	3.87
Patel, D.N.	122	9	468	12	39.00	3-36	–	3.83
Rutherford, K.R.	1.4	0	11	0	–	–	–	6.60
Snedden, M.C.	81.5	6	455	10	45.50	2-36	–	5.56
Stott, L.W.	12	1	48	3	16.00	3-48	–	4.00
Troup, G.B.	32	3	104	4	26.00	2-36	–	3.25
Watson, W.	132	14	571	19	30.05	3-37	–	4.32

WORLD CUP REGISTER

INDIA

India's World Cup selections had not been released at the time of going to press. All career statistics are up to the end of the 1995 season (18 September). Key to abbreviations on page 32.

AZHARUDDIN, Mohammed (Hyderabad)
Born Hyderabad 8 Feb 1963. 5′ 11″. Educated at Nizam College; Osmania University. Right-hand batsman, right-arm medium pace/leg-break bowler. First-class debut 1981-82. Derbyshire 1991 and 1994 (cap 1991). One of *Wisden's* Five Cricketers of 1990. **TESTS:** 65 (1984-85 to 1994-95, 31 as captain). 4198 runs (av 46.64), 14 hundreds; 0 wkts; 68 ct. HS 199 v SL (Kanpur) 1986-87. **L-O INTERNATIONALS:** 194 (1984-85 to 1994-95, 96 as captain). 5288 runs (av 36.72), 3 hundreds; 12 wkts (av 39.00); 80 ct. HS 108* v NZ (Baroda) 1988-89. BB 3-19 v A (Delhi) 1987-88.

BEDADE, Atul Chandrakant (Baroda)
Born Bombay 24 Sep 1966. Left-hand batsman, right-arm medium pace bowler. First-class debut 1990-91. **TESTS:** 0. **L-O INTERNATIONALS:** 12 (1993-94 to 1994-95). 158 runs (av 22.57); 4 ct. HS 51 v WI (Faridabad) 1994-95.

BHUPINDER SINGH (Punjab)
Born Tarantaran 19 Nov 1970. Right-hand batsman. First-class debut 1989-90. **TESTS:** 0. **L-O INTERNATIONALS:** 2 (1993-94). 6 runs (av 6.00); 3 wkts (av 26.00); 0 ct. HS 6. BB 3-34 v UAE (Sharjah) 1993-94 – on debut.

CHATTERJEE, Utpal (Bengal)
Born Calcutta 13 Jul 1964. Left-hand batsman, left-arm orthodox slow bowler. First-class debut 1984-85. **TESTS:** 2 (1994-95). 3 runs (av –); 3 wkts (av 21.00); 1 ct. HS 3* and BB 2-35 v P (Sharjah) 1994-95.

CHAUHAN, Rajesh Kumar (Madhya Pradesh)
Born Ranchi 19 Dec 1966. Right-hand batsman, off-break bowler. First-class debut 1988-89. **TESTS:** 13 (1992-93 to 1994-95). 64 runs (av 9.14); 33 wkts (av 34.87); 8 ct. HS 15* v SL (PSS, Colombo) 1993-94. BB 3-8 v SL (Ahmedabad) 1993-94. **L-O INTERNATIONALS:** 20 (1993-94 to 1994-95). 73 runs (av 14.60); 21 wkts (av 34.00);5 ct. HS 26* v SL (Jalandhar). BB3-29 v P (Sharjah) 1993-94.

HIRWANI, Narendra Deepchand (Madhya Pradesh)
Born Gorakhpur 18 Oct 1968. Right-hand batsman, right-arm leg-break and googly bowler. First-class debut 1984-85. **TESTS:** 14 (1987-88 to 1990-91). 45 runs (av 5.62); 58 wkts (av 31.01), 5 wkts/inns (3), 10 wkts/match (1); 5 ct. HS 17 v NZ (Hyderabad) 1988-89. BB 8-61 (16-136 match) v WI (Madras) 1987-88 – on debut. **L-O INTERNATIONALS:** 18 (1987-88 to 1991-92). 8 runs (av 2.00); 23 wkts (av 31.26); 2 ct. HS 4. BB 4-43 v NZ (Sharjah) 1987-88.

JADEJA, Ajaysinhji Daulatsinhji (Haryana)
Born Jamnagar 1 Feb 1971. Right-hand batsman, right-arm medium pace bowler. First-class debut 1988-89. **TESTS:** 3 (1992-93). 99 runs (av 24.75); 0 ct. HS 43 v SA (Johannesburg) 1992-93. **L-O INTERNATIONALS:** 37 (1991-92 to 1994-95). 1032 runs (av 32.25), 1 hundred; 8 wkts (av 54.25); 12 ct. HS 104 v WI (Cuttack) 1994-95. BB 2-16 v SA (Chandigarh) 1993-94.

KAMBLI, Vinod Ganpat (Bombay)
Born Bombay 18 Jan 1972. Left-hand batsman, off-break bowler. First-class debut 1989-90.
TESTS: 14 (1992-93 to 1994-95). 1029 runs (av 57.16), 4 hundreds; 6 ct. HS 227 v Z
(Delhi) 1992-93. **L-O INTERNATIONALS:** 57 (1991-92 to 1994-95). 1620 runs (av
41.53), 1 hundred; 1 wkt (av 7.00); 10 ct. HS 100* v E (Jaipur) 1992-93. BB 1-7.

KAPOOR, Aashish Rakesh (Punjab)
Born Madras 25 Mar 1971. Right-hand batsman, off-break bowler. First-class debut
1989-90. **TESTS:** 1 (1994-95). 16 runs (av 8.00); 1 wkt (av 122.00); 1 ct. HS 15 and BB
1-90 v WI (Chandigarh) 1994-95. **L-O INTERNATIONALS:** 3 (1994-95). Did not bat; 0
wkts;0 ct.

KUMBLE, Anil (Karnataka)
Born Bangalore 17 Oct 1970. 6′ 1½″. Educated at National High School; R.V. Engineering
C, Bangalore. Right-hand batsman, right-arm leg-break and googly bowler. First-class
debut 1989-90. Northamptonshire 1995 (cap 1995) – taking 105 f-c wickets. **TESTS:** 20
(1990 to 1994-95). 249 runs (av 14.64); 99 wkts (av 25.35), 5 wkts/inns (5), 10 wkts/match
(1); 9 ct. HS 52* v WI (Nagpur) 1994-95. BB 7-59 (11-128 match) v SL (Lucknow)
1993-94. **L-O INTERNATIONALS:** 66 (1989-90 to 1994-95). 155 runs (av 9.11); 81 wkts
(av 29.93); 21 ct. HS 24 v E (Bangalore) 1992-93. BB6-12 v WI (Calcutta) 1993-94.

MANJREKAR, Sanjay Vijay (Bombay)
Born Mangalore 12 Jul 1965. Right-hand batsman, off-break bowler. First-class debut
1984-85. **TESTS:** 33 (1987-88 to 1994-95). 1855 runs (av 38.64), 4 hundreds; 0 wkts; 21 ct,
1 st. HS 218 v P (Lahore) 1989-90. **L-O INTERNATIONALS:** 55 (1987-88 to 1994-95).
1469 runs (av 33.38), 1 hundred; 1 wkt (av 6.00); 17 ct. HS 105 v SA (Delhi) 1991-92. BB
1-2.

MONGIA, Nayan Ramlal (Baroda)
Born Baroda 19 Dec 1969. Right-hand batsman, wicket-keeper. First-class debut 1989-90.
TESTS: 7 (1993-94 to 1994-95). 342 runs (av 34.20); 16 ct, 2 st. HS 80 v WI (Bombay)
1994-95. **L-O INTERNATIONALS:** 29 (1993-94 to 1994-95). 157 runs (av 19.62); 36 ct,
9 st. HS 40* v NZ (Christchurch) 1993-94.

PRABHAKAR, Manoj (Delhi)
Born Ghaziabad 15 Apr 1963. 5′ 8½″. Educated at Ghaziabad Secondary School; Delhi
College. Right-hand batsman, right-arm medium pace bowler. First-class debut 1982-83.
Durham 1995. **TESTS:** 36 (1984-85 to 1994-95). 1490 runs (av 32.39), 1 hundred; 94 wkts
(av 37.58), 5 wkts/inns (3); 19 ct. HS 120 v WI (Chandigarh) 1994-95. BB 6-132 v P
(Faisalabad) 1989-90. **L-O INTERNATIONALS:** 120 (1983-84 to 1994-95). 1699 runs
(av 24.27), 2 hundreds; 147 wkts (av 28.50); 25 ct. HS 106 v P (Jamshedpur) 1986-87. BB
5-35 v SL (Hyderabad) 1993-94.

PRASAD, Bapu Krishnarao Venkatesh (Karnataka)
Born Bangalore 5 Aug 1969. Right-hand batsman, right-arm medium-fast bowler. First-
class debut 1990-91. **TESTS:** 0. **L-O INTERNATIONALS:** 16 (1993-94 to 1994-95). 8
runs (av 2.66); 14 wkts (av 38.42); 5 ct. HS 5*. BB 3-36 v WI (Bombay) 1994-95.

RAJU, Sagi Lakshmi Venkatapathy (Hyderabad)
Born Hyderabad 9 Jul 1969. Right-hand batsman, left-arm orthodox slow bowler. First-
class debut 1985-86. **TESTS:** 21 (1989-90 to 1994-95). 228 runs (av 12.66); 81 wkts (av
28.06), 5 wkts/inns (5), 10 wkts/match (1); 5 ct. HS 31 v A (Melbourne) 1991-92. BB 6-12 v
SL (Chandigarh) 1990-91. **L-O INTERNATIONALS:** 42 (1989-90 to 1994-95). 29 runs
(av 4.14); 45 wkts (av 33.28); 7 ct. HS 8. BB 4-46 v WI (Jaipur) 1994-95.

SIDHU, Navjot Singh (Punjab)
Born Patiala 20 Oct 1963. Right-hand batsman, right-arm medium pace bowler. First-class debut 1981-82. **TESTS:** 34 (1983-84 to 1994-95). 2013 runs (av 40.26), 6 hundreds; 0 wkts; 8 ct. HS 124 v SL (Lucknow) 1993-94. **L-O INTERNATIONALS:** 90 (1987-88 to 1994-95). 3447 runs (av 43.63), 5 hundreds; 0 wkts; 15 ct. HS 134* v E (Gwalior) 1992-93.

SRINATH, Javagal (Karnataka)
Born Mysore 31 Aug 1969. 6' 3". Right-hand batsman, right-arm fast-medium bowler. First-class debut 1989-90. **TESTS:** 15 (1991-92 to 1994-95). 227 runs (av 22.70); 41 wkts (av 37.78); 7 ct. HS 60 v WI (Bombay) 1994-95. BB 4-33 v SA (Cape Town) 1992-93. **L-O INTERNATIONALS:** 77 (1991-92 to 1994-95). 153 runs (av 8.05); 112 wkts (av 25.11); 9 ct. HS 37 v SA (Hamilton) 1994-95. BB 5-24 v SL (Kanpur) 1993-94.

TENDULKAR, Sachin Ramesh (Bombay)
Born Bombay 24 Apr 1973. Right-hand batsman, right-arm medium pace bowler. First-class debut 1988-89. Yorkshire 1992 (cap 1992). **TESTS:** 35 (1989-90 to 1994-95). 2425 runs (av 52.71), 8 hundreds; 4 wkts (av 47.75); 28 ct. HS 179 v WI (Nagpur) 1994-95. BB 2-10 v A (Adelaide) 1991-92. **L-O INTERNATIONALS:** 96 (1989-90 to 1994-95). 3059 runs (av 36.85), 4 hundreds; 31 wkts (av 52.19); 28 ct. HS 115 v NZ (Baroda) 1994-95. BB 4-34 v WI (Sharjah) 1991-92.

VAIDYA, Prashant Sridhar (Bengal)
Born Nagpur 23 Sep 1967. Right-hand batsman, right-arm medium-fast bowler. First-class debut 1987-88. **TESTS:** 0. **L-O INTERNATIONALS:** 2 (1994-95). Did not bat; 3 wkts (av 25.66); 2 ct. BB 2-41 v Bangladesh (Sharjah) 1994-95.

YADAV, Vijay (Haryana)
Born Gonda 14 Mar 1967. Right-hand batsman, wicket-keeper. First-class debut 1987-88. **TESTS:** 1 (1992-93). 30 runs (av 30.00); 1 ct. HS 30 v Z (Delhi) 1992-93 – on debut. **L-O INTERNATIONALS:** 19 (1992-93 to 1994-95). 118 runs (av 11.80); 12 ct, 7 st. HS 34* v SA (East London) 1992-93.

WORLD CUP CAREER RECORDS

INDIA – BATTING AND FIELDING

	M	I	NO	HS	Runs	Avge	100	50	Ct/St
Abid Ali, S.	3	1	–	70	70	70.00	–	1	–
Amarnath, M.	14	12	–	80	254	21.16	–	1	2
Amre, P.K.	4	3	1	22	27	13.50	–	–	–
Azad, K.	3	2	–	15	15	7.50	–	–	–
Azharuddin, M.	15	12	2	93	522	52.20	–	6	3
Banerjee, S.T.	2	2	1	25*	36	36.00	–	–	2
Bedi, B.S.	5	4	1	13	25	8.33	–	–	–
Binny, R.M.H.	9	7	–	27	73	10.42	–	–	2
Engineer, F.M.	3	2	1	54*	78	78.00	–	1	2
Gaekwad, A.D.	6	5	–	37	113	22.60	–	–	2
Gavaskar, S.M.	19	19	3	103*	561	35.06	1	4	4
Ghavri, K.D.	4	3	–	20	35	11.66	–	–	–

	M	I	NO	HS	Runs	Avge	100	50	Ct/St
Jadeja, A.D.	6	5	1	46	93	23.25	–	–	2
Kambli, V.G.	5	4	–	24	29	7.25	–	–	–
Kapil Dev	26	24	6	175*	669	37.16	1	1	12
Khanna, S.C.	3	3	–	10	17	5.66	–	–	1
Kirmani, S.M.H.	8	6	1	24*	61	12.20	–	–	12/2
Madan Lal	11	7	3	27	122	30.50	–	–	1
Maninder Singh	7	2	1	4	4	4.00	–	–	1
Manjrekar, S.V.	6	6	–	47	154	25.66	–	–	3
More, K.S.	14	10	5	42*	100	20.00	–	–	12/6
Pandit, C.S.	2	1	–	24	24	24.00	–	–	1
Patel, B.P.	6	5	1	38	88	22.00	–	–	1
Patil, S.M.	8	8	1	51*	216	30.85	–	2	2
Prabhakar, M.	15	8	2	11*	34	5.66	–	–	2
Raju, S.L.V.	7	2	–	1	1	0.50	–	–	1
Sandhu, B.S.	8	4	2	11*	28	14.00	–	–	1
Sharma, C.	4	1	–	0	0	0.00	–	–	–
Shastri, R.J.	14	11	1	57	185	18.50	–	1	6
Sidhu, N.S.	7	5	–	75	276	55.20	–	4	3
Sivaramakrishnan, L.	2	–	–	–	–	–	–	–	1
Solkar, E.D.	3	2	–	13	21	10.50	–	–	1
Srikkanth, K.	23	23	1	75	521	23.68	–	2	9
Srinath, J.	8	6	5	11	34	34.00	–	–	1
Tendulkar, S.R.	8	7	1	84	283	47.16	–	3	2
Vengsarkar, D.B.	11	10	3	63	252	36.00	–	1	3
Venkataraghavan, S.	6	4	3	26*	49	49.00	–	–	1
Viswanath, G.R.	6	5	–	75	145	29.00	–	1	–
Yashpal Sharma	8	8	1	89	240	34.28	–	2	2

INDIA – BOWLING

	O	M	R	W	Avge	Best	4w	R/O
Abid Ali, S.	36	7	115	6	19.16	2-22	–	3.19
Amarnath, M.	110.3	9	431	16	26.93	3-12	–	3.90
Azad, K.	17	1	42	1	42.00	1-28	–	2.47
Azharuddin, M.	23.5	0	109	5	21.80	3-19	–	4.57
Banerjee, S.T.	13	1	85	1	85.00	1-45	–	6.53
Bedi, B.S.	60	17	148	2	74.00	1- 6	–	2.46
Binny, R.M.H.	95	9	382	19	20.10	4-29	1	4.02
Ghavri, K.D.	43	4	195	0	–	–	–	4.53
Jadeja, A.D.	7.2	0	39	0	–	–	–	5.31
Kapil Dev	237	27	892	28	31.85	5-43	1	3.76
Madan Lal	116.2	12	426	22	19.36	4-20	1	3.66
Maninder Singh	70	1	280	14	20.00	3-21	–	4.00
Patil, S.M.	9	0	61	0	–	–	–	6.77
Prabhakar, M.	116.1	9	480	21	22.85	4-19	1	4.13
Raju, S.L.V.	48.1	3	208	5	41.60	2-38	–	4.31
Sandhu, B.S.	83	10	297	8	37.12	2-26	–	3.57
Sharma, C.	36.1	2	170	6	28.33	3-51	–	4.70
Shastri, R.J.	92.3	5	389	12	32.41	3-26	–	4.20
Sivaramakrishnan, L.	17	0	70	1	70.00	1-36	–	4.11
Solkar, E.D.	4	0	28	0	–	–	–	7.00
Srikkanth, K.	2.1	0	15	0	–	–	–	6.92
Srinath, J.	53.1	3	249	8	31.12	2-23	–	4.68
Tendulkar, S.R.	41	0	180	2	90.00	1-35	–	4.39
Venkataraghavan, S.	72	7	217	0	–	–	–	3.01

WORLD CUP REGISTER

PAKISTAN

All career statistics are up to the end of the 1995 season (18 September). Key to abbreviations on page 32. Pakistan's selected 20 players for the Wills World Cup are:

AAMIR SOHAIL (Lahore)
Born Lahore 14 Sep 1966. Left-hand batsman, left-arm orthodox slow bowler. First-class debut 1983-84. **TESTS**: 23 (1992 to 1994-95). 1508 runs (av 35.90), 2 hundreds; 8 wkts (av 36.87); 26 ct. HS 205 v E (Manchester) 1992. BB 2-5 v Z (Bulawayo) 1994-95. **L-O INTERNATIONALS**: 76 (1990-91 to 1994-95). 2353 runs (av 31.79), 3 hundreds; 48 wkts (av 36.72); 21 ct. HS 134 v NZ (Sharjah) 1993-94. BB 3-33 v Z (Harare) 1994-95.

AQIB JAVED (Islamabad)
Born Sheikhupura 5 Aug 1972. Right-hand batsman, right-arm fast-medium bowler. First-class debut 1984-85. Hampshire 1991 (uncapped). **TESTS**: 18 (1988-89 to 1994-95). 38 runs (av 2.37); 38 wkts (av 38.76); 1 ct. HS 10 v SL (Faisalabad) 1991-92. BB 4-64 v Z (Harare) 1994-95. **L-O INTERNATIONALS**: 110 (1988-89 to 1994-95). 81 runs (av 6.75); 123 wkts (av 30.56);14 ct. HS 17 v A (Lahore) 1994-95. BB 7-37 v I (Sharjah) 1991-92 – LOI world record analysis.

ATA-UR-REHMAN (Lahore)
Born Lahore 28 Mar 1975. Right-hand batsman, right-arm fast-medium bowler. First-class debut 1990-91. **TESTS**: 9 (1992 to 1994-95). 48 runs (av 8.00); 21 wkts (av 34.28); 2 ct. HS 19 and BB 3-28 v WI (Port-of-Spain) 1992-93. **L-O INTERNATIONALS**: 23 (1992-93 to 1994-95). 21 runs (av 5.25); 17 wkts (av 52.23); 0 ct. HS 11* v NZ (Auckland) 1993-94. BB3-32 v UAE (Sharjah) 1993-94.

BASIT ALI (Karachi Whites; United Bank)
Born Karachi 13 Dec 1970. Right-hand batsman, off-break bowler. First-class debut 1985-86. **TESTS**: 14 (1992-93 to 1994-95). 757 runs (av 34.40), 1 hundred; 0 wkts; 4 ct. HS 103 v NZ (Christchurch) 1993-94. **L-O INTERNATIONALS**: 38 (1992-93 to 1994-95). 1057 runs (av 37.75), 1 hundred; 1 wkt (av 21.00); 7 ct. HS 127* v WI (Sharjah) 1993-94. BB 1-17.

IJAZ AHMED ('sr') (Habib Bank)
Born Sialkot 20 Sep 1968. Right-hand batsman, left-arm medium pace bowler. First-class debut 1983-84. **TESTS**: 24 (1986-87 to 1994-95). 1056 runs (av 31.05), 2 hundreds; 1 wkt (av 18.00); 20 ct. HS 122 v A (Faisalabad) 1988-89. BB 1-9. **L-O INTERNATIONALS**: 118 (1986-87 to 1994-95). 2326 runs (av 26.73), 4 hundreds; 3 wkts (av 90.66); 39 ct. HS 124* v Bangladesh (Chittagong) 1988-89. BB 2-31 v SL (Sialkot) 1990-91. *(No relation to Ijaz Ahmed ('jr') of Faisalabad and Railways, born Lyallpur 2 Feb 1969, who made his international debut against Sri Lanka in September 1995).*

INZAMAM-UL-HAQ (United Bank)
Born Multan 3 Mar 1970. Right-hand batsman, left-arm orthodox slow bowler. First-class debut 1985-86. **TESTS**: 23 (1992 to 1994-95). 1541 runs (av 48.15), 4 hundreds; 22 ct. HS 135* v NZ (Wellington) 1993-94. **L-O INTERNATIONALS**: 87 (1991-92 to 1994-95). 2981 runs (av 41.40), 4 hundreds; 2 wkts (av 21.00); 24 ct. HS 137* v NZ (Sharjah) 1993-94. BB 1-4.

JAVED MIANDAD (Habib Bank)
Born Karachi 12 Jun 1957. Right-hand batsman, right-arm leg-break bowler. First-class debut 1973-74. Glamorgan 1980 to 1985 (cap 1980). **TESTS:** 124 (1976-77 to 1993-94, 34 as captain). 8832 runs (av 52.57), 23 hundreds; 17 wkts (av 40.11); 93 ct, 1 st. HS 280* v I (Hyderabad, Pakistan) 1982-83. BB 3-74 v NZ (Hyderabad) 1976-77. **L-O INTERNATIONALS:** 228 (1975-76 to 1993-94, 62 as captain). 7327 runs (av 41.86), 8 hundreds; 7 wkts (av 42.42); 68 ct, 2 st. HS 119* v I (Lahore) 1982-83. BB 2-22 v SL (Nottingham) 1975.

KABIR KHAN (HBFC)
Born Peshawar 12 Apr 1974. Right-hand batsman, left-arm fast-medium bowler. First-class debut 1990-91. **TESTS:** 4 (1994-95). 24 runs (av 8.00); 9 wkts (av 41.11); 1 ct. HS 10 v SA (Johannesburg) 1994-95. BB 3-26 v Z (Bulawayo) 1994-95. **L-O INTERNATIONALS:** 2 (1994-95). Did not bat; 3 wkts (av 22.00); 0 ct. BB 2-32 v NZ (East London) 1994-95.

MOHAMMAD AKRAM (Rawalpindi)
Born Islamabad 10 Sep 1974. Right-hand batsman, right-arm fast-medium bowler. First-class debut 1992-93. **TESTS:** 0. **L-O INTERNATIONALS:** 0.

MOIN KHAN (Karachi Whites; PIA)
Born Rawalpindi 23 Sep 1971. Right-hand batsman, wicket-keeper. First-class debut 1986-87. **TESTS:** 13 (1990-91 to 1994-95). 309 runs (av 19.31), 1 hundred; 34 ct, 2 st. HS 115* v A (Lahore) 1994-95. **L-O INTERNATIONALS:** 33 (1990-91 to 1994-95, 2 as captain). 197 runs (av 14.07); 41 ct, 8 st. HS 23 v WI (Multan) 1990-91.

MUSHTAQ AHMED (United Bank)
Born Sahiwal 28 Jun 1970. 5' 5". Right-hand batsman, right-arm leg-break and googly bowler. First-class debut 1986-87. Somerset debut/cap 1993. **TESTS:** 18 (1989-90 to 1994-95). 163 runs (av 8.15); 44 wkts (av 36.47); 5 ct. HS 27 and BB 4-121 v A (Lahore) 1994-95. **L-O INTERNATIONALS:** 82 (1988-89 to 1994-95). 203 runs (av 8.12); 92 wkts (av 32.76); 18 ct. HS 17* v A (Sharjah) 1989-90. BB 3-14 v SL (Sharjah) 1990-91.

RAMIZ RAJA (Islamabad; Lahore)
Born Lyallpur 14 Aug 1962. Right-hand batsman, right-arm leg-break bowler. First-class debut 1977-78. **TESTS:** 48 (1983-84 to 1992-93). 2243 runs (av 30.72), 2 hundreds; 27 ct. HS 122 v SL (PSS, Colombo) 1985-86. **L-O INTERNATIONALS:** 159 (1984-85 to 1992-93, 1 as captain). 4915 runs (av 33.43), 8 hundreds; 0 wkts; 23 ct. HS 119* v NZ (Christchurch) 1991-92.

RASHID LATIF (Karachi Whites; United Bank)
Born Karachi 14 Oct 1968. Right-hand batsman, wicket-keeper. First-class debut 1986-87. **TESTS:** 16 (1992 to 1994-95). 533 runs (av 26.65); 0 wkts; 44 ct, 5 st. HS 68* v Z (Karachi) 1993-94. **L-O INTERNATIONALS:** 66 (1992-93 to 1994-95). 478 runs (av 14.93); 64 ct, 18 st. HS 39 v A (Hobart) 1992-93.

SAEED ANWAR (ADBP)
Born Karachi 6 Sep 1968. Left-hand batsman, left-arm orthodox slow bowler. First-class debut 1986-87. **TESTS:** 12 (1990-91 to 1994-95). 884 runs (av 40.18), 2 hundreds; 0 wkts; 4 ct. HS 169 v NZ (Wellington) 1993-94. **L-O INTERNATIONALS:** 80 (1988-89 to 1994-95, 2 as captain). 2509 runs (av 34.36), 8 hundreds; 2 wkts (av 60.50); 19 ct. HS 131 v WI (Sharjah) 1993-94. BB 1-15.

SALIM ELAHI
Born Sahiwal 21 Nov 1976. Brother of Manzoor Elahi. Right-hand batsman, off-break bowler. Awaiting first-class debut. Represented Lahore in Wills Trophy 1994-95. **TESTS:** 0. **L-O INTERNATIONALS:** 0. *(Made debut v SL at Gujranwala on 29 September 1995 scoring 102* and becoming the fourth batsman after D.L.Amiss (E), D.L.Haynes (WI) and A.Flower (Z) to score 100 on debut in LOIs).*

SALIM MALIK (Habib Bank)
Born Lahore 16 Apr 1963. Right-hand batsman, right-arm leg-break bowler. First-class debut 1978-79. **TESTS:** 84 (1981-82 to 1994-95, 12 as captain). 4804 runs (av 45.75), 13 hundreds; 5 wkts (av 49.20); 54 ct. HS 237 v A (Rawalpindi) 1994-95. BB 1-3. **L-O INTERNATIONALS:** 210 (1981-82 to 1994-95, 34 as captain). 5271 runs (av 32.33), 5 hundreds; 54 wkts (av 32.33); 64 ct. HS 102 v I (Sharjah) 1989-90 and 102 v SL (Rawalpindi) 1991-92. BB 5-35 v NZ (Lahore) 1990-91.

SAQLAIN MUSHTAQ (PIA; Islamabad)
Born Lahore 27 Nov 1976. Right-hand batsman, off-break bowler. First-class debut 1994-95 taking 52 wickets in first season. **TESTS:** 0. **L-O INTERNATIONALS:** 0. *(Made international debut against Sri Lanka in September 1995).*

SHAHID ANWAR (Lahore; National Bank)
Born Multan 5 Jul 1968. Right-hand batsman, right-arm medium pace bowler. First-class debut 1983-84. **TESTS:** 0. **L-O INTERNATIONALS:** 0.

WAQAR YOUNIS (United Bank)
Born Vehari 16 Nov 1971. 6′ 0″. Educated at Government College, Vehari. Right-hand batsman, right-arm fast bowler. First-class debut 1987-88. Surrey 1990 to 1993 (cap 1990). One of *Wisden*'s Five Cricketers of 1991. **TESTS:** 33 (1989-90 to 1994-95, 1 as captain). 312 runs (av 8.91); 190 wkts (av 19.15), 5 wkts/inns (19), 10 wkts/match (4); 4 ct. HS 29 v WI (Bridgetown) 1992-93. BB 7-76 v NZ (Faisalabad) 1990-91. **L-O INTERNATIONALS:** 104 (1989-90 to 1994-95, 1 as captain). 312 runs (av 10.40); 176 wkts (av 21.59); 10 ct. HS 37 v WI (Johannesburg) 1992-93. BB 6-26 v SL (Sharjah) 1989-90.

WASIM AKRAM (PIA)
Born Lahore 3 Jun 1966. 6′ 3″. Educated at Islamia College. Left-hand batsman, left-arm fast bowler. First-class debut 1984-85. Lancashire debut 1988 (cap 1989). One of *Wisden*'s Five Cricketers of 1992. **TESTS:** 61 (1984-85 to 1994-95, 5 as captain). 1401 runs (av 19.73), 1 hundred; 261 wkts (av 23.20), 5 wkts/inns (18), 10 wkts/match (3); 21 ct. HS 123 v A (Adelaide) 1989-90. BB 7-119 v NZ (Wellington) 1993-94. **L-O INTERNATIONALS:** 189 (1984-85 to 1994-95, 23 as captain). 1680 runs (av 14.35); 273 wkts (av 22.57); 33 ct. HS 86 v A (Melbourne) 1989-90. BB 5-15 v Z (Karachi) 1993-94.

WORLD CUP CAREER RECORDS

PAKISTAN – BATTING AND FIELDING

	M	I	NO	HS	Runs	Avge	100	50	Ct/St
Aamir Sohail	10	10	–	114	326	32.60	1	2	3
Abdul Qadir	13	9	7	41*	118	59.00	–	–	3
Aqib Javed	10	2	2	1*	2	–	–	–	2
Asif Iqbal	5	4	–	61	182	45.50	–	3	5
Asif Masood	3	1	–	6	6	6.00	–	–	–
Haroon Rashid	4	4	1	37*	69	23.00	–	–	–
Ijaz Ahmed	14	11	2	59	143	15.88	–	1	5
Ijaz Faqih	6	5	1	42*	61	15.25	–	–	1
Imran Khan	28	24	5	102*	666	35.05	1	4	6
Inzamam-ul-Haq	10	10	–	60	225	22.50	–	1	4
Iqbal Sikander	4	1	1	1*	1	–	–	–	–
Javed Miandad	28	27	4	103	1029	44.73	1	8	7/1
Majid Khan	7	7	–	84	359	51.28	–	5	1
Mansoor Akhtar	8	8	–	33	108	13.50	–	–	2
Manzoor Elahi	1	1	1	4*	4	–	–	–	–
Mohsin Khan	7	7	–	82	223	31.85	–	2	3
Moin Khan	10	5	2	20*	44	14.66	–	–	11/3
Mudassar Nazar	12	10	1	40	149	16.55	–	–	6
Mushtaq Ahmed	9	4	1	17	27	9.00	–	–	2
Mushtaq Mohammad	3	3	–	55	89	29.66	–	1	1
Naseer Malik	3	1	1	0*	0	–	–	–	–
Parvez Mir	2	2	1	4*	8	8.00	–	–	1
Ramiz Raja	15	15	2	119*	698	53.69	3	2	4
Rashid Khan	7	1	–	9	9	9.00	–	–	1
Sadiq Mohammad	7	7	1	74	189	31.50	–	2	3
Salim Jaffer	5	3	2	8*	9	9.00	–	–	–
Salim Malik	17	16	4	100	439	36.58	1	3	4
Salim Yousuf	7	6	3	56	112	37.33	–	1	9
Sarfraz Nawaz	11	8	1	17	65	9.28	–	–	2
Shahid Mahboob	5	3	–	77	100	33.33	–	1	1
Shoaib Mohammad	1	1	–	0	0	0.00	–	–	–
Sikander Bakht	4	2	1	2	3	3.00	–	–	1
Tahir Naqqash	1	1	1	0*	0	–	–	–	1
Tausif Ahmed	6	2	–	1	1	0.50	–	–	1
Wasim Akram	17	14	2	39	147	12.25	–	–	2
Wasim Bari	14	8	4	34	87	21.75	–	–	18/4
Wasim Haider	3	2	–	13	26	13.00	–	–	–
Wasim Raja	8	8	–	58	154	19.25	–	1	4
Zaheer Abbas	14	14	2	103*	597	49.75	1	4	7
Zahid Fazal	2	2	–	11	13	6.50	–	–	1

PAKISTAN – BOWLING

	O	M	R	W	Avge	Best	4w	R/O
Aamir Sohail	40	2	184	4	46.00	2-26	–	4.60
Abdul Qadir	135.4	8	506	24	21.08	5-44	3	3.72
Aqib Javed	84.5	11	328	11	29.81	3-21	–	3.86
Asif Iqbal	59	5	215	10	21.50	4-56	1	3.64
Asif Masood	30	3	128	2	64.00	1-50	–	4.26
Ijaz Ahmed	36	1	149	1	149.00	1-28	–	4.13
Ijaz Faqih	37	2	125	0	–	–	–	3.37
Imran Khan	169.3	18	655	34	19.26	4-37	2	3.86
Iqbal Sikander	35	2	147	3	49.00	1-30	–	4.20
Javed Miandad	22	2	73	4	18.25	2-22	–	3.31
Majid Khan	47	8	117	7	16.71	3-27	–	2.48
Mansoor Akhtar	17	2	75	2	37.50	1- 7	–	4.41
Manzoor Elahi	9.4	0	32	1	32.00	1-32	–	3.31
Mohsin Khan	1	0	3	0	–	–	–	3.00
Mudassar Nazar	105	8	397	8	49.62	3-43	–	3.78
Mushtaq Ahmed	78	3	311	16	19.43	3-41	–	3.98
Mushtaq Mohammad	7	0	23	0	–	–	–	3.28
Naseer Malik	30	5	98	5	19.60	2-37	–	3.26
Parvez Mir	15	2	59	2	29.50	1-17	–	3.93
Rashid Khan	71	11	266	8	33.25	3-47	–	3.74
Sadiq Mohammad	6	1	20	2	10.00	2-20	–	3.33
Salim Jaffar	39.4	0	210	5	42.00	3-30	–	5.29
Salim Malik	35	1	175	1	175.00	1-22	–	5.00
Sarfraz Nawaz	119	15	435	16	27.18	4-44	1	3.65
Shahid Mahboob	52	4	228	4	57.00	1-37	–	4.38
Sikander Bakht	41	10	108	7	15.42	3-32	–	2.63
Tahir Naqqash	8	0	49	1	49.00	1-49	–	6.12
Tausif Ahmed	60	4	230	5	46.00	1-35	–	3.83
Wasim Akram	153	4	633	25	25.32	4-32	1	4.13
Wasim Haider	19	1	79	1	79.00	1-36	–	4.15
Wasim Raja	13.4	4	46	1	46.00	1- 7	–	3.36
Zaheer Abbas	19.4	2	74	2	37.00	1- 8	–	3.76

WORLD CUP REGISTER

SRI LANKA

Sri Lanka's World Cup selections had not been released at the time of going to press. All career statistics are up to the end of the 1995 season (18 September). Key to abbreviations on page 32.

DASSANAYAKE, Pubudu Bathiya **(Central Province)**
Born Kandy 11 Jul 1970. Right-hand batsman, wicket-keeper. First-class debut 1993-94. **TESTS:** 11 (1993-94 to 1994-95). 196 runs (av 13.06); 19 ct, 5 st. HS 36 v I (Lucknow) 1993-94. **L-O INTERNATIONALS:** 15 (1993-94 to 1994-95). 85 runs (av 10.62); 9 ct, 4 st. HS 20* v I (Jalandhar) 1993-94.

De SILVA, Pinnaduwage Aravinda (Nondescripts; Western Province North)
Born Colombo 17 Oct 1965. 5' 3½". Right-hand batsman, off-break bowler. First-class debut 1983-84. **TESTS:** 48 (1984 to 1994-95, 4 as captain). 2965 runs (av 37.53), 7 hundreds; 11 wkts (av 38.54), 22 ct. HS 267 v I (Wellington) 1990-91. BB 3-39 v SA (SSC, Colombo) 1993-94. **L-O INTERNATIONALS:** 156 (1983-84 to 1994-95, 13 as captain). 4387 runs (av 31.78), 3 hundreds; 35 wkts (av 46.05); 43 ct. HS 107* v Z (Harare) 1994-95. BB 3-58 v A (Perth) 1987-88. **F-C CAREER:** 10,007 runs (av 48.57), 27 hundreds, 1000 runs/season (2). HS 267; 66 wkts (av 34.15), 5 wkts/inns (4), BB 7-24; 79 ct.

DHARMASENA, Handunettige Deepthi Priyantha Kumara (Western Province City)
Born Colombo 24 Apr 1971. Right-hand batsman, off-break bowler. First-class debut 1988-89. **TESTS:** 6 (1993-94 to 1994-95). 139 runs (av 13.90); 17 wkts (av 37.47), 5 wkts/inns (1); 2 ct. HS 54 v Z (Bulawayo) 1994-95. BB 6-99 v P (SSC, Colombo) 1994-95. **L-O INTERNATIONALS:** 9 (1994-95). 76 runs (av 38.00); 8 wkts (av 33.87); 1 ct. HS 30 v I (Sharjah) 1994-95. BB 4-37 v SA (Port Elizabeth) 1994-95.

DUNUSINGHE, Chamara I. (Western Province North)
Born 19 Oct 1970. Right-hand batsman, wicket-keeper. First-class debut 1990-91. **TESTS:** 2 (1994-95). 113 runs (av 28.25); 8 ct. HS 91 v NZ (Napier) 1994-95 – on debut. **L-O INTERNATIONALS:** 1 (1994-95). 1 run (av 1.00); 1 ct, 1 st. HS 1.

GURUSINHA, Asanka Pradeep **(Sinhalese SC; Western Province City)**
Born Colombo 16 Sep 1966. 6' 0". Educated at Nalanda Collge. Left-hand batsman, right-arm medium pace bowler. First-class debut 1984-85. **TESTS:** 33 (1985-86 to 1994-95). 1952 runs (av 39.83), 6 hundreds; 18 wkts (av 33.50); 26 ct. HS 137 v A (SSC, Colombo) I922-93. BB 2-7 v E (SSC, Colombo) 1992-93. **L-O INTERNATIONALS:** 10 (1985-86 to 1994-95). 2889 runs (av 28.04), 2 hundreds; 26 wkts (av 49.23); 38 ct. HS 117* v NZ (Auckland) 1994-95. BB 2-25 v NZ (RPS, Colombo) 1992-93.

HATHURUSINGHE, Upul Chandika (Tamil Union; Western Province City)
Born Colombo 13 Sep 1968. 5' 7". Educated at Ananda College. Right-hand batsman, right-arm medium pace bowler. First-class debut 1988-89. **TESTS:** 18 (1990-91 to 1994-95). 840 runs (av 28.96); 16 wkts (av 35.00); 2 ct. HS 81 v NZ (Hamilton) 1994-95 – on debut. BB 4-66 v A (SSC, Colombo) 1992-93. **L-O INTERNATIONALS:** 26 (1991-92 to 1994-95). 589 runs (av 24.54); 9 wkts (av 43.88); 4 ct. HS 66 v Z (Sharjah) 1992-93. BB 4-57 v WI (Berri, S Australia) 1991-92.

JAYASURIYA, Sanath Teran **(Southern Province)**
Born Matara 30 Jun 1969. 5' 6". Educated at St Seruatius College. Left-hand batsman, left-arm orthodox slow bowler. First-class debut 1988-89. **TESTS:** 16 (1990-91 to 1994-95). 611 runs (av 30.55); 4 wkts (av 86.25); 17 ct. HS 81 v P (Faisalabad) 1991-92. BB 2-46 v E (SSC, Colombo) 1994-95. **L-O INTERNATIONALS:** 80 (1989-90 to 1994-95). 1396 runs (av 19.38), 1 hundred; 59 wkts (av 31.32); 30 ct. HS 140 v NZ (Bloemfontein) 1994-95. BB 6-29 v E (Moratuwa) 1992-93.

KALPAGE, Ruwan Senani (**Nondescripts; Central Province**)
Born Kandy 19 Feb 1970. Left-hand batsman, off-break bowler. First-class debut 1988-89.
TESTS: 8 (1993-94 to 1994-95). 265 runs (av 20.38); 6 wkts (av 67.50); 6 ct. HS 63 v I
(Bangalore) 1993-94. BB 2-27 v WI (Moratuwa) 1993-94. **L-O INTERNATIONALS:** 67
(1991-92 to 1994-95). 706 runs (av 23.53); 64 wkts (av 37.12); 21 ct. HS 51 v I (Hyderabad)
1993-94. BB 4-36 v P (RPS, Colombo) 1994-95.

KALUWITHARANA, Romesh Shantha (**Sebastianites; Western Province South**)
Born Colombo 24 Nov 1969. Right-hand batsman, wicket-keeper. First-class debut 1988-
89. **TESTS:** 3 (1992-93 to 1994-95). 177 runs (av 59.00), 1 hundred; 6 ct. HS 132* v A
(SSC, Colombo) 1992-93 – on debut. **L-O INTERNATIONALS:** 22 (1990-91 to 1994-
95). 180 runs (av 10.58); 9 ct, 7 st. HS 31 v P (Sharjah) 1993-94.

MAHANAMA, Roshan Siriwardene (**Colombo CC; Western Province North**)
Born Colombo 31 May 1966. 5′ 10″. Educated at Nalanda College. Right-hand batsman.
First-class debut 1984-85. **TESTS:** 32 (1985-86 to 1994-95). 1687 runs (av 31.83), 3
hundreds; 0 wkts; 19 ct. HS 153 v NZ (Moratuwa) 1992-93. **L-O INTERNATIONALS:**
119 (1985-86 to 1994-95, 2 as captain). 3045 runs (av 29.27), 3 hundreds; 0 wkts; 66 ct. HS
119* v Z (Harare) 1994-95.

MUNASINGH, Manjula (**Sinhalese SC; Western Province North**)
Born Colombo 10 Dec 1971. Right-hand batsman, right-arm fast-medium bowler. First-
class debut 1990-91. **TESTS:** 0. **L-O INTERNATIONALS:** 1 (1993-94). 2 runs (av 2.00);
0 wkts; 0 ct. HS 2.

MURALITHARAN, Muthiah (**Tamil Union; Central Province**)
Born Kandy 17 Apr 1972. 5′ 5″. Educated at St Anthony's College, Kandy. Right-hand
batsman, off-break bowler. First-class debut 1989-90. **TESTS:** 18 (1992-93 to 1994-95).
161 runs (av 16.10); 63 wkts (av 31.53), 5 wkts/inns (4); 7 ct. HS 20* v I (Bangalore)
1993-94 and 20* v P (PSS, Colombo) 1994-95. BB 5-64 v NZ (Napier) 1994-95. **L-O
INTERNATIONALS:** 25 (1993-94 to 1994-95). 20 runs (av 5.00); 25 wkts (av 36.12); 8 ct.
HS 8. BB 4-23 v Bangladesh (Sharjah) 1994-95.

PUSHPAKUMARA, Karuppiahyage Ravindra (**Western Province South**)
Born Panadura 21 Jul 1975. Right-hand batsman, right-arm fast-medium bowler. First-class
debut 1992-93. **TESTS:** 5 (1994-95). 39 runs (av 7.80); 14 wkts (av 29.50), 5 wkts/inns (1);
0 ct. HS 17* v NZ (Dunedin) 1994-95. BB 7-116 v Z (Harare) 1994-95. **L-O INTER-
NATIONALS:** 12 (1993-94 to 1994-95). 20 runs (av 20.00); 11 wkts (av 41.63); 3 ct. HS 14
v P (Verwoerdburg) 1994-95. BB 3-25 v Z (Harare) 1994-95.

RANATUNGA, Arjuna (**Western Province North**)
Born Colombo 1 Dec 1963. 5′ 8″. Educated at Ananda College. Left-hand batsman,
right-arm medium-pace bowler. First-class debut 1981-82. **TESTS:** 56 (1981-82 to 1994-
95, 29 as captain). 3134 runs (av 35.21), 4 hundreds; 14 wkts (av 67.28); 22 ct. HS 135* v P
(PSS, Colombo) 1985-86. BB 2-17 v NZ (Kandy) 1983-84. **L-O INTERNATIONALS:**
164 (1981-82 to 1994-95, 88 as captain). 4536 runs (av 35.43), 1 hundred; 70 wkts (av
49.08); 35 ct. HS 101* v P (Durban) 1994-95. BB 4-14 v I (Kanpur) 1986-87.

RANATUNGA, Sanjeeva (**Nondescripts; Western Province North**)
Born Colombo 25 Apr 1969. Left-hand batsman, off-break bowler. First-class debut
1988-89. **TESTS:** 6 (1994-95). 346 runs (av 34.60), 2 hundreds; 2 ct. HS 118 v Z (Harare)
1994-95. **L-O INTERNATIONALS:** 11 (1994-95). 248 runs (av 24.80); 2 ct. HS 70 v P
(RPS, Colombo) 1994-95.

SILVA, Kelaniyage **Jayantha (Western Province South)**
Born 2 Jun 1973. Right-hand batsman, left-arm orthodox slow bowler. First-class debut 1991-92. **TESTS:** 0. **L-O INTERNATIONALS:** 1 (1994-95). 1 run (av –); 0 wkt; 0 ct. HS 1*.

TILLEKERATNE, Hashan Prasantha **(Nondescripts; Southern Districts)**
Born Colombo 14 Jul 1967. 5'6". Educated at D.S.Senanayake College. Left-hand batsman, occasional right-arm medium pace, wicket-keeper. First-class debut 1984-85. **TESTS:** 30 (1989-90 to 1994-95). 1640 runs (av 39.04), 2 hundreds; 0 wkts; 66 ct. HS 116 v Z (Harare) 1994-95. **L-O INTERNATIONALS:** 104 (1986-87 to 1994-95). 1938 runs (av 28.08), 1 hundred; 2 wkts (av 33.00); 54 ct, 5 st. HS 104 v WI (Bombay) 1993-94. BB 1-3.

UPASHANTHA, Eric **(Colts)**
Born 1972. Right-hand batsman, right-arm fast-medium bowler. First-class debut 1990-91. **TESTS:** 0. **L-O INTERNATIONALS:** 0.

VAAS, Warnakulasooriya Patabendige Ushantha **Chaminda** Joseph **(Western Province North)**
Born Colombo 27 Jan 1974. Left-hand batsman, left-arm medium-fast bowler. First-class debut 1990-91. **TESTS:** 6 (1994-95). 160 runs (av 22.85); 26 wkts (av 18.92), 5 wkts/inns (3), 10 wkts/match (1); 0 ct. HS 51 and BB 6-87 v NZ (Dunedin) 1994-95. **L-O INTERNATIONALS:** 29 (1993-94 to 1994-95). 105 runs (av 21.00); 34 wkts (av 27.67); 4 ct. HS 33 v P (SSC, Colombo) 1994-95. BB 4-20 v Z (Harare) 1994-95.

WICKREMASINGHE, Gallage **Pramodya (Sinhalese SC; Western Province South)**
Born Matara 14 Aug 1971. Right-hand batsman, right-arm fast-medium bowler. First-class debut 1988-89. **TESTS:** 17 (1991-92 to 1994-95). 199 runs (av 9.04); 32 wkts (av 50.09), 5 wkts/inns (1); 7 ct. HS 22 v I (Ahmedabad) 1993-94. BB 5-73 v P (Faisalabad) 1991-92. **L-O INTERNATIONALS:** 61 (1990-91 to 1994-95). 105 runs (av 7.50); 48 wkts (av 39.41); 12 ct. HS 21* v WI (Berri, S Australia) 1991-92. BB 3-28 v I (RPS, Colombo) 1994-95.

WORLD CUP CAREER RECORDS

SRI LANKA – BATTING AND FIELDING

	M	I	NO	HS	Runs	Avge	100	50	Ct/St
Anurasiri, S.D.	11	5	2	11	21	7.00	–	–	3
De.Alwis, R.G.	6	6	3	59*	167	55.66	–	2	5
De Mel, A.L.F.	9	7	–	27	66	9.42	–	–	1
De Silva, D.L.S.	2	1	–	10	10	10.00	–	–	–
De Silva, D.S.	11	10	1	35	148	16.44	–	–	2
De Silva, G.R.A.	2	2	1	2*	2	2.00	–	–	–
De Silva, P.A.	14	13	2	62	276	25.09	–	1	3
Dias, R.L.	10	10	–	80	310	34.44	–	3	5
Fernando, E.R.	3	3	–	22	47	15.66	–	–	–
Goonatillake, F.R.M.	1	–	–	–	–	–	–	–	–
Gurusinha, A.P.	12	11	–	37	181	16.45	–	1	2
Hathurusinghe, U.C.	4	3	–	16	26	8.66	–	–	1
Heyn, P.D.	2	2	–	2	3	1.50	–	–	1
Jayasinghe, S.A.	2	1	–	1	1	1.00	–	–	2
Jayasuriya, S.T.	6	5	–	32	74	14.80	–	–	4
Jeganathan, S.	3	3	1	20*	24	12.00	–	–	1
John, V.B.	11	9	7	15	46	23.00	–	–	4
Kalpage, R.S.	7	6	2	14	67	16.75	–	–	3

	M	I	NO	HS	Runs	Avge	100	50	Ct/St
Kaluperuma, L.W.S.	3	2	2	13*	19	–	–	–	–
Kuruppu, D.S.B.P.	11	11	–	72	251	22.81	–	2	4/1
Labrooy, G.F.	1	1	–	19	19	19.00	–	–	–
Madugalle, R.S.	11	10	–	60	193	19.30	–	1	4
Mahanama, R.S.	14	13	–	89	380	29.23	–	4	5
Mendis, L.R.D.	16	16	2	64	412	29.42	–	3	2
Opatha, A.R.M.	5	3	–	18	29	9.66	–	–	3
Pasqual, S.P.	2	2	1	23*	24	24.00	–	–	–
Pieris, H.S.M.	3	3	1	16	19	9.50	–	–	
Ramanayake, C.P.H.	8	6	2	12	25	6.25	–	–	4
Ranasinghe, A.N.	3	3	1	14*	23	11.50	–	–	
Ranatunga, A.	19	18	4	88*	594	42.42	–	5	5
Ratnayake, R.J.	9	8	2	20*	81	13.50	–	–	3
Ratnayeke, J.R.	6	5	–	22	52	10.40	–	–	
Samarasekera, M.A.R.	8	8	–	75	224	28.00	–	1	1
Tennekoon, A.P.B.	4	4	–	59	137	34.25	–	1	3
Tillekeratne, H.P.	8	7	1	25*	80	13.33	–	–	6/1
Tissera, M.H.	3	3	–	52	78	26.00	–	1	–
Warnapura, B.	5	5	–	31	79	15.80	–	–	
Wettimuny, S.	6	6	–	50	128	21.33	–	1	–
Wettimuny, S.R.de S.	3	3	1	67	136	68.00	–	2	–
Wickremasinghe, G.P.	8	3	3*	21*	30	–	–	–	–
Wijegunawardene, K.I.W.	3								

SRI LANKA – BOWLING

	O	M	R	W	Avge	Best	4w	R/O
Anurasiri, S.D.	105	4	455	9	50.55	3-41	–	4.33
De Mel, A.L.F.	90.2	13	449	18	24.94	5-32	2	4.97
De Silva, D.L.S.	20	2	54	2	27.00	2-36	–	2.70
De Silva, D.S.	110	12	463	10	46.30	3-29	–	4.20
De Silva, G.R.A.	19	2	85	1	85.00	1-39	–	4.47
De Silva, P.A.	43	0	223	3	74.33	2-43	–	5.18
Goonatillake, F.R.M	9	1	34	0	–	–	–	3.77
Gurusinha, A.P.	53	0	307	7	43.85	2-67	–	5.79
Hathurusinghe, U.C.	17	0	97	5	19.40	4-57	1	5.70
Jayasuriya, S.T.	6	0	44	0	–	–	–	7.33
Jeganathan, S.	29	2	123	4	30.75	2-45	–	4.24
John, V.B.	99.2	10	477	4	119.25	1-49	–	4.80
Kalpage, R.S.	50	0	241	4	60.25	2-33	–	4.82
Kaluperuma, L.W.S.	27.4	2	102	1	102.00	1-50	–	3.68
Labrooy, G.F.	10	1	68	1	68.00	1-68	–	6.80
Opatha, A.R.M.	42.1	1	180	5	36.00	3-31	–	4.26
Pasqual, S.P.	4.4	0	20	0	–	–	–	4.28
Pieris, H.S.M.	22	0	135	2	67.50	2-68	–	6.13
Ramanayake, C.P.H.	64.4	6	265	5	53.00	2-37	–	4.09
Ranasinghe, A.N.	10	0	65	0	–	–	–	6.50
Ranatunga, A.	70.1	2	392	4	98.00	2-26	–	5.58
Ratnayake, R.J.	89	6	437	12	36.41	2-18	–	4.91
Ratnayeke, J.R.	54	2	313	10	31.30	3-41	–	5.79
Samarasekera, M.A.R.	16.2	2	71	0	–	–	–	4.34
Warnapura, B.	36	0	159	4	39.75	3-42	–	4.41
Wettimuny, S.	3	0	15	0	–	–	–	5.00
Wickremasinghe, G.P.	60.1	5	276	7	39.42	2-29	–	4.57
Wijegunawardene, K.I.W.	17	1	88	0	–	–	–	5.17

WORLD CUP REGISTER

ZIMBABWE

Zimbabwe's World Cup selections had not been released at the time of going to press. All career statistics are up to the end of the 1995 season (18 September). Key to abbreviations on page 32.

BRAIN, David Hayden **(Mashonaland)**
Born Salisbury 4 Oct 1964. 6′ 4″. Educated at Churchill High School. Left-hand batsman, left-arm medium-fast bowler. First-class debut 1986-87. **TESTS:** 9 (1992-93 to 1994-95). 115 runs (av 10.45); 30 wkts (av 30.50), 5 wkts/inns (1); 1 ct. HS 28 and BB 5-42 v P (Lahore) 1993-94. **L-O INTERNATIONALS:** 22 (1992-93 to 1994-95). 105 runs (av 7.50); 21 wkts (av 39.09); 5 ct. HS 27 v I (Faridabad) 1992-93. BB 3-51 v P (Sharjah) 1992-93.

BRANDES, Eddo Andre **(Mashonaland County Districts)**
Born Port Shepstone, South Africa 5 Mar 1963. Right-hand batsman, right-arm fast-medium bowler. First-class debut 1985-86. **TESTS:** 6 (1992-93 to 1993-94). 60 runs (av 6.66); 17 wkts (av 35.17); 3 ct. HS 18 v P (Rawalpindi) 1993-94. BB 3-45 v P (Lahore) 1993-94. **L-O INTERNATIONALS:** 24 (1987-88 to 1994-95). 182 runs (av 12.13); 29 wkts (av 35.03); 6 ct. HS 55 v SL (Sharjah) 1992-93. BB 4-21 v E (Albury) 1991-92.

BURMESTER, Mark Greville **(Mashonaland)**
Born Durban, South Africa 24 Jan 1968. Right-hand batsman, right-arm medium pace bowler. First-class debut 1990-91. **TESTS:** 3 (1992-93). 54 runs (av 27.00); 3 wkts (av 75.66); 1 ct. HS 30 v NZ (Harare) 1992-93. BB 3-78 v I (Harare) 1992-93 – on debut. **L-O INTERNATIONALS:** 8 (1991-92 to 1994-95). 109 runs (av 18.16); 5 wkts (av 42.40); 2 ct. HS 39 v P (Harare) 1994-95. BB 3-36 v I (Hamilton) 1991-92.

CAMPBELL, Alistair Douglas Ross **(Mashonaland County Districts)**
Born Salisbury 23 Sep 1972. 6′ 1″. Educated at Eaglesvale High School. Left-hand batsman, right-arm leg-break bowler. First-class debut 1990-91. **TESTS:** 13 (1992-93 to 1994-95). 732 runs (av 36.60); 0 wkts; 9 ct. HS 99 v SL (Harare) 1994-95. **L-O INTERNATIONALS:** 26 (1991-92 to 1994-95). 489 runs (av 21.26), 1 hundred; 0 wkts; 6 ct. HS 131* v SL (Harare) 1994-95.

CARLISLE, Stuart Vance **(Mashonaland Under 24)**
Born Salisbury 10 May 1972. Right-hand batsman, right-arm medium pace bowler. First-class debut 1993-94. **TESTS:** 3 (1994-95). 78 runs (av 26.00); 5 ct. HS 46* v P (Bulawayo) 1994-95. **L-O INTERNATIONALS:** 3 (1994-95). 13 runs (av 6.50); 2 ct. HS 9* v P (Harare) 1994-95.

DEKKER, Mark Hamilton **(Matebeleland)**
Born Gatooma 5 Dec 1969. Right-hand batsman, left-arm medium pace/orthodox slow bowler. First-class debut 1990-91. **TESTS:** 8 (1993-94 to 1994-95). 208 runs (av 20.80); 0 wkts; 10 ct. HS 68* v P (Rawalpindi) 1993-94. **L-O INTERNATIONALS:** 19 (1992-93 to 1994-95). 339 runs (av 19.94); 9 wkts (av 26.77); 5 ct. HS 79 v NZ (Bulawayo) 1992-93 – on debut. BB 2-16 v P (Rawalpindi) 1993-94.

EVANS, Craig Neil **(Mashonaland Under 24)**
Born Salisbury 29 Nov 1969. Right-hand batsman, right-arm medium pace bowler. First-class debut 1990-91. **TESTS:** 0. **L-O INTERNATIONALS:** 3 (1992-93). 35 runs (av 11.66); 1 ct. HS 22 v NZ (Bulawayo) 1992-93.

FLOWER, Andrew (Mashonaland)
Born Cape Town, South Africa 28 Apr 1968. 5' 10". Brother of Grant. Educated at Jainona High School. Left-hand batsman, occasional right-arm medium pace bowler, wicket-keeper. First-class debut 1986-87. **TESTS:** 13 (1992-93 to 1994-95, 9 as captain). 835 runs (av 49.11), 2 hundreds; 0 wkts; 29 ct, 2 st. HS 156 v P (Harare) 1994-95 sharing with G.W.Flower in fourth wicket partnership of 269, the highest stand between brothers in Test cricket. **L-O INTERNATIONALS:** 34 (1991-92 to 1994-95, 17 as captain). 1028 runs (av 33.16), 1 hundred; 0 wkts; 24 ct, 5 st. HS 115* v SL (New Plymouth) 1991-92 – on debut.

FLOWER, Grant William (Mashonaland)
Born Salisbury 20 Dec 1970. 5' 10". Brother of Andrew. Educated at St George's College. Right-hand batsman, left-arm orthodox slow bowler. First-class debut 1989-90. **TESTS:** 13 (1992-93 to 1994-95). 627 runs (av 31.35), 1 hundred; 2 wkts (av 86.50); 6 ct. HS 201* v P (Harare) 1994-95 sharing with G.W.Flower in fourth wicket partnership of 269, the highest stand between brothers in Test cricket. BB 1-8. **L-O INTERNATIONALS:** 24 (1992-93 to 1994-95). 584 runs (av 27.80); 13 wkts (av 34.15); 14 ct. HS 84* v E (Sydney) 1994-95. BB 3-15 v A (Perth) 1994-95.

HOUGHTON, David Laud (Mashonaland)
Born Bulawayo 23 Jun 1957. 5' 10". Educated at Prince Edward School. Right-hand batsman, occasional off-break bowler, wicket-keeper. First-class debut 1978-79. **TESTS:** 13 (1992-93 to 1994-95, 4 as captain). 912 runs (av 48.00), 3 hundreds; 0 wkts; 9 ct. HS 266 v SL (Bulawayo) 1994-95 – record first-class score in Zimbabwe. **L-O INTERNATIONALS:** 45 (1983 to 1994-95, 17 as captain). 1245 runs (av 29.64), 1 hundred; 1 wkt (av 19.00); 22 ct, 2 st. HS 142 v NZ (Hyderabad, India) 1987-88. BB 1-19.

JAMES, Wayne Robert (Matebeleland)
Born Bulawayo 27 Aug 1965. Educated at Plumtree High School. Right-hand batsman, wicket-keeper. First-class debut 1986-87. **TESTS:** 4 (1993-94 to 1994-95). 61 runs (av 15.25); 16 ct. HS 33 v SL (Bulawayo) 1994-95. **L-O INTERNATIONALS:** 10 (1991-92 to 1994-95). 101 runs (av 14.42); 6 ct. HS 29 v SL (Harare) 1994-95.

LOCK, Alan Patrick Charles
Born Salisbury 10 Sep 1962. Right-hand batsman, right-arm fast-medium bowler. First-class debut 1987-88. **TESTS:** 0. **L-O INTERNATIONALS:** 0.

OLONGA, Henry Rhaaba (Matebeleland)
Born Lusaka, Zambia 3 Jul 1976. Right-hand batsman, right-arm fast-medium bowler. First-class debut 1993-94. **TESTS:** 1 (1994-95). Did not bat; 1 wkt (av 27.00); 0 ct. BB 1-27. **L-O INTERNATIONALS:** 0.

PEALL, Stephen Guy (Mashonaland Country Districts)
Born Salisbury 2 Sep 1970. 5' 9". Educated at Falcon College. Left-hand batsman, off-break bowler. First-class debut 1990-91. **TESTS:** 4 (1993-94 to 1994-95). 60 runs (av 15.00); 4 wkts (av 75.75); 1 ct. HS 30 v SL (Bulawayo) 1994-95. BB 2-89 v P (Karachi) 1993-94 – on debut. **L-O INTERNATIONALS:** 15 (1992-93 to 1994-95). 82 runs (av 7.45); 6 wkts (av 88.16); 0 ct. HS 21 v SL (Harare) 1994-95. BB 3-54 v I (Indore) 1993-94.

SHAH, Ali Hassimshah (Mashonaland)
Born Salisbury 7 Aug 1959. Left-hand batsman, right-arm medium pace bowler. First-class debut 1979-80. **TESTS:** 2 (1992-93). 59 runs (av 19.66); 1 wkt (av 125.00); 0 ct. HS 28 and BB 1-46 v NZ (Bulawayo) 1992-93 – on debut. **L-O INTERNATIONALS:** 26 (1983-84 to 1993-94). 390 runs (av 16.25); 18 wkts (av 44.11); 6 ct. HS 60* v WI (Brisbane) 1991-92. BB 3-33 v P (Sharjah) 1992-93.

STRANG, Bryan Colin **(Mashonaland Country Districts)**
Born Bulawayo 9 Jun 1972. Brother of Paul. Right-hand batsman, left-arm fast-medium bowler. First-class debut 1994-95. **TESTS:** 2 (1994-95). 6 runs (av 2.00); 9 wkts (av 13.33); 1 ct. HS 6 and BB 3-43 v P (Harare) 1994-95. **L-O INTERNATIONALS:** 3 (1994-95). 4 runs (av –); 7 wkts (av 10.42); 3 ct. HS 4*. BB 4-36 v P (Harare) 1994-95 – on debut.

STRANG, Paul Andrew **(Mashonaland Country Districts)**
Born Bulawayo 28 Jul 1970. Brother of Bryan. Educated at Falcon College; Cape Town University. Right-hand batsman, right-arm leg-break bowler. First-class debut 1992-93. **TESTS:** 4 (1994-95). 74 runs (av 14.80); 4 wkts (av 58.50); 3 ct. HS 32 v P (Bulawayo) 1994-95. BB 3-65 v SL (Harare) 1994-95 – on debut. **L-O INTERNATIONALS:** 7 (1994-95). 67 runs (av 16.75); 8 wkts (av 33.62); 2 ct. HS 21* v A (Hobart) 1994-95. BB 3-42 v P (Harare) 1994-95.

STREAK, Heath Hilton **(Matebeleland)**
Born Bulawayo 16 Mar 1974. 6′ 1″. Educated at Falcon College. Right-hand batsman, right-arm fast-medium bowler. First-class debut 1992-93. Hampshire 1995 (uncapped). **TESTS:** 9 (1993-94 to 1994-95). 103 runs (av 10.30); 43 wkts (av 20.60), 5 wkts/inns (3); 3 ct. HS 30* v P (3rd) (Harare) 1994-95. BB 6-90 v P (1st) (Harare) 1994-95. **L-O INTERNATIONALS:** 16 (1993-94 to 1994-95). 98 runs (av 12.25); 19 wkts (av 30.63); 2 ct. HS 18*. BB 4-44.

WALLER, Andrew Christopher **(Mashonaland Country Districts)**
Born Salisbury 25 Sep 1959. Right-hand batsman, right-arm medium pace bowler. First-class debut 1984-85. **TESTS:** 0. **L-O INTERNATIONALS:** 22 (1987-88 to 1994-95). 488 runs (av 27.11); 8 ct. HS 83* v SL (New Plymouth) 1991-92.

WHITTALL, Guy James **(Matebeleland)**
Born Chipingi 5 Sep 1972. 5′ 8″. Educated at Falcon College. Right-hand batsman, right-arm medium pace bowler. First-class debut 1990-91. **TESTS:** 9 (1993-94 to 1994-95). 304 runs (av 27.63), 1 hundred; 18 wkts (av 32.66); 5 ct. HS 113* v P (Harare) 1994-95. BB 4-70 v SL (Harare) 1994-95. **L-O INTERNATIONALS:** 15 (1993-94 to 1994-95). 263 runs (av 20.23); 13 wkts (av 26.69); 6 ct. HS 53 v E (Brisbane) 1994-95. BB 3-46 v P (Harare) 1994-95.

WISHART, Craig Brian **(Mashonaland Under 24)**
Born Salisbury 9 Jan 1974. Right-hand batsman, right-arm medium pace bowler. First-class debut 1992-93. **TESTS:** 0. **L-O INTERNATIONALS:** 0.

WORLD CUP CAREER RECORDS

ZIMBABWE – BATTING AND FIELDING

	M	I	NO	HS	Runs	Avge	100	50	Ct/St
Arnott, K.J.	9	8	1	60	206	29.42	–	3	2
Brandes, E.A.	12	9	3	23	92	15.33	–	–	4
Brown, R.D.	7	7	–	38	110	15.71	–	–	5
Burmester, M.G.	4	3	1	12	17	8.50	–	–	1
Butchart, I.P.	17	14	2	54	240	20.00	–	1	4
Campbell, A.D.R.	4	3	–	8	13	4.33	–	–	1
Curran, K.M.	11	11	–	73	287	26.09	–	2	1
Duers, K.G.	6	2	1	5	7	7.00	–	–	2
Fletcher, D.A.G.	6	6	2	71*	191	47.75	–	2	–
Flower, A.	8	8	2	115*	246	41.00	1	–	6/1
Heron, J.G.	6	6	–	18	50	8.33	–	–	1
Hogg, V.R.	2	1	1	7*	7	–	–	–	–
Houghton, D.L.	20	19	–	142	567	29.84	1	4	14/2
James, W.R.	4	3	–	17	35	11.66	–	–	1
Jarvis, M.P.	10	5	3	17	37	18.50	–	–	1
Meman, M.A.	1	1	–	19	19	19.00	–	–	–
Paterson, G.A.	10	10	–	27	123	12.30	–	–	2
Peckover, G.E.	3	3	1	16*	33	16.50	–	–	–
Pycroft, A.J.	20	19	2	61	295	17.35	–	2	6
Rawson, P.W.E.	10	8	3	24*	80	16.00	–	–	4
Shah, A.H.	16	16	1	60*	266	17.73	–	1	3
Traicos, A.J.	20	12	5	19	70	10.00	–	–	2
Waller, A.C.	14	14	3	83*	317	28.81	–	1	3

ZIMBABWE – BOWLING

	O	M	R	W	Avge	Best	4w	R/O
Brandes, E.A.	103.1	11	509	16	31.81	4-21	1	4.93
Burmester, M.G.	21.5	0	138	4	34.50	3-36	–	6.32
Butchart, I.P.	117	6	640	12	53.33	3-57	–	5.47
Curran, K.M.	84.2	3	398	9	44.22	3-65	–	4.71
Duers, K.G.	50	2	256	3	85.33	1-17	–	5.12
Fletcher, D.A.G.	50.1	5	221	7	31.57	4-42	1	4.40
Hogg, V.R.	15	4	49	0	–	–	–	3.26
Houghton, D.L.	2	0	19	1	19.00	1-19	–	9.50
Jarvis, M.P.	83.1	5	384	7	54.85	1-21	–	4.61
Meman, M.A.	6.5	0	34	0	–	–	–	4.97
Rawson, P.W.E.	95.1	10	427	12	35.58	3-47	–	4.48
Shah, A.H.	104.3	9	456	11	41.45	2-17	–	4.36
Traicos, A.J.	188	13	671	16	42.06	3-35	–	3.57

WORLD CUP REGISTER

HOLLAND

HOLLAND will be playing their first Limited-Overs International match when they meet New Zealand at Baroda on 17 February. All career statistics are up to the end of the 1995 season (18 September). Key to abbreviations on page 32. Holland's selected 20 players for the Wills World Cup are:

APONSO, Flavian (Amsterdam CC)
Born Ceylon 28 Oct 1952. Left-hand batsman, off-break bowler. Played most of his cricket in Sri Lanka. Professional coach in Holland since 1984. Holland debut 1989. Employee of the Sri Lankan Embassy. **HOLLAND CAREER:** 49 matches; 895 runs (av 23.55), 1 hundred, HS 100; 41 wkts (av 29.75); 9 ct.

BAKKER, Paul-Jan (Quick CC, The Hague)
Born Vlaardingen 19 Aug 1957. 5′ 11″. Educated at Hugo De Groot College, The Hague. Right-hand lower-order batsman, right-arm medium-fast opening bowler. Holland debut 1983. Hampshire 1986 to 1992 (cap 1989). First Dutchman to play county cricket. Manager of Quick Cricket Club. **F-C CAREER:** 333 runs (av 9.51); 193 wkts (av 28.01), 5 wkts/inns (7), 10 wkts/match (0), 50 wkts in a season (1): 77 (1989); 9 ct. HS 22 Hampshire v Yorks (Southampton) 1989 and v Glamorgan (Portsmouth) 1992. BB 7-31 Hampshire v Kent (Bournemouth) 1987. **HOLLAND CAREER:** 39 matches; 147 runs (av 13.36), HS 25; 70 wkts (av 15.74); 5 ct.

BOERSTRA, Hans (Voorburg CC)
Born 6 Jan 1965. Right-hand lower-order batsman, right-arm medium pace bowler. Holland debut 1991. Played first grade cricket in Sydney 1992-93 to 1994-95. Chemical Engineer. **HOLLAND CAREER:** 13 matches; 97 runs (av 13.85), HS 26; 11 wkts (av 39.54); 0 ct.

CANTRELL, Peter Edward (Kampong CC, Utrecht)
Born Gunnedah, NSW, Australia 28 Oct 1962. Right-hand opening batsman, off-break bowler. Queensland 1988-89 to 1990-91. Holland debut 1992. Golf professional. **F-C CAREER:** 1827 runs (av 32.62), 3 hundreds; 27 wkts (av 63.00); 43 ct. HS 176* Queensland v South Australia (Brisbane) 1990-91. BB 4-52 Queensland v Victoria (Brisbane) 1988-89. Fielded substitute for Australia in first Test v England (Brisbane) 1990-91 holding two catches at gully. **HOLLAND CAREER:** 30 matches; 1473 runs (av 58.92), 2 hundreds, HS 112*; 13 wkts (av 42.76); 14 ct.

CLARKE, Nolan Ewatt (Sparta CC, Rotterdam)
Born St Michael, Barbados 22 Jun 1948. Right-hand opening batsman, occasional leg-break and googly bowler. Barbados 1969-70 to 1976-77. Holland debut 1989. Professional cricketer and coach. Leading six-hitter at Hong Kong 'Sixes' 1994. **F-C CAREER:** 1331 runs (av 31.69), 2 hundreds; 0 wkts; 27 ct. HS 159 Barbados v MCC (Bridgetown) 1973-74. **HOLLAND CAREER:** 87 matches; 3164 runs (av 41.63), 7 hundreds *(record)*, HS 154; 12 wkts (av 36.33); 33 ct.

De LEEDE, Timotheus Bernardus Maria (Voorburg CC)
Born Leidschendam 25 Jan 1968. Right-hand batsman, right-arm medium pace bowler. Holland debut 1990. Northamptonshire 2nd XI 1990. Sussex 2nd XI 1990 and 1991. Surrey 2nd XI 1993. Melbourne first grade cricket 1988-89 to 1990-91. Cricket goods representative. **HOLLAND CAREER:** 81 matches; 1871 runs (av 31.18), 3 hundreds, HS 114; 66 wkts (av 25.00); 24 ct.

FRANK, Eldert (VOC CC, Rotterdam)
Born Rotterdam 22 Oct 1972. Right-hand lower-order batsman, left-arm orthodox slow bowler. Awaiting Holland debut.

GOUKA, Eric (Excelsior CC, Schiedam)
Born 29 Jan 1970. Right-hand batsman, right-arm medium pace bowler. Holland debut 1989. Has toured Zimbabwe, Dubai, Namibia and India. University student. **HOLLAND CAREER:** 21 matches; 225 runs (av 17.30), HS 40; 10 wkts (av 27.60); 8 ct.

GRAVESANDE, Gary (VRA CC, Amsterdam)
Born 6 Nov 1976. Right-hand batsman, right-arm medium pace bowler, occasional wicket-keeper. Awaiting Holland debut.

JANSEN, Floris (Kampong CC, Utrecht)
Born 10 Jun 1962. Right-hand lower-order batsman, right-arm medium pace swing bowler. Holland debut 1987. Publishing executive. **HOLLAND CAREER:** 84 matches; 281 runs (av 10.03), HS 32; 128 wkts (av 21.57); 18 ct.

KHAN, K. Asim (VRA CC, Amsterdam)
Born Lahore, Pakistan 14 Feb 1962. Right-hand lower-order batsman, right-arm medium pace opening swing bowler. Holland debut 1994. **HOLLAND CAREER:** 9 matches; 32 runs (av 10.66), HS 14*; 7 wkts (av 41.85); 2 ct.

LEFEBVRE, Roland Philippe **(Glamorgan; VOC CC, Rotterdam)**
Born Rotterdam 7 Feb 1963. 6' 1". Educated at Montessori Lyceum, Rotterdam; Hague Accademie of Physiotherapy. Right-hand batsman, right-arm medium-fast bowler. Somerset 1990 to 1992 (cap 1991). Glamorgan debut/cap 1993. Holland debut 1983. Canterbury (NZ) 1990-91. **F-C CAREER:** 1494 runs (av 20.46), 1 hundred; 149 wkts (av 36.23), 5 wkts/inns (3); 36 ct. HS 100 Somerset v Worcs (Weston-super-Mare) 1991. Glamorgan HS 50 v Worcs (Worcester) 1993. BB 6-45 Glamorgan v Oxford U (Oxford) 1995. Championship BB 5-30 Somerset v Glos (Taunton) 1990. **1995 SEASON** (f-c): 55 runs (av 18.33); 6 wkts (av 29.83), 5 wkts/inns (1); 0 ct. **HOLLAND CAREER:** 90 matches; 2183 runs (av 30.74), 2 hundreds, HS 134; 92 wkts (av 20.28); 47 ct.

LUBBERS, Steven W. (CAPTAIN) (Hermes DVS, Schiedam)
Born 24 Mar 1953. Right-handed upper-order batsman, off-break bowler. Holland debut 1972. Captain 1988 to date. Only cricketer to gain 100 Dutch caps. Physical education teacher. **HOLLAND CAREER:** 163 matches *(record)*; 3195 runs *(record)* (av 25.56), 2 hundreds, HS 118; 135 wkts (av 26.28); 85 ct *(record by non wicket-keeper)*.

SCHEWE, Marcel (Excelsior CC, Schiedam)
Born 10 May 1969. Aggressive right-hand middle-order batsman, wicket-keeper. Holland debut 1994. Toured Kenya and India. Metal worker. **HOLLAND CAREER:** 15 matches; 218 runs (av 24.22), HS 80; has not bowled; 17 ct.

SCHIFERLI, Edgar (Quick CC, The Hague)
Born The Hague 17 May 1976. Right-hand middle-order batsman, right-arm medium pace bowler. Awaiting Holland debut.

SCHOLTE, Reinout H. (VICE-CAPTAIN) (HBS CC, The Hague)
Born 10 Aug 1967. Right-hand middle-order batsman, wicket-keeper. Holland debut 1987.
Has captained on several occasions. Bank officer. **HOLLAND CAREER:** 64 matches; 708
runs (av 19.66), HS 90*; has not bowled; 50 ct, 4 st.

SMITS, Jeroen (HCC CC, The Hague)
Born The Hague 21 Jun 1972. Right-hand lower-order batsman, exceptionally promising
wicket-keeper. Holland debut 1992. **HOLLAND CAREER:** 10 matches; 4 runs (av 4.00),
HS 4*; has not bowled; 6 ct, 4 st.

Van NOORTWIJK, Klaas Jan (VOC CC, Rotterdam)
Born Rotterdam 10 Jul 1970. Hard-hitting right-hand middle-order batsman who impressed
at the 1995 Hong Kong 'Sixes'. Holland debut 1994. **HOLLAND CAREER:** 17 matches;
258 runs (av 25.80), HS 68; 2 wkts (av 18.00); 4 ct.

Van OOSTEROM, Robert F. (HBS CC, The Hague)
Born The Hague 16 Oct 1968. Right-hand opening batsman. Holland debut 1990.
HOLLAND CAREER: 60 matches; 1061 runs (av 21.65), HS 87; has not bowled; 19 ct.

ZUIDERENT, Bastiaan ('Bas') (VOC CC, Rotterdam)
Born Rotterdam 3 Mar 1977. Right-hand upper-order batsman and right-arm medium pace
bowler. Holland debut 1994. **HOLLAND CAREER:** 9 matches; 106 runs (av 13.25), HS
39; 1 wkt (av 35.00); 5 ct.

WORLD CUP REGISTER

KENYA

All career statistics are up to the end of the 1995 season (18 September). Key to abbreviations on page 32. Kenya's selected 20 players for the Wills World Cup are:

ALI, Rajab (Simba Union)
Born 1965. Right-hand batsman, right-arm fast-medium opening bowler.

ANGARA, Joseph (Swamibapa Sports Club)
Born 8 Nov 1971. Right-arm medium-fast bowler.

ASIF KARIM (Jaffery Sports Club)
Born 15 Dec 1963. Right-hand batsman, orthodox left-arm slow bowler. **F-C CAREER:** 11 runs (av 11.00); 6 wkts (av 19.83); 0 ct. HS 11 and BB 3-40 Kenya v Pakistan B (Nairobi) 1986-87.

CHUDASAMA, Dipak (Nairobi Gymkhana)
Born 20 May 1963. Right-hand opening batsman.

GUPTA, Sandip (Nairobi Gymkhana)
Born 7 Apr 1967. Right-hand batsman, wicket-keeper.

MacDONALD, Daniel (Aga Khan Club)
Born 27 Nov 1962. Right-hand opening batsman, right-arm medium-fast bowler. **F-C CAREER:** 37 runs (av 18.50); 0 ct. HS 32 Kenya v Pakistan B (Nairobi) 1986-87.

MODI, Hitesh (Nairobi Gymkhana)
Born 13 Oct 1971. Left-hand batsman, off-break bowler.

ODOYO, Thomas (Nairobi Gymkhana)
Born 12 May 1978. Right-hand batsman, right-arm medium-fast bowler.

ODUMBE, Edward (Aga Khan Club)
Born 19 May 1965. Right-hand batsman, right-arm medium-fast bowler.

ODUMBE, Martin Oriwo (Swamibapa Sports Club)
Born 19 May 1968. Right-hand batsman, right-arm fast-medium opening bowler.

ODUMBE, Maurice (Aga Khan Club)
Born 15 Jun 1969. Right-hand batsman, off-break bowler.

ONDIK, O.S. (Aga Khan Club)
Born 5 Feb 1976. Right-hand batsman, right-arm medium-fast bowler.

ONYANGO, Lameck (Swamibapa Sports Club)
Born 22 Sep 1973. Right-hand batsman, right-arm medium-fast bowler.

OTIENO, Kennedy (Aga Khan Club)
Born 11 Mar 1973. Right-hand opening batsman, wicket-keeper.

PATEL, Brijal (Premier Club)
Born 14 Nov 1977. Right-hand batsman, orthodox left-arm slow bowler.

SUJI, Martin (Aga Khan Club)
Born 2 Jun 1971. Right-hand batsman, right-arm fast-medium opening bowler.

TARIQ IQBAL (Swamibapa Sports Club)
Born 1962. Right-hand opening batsman, wicket-keeper.

TIKOLO, David (Swamibapa Sports Club)
Born 27 Dec 1964. Right-hand batsman, right-arm medium pace bowler.

TIKOLO, Steven (Swamibapa Sports Club)
Born 25 Jun 1971. Right-hand batsman, off-break bowler.

VADER, Alpesh (Premier Club)
Born 7 Sep 1974. Right-hand middle-order batsman.

KENYA TEAM OFFICIALS

JASMER SINGH (Tour Manager)
Former Chairman of Kenya Cricket Association. Manager of 1975 East Africa World Cup team. Elected honorary life member of MCC for services to cricket in Kenya.

HARILAL Raishi **SHAH (Team Manager)**
Born Kenya 1943. Right-hand batsman, right-arm medium pace bowler. **TOUR:** East Africa to England 1975 (captain). **F-C CAREER:** 92 runs (av 46.00); 0 wkts; 0 ct. HS 59 East Africa v Sri Lanka (Taunton) 1975 – his only f-c match. A hard-hitting middle-order batsman and excellent cover fielder, he captained East Africa in the inaugural World Cup. He is chairman of Kenya's World Cup Preparations Committee and Vice-Chairman of the Kenya Cricket Association.

HANUMANT SINGH (Coach)
(Maharajkumar of Banswara.) Born Banswara, India 29 Mar 1939. Nephew of K.S.Duleepsinhji (Sussex and England). Right-hand middle-order batsman, leg-break bowler. Madhya Bharat 1956-57. Rajasthan 1957-58 to 1978-79. **TESTS (India):** 14 (1963-64 to 1969-70). 686 runs (av 31.18), 1 hundred; 0 wkts; 11 ct. HS 105 v England (Delhi) 1963-64 – on Test debut. **TOUR:** India to England 1967. **F-C CAREER:** 12,338 runs (av 43.90), 29 hundreds (inc 4 doubles), 1000 runs in a season (3); most – 1586 (1966-67); 56 wkts (av 40.94), 5 wkts/inns (1); 110 ct. HS 213* Rajasthan v Bombay (Bombay) 1966-67. BB 5-48. ICC referee for West Indies v Australia Limited-Overs International series 1994-95.

WORLD CUP REGISTER

UNITED ARAB EMIRATES

Career statistics, provided by the Emirates Cricket Board, incorporate the following tournaments and tours and are up to the end of the 1995 season (18 September).

ICC Trophy	February/March 1994
Australasia Cup	April 1994
UAE Interface Tournament	December 1994
UAE ABN AMRO	December 1994
Sail Trophy	January 1995
India-Kenya tournament	February 1995
UAE v India	April 1995
Pakistan tour	June 1995

Key to abbreviations on page 32.

The Emirates' selected 20 players for the Wills World Cup are:

ARSHAD LAIQ
Born Karachi, Pakistan 28 Nov 1970. Right-hand batsman, right-arm fast-medium bowler. **L-O INTERNATIONALS:** 2 (1993-94). 35 runs (av 17.50), HS 31; 0 wkts; 1 ct. **UAE CAREER:** 402 runs (av 40.20), HS 70*; 24 wkts (av 33.33).

AZHAR SAEED, Syed
Born Lahore, Pakistan 25 Dec 1968. Left-hand batsman, left-arm orthodox slow bowler. **L-O INTERNATIONALS:** 2 (1993-94). 3 runs (av 1.50), HS 3; 0 wkts; 0 ct. **UAE CAREER:** 662 runs (av 34.84), HS 126; 18 wkts (av 40.61); ct.

BANGERA, Daynanand
Born 1 Jun 1963. Batsman, wicket-keeper. **L-O INTERNATIONALS:** 0. **UAE CAREER:** 152 runs (av 38.00), HS 59.

DUKANWALA, Shaukat
Born 10 Feb 1964. Bowler. **L-O INTERNATIONALS:** 0. **UAE CAREER:** 9 runs (av 9.00), HS 9*; 0 wkts.

FERNANDO, Shane
Born 21 Oct 1965. Batsman, wicket-keeper. **L-O INTERNATIONALS:** 0. **UAE CAREER:** 189 runs (av 27.00), HS 78.

IMTIAZ ABBASI
Born Poonch, Pakistan 6 Feb 1968. Right-hand batsman, wicket-keeper. **L-O INTERNATIONALS:** 2 (1993-94). 8 runs (av 8.00), HS 6*; 2 ct. **UAE CAREER:** 30 runs (av 4.28), HS 8.

MAZHAR HUSSAIN, Sheikh
Born Lahore, Pakistan 25 Oct 1967. Right-hand batsman, right-arm leg-break bowler. **L-O INTERNATIONALS:** 2 (1993-94). 80 runs (av 40.00), HS 70; 0 ct. **UAE CAREER:** 603 runs (av 33.50), HS 122; 0 wkts.

MEHRA, Vijay
Born India 17 Oct 1963. Batsman. **L-O INTERNATIONALS:** 2 (1993-94). 48 runs (av 24.00), HS 43; 0 ct. **UAE CAREER:** 522 runs (av 27.47), HS 50.

MOHAMMAD ASLAM
Batsman. **L-O INTERNATIONALS:** 0. **UAE CAREER:** 155 runs (av 77.50), HS 115*.

MOHAMMAD ISHAQ
Born Lahore, Pakistan 7 Mar 1963. Right-hand batsman, right-arm medium pace bowler. **L-O INTERNATIONALS:** 2 (1993-94). 27 runs (av 13.50), HS 23. 0 ct. **UAE CAREER:** 546 runs (av 34.12), HS 89.

MYLVAGANAM, Ganesh
Born 1 Aug 1966. Batsman. **L-O INTERNATIONALS:** 0. **UAE CAREER:** 261 runs (av 37.28), HS 93.

PERERA, Vijay
All-rounder. **L-O INTERNATIONALS:** 0. **UAE CAREER:** –

PRASAD, Rajinder
All-rounder. **L-O INTERNATIONALS:** 0. **UAE CAREER:** –

SALIM RAZA
Born Lahore, Pakistan 5 Jul 1964. Right-hand batsman, off-break bowler. **L-O INTERNATIONALS:** 2 (1993-94). 22 runs (av 11.00), HS 16 ; 2 wkts (av 35.50), BB 1-17; 0 ct. **UAE CAREER:** 504 runs (av 29.64), HS 78; 18 wkts (av 44.38).

SAMARASEKERA, Johanne Abeyratne
Born Colombo, Sri Lanka 22 Feb 1968. Right-hand batsman, right-arm medium-fast bowler. **L-O INTERNATIONALS:** 2 (1993-94). 34 runs (av 34.00), HS 31*; 1 wkts (av 79.00), BB 1-48; 1 ct. **UAE CAREER:** 107 runs (av 26.75), HS 31; 16 wkts (av 25.68).

SHAHZAD ALTAF
Born 6 Oct 1957. Bowler. **L-O INTERNATIONALS:** 0. **UAE CAREER:** 22 runs (av 5.50), HS 18; 11 wkts (av 37.09).

SHAHZAD KHAN
Born 1964. Bowler. **L-O INTERNATIONALS:** 0. **UAE CAREER:** Did not bat; 3 wkts (av 17.33).

SHENOY, Subraya
Born 17 Apr 1971. Bowler. **L-O INTERNATIONALS:** 0. **UAE CAREER:** 71 runs (av 71.00), HS 63; 0 wkts.

SULTAN ZARAWANI
Born 24 Jan 1961. Bowler. **L-O INTERNATIONALS:** 2 (1993-94). 10 runs (av 5.00), HS 6; 1 wkt (av 48.00), BB 1-22; 0 ct. **UAE CAREER:** 134 runs (av 13.40), HS 32; 13 wkts (av 49.00).

TUAN AHAMATH
Born 12 Sep 1963. Bowler. **L-O INTERNATIONALS:** 0. **UAE CAREER:** 25 runs (av 25.00), HS 14; 6 wkts (av 18.33).

CANADA
BATTING AND FIELDING

	M	I	NO	HS	Runs	Avge	100	50	Ct/St
Baksh, S.	1	1	–	0	0	0.00	–	–	–
Callender, R.G.	2	2	–	0	0	0.00	–	–	–
Chappell, C.J.D.	3	3	–	19	38	12.66	–	–	–
Dennis, F.A.	3	3	–	25	47	15.66	–	–	–
Henry, C.C.	2	2	1	5	6	6.00	–	–	–
Marshall, C.A.	2	2	–	8	10	5.00	–	–	–
Mauricette, B.M.	3	3	–	15	20	6.66	–	–	–
Patel, J.M.	3	3	–	2	3	1.00	–	–	–
Sealy, G.R.	3	3	–	45	73	24.33	–	–	–
Stead, M.P.	2	2	–	10	10	5.00	–	–	–
Tariq Javed	3	3	–	8	15	5.00	–	–	–
Valentine, J.N.	3	2	2	3*	3	–	–	–	1
Vaughan, J.C.B.	3	3	–	29	30	10.00	–	–	–

BOWLING

	O	M	R	W	Avge	Best	4w	R/O
Callender, R.G.	9	1	26	1	26.00	1-14	–	2.88
Henry, C.C.	15	0	53	2	26.50	2-27	–	3.53
Patel, J.M.	15.1	0	47	0	–	–	–	3.09
Sealy, G.R.	6	0	21	0	–	–	–	3.50
Stead, M.P.	4.5	0	24	0	–	–	–	4.96
Valentine, J.N.	19	5	66	3	22.00	1-18	–	3.47
Vaughan, J.C.B.	11	1	36	0	–	–	–	3.27

EAST AFRICA
BATTING AND FIELDING

	M	I	NO	HS	Runs	Avge	100	50	Ct/St
Frasat Ali	3	3	–	45	57	19.00	–	–	–
Harilal Shah	3	3	–	6	6	2.00	–	–	–
Jawahir Shah	3	3	–	37	46	15.33	–	–	–
McLeod, H.	2	2	–	5	5	2.50	–	–	–
Mehmood Quaraishy	3	3	1	19	41	20.50	–	–	–
Nagenda, J.	1	–	–	0	–	–	–	–	–
Nana, P.G.	3	3	2	8*	9	9.00	–	–	2
Praful Mehta	1	1	–	12	12	12.00	–	–	–
Pringle, D.	2	2	–	3	5	2.50	–	–	–
Ramesh Sethi	3	3	–	30	54	18.00	–	–	1
Shiraz Sumar	1	1	–	4	4	4.00	–	–	–
Walusimba, S.	3	3	–	16	38	12.66	–	–	1
Yunus Badat	2	2	–	1	1	0.50	–	–	–
Zulfiqar Ali	3	3	1	30	39	19.50	–	–	1

BOWLING

	O	M	R	W	Avge	Best	4w	R/O
Frasat Ali	24	1	107	0	–	–	–	4.45
Mehmood Quaraishy	18	0	94	3	31.33	2-55	–	5.22
Nagenda, J.	9	1	50	1	50.00	1-50	–	5.55
Nana, P.G.	28.5	4	116	1	116.00	1-34	–	4.02
Pringle, D.	15	0	55	0	–	–	–	3.66
Ramesh Sethi	20	1	100	1	100.00	1-51	–	5.00
Zulfiqar Ali	35	3	166	4	41.50	3-63	–	4.74

THE 1975 WORLD CUP

The inaugural World Cup tournament was held within five years of the birth of limited-overs internationals, the very first of which had been a hastily arranged affair played on the final day (5 January 1971) of a rain-aborted Melbourne Test match to appease the disappointed local public. Like all of England's home one-day matches between the first in 1972 and the end of the third World Cup in 1983, the competition was sponsored by Prudential Assurance who contributed over £100,000 for the privilege.

This initial competition was a very modest affair, consisting of just 15 matches on only five playing days. That it was such a resounding success was due as much to the fact that its 15-day span coincided with the start of one of Britain's rare long, hot summers, as to the standard of cricket played. For that number of 60-overs matches to be completed without the loss of a single minute to inclement weather in Britain in June constituted a miracle of major proportions, particularly as an inch-deep covering of snow had prevented play in a county match at Buxton just five days before the tournament began. Pessimistically, the organisers had set aside three days for each contest. All 15 matches were staged at Test match venues, with Edgbaston, Headingley and The Oval each hosting three games and Lord's, Old Trafford and Trent Bridge two apiece.

The six current Test-playing countries were joined by two associate members, Sri Lanka and East Africa, the eight teams being divided into two groups of four, each playing the other once, but with England and Australia seeded. Group A comprised England, East Africa, India and New Zealand, while Pakistan, Sri Lanka and West Indies joined Australia in Group B. The leading two teams in each group qualified for the semi-finals.

A crowd of almost 20,000 (receipts £19,000) watched England amass 334 for 4, then the highest total in a 60-over match in Britain, with Dennis Amiss (137) recording the first World Cup hundred and the left-handed Chris Old scoring an undefeated 51 off 30 balls. The game was reduced to farcical boredom when India decided that the target on a slow pitch was totally beyond them and played for a draw! The chief culprit was opening batsman Sunil Gavaskar who took it upon himself to use the 60 overs for batting practice and managed to score just 36 runs from 174 balls, a performance which incurred the public wrath of both his manager, G.S.Ramchand, and his captain, Srini Venkataraghavan. England's margin of victory, 202 runs, remains the largest by any side batting first in World Cup matches.

Australia's clash with Pakistan attracted Headingley's first full house for nine years (21,000 plus). Chasing 279, Pakistan looked set for a sensational win at 181 for 4, but their last six wickets clattered for 24 runs, Dennis Lillee returning the competition's first five-wicket haul. His partner in pace, Jeff Thomson, could find no rhythm and was no-balled 12 times, five of them in the first over.

Sri Lanka were totally outclassed by West Indies, being dismissed in 37.2 overs on a blameless pitch for just 86, the lowest total of this tournament. As the match was completed by 3.30pm, the players entertained a disappointed Old Trafford crowd with a 20-over exhibition game.

East Africa fared little better against New Zealand, thanks to an exceptional batting display by Glenn Turner. Imperious driving featured prominently in the Worcestershire opener's unbeaten 171, the World Cup's highest score until Kapil Dev surpassed it four years later.

The Kiwis' captain was unable to reproduce this form in the second round of matches and his team was easily beaten by England. At Headingley, India's ten-wicket defeat of East Africa attracted a paying attendance of only 720. Lancashire-born Don Pringle, father of future England and Essex all-rounder Derek, made his World Cup debut for East Africa.

West Indies and Pakistan produced an epic match at Edgbaston, the eventual champions scraping home by one wicket with two balls to spare thanks to a last-wicket partnership of 64 in 14 overs between Deryck Murray and Andy Roberts. At The Oval, Sri Lanka, facing a daunting total of 328 (Alan Turner contributing the only pre-lunch hundred in World Cup matches), batted with extraordinary bravery against a hostile Australian attack. Remember that this was before the introduction of helmets and arm guards. Despite two of their batsmen being put in hospital by Thomson, they fell only 52 runs short of their target and lost just four wickets. This outstanding performance gained Sri Lanka considerable support in their quest for Test-playing status, eventually granted six years later.

Sri Lanka and East Africa were emphatically beaten by Pakistan and England respectively in the final round of matches, while New Zealand beat India by four wickets with seven balls to spare thanks to another magnificent hundred by their captain, Glenn Turner. From the time the draw was made a year earlier, the most eagerly awaited contest was that between the favourites, West Indies and Australia. Although it produced some marvellously entertaining action, the encounter failed to provide a memorable finish, West Indies cantering home by seven wickets with 14 overs to spare. This was the first time I had scored an international match not involving England, a curious experience. The main recollection is of the diminutive and hatless Alvin Kallicharran hooking and cutting a succession of ferocious short-pitched deliveries from Lillee to the tune of 35 runs from ten balls: 4 4 4 4 1 4 6 0 4.

The final group placings eliminated India, Pakistan and the two associate member teams:

GROUP A	P	W	L	Pts	GROUP B	P	W	L	Pts
ENGLAND	3	3	0	12	WEST INDIES	3	3	0	12
NEW ZEALAND	3	2	1	8	AUSTRALIA	3	2	1	8
India	3	1	2	4	Pakistan	3	1	2	4
East Africa	3	0	3	0	Sri Lanka	3	0	3	0

A typical Headingley pitch produced a low-scoring semi-final and 65 overs of frenzied excitement. Put in by Ian Chappell in ideal bowling conditions, a heavy atmosphere allied to a damp, green pitch which had staged the Australia–Pakistan match eleven days previously, England were dismissed in the 37th over for 93, Gary Gilmour returning the tournament's first six-wicket analysis. Bowling left-arm fast-medium, he took full advantage of those conditions to swing the ball late and seam it either way. At one stage England were 37 for 7. Although Chris Old, John Snow and Geoff Arnold inflicted similar damage, reducing Australia to 39 for 6, Gilmour, at 24 the team's youngest member, completed an outstanding day by contributing 28, the game's highest innings, to an unbroken winning partnership of 55 with Doug Walters.

At The Oval, West Indies coasted to the final, defeating New Zealand by five wickets with almost 20 overs in hand. At lunch, New Zealand, 92 for 1 after 29 overs and with Glenn Turner and Geoff Howarth (on the ground of his adopted county) in prime form, were promisingly placed after being put in to bat. An astonishing slip catch by the 39-year-old Rohan Kanhai ended their 90-run stand in the first over after the interval and the remaining eight wickets could add only 60 runs. Gordon Greenidge and Alvin Kallicharran provided rich entertainment with their second-wicket stand of 125, New Zealand gaining some consolation from an aggressive display of left-arm fast bowling by Richard Collinge.

89

It was fortunate that the first World Cup final was played on the longest day of the year as this epic battle fully absorbed its vast audience, with millions viewing on television, from 11am until 8.42pm, the most protracted day's cricket at international level. Australia, having elected to bowl, made an early if freakish breakthrough when Roy Fredericks slipped while hooking a Lillee bouncer and kicked his wicket as the ball soared over the long-leg boundary. At 50 for 3 in the 19th over and with their semi-final heroes Greenidge and Kallicharran both out, West Indies were under pressure. Clive Lloyd swiftly swung the match with a breathtaking exhibition of hooking and effortless driving off the back foot. Tall, strong-wristed and armed with one of cricket's most weighty bats, its handle adorned with five rubber grips, he survived a chance at mid-wicket when he had made 26, reached fifty from 52 balls and completed his hundred just 30 balls later. His timing, and power of stroke prompted radio commentator John Arlott, for whom I was privileged to be scoring, to describe one pull as being played with 'the ease of a man knocking off a thistle-top with a walking stick' and to label a delivery which failed to produce a run as 'a maiden ball'.

Lloyd's partnership with his fellow Guyanan, Kanhai, added 149 in 26 overs, the latter playing a passive anchor role and remaining on 16 for ten overs. The West Indies captain batted 148 minutes during which he faced just 85 balls, hitting two sixes and a dozen fours. Although Richards failed (one of another five wickets for Gilmour), Keith Boyce and Bernard Julien added 50 from ten overs to take West Indies towards their highest total so far in limited-overs internationals.

Undaunted by their immense task, Australia maintained their challenge to the end and might well have achieved a remarkable win if half their wickets had not fallen to run outs, three by Richards, including direct hits from mid-wicket and cover. A defiant last-wicket partnership of 41 between Thomson and Lillee took Australia within range of their target before Thomson, sent back when attempting a bye to the keeper, was beaten by Murray's underarm lob.

Most of the crowd swarmed on to the field and the huge Caribbean element produced their own carnival of dances and song as, shortly before 9pm, HRH the Duke of Edinburgh presented the Prudential Cup to Clive Lloyd. Made in 1890, the elegant 18½ inch-high trophy was styled on the work of Paul de Lamerie (1688-1751), one of the most renowned silversmiths of all time.

That this tournament proved to be an outstanding success was a great relief to the organisers. The ICC had carefully avoided the title 'World Cup' and had designated the series as 'International Championship Cricket'. Unlike soccer's similar competition, this had involved only eight of the 21 member nations of the ICC. Indeed it had been referred to as the 'World without South Africa Cup'.

Overall takings (excluding the sponsor's fee of £100,000 which covered the cost of staging the matches plus fares and a month's subsistence for the teams) exceeded £200,000, the total attendance for the 15 games being 158,000. The Lord's final accounted for 26,000 and gross receipts of £66,950, then a record for a one-day match in Britain. The winners received £4,000, runners-up Australia gained £2,000 and the two losing semi-finalists, England and New Zealand won £1,000 each. As hosts, the Test and County Cricket Board received 10% of the profits, the other seven participants each receiving 7½%. The ICC distributed the balance to the non-participating associate member countries, the international coaching fund and to the reserve for promoting the next World Cup in 1979.

When the ICC membership congregated for its AGM in London soon after the final, suggestions were invited for the next tournament. Although India were keen to act as hosts, it was thought that England with its longer period of daylight in midsummer was the ideal venue for 60-over matches.

ENGLAND v INDIA

At Lord's, London, on 7 June 1975.   Toss: England.
Result: **ENGLAND** won by 202 runs.   Award: D.L.Amiss.
LOI debuts: India – M.Amarnath, A.D.Gaekwad, K.D.Ghavri.

ENGLAND		Runs	Balls	4/6
J.A.Jameson	c Venkataraghavan b Amarnath	21	42	2
D.L.Amiss	b Madan Lal	137	147	18
K.W.R.Fletcher	b Abid Ali	68	107	4/1
A.W.Greig	lbw b Abid Ali	4	8	–
*M.H.Denness	not out	37	31	2/1
C.M.Old	not out	51	30	4/2
B.Wood				
†A.P.E.Knott				
J.A.Snow				
P.Lever				
G.G.Arnold				
Extras	(LB12, W2, NB2)	16		
TOTAL	(60 overs; 4 wickets)	334		

INDIA		Runs	Balls	4/6
S.M.Gavaskar	not out	36	174	1
E.D.Solkar	c Lever b Arnold	8	34	–
A.D.Gaekwad	c Knott b Lever	22	46	2
G.R.Viswanath	c Fletcher b Old	37	59	5
B.P.Patel	not out	16	57	–
M.Amarnath				
†F.M.Engineer				
S.Abid Ali				
Madan Lal				
*S.Venkataraghavan				
K.D.Ghavri				
Extras	(LB3, W1, NB9)	13		
TOTAL	(60 overs; 3 wickets)	132		

INDIA	O	M	R	W		FALL OF WICKETS		
Madan Lal	12	1	64	1		Wkt	E	I
Amarnath	12	2	60	1		1st	54	21
Abid Ali	12	0	58	2		2nd	230	50
Ghavri	11	1	83	0		3rd	237	108
Venkataraghavan	12	0	41	0		4th	245	–
Solkar	1	0	12	0		5th	–	–
						6th	–	–
ENGLAND						7th	–	–
Snow	12	2	24	0		8th	–	–
Arnold	10	2	20	1		9th	–	–
Old	12	4	26	1		10th	–	–
Greig	9	1	26	0				
Wood	5	2	4	0				
Lever	10	0	16	1				
Jameson	2	1	3	0				

Umpires: D.J.Constant (4) and J.G.Langridge (1).

NEW ZEALAND v EAST AFRICA

At Edgbaston, Birmingham, on 7 June 1975.   Toss: New Zealand.
Result: **NEW ZEALAND** won by 181 runs.   Award: G.M.Turner.
LOI debuts: New Zealand – B.J.McKechnie; East Africa – all.

NEW ZEALAND		Runs	Balls	4/6
*G.M.Turner	not out	171		16/2
J.F.M.Morrison	c and b Nana	14		–
G.P.Howarth	b Mehmood	20		2
J.M.Parker	c Zulfiqar b Ramesh	66		7
B.F.Hastings	c Ramesh b Zulfiqar	8		1
†K.J.Wadsworth	b Nagenda	10		–/1
R.J.Hadlee	not out	6		
B.J.McKechnie				
D.R.Hadlee				
H.J.Howarth				
R.O.Collinge				
Extras	(B1, LB8, W5)	14		
TOTAL	(60 overs; 5 wickets)	309		

EAST AFRICA		Runs	Balls	4/6
Frasat Ali	st Wadsworth b H.J.Howarth	45		1/1
S.Walusimba	b D.R.Hadlee	15		1
Ramesh Sethi	run out	1		–
Shiraz Sumar	b D.R.Hadlee	4		–
Jawahir Shah	c and b H.J.Howarth	5		–
*Harilal Shah	lbw b H.J.Howarth	0		–
Mehmood Quaraishy	not out	16		–
Zulfiqar Ali	b D.R.Hadlee	30		4
†H.McLeod	b Collinge	5		–
P.G.Nana	not out	1		–
J.Nagenda				
Extras	(LB5, NB1)	6		
TOTAL	(60 overs; 8 wickets)	128		

EAST AFRICA	O	M	R	W		FALL OF WICKETS		
					Wkt	NZ	EA	
Nagenda	9	1	50	1	1st	51	30	
Frasat Ali	9	0	50	0	2nd	103	32	
Nana	12	2	34	1	3rd	252	36	
Ramesh Sethi	10	1	51	1	4th	278	59	
Zulfiqar Ali	12	0	71	1	5th	292	59	
Mehmood Quaraishy	8	0	39	1	6th	–	84	
					7th	–	121	
NEW ZEALAND					8th	–	126	
Collinge	12	5	23	1	9th	–	–	
R.J.Hadlee	12	6	10	0	10th	–	–	
McKechnie	12	2	39	0				
D.R.Hadlee	12	1	21	3				
H.J.Howarth	12	3	29	3				

Umpires: H.D.Bird (4) and A.E.Fagg (3).

AUSTRALIA v PAKISTAN

At Headingley, Leeds, on 7 June 1975.   Toss: Australia.
Result: **AUSTRALIA** won by 73 runs.   Award: D.K.Lillee.
LOI debuts: Australia – R.B.McCosker, A.Turner; Pakistan – Naseer Malik.

AUSTRALIA		**Runs**	**Balls**	**4/6**
A.Turner	c Mushtaq b Asif Iqbal	46	54	4
R.B.McCosker	c Wasim Bari b Naseer	25	76	2
*I.M.Chappell	c Wasim Raja b Sarfraz	28	30	5
G.S.Chappell	c Asif Iqbal b Imran	45	56	5
K.D.Walters	c Sarfraz b Naseer	2	13	–
R.Edwards	not out	80	94	6
†R.W.Marsh	c Wasim Bari b Imran	1	5	–
M.H.N.Walker	b Asif Masood	18	28	2
J.R.Thomson	not out	20	14	2/1
A.A.Mallett				
D.K.Lillee				
Extras	(LB7, NB6)	13		
TOTAL	(60 overs; 7 wickets)	278		

PAKISTAN		**Runs**	**Balls**	**4/6**
Sadiq Mohammad	b Lillee	4	12	–
Majid Khan	c Marsh b Mallett	65	76	11
Zaheer Abbas	c Turner b Thomson	8	10	2
Mushtaq Mohammad	c G.S.Chappell b Walters	8	32	–
*Asif Iqbal	b Lillee	53	95	8
Wasim Raja	c Thomson b Walker	31	57	4
Imran Khan	c Turner b Walker	9	19	1
Sarfraz Nawaz	c Marsh b Lillee	0	2	–
†Wasim Bari	c Marsh b Lillee	2	18	–
Asif Masood	c Walker b Lillee	6	7	1
Naseer Malik	not out	0	13	–
Extras	(LB4, W3, NB12)	19		
TOTAL	(53 overs)	205		

PAKISTAN	O	M	R	W		**FALL OF WICKETS**	
Naseer Malik	12	2	37	2	Wkt	A	P
Asif Masood	12	0	50	1	1st	63	15
Sarfraz Nawaz	12	0	63	1	2nd	99	27
Asif Iqbal	12	0	58	1	3rd	110	68
Imran Khan	10	0	44	2	4th	124	104
Wasim Raja	2	0	13	0	5th	184	181
					6th	195	189
AUSTRALIA					7th	243	189
Lillee	12	2	34	5	8th	–	195
Thomson	8	2	25	1	9th	–	203
Walker	12	3	32	2	10th	–	205
Mallett	12	1	49	1			
Walters	6	0	29	1			
G.S.Chappell	3	0	17	0			

Umpires: W.E.Alley (2) and T.W.Spencer (3).

WEST INDIES v SRI LANKA

At Old Trafford, Manchester, on 7 June 1975.   Toss: West Indies.
Result: **WEST INDIES** won by 9 wickets.   Award: B.D.Julien.
LOI debuts: West Indies – I.V.A.Richards, A.M.E.Roberts; Sri Lanka – all.

SRI LANKA		Runs	Balls	4/6
†E.R.Fernando	c Murray b Julien	4		–
B.Warnapura	c Murray b Boyce	8		2
*A.P.B.Tennekoon	c Murray b Julien	0		–
P.D.Heyn	c Lloyd b Roberts	2		–
M.H.Tissera	c Kallicharran b Julien	14		1
L.R.D.Mendis	c Murray b Boyce	8		1
A.N.Ranasinghe	b Boyce	0		–
H.S.M.Pieris	c Lloyd b Julien	3		–
A.R.M.Opatha	b Roberts	11		1
D.S.de Silva	c Lloyd b Holder	21		2
L.W.S.Kaluperuma	not out	6		–
Extras	(B3, LB3, NB3)	9		
TOTAL	(37.2 overs)	86		

WEST INDIES		Runs	Balls	4/6
R.C.Fredericks	c Warnapura b De Silva	33		4
†D.L.Murray	not out	30		2/1
A.I.Kallicharran	not out	19		–
R.B.Kanhai				
*C.H.Lloyd				
I.V.A.Richards				
B.D.Julien				
K.D.Boyce				
V.A.Holder				
A.M.E.Roberts				
L.R.Gibbs				
Extras	(B2, LB1, W1, NB1)	5		
TOTAL	(20.4 overs; 1 wicket)	87		

WEST INDIES	O	M	R	W		FALL OF WICKETS	
					Wkt	SL	WI
Roberts	12	5	16	2	1st	5	52
Boyce	8	1	22	3	2nd	5	–
Julien	12	3	20	4	3rd	16	–
Gibbs	4	0	17	0	4th	21	–
Holder	1.2	0	2	1	5th	41	–
					6th	41	–
SRI LANKA					7th	42	–
Opatha	4	0	19	0	8th	48	–
De Silva	8	1	33	1	9th	58	–
Pieris	2	0	13	0	10th	86	–
Kaluperuma	6.4	1	17	0			

Umpires: W.L.Budd (2) and A.Jepson (2).

ENGLAND v NEW ZEALAND

At Trent Bridge, Nottingham, on 11 June 1975.   Toss: New Zealand.
Result: **ENGLAND** won by 80 runs.   Award: K.W.R.Fletcher.
LOI debuts: None.

ENGLAND		Runs	Balls	4/6
J.A.Jameson	c Wadsworth b Collinge	11	31	–
D.L.Amiss	b Collinge	16	18	3
K.W.R.Fletcher	run out	131	147	13
F.C.Hayes	lbw b R.J.Hadlee	34	80	5
*M.H.Denness	c Morrison b D.R.Hadlee	37	52	1/1
A.W.Greig	b D.R.Hadlee	9	19	–
C.M.Old	not out	20	16	–/1
†A.P.E.Knott				
D.L.Underwood				
G.G.Arnold				
P.Lever				
Extras	(LB6, W1, NB1)	8		
TOTAL	(60 overs; 6 wickets)	266		

NEW ZEALAND		Runs	Balls	4/6
J.F.M.Morrison	c Old b Underwood	55	85	6/1
*G.M.Turner	b Lever	12	34	1
B.G.Hadlee	b Greig	19	77	1
J.M.Parker	b Greig	1	8	–
B.F.Hastings	c Underwood b Old	10	26	1
†K.J.Wadsworth	b Arnold	25	24	3
R.J.Hadlee	b Old	0	6	–
B.J.McKechnie	c Underwood b Greig	27	50	4
D.R.Hadlee	c Arnold b Greig	20	42	2
H.J.Howarth	not out	1	7	–
R.O.Collinge	b Underwood	6	6	–/1
Extras	(B1, LB4, W1, NB4)	10		
TOTAL	(60 overs)	186		

NEW ZEALAND	O	M	R	W
Collinge	12	2	43	2
R.J.Hadlee	12	2	66	1
D.R.Hadlee	12	1	55	2
McKechnie	12	2	38	0
Howarth	12	2	56	0
ENGLAND				
Arnold	12	3	35	1
Lever	12	0	37	1
Old	12	2	29	2
Greig	12	0	45	4
Underwood	12	2	30	2

FALL OF WICKETS		
Wkt	E	NZ
1st	27	30
2nd	28	83
3rd	111	91
4th	177	95
5th	200	129
6th	266	129
7th	–	129
8th	–	177
9th	–	180
10th	–	186

Umpires: W.E.Alley (3) and T.W.Spencer (4).

INDIA v EAST AFRICA

At Headingley, Leeds, on 11 June 1975.   Toss: East Africa.
Result: **INDIA** won by 10 wickets.   Award: F.M.Engineer.
LOI debuts: East Africa – Praful Mehta, D.Pringle, Yunus Badat.

EAST AFRICA		Runs	Balls	4/6
Frasat Ali	b Abid Ali	12		1
S.Walusimba	lbw b Abid Ali	16		1
†Praful Mehta	run out	12		–
Yunus Badat	b Bedi	1		–
Jawahir Shah	b Amarnath	37		5
*Harilal Shah	c Engineer b Amarnath	0		–
Ramesh Sethi	c Gaekwad b Madan Lal	23		2
Mehmood Quaraishy	run out	6		–
Zulfiqar Ali	not out	2		–
P.G.Nana	lbw b Madan Lal	0		–
D.Pringle	b Madan Lal	2		–
Extras	(LB8, NB1)	9		
TOTAL	(55.3 overs)	120		

INDIA		Runs	Balls	4/6
S.M.Gavaskar	not out	65		9
†F.M.Engineer	not out	54		7
A.D.Gaekwad				
G.R.Viswanath				
B.P.Patel				
E.D.Solkar				
S.Abid Ali				
Madan Lal				
M.Amarnath				
*S.Venkataraghavan				
B.S.Bedi				
Extras	(B4)	4		
TOTAL	(29.5 overs; 0 wickets)	123		

INDIA	O	M	R	W	FALL OF WICKETS		
Abid Ali	12	5	22	2	Wkt	EA	I
Madan Lal	9.3	2	15	3	1st	26	–
Bedi	12	8	6	1	2nd	36	–
Venkataraghavan	12	4	29	0	3rd	37	–
Amarnath	10	0	39	2	4th	56	–
					5th	56	–
EAST AFRICA					6th	98	–
Frasat Ali	6	1	17	0	7th	116	–
Pringle	3	0	14	0	8th	116	–
Zulfiqar Ali	11	3	32	0	9th	116	–
Nana	4.5	0	36	0	10th	120	–
Ramesh Sethi	5	0	20	0			

Umpires: H.D.Bird (5) and A.Jepson (3).

AUSTRALIA v SRI LANKA

At Kennington Oval, London, on 11 June 1975.   Toss: Sri Lanka.
Result: **AUSTRALIA** won by 52 runs.   Award: A.Turner.
LOI debuts: Sri Lanka – S.R.de S.Wettimuny.

AUSTRALIA		Runs	Balls	4/6
R.B.McCosker	b De Silva	73	111	2
A.Turner	c Mendis b De Silva	101	113	9/1
*I.M.Chappell	b Kaluperuma	4	7	1
G.S.Chappell	c Opatha b Pieris	50	50	5/1
K.D.Walters	c Tennekoon b Pieris	59	66	5
J.R.Thomson	not out	9	7	–
†R.W.Marsh	not out	9	7	–
R.Edwards				
M.H.N.Walker				
D.K.Lillee				
A.A.Mallett				
Extras	(B1, LB20, W1, NB1)	23		
TOTAL	(60 overs; 5 wickets)	328		

SRI LANKA		Runs	Balls	4/6
S.R.de S.Wettimuny	retired hurt	53	102	7
†E.R.Fernando	b Thomson	22	18	4
B.Warnapura	st Marsh b Mallett	31	39	5
L.R.D.Mendis	retired hurt	32	45	5
*A.P.B.Tennekoon	b I.M.Chappell	48	71	6
M.H.Tissera	c Turner b I.M.Chappell	52	72	7
A.N.Ranasinghe	not out	14	18	3
H.S.M.Pieris	not out	0	3	–
A.R.M.Opatha				
D.S.de Silva				
L.W.S.Kaluperuma				
Extras	(B6, LB8, W8, NB2)	24		
TOTAL	(60 overs; 4 wickets)	276		

SRI LANKA	O	M	R	W		FALL OF WICKETS	
Opatha	9	0	32	0	Wkt	A	SL
Pieris	11	0	68	2	1st	182	30
Warnapura	9	0	40	0	2nd	187	84
Ranasinghe	7	0	55	0	3rd	191	246
De Silva	12	3	60	2	4th	308	268
Kaluperuma	12	0	50	1	5th	308	–
					6th	–	–
AUSTRALIA					7th	–	–
Lillee	10	0	42	0	8th	–	–
Thomson	12	5	22	1	9th	–	–
Mallett	12	0	72	1	10th	–	–
Walters	6	1	33	0			
Walker	12	1	44	0			
G.S.Chappell	4	0	25	0			
I.M.Chappell	4	0	14	2			

Umpires: W.L.Budd (3) and A.E.Fagg (4).

WEST INDIES v PAKISTAN

At Edgbaston, Birmingham, on 11 June 1975.　Toss: Pakistan.
Result: **WEST INDIES** won by 1 wicket.　Award: Sarfraz Nawaz.
LOI debuts: Pakistan – Javed Miandad, Parvez Mir; West Indies – C.G.Greenidge.

PAKISTAN		Runs	Balls	4/6
*Majid Khan	c Murray b Lloyd	60		6
Sadiq Mohammad	c Kanhai b Julien	7		1
Zaheer Abbas	lbw b Richards	31		4
Mushtaq Mohammad	b Boyce	55		3
Wasim Raja	b Roberts	58		6
Javed Miandad	run out	24		2
Parvez Mir	run out	4		–
†Wasim Bari	not out	1		–
Sarfraz Nawaz	not out	0		–
Asif Masood				
Naseer Malik				
Extras	(B1, LB15, W4, NB6)	26		
TOTAL	(60 overs; 7 wickets)	266		

WEST INDIES		Runs	Balls	4/6
R.C.Fredericks	lbw b Sarfraz	12		2
C.G.Greenidge	c Wasim Bari b Sarfraz	4		1
A.I.Kallicharran	c Wasim Bari b Sarfraz	16		1
R.B.Kanhai	b Naseer	24		3
*C.H.Lloyd	c Wasim Bari b Miandad	53		8
I.V.A.Richards	c Zaheer b Parvez	13		2
B.D.Julien	c Miandad b Asif	18		2
†D.L.Murray	not out	61		6
K.D.Boyce	b Naseer	7		–
V.A.Holder	c Parvez b Sarfraz	16		1
A.M.E.Roberts	not out	24		3
Extras	(LB10, W1, NB8)	19		
TOTAL	(59.4 overs; 9 wickets)	267		

WEST INDIES	O	M	R	W		FALL OF WICKETS	
Roberts	12	1	47	1	Wkt	P	WI
Boyce	12	2	44	1	1st	21	6
Julien	12	1	41	1	2nd	83	31
Holder	12	3	56	0	3rd	140	36
Richards	4	0	21	1	4th	202	84
Lloyd	8	1	31	1	5th	249	99
					6th	263	145
PAKISTAN					7th	265	151
Asif Masood	12	1	64	1	8th	–	166
Sarfraz Nawaz	12	1	44	4	9th	–	203
Naseer Malik	12	2	42	2	10th	–	–
Parvez Mir	9	1	42	1			
Javed Miandad	12	0	46	1			
Mushtaq Mohammad	2	0	7	0			
Wasim Raja	0.4	0	3	0			

Umpires: D.J.Constant (5) and J.G.Langridge (2).

ENGLAND v EAST AFRICA

At Edgbaston, Birmingham, on 14 June 1975.　Toss: East Africa.
Result: **ENGLAND** won by 196 runs.　Award: J.A.Snow.
LOI debuts: None.

ENGLAND		Runs	Balls	4/6
B.Wood	b Mehmood	77		6
D.L.Amiss	c Nana b Zulfiqar	88		7
F.C.Hayes	b Zulfiqar	52		3/2
A.W.Greig	lbw b Zulfiqar	9		
†A.P.E.Knott	not out	18		
C.M.Old	b Mehmood	18		3
*M.H.Denness	not out	12		1
K.W.R.Fletcher				
J.A.Snow				
P.Lever				
D.L.Underwood				
Extras	(B7, LB7, W1, NB1)	16		
TOTAL	(60 overs; 5 wickets)	290		

EAST AFRICA		Runs	Balls	4/6
Frasat Ali	b Snow	0		–
S.Walusimba	lbw b Snow	7		–
Yunus Badat	b Snow	0		–
Jawahir Shah	lbw b Snow	4		–
Ramesh Sethi	b Lever	30		3
*Harilal Shah	b Greig	6		–
Mehmood Quaraishy	c Amiss b Greig	19		2
Zulfiqar Ali	b Lever	7		–
†H.McLeod	b Lever	0		–
P.G.Nana	not out	8		–
D.Pringle	b Old	3		–
Extras	(LB6, W1, NB3)	10		
TOTAL	(52.3 overs)	94		

EAST AFRICA	O	M	R	W	FALL OF WICKETS		
Frasat Ali	9	0	40	0	Wkt	E	EA
Pringle	12	0	41	0	1st	158	7
Nana	12	2	46	0	2nd	192	7
Ramesh Sethi	5	0	29	0	3rd	234	15
Zulfiqar Ali	12	0	63	3	4th	244	21
Mehmood Quaraishy	10	0	55	2	5th	277	42
					6th	–	72
ENGLAND					7th	–	76
Snow	12	6	11	4	8th	–	79
Lever	12	3	32	3	9th	–	88
Underwood	10	5	11	0	10th	–	94
Wood	7	3	10	0			
Greig	10	1	18	2			
Old	1.3	0	2	1			

Umpires: W.E.Alley (4) and J.G.Langridge (3).

NEW ZEALAND v INDIA

At Old Trafford, Manchester, on 14 June 1975.   Toss: India.
Result: **NEW ZEALAND** won by 4 wickets.   Award: G.M.Turner.
LOI debuts: None.

INDIA		Runs	Balls	4/6
S.M.Gavaskar	c R.J.Hadlee b D.R.Hadlee	12		2
†F.M.Engineer	lbw b R.J.Hadlee	24		3
A.D.Gaekwad	c Hastings b R.J.Hadlee	37		3
G.R.Viswanath	lbw b McKechnie	2		–
B.P.Patel	c Wadsworth b H.J.Howarth	9		1
E.D.Solkar	c Wadsworth b H.J.Howarth	13		2
S.Abid Ali	c H.J.Howarth b McKechnie	70		5/1
Madan Lal	c and b McKechnie	20		4
M.Amarnath	c Morrison b D.R.Hadlee	1		–
*S.Venkataraghavan	not out	26		3
B.S.Bedi	run out	6		–
Extras	(B5, W1, NB4)	10		
TOTAL	(60 overs)	230		

NEW ZEALAND		Runs	Balls	4/6
*G.M.Turner	not out	114		13
J.F.M.Morrison	c Engineer b Bedi	17		2
G.P.Howarth	run out	9		–
J.M.Parker	lbw b Abid Ali	1		–
B.F.Hastings	c Solkar b Amarnath	34		3
†K.J.Wadsworth	lbw b Madan Lal	22		3
R.J.Hadlee	b Abid Ali	15		2
D.R.Hadlee	not out	8		2
B.J.McKechnie				
H.J.Howarth				
R.O.Collinge				
Extras	(B8, LB5)	13		
TOTAL	(58.5 overs; 6 wickets)	233		

NEW ZEALAND	O	M	R	W		FALL OF WICKETS	
Collinge	12	2	43	0	Wkt	I	NZ
R.J.Hadlee	12	2	48	2	1st	17	45
D.R.Hadlee	12	3	32	2	2nd	48	62
McKechnie	12	1	49	3	3rd	59	70
H.J.Howarth	12	0	48	2	4th	81	135
					5th	94	185
INDIA					6th	101	224
Madan Lal	11.5	1	62	1	7th	156	–
Amarnath	8	1	40	1	8th	157	–
Bedi	12	6	28	1	9th	217	–
Abid Ali	12	2	35	2	10th	230	–
Venkataraghavan	12	0	39	0			
Solkar	3	0	16	0			

Umpires: W.L.Budd (4) and A.E.Fagg (5).

AUSTRALIA v WEST INDIES

At Kennington Oval, London, on 14 June 1975.   Toss: West Indies.
Result: **WEST INDIES** won by 7 wickets.   Award: A.I.Kallicharran.
LOI debuts: None.

AUSTRALIA		Runs	Balls	4/6
R.B.McCosker	c Fredericks b Julien	0	3	–
A.Turner	lbw b Roberts	7	18	–
*I.M.Chappell	c Murray b Boyce	25	63	–
G.S.Chappell	c Murray b Boyce	15	33	–
K.D.Walters	run out	7	18	–
R.Edwards	b Richards	58	74	6
†R.W.Marsh	not out	52	84	4
M.H.N.Walker	lbw b Holder	8	22	1
J.R.Thomson	c Holder b Richards	1	3	–
D.K.Lillee	b Roberts	3	12	–
A.A.Mallett	c Murray b Roberts	0	1	–
Extras	(LB9, W1, NB6)	16		
TOTAL	(53.4 overs)	192		

WEST INDIES		Runs	Balls	4/6
R.C.Fredericks	c Marsh b Mallett	58	105	5
C.G.Greenidge	lbw b Walker	16	18	2
A.I.Kallicharran	c Mallett b Lillee	78	83	14/1
I.V.A.Richards	not out	15	38	2
R.B.Kanhai	not out	18	33	1
*C.H.Lloyd				
B.D.Julien				
†D.L.Murray				
K.D.Boyce				
V.A.Holder				
A.M.E.Roberts				
Extras	(B4, LB2, W3, NB1)	10		
TOTAL	(46 overs; 3 wickets)	195		

WEST INDIES	O	M	R	W		FALL OF WICKETS		
Julien	12	2	31	1	Wkt	A	WI	
Roberts	10.4	1	39	3	1st	0	29	
Boyce	11	0	38	2	2nd	21	153	
Holder	10	0	31	1	3rd	49	159	
Lloyd	4	1	19	0	4th	56	–	
Richards	6	0	18	2	5th	61	–	
					6th	160	–	
AUSTRALIA					7th	173	–	
Lillee	10	0	66	1	8th	174	–	
Thomson	6	1	21	0	9th	192	–	
Walker	12	2	41	1	10th	192	–	
G.S.Chappell	4	0	13	0				
Mallett	11	2	35	1				
I.M.Chappell	3	1	9	0				

Umpires: H.D.Bird (6) and D.J.Constant (6).

PAKISTAN v SRI LANKA

At Trent Bridge, Nottingham, on 14 June 1975.   Toss: Sri Lanka.
Result: **PAKISTAN** won by 192 runs.   Award: Zaheer Abbas.
LOI debuts: Sri Lanka – G.R.A.de Silva.

PAKISTAN		Runs	Balls	4/6
Sadiq Mohammad	c Opatha b Warnapura	74		12/1
*Majid Khan	c Tennekoon b D.S.de Silva	84		9/1
Zaheer Abbas	b Opatha	97		10/1
Mushtaq Mohammad	c Heyn b Warnapura	26		2
Wasim Raja	c Opatha b Warnapura	2		–
Javed Miandad	not out	28		1
Imran Khan	b Opatha	0		–
Parvez Mir	not out	4		–
†Wasim Bari				
Asif Masood				
Naseer Malik				
Extras	(B4, LB4, W2, NB5)	15		
TOTAL	(60 overs; 6 wickets)	330		

SRI LANKA		Runs	Balls	4/6
†E.R.Fernando	c and b Miandad	21		3
B.Warnapura	b Imran	2		–
*A.P.B.Tennekoon	lbw b Naseer	30		4
M.H.Tissera	c Wasim Bari b Sadiq	12		2
P.D.Heyn	c Zaheer b Miandad	1		–
A.N.Ranasinghe	b Wasim Raja	9		–
H.S.M.Pieris	lbw b Parvez	16		2
A.R.M.Opatha	c Zaheer b Sadiq	0		–
D.S.de Silva	b Imran	26		4
L.W.S.Kaluperuma	not out	13		1
G.R.A.de Silva	c Wasim Raja b Imran	0		–
Extras	(LB1, W3, NB4)	8		
TOTAL	(50.1 overs)	138		

SRI LANKA	O	M	R	W		FALL OF WICKETS		
					Wkt	P	SL	
Opatha	12	0	67	2	1st	159	5	
Pieris	9	0	54	0	2nd	168	44	
G.R.A.de Silva	7	1	46	0	3rd	256	60	
D.S.de Silva	12	1	61	1	4th	268	61	
Kaluperuma	9	1	35	0	5th	318	75	
Warnapura	8	0	42	3	6th	318	79	
Ranasinghe	3	0	10	0	7th	–	90	
PAKISTAN					8th	–	113	
Asif Masood	6	2	14	0	9th	–	135	
Imran Khan	7.1	3	15	3	10th	–	138	
Javed Miandad	7	2	22	2				
Naseer Malik	6	1	19	1				
Sadiq Mohammad	6	1	20	2				
Wasim Raja	7	4	7	1				
Mushtaq Mohammad	5	0	16	0				
Parvez Mir	6	1	17	1				

Umpires: A.Jepson (4) and T.W.Spencer (5).

ENGLAND v AUSTRALIA (SEMI-FINAL)

At Headingley, Leeds, on 18 June 1975.   Toss: Australia.
Result: **AUSTRALIA** won by 4 wickets.   Award: G.J.Gilmour.
LOI debuts: None.

ENGLAND		Runs	Balls	4/6
D.L.Amiss	lbw b Gilmour	2	7	–
B.Wood	b Gilmour	6	19	1
K.W.R.Fletcher	lbw b Gilmour	8	45	–
A.W.Greig	c Marsh b Gilmour	7	25	1
F.C.Hayes	lbw b Gilmour	4	6	1
*M.H.Denness	b Walker	27	60	1
†A.P.E.Knott	lbw b Gilmour	0	5	–
C.M.Old	c G.S.Chappell b Walker	0	3	–
J.A.Snow	c Marsh b Lillee	2	14	–
G.G.Arnold	not out	18	30	2
P.Lever	lbw b Walker	5	13	–
Extras	(LB5, W7, NB2)	14		
TOTAL	(36.2 overs)	93		

AUSTRALIA		Runs	Balls	4/6
A.Turner	lbw b Arnold	7	20	–
R.B.McCosker	b Old	15	50	–
*I.M.Chappell	lbw b Snow	2	19	–
G.S.Chappell	lbw b Snow	4	9	1
K.D.Walters	not out	20	43	2
R.Edwards	b Old	0	3	–
†R.W.Marsh	b Old	5	8	–
G.J.Gilmour	not out	28	28	5
M.H.N.Walker				
D.K.Lillee				
J.R.Thomson				
Extras	(B1, LB6, NB6)	13		
TOTAL	(28.4 overs; 6 wickets)	94		

AUSTRALIA	O	M	R	W		FALL OF WICKETS		
Lillee	9	3	26	1	Wkt	E	A	
Gilmour	12	6	14	6	1st	2	17	
Walker	9.2	3	22	3	2nd	11	24	
Thomson	6	0	17	0	3rd	26	32	
					4th	33	32	
ENGLAND					5th	35	32	
Arnold	7.4	2	15	1	6th	36	39	
Snow	12	0	30	2	7th	37	–	
Old	7	2	29	3	8th	52	–	
Lever	2	0	7	0	9th	73	–	
					10th	93	–	

Umpires: W.E.Alley (5) and D.J.Constant (7).

WEST INDIES v NEW ZEALAND (SEMI-FINAL)

At Kennington Oval, London, on 18 June 1975. Toss: West Indies.
Result: **WEST INDIES** won by 5 wickets. Award: A.I.Kallicharran.
LOI debuts: None.

NEW ZEALAND		Runs	Balls	4/6
*G.M.Turner	c Kanhai b Roberts	36	74	3
J.F.M.Morrison	lbw b Julien	5	26	–
G.P.Howarth	c Murray b Roberts	51	93	3
J.M.Parker	b Lloyd	3	12	–
B.F.Hastings	not out	24	57	4
†K.J.Wadsworth	c Lloyd b Julien	11	21	1
B.J.McKechnie	lbw b Julien	1	9	–
D.R.Hadlee	c Holder b Julien	0	10	–
B.L.Cairns	b Holder	10	14	1
H.J.Howarth	b Holder	0	1	–
R.O.Collinge	b Holder	2	4	–
Extras	(B1, LB5, W2, NB7)	15		
TOTAL	(52.2 overs)	**158**		

WEST INDIES		Runs	Balls	4/6
R.C.Fredericks	c Hastings b Hadlee	6	14	–
C.G.Greenidge	lbw b Collinge	55	95	9/1
A.I.Kallicharran	c and b Collinge	72	92	7/1
I.V.A.Richards	lbw b Collinge	5	10	1
R.B.Kanhai	not out	12	18	2
*C.H.Lloyd	c Hastings b McKechnie	3	8	–
B.D.Julien	not out	4	5	1
†D.L.Murray				
K.D.Boyce				
V.A.Holder				
A.M.E.Roberts				
Extras	(LB1, NB1)	2		
TOTAL	(40.1 overs; 5 wickets)	**159**		

WEST INDIES	O	M	R	W		FALL OF WICKETS	
					Wkt	NZ	WI
Julien	12	5	27	4	1st	8	8
Roberts	11	3	18	2	2nd	98	133
Holder	8.2	0	30	3	3rd	105	139
Boyce	9	0	31	0	4th	106	142
Lloyd	12	1	37	1	5th	125	151
					6th	133	–
NEW ZEALAND					7th	139	–
Collinge	12	4	28	3	8th	155	–
Hadlee	10	0	54	1	9th	155	–
Cairns	6.1	2	23	0	10th	158	–
McKechnie	8	0	37	1			
H.J.Howarth	4	0	15	0			

Umpires: W.L.Budd (5) and A.E.Fagg (6).

AUSTRALIA v WEST INDIES (FINAL)

At Lord's, London, on 21 June 1975.   Toss: Australia.
Result: **WEST INDIES** won by 17 runs.   Award: C.H.Lloyd.
LOI debuts: None.

WEST INDIES		Runs	Balls	4/6
R.C.Fredericks	hit wicket b Lillee	7	13	–
C.G.Greenidge	c Marsh b Thomson	13	61	1
A.I.Kallicharran	c Marsh b Gilmour	12	18	2
R.B.Kanhai	b Gilmour	55	105	8
*C.H.Lloyd	c Marsh b Gilmour	102	85	12/2
I.V.A.Richards	b Gilmour	5	11	1
K.D.Boyce	c G.S.Chappell b Thomson	34	37	3
B.D.Julien	not out	26	37	1
†D.L.Murray	c and b Gilmour	14	10	1/1
V.A.Holder	not out	6	2	1
A.M.E.Roberts				
Extras	(LB6, NB11)	17		
TOTAL	(60 overs; 8 wickets)	291		

AUSTRALIA		Runs	Balls	4/6
A.Turner	run out	40	24	1
R.B.McCosker	c Kallicharran b Boyce	7	54	4
*I.M.Chappell	run out	62	93	6
G.S.Chappell	run out	15	23	2
K.D.Walters	b Lloyd	35	51	5
†R.W.Marsh	b Boyce	11	24	–
R.Edwards	c Fredericks b Boyce	28	37	2
G.J.Gilmour	c Kanhai b Boyce	14	11	2
M.H.N.Walker	run out	7	9	1
J.R.Thomson	run out	21	21	2
D.K.Lillee	not out	16	19	1
Extras	(B2, LB9, NB7)	18		
TOTAL	(58.4 overs)	274		

AUSTRALIA	O	M	R	W	FALL OF WICKETS		
					Wkt	WI	A
Lillee	12	1	55	1	1st	12	25
Gilmour	12	2	48	5	2nd	27	81
Thomson	12	1	44	2	3rd	50	115
Walker	12	1	71	0	4th	199	162
G.S.Chappell	7	0	33	0	5th	206	170
Walters	5	0	23	0	6th	209	195
					7th	261	221
WEST INDIES					8th	285	231
Julien	12	0	58	0	9th	–	233
Roberts	11	1	45	0	10th	–	274
Boyce	12	0	50	4			
Holder	11.4	0	65	0			
Lloyd	12	1	38	1			

Umpires: H.D.Bird (7) and T.W.Spencer (6).

THE 1979 WORLD CUP

Without being graced with the exemplary weather of the initial venture, the second World Cup series proved another outstanding success. Once again West Indies, the favourites, won the Prudential Cup but against different finalists.

The tournament was run on similar lines to its predecessor with eight teams playing 15 matches spread over as many days and according to 60-over Gillette Cup rules. Again only Test match grounds were used but with a different distribution: Headingley, Old Trafford and Trent Bridge each hosting three games, while Edgbaston, Lord's and The Oval staged two apiece.

This time a special mini-tournament of 60-over matches for the ICC Trophy was held on Midlands club grounds to determine which two associate members would qualify to join the six Test-playing countries in the Prudential World Cup. Fifteen associates (all except West Africa and Hong Kong) entered this qualifying tournament and were divided into three groups. When Gibraltar withdrew they were replaced by Wales, who, not being an associate ICC member were ineligible for the competition. They did not compete for a place in the semi-finals but points scored against them counted. The three group winners plus the best of the runners-up qualified for the semi-finals. Denmark (16), Bermuda (14) and Canada (12) were joined by Sri Lanka (10), the latter being equal on points with East Africa and USA but having a superior run-rate.

Apart from the final, which was staged two days prior to the World Cup final itself, all the matches were played during the fortnight immediately preceding the major tournament. Unfortunately those two weeks attracted an abnormal amount of rain and six matches were abandoned. The competition did not escape political interference, Israel gaining four points when the Sri Lanka team 'withdrew from the game'.

The two victorious semi-finalists were Sri Lanka (predictably) who thrashed Denmark by 208 runs and Canada who beat Bermuda by four wickets with seven balls to spare. The final, at the Worcester County Ground, produced an exhilarating match in which 588 runs were scored, Sri Lanka (324-8) triumphing over Canada (264-5) by 60 runs to become the ICC Trophy's first holders.

As in 1975, the eight teams contesting the Prudential Cup were divided into two groups of four, each playing the others once, but this time England and Australia were not seeded. The draw, made at the ICC meeting at Lord's in July 1978, put Australia, England and Pakistan in Group A, while West Indies, India and New Zealand were in Group B. The leading two teams in each group qualified for the semi-finals.

The final group placings again eliminated India and the two associate members, but this time they were joined by an Australian team still bereft of its Packer players. Sri Lanka provided the group stage's major highlight when they gained their first World Cup victory, defeating India by 47 runs at Old Trafford.

GROUP A	P	W	L	Pts	GROUP B	P	W	L	NR	Pts
ENGLAND	3	3	0	12	WEST INDIES	3	2	0	1	10
PAKISTAN	3	2	1	8	NEW ZEALAND	3	2	1	0	8
Australia	3	1	2	4	Sri Lanka	3	1	1	1	6
Canada	3	0	3	0	India	3	0	3	0	0

Graced by brilliant weather, the semi-finals produced two vintage matches. At Old Trafford England scraped home against New Zealand by just 9 runs, at that time the narrowest margin of victory in a World Cup match. The holders' clash with Pakistan at The Oval provided a run feast, 543 runs coming from 116.2 overs.

Despite a magnificent second-wicket partnership of 166 between Majid Khan (81) and Zaheer Abbas (93), Pakistan failed by 43 runs to match the record West Indies World Cup total of 293.

The final was blessed with fine weather and an all-ticket capacity crowd of 25,000. They saw Clive Lloyd's team retain the World Cup with an emphatic 92-run victory after Viv Richards and Collis King rescued them from a tottering start. Richards contributed 136 not out but it was King's innings which stays in the memory, his 86 coming off just 66 balls and including 3 sixes and 10 fours. England had opted to go into the match with only four specialist bowlers, the remaining 12 overs being shared by Geoff Boycott, Graham Gooch and Wayne Larkins and producing 86 runs. Although Mike Brearley and Boycott scored 129 for the first wicket, they fell a long way behind the asking rate, the Yorkshireman taking 17 overs to reach double figures. Brearley's dismissal left England wanting 158 from the last 22 overs and the giant Joel Garner, with five wickets for 4 runs from 11 balls made sure that they were disappointed.

Although the total attendance for the competition was down by 28,000 (132,000 compared with 160,000 in 1975), the fall was caused by the poor weather. Increased prices meant that gate receipts amounted to £359,700, almost double the £188,000 for the first Prudential Cup. Profits amounted to £350,000.

At their annual meeting following this tournament, the ICC agreed to make the competition a four-yearly event with the 1983 Cup again being staged in England.

WEST INDIES v INDIA

At Edgbaston, Birmingham, on 9 June 1979.　Toss: West Indies.
Result: **WEST INDIES** won by 9 wickets.　Award: C.G.Greenidge.
LOI debuts: India – S.C.Khanna.

INDIA		Runs	Balls	4/6
S.M.Gavaskar	c Holding b Roberts	8		
A.D.Gaekwad	c King b Holding	11		
D.B.Vengsarkar	c Kallicharran b Holding	7		
G.R.Viswanath	b Holding	75		
B.P.Patel	run out	15		
M.Amarnath	c Murray b Croft	8		
Kapil Dev	b King	12		
†S.C.Khanna	c Haynes b Holding	0		
K.D.Ghavri	c Murray b Garner	12		
*S.Venkataraghavan	not out	13		
B.S.Bedi	c Lloyd b Roberts	13		
Extras	(B6, LB3, W3, NB4)	16		
TOTAL	(53.1 overs)	190		

WEST INDIES		Runs	Balls	4/6
C.G.Greenidge	not out	106		
D.L.Haynes	lbw b Kapil Dev	47		
I.V.A.Richards	not out	28		
A.I.Kallicharran				
*C.H.Lloyd				
C.L.King				
†D.L.Murray				
A.M.E.Roberts				
J.Garner				
M.A.Holding				
C.E.H.Croft				
Extras	(LB6, NB7)	13		
TOTAL	(51.3 overs; 1 wicket)	194		

WEST INDIES	O	M	R	W		FALL OF WICKETS	
Roberts	9.1	0	32	2	Wkt	I	WI
Holding	12	2	33	4	1st	10	138
Garner	12	1	42	1	2nd	24	–
Croft	10	1	31	1	3rd	29	–
King	10	1	36	1	4th	56	–
					5th	77	–
INDIA					6th	112	–
Kapil Dev	10	1	46	1	7th	119	–
Ghavri	10	2	25	0	8th	155	–
Venkataraghavan	12	3	30	0	9th	163	–
Bedi	12	0	45	0	10th	190	–
Amarnath	7.3	0	35	0			

Umpires: D.G.L.Evans (1) and J.G.Langridge (5).

NEW ZEALAND v SRI LANKA

At Trent Bridge, Nottingham, on 9 June 1979. Toss: New Zealand.
Result: NEW ZEALAND won by 9 wickets. Award: G.P.Howarth.
LOI debuts: New Zealand – J.V.Coney, W.K.Lees, L.W.Stott; Sri Lanka – D.L.S.de Silva,
R.L.Dias, S.A.Jayasinghe, S.P.Pasqual.

SRI LANKA		Runs	Balls	4/6
B.Warnapura	c and b McKechnie	20		
S.R.de S.Wettimuny	b Cairns	16		
*A.P.B.Tennekoon	b Stott	59		
R.L.Dias	c and b Stott	25		
L.R.D.Mendis	c Turner b Troup	14		
D.S.de Silva	c Burgess b Stott	6		
†S.A.Jayasinghe	run out	1		
S.P.Pasqual	b Hadlee	1		
A.R.M.Opatha	b McKechnie	18		
D.L.S.de Silva	c Wright b McKechnie	10		
G.R.A.de Silva	not out	2		
Extras	(LB13, W2, NB2)	17		
TOTAL	(56.5 overs)	189		

NEW ZEALAND		Runs	Balls	4/6
G.M.Turner	not out	83		
J.G.Wright	c Tennekoon b G.R.A.de Silva	34		
G.P.Howarth	not out	63		
J.V.Coney				
*M.G.Burgess				
†W.K.Lees				
B.J.McKechnie				
B.L.Cairns				
R.J.Hadlee				
L.W.Stott				
G.B.Troup				
Extras	(LB7, W2, NB1)	10		
TOTAL	(47.4 overs; 1 wicket)	190		

NEW ZEALAND	O	M	R	W		FALL OF WICKETS		
Hadlee	12	3	24	1	Wkt	SL	NZ	
Troup	10	0	30	1	1st	26	64	
Cairns	12	1	45	1	2nd	57	–	
McKechnie	10.5	2	25	3	3rd	107	–	
Stott	12	1	48	3	4th	137	–	
					5th	149	–	
SRI LANKA					6th	150	–	
Opatha	7	1	31	0	7th	150	–	
D.L.S.de Silva	8	2	18	0	8th	154	–	
Warnapura	7	0	30	0	9th	178	–	
D.S.de Silva	9	0	42	0	10th	189	–	
G.R.A.de Silva	12	1	39	1				
Pasqual	4.4	0	20	0				

Umpires: W.L.Budd (9) and K.E.Palmer (3).

ENGLAND v AUSTRALIA

At Lord's, London, on 9 June 1979.   Toss: England.
Result: **ENGLAND** won by 6 wickets.   Award: G.A.Gooch.
LOI debuts: None.

AUSTRALIA		Runs	Balls	4/6
A.M.J.Hilditch	b Boycott	47	108	2
W.M.Darling	lbw b Willis	25	61	3
A.R.Border	c Taylor b Edmonds	34	74	4
*K.J.Hughes	c Hendrick b Boycott	6	13	1
G.N.Yallop	run out	10	20	1
G.J.Cosier	run out	6	20	–
T.J.Laughlin	run out	8	22	–
†K.J.Wright	lbw b Old	6	15	–
G.Dymock	not out	4	12	–
R.M.Hogg	run out	0	5	–
A.G.Hurst	not out	3	10	–
Extras	(B4, LB5, W1)	10		
TOTAL	(60 overs; 9 wickets)	159		

ENGLAND		Runs	Balls	4/6
*J.M.Brearley	c Wright b Laughlin	44	147	2
G.Boycott	lbw b Hogg	1	5	–
D.W.Randall	c Wright b Hurst	1	3	–
G.A.Gooch	lbw b Laughlin	53	96	6
D.I.Gower	not out	22	30	2
I.T.Botham	not out	18	14	2
P.H.Edmonds				
†R.W.Taylor				
C.M.Old				
M.Hendrick				
R.G.D.Willis				
Extras	(LB10, NB11)	21		
TOTAL	(47.1 overs; 4 wickets)	160		

ENGLAND	O	M	R	W		FALL OF WICKETS	
Willis	11	2	20	1	Wkt	A	E
Hendrick	12	2	24	0	1st	56	4
Old	12	2	33	1	2nd	97	5
Botham	8	0	32	0	3rd	111	113
Edmonds	11	1	25	1	4th	131	124
Boycott	6	0	15	2	5th	132	–
					6th	137	–
AUSTRALIA					7th	150	–
Hogg	9	1	25	1	8th	153	–
Hurst	10	3	33	1	9th	153	–
Dymock	11	2	19	0	10th	–	–
Cosier	8	1	24	0			
Laughlin	9.1	0	38	2			

Umpires: D.J.Constant (12) and B.J.Meyer (3).

PAKISTAN v CANADA

At Headingley, Leeds, on 9 June 1979.   Toss: Canada.
Result: **PAKISTAN** won by 8 wickets.   Award: Sadiq Mohammad.
LOI debuts: Canada – all.

CANADA		Runs	Balls	4/6
C.J.D.Chappell	c and b Sikander	14		
G.R.Sealy	c and b Asif	45		
F.A.Dennis	c Wasim b Sarfraz	25		
M.P.Stead	c Zaheer b Asif	10		
C.A.Marshall	b Imran	8		
J.C.B.Vaughan	c and b Asif	0		
*†B.M.Mauricette	c Zaheer b Sarfraz	15		
Tariq Javed	st Wasim b Majid	3		
J.M.Patel	b Sarfraz	0		
C.C.Henry	not out	1		
J.N.Valentine				
Extras	(LB10, W5, NB3)	18		
TOTAL	(60 overs; 9 wickets)	139		
PAKISTAN		Runs	Balls	4/6
Majid Khan	b Valentine	1		
Sadiq Mohammad	not out	57		
Zaheer Abbas	run out	36		
Haroon Rashid	not out	37		
Javed Miandad				
*Asif Iqbal				
Mudassar Nazar				
Imran Khan				
†Wasim Bari				
Sarfraz Nawaz				
Sikander Bakht				
Extras	(B1, LB3, W1, NB4)	9		
TOTAL	(40.1 overs; 2 wickets)	140		

PAKISTAN	O	M	R	W	FALL OF WICKETS		
Imran Khan	11	1	27	1	Wkt	C	P
Sarfraz Nawaz	10	1	26	3	1st	54	4
Mudassar Nazar	4	1	11	0	2nd	85	61
Sikander Bakht	12	5	18	1	3rd	103	–
Majid Khan	11	4	11	1	4th	110	–
Asif Iqbal	12	2	28	3	5th	110	–
CANADA					6th	129	–
Valentine	9	3	18	1	7th	134	–
Vaughan	5	1	21	0	8th	138	–
Henry	5	0	26	0	9th	139	–
Patel	11.1	0	27	0	10th	–	–
Sealy	6	0	21	0			
Stead	4	0	18	0			

Umpires: H.D.Bird (12) and A.G.T.Whitehead (1).

SECOND WORLD CUP (5th Match): WEST INDIES v SRI LANKA
At Kennington Oval, London, on 13, 14, 15 June 1979. Toss: –
No result – match abandoned without a ball bowled (2 points each).

NEW ZEALAND v INDIA

At Headingley, Leeds, on 13 June 1979.   Toss: New Zealand.
Result: **NEW ZEALAND** won by 8 wickets.   Award: B.A.Edgar.
LOI debuts: None.

INDIA		Runs	Balls	4/6
S.M.Gavaskar	c Lees b Hadlee	55		
A.D.Gaekwad	b Hadlee	10		
D.B.Vengsarkar	c Lees b McKechnie	1		
G.R.Viswanath	c Turner b Cairns	9		
B.P.Patel	b Troup	38		
M.Amarnath	b Troup	1		
Kapil Dev	c and b Cairns	25		
K.D.Ghavri	c Coney b McKechnie	20		
†S.C.Khanna	c Morrison b McKechnie	7		
*S.Venkataraghavan	c Lees b Cairns	1		
B.S.Bedi	not out	1		
Extras	(LB8, W5, NB1)	14		
TOTAL	(55.5 overs)	182		

NEW ZEALAND		Runs	Balls	4/6
J.G.Wright	c and b Amarnath	48		
B.A.Edgar	not out	84		
B.L.Cairns	run out	2		
G.M.Turner	not out	43		
J.V.Coney				
*M.G.Burgess				
J.F.M.Morrison				
B.J.McKechnie				
†W.K.Lees				
R.J.Hadlee				
G.B.Troup				
Extras	(LB3, NB3)	6		
TOTAL	(57 overs; 2 wickets)	183		

NEW ZEALAND	O	M	R	W		FALL OF WICKETS	
					Wkt	I	NZ
Hadlee	10	2	20	2	1st	27	100
Troup	10	2	36	2	2nd	38	103
Cairns	11.5	0	36	3	3rd	53	–
McKechnie	12	1	24	3	4th	104	–
Coney	7	0	33	0	5th	107	–
Morrison	5	0	19	0	6th	147	–
INDIA					7th	153	–
Amarnath	12	1	39	1	8th	180	–
Bedi	12	1	32	0	9th	182	–
Venkataraghavan	12	0	34	0	10th	182	–
Ghavri	10	1	34	0			
Kapil Dev	11	3	38	0			

Umpires: W.L.Budd (10) and A.G.T.Whitehead (2).

AUSTRALIA v PAKISTAN

At Trent Bridge, Nottingham, on 13, 14 June 1979.   Toss: Australia.
Result: **PAKISTAN** won by 89 runs.   Award: Asif Iqbal.
LOI debuts: Australia – J.K.Moss, G.D.Porter.

PAKISTAN		Runs	Balls	4/6
Sadiq Mohammad	c Moss b Porter	27	73	2
Majid Khan	b Dymock	61	100	7/1
Zaheer Abbas	c and b Cosier	16	32	1
Haroon Rashid	c Wright b Cosier	16	42	2
Javed Miandad	c Border b Cosier	46	46	4
*Asif Iqbal	c sub (D.F.Whatmore) b Hurst	61	57	7
Wasim Raja	c Moss b Border	18	12	2/1
Imran Khan	not out	15	9	–
Mudassar Nazar	not out	1	1	–
†Wasim Bari				
Sikander Bakht				
Extras	(B6, LB4, W5, NB10)	25		
TOTAL	(60 overs; 7 wickets)	286		

AUSTRALIA		Runs	Balls	4/6
W.M.Darling	c Wasim Bari b Imran	13	25	1
A.M.J.Hilditch	c Sadiq b Mudassar	72	129	4
A.R.Border	b Sikander	0	5	–
*K.J.Hughes	lbw b Sikander	15	37	2
G.N.Yallop	b Majid	37	64	2
J.K.Moss	run out	7	16	–
G.J.Cosier	c and b Majid	0	1	–
†K.J.Wright	c Wasim Bari b Imran	23	37	–
G.D.Porter	c Sadiq b Majid	3	9	–
G.Dymock	lbw b Sikander	10	18	–
A.G.Hurst	not out	3	2	–
Extras	(B1, LB5, W8)	14		
TOTAL	(57.1 overs)	197		

AUSTRALIA	O	M	R	W
Porter	12	3	20	1
Dymock	12	3	28	1
Cosier	12	1	54	3
Hurst	12	0	65	1
Yallop	8	0	56	0
Border	4	0	38	1
PAKISTAN				
Asif Iqbal	12	0	36	0
Majid Khan	12	0	53	3
Mudassar Nazar	12	0	31	1
Imran Khan	10.1	2	29	2
Sikander Bakht	11	1	34	3

FALL OF WICKETS		
Wkt	P	A
1st	99	22
2nd	99	24
3rd	133	46
4th	152	117
5th	239	136
6th	268	137
7th	274	172
8th	–	175
9th	–	193
10th	–	197

Umpires: H.D.Bird (13) and K.E.Palmer (4).

ENGLAND v CANADA

At Old Trafford, Manchester, on 13 *(no play)*, 14 June 1979. Toss: Canada.
Result: **ENGLAND** won by 8 wickets.   Award: C.M.Old.
LOI debuts: Canada – R.G.Callender.

CANADA		Runs	Balls	4/6
G.R.Sealy	c Botham b Hendrick	3	9	–
C.J.D.Chappell	lbw b Botham	5	31	–
F.A.Dennis	hit wicket b Willis	21	99	2
Tariq Javed	lbw b Old	4	40	–
J.C.B.Vaughan	b Old	1	10	–
C.A.Marshall	b Old	2	7	–
*†B.M.Mauricette	b Willis	0	8	–
M.P.Stead	b Old	0	12	–
J.M.Patel	b Willis	1	14	–
R.G.Callender	b Willis	0	3	–
J.N.Valentine	not out	3	11	–
Extras	(LB4, NB1)	5		
TOTAL	(40.3 overs)	45		

ENGLAND		Runs	Balls	4/6
*J.M.Brearley	lbw b Valentine	0	10	–
G.Boycott	not out	14	36	–
D.W.Randall	b Callender	5	11	1
G.A.Gooch	not out	21	31	2/1
D.I.Gower				
I.T.Botham				
G.Miller				
†R.W.Taylor				
C.M.Old				
R.G.D.Willis				
M.Hendrick				
Extras	(W3, NB3)	6		
TOTAL	(13.5 overs; 2 wickets)	46		

ENGLAND	O	M	R	W		FALL OF WICKETS		
Willis	10.3	3	11	4	Wkt		C	E
Hendrick	8	4	5	1	1st		5	3
Botham	9	5	12	1	2nd		13	11
Miller	2	1	1	0	3rd		25	
Boycott	1	0	3	0	4th		29	
Old	10	5	8	4	5th		37	
					6th		38	
CANADA					7th		41	
Valentine	7	2	20	1	8th		41	
Callender	6	1	14	1	9th		42	
Stead	0.5	0	6	0	10th		45	

Umpires: J.G.Langridge (6) and B.J.Meyer (4).

INDIA v SRI LANKA

At Old Trafford, Manchester, on 16, 18 June 1979.   Toss: India.
Result: **SRI LANKA** won by 47 runs.   Award: L.R.D.Mendis.
LOI debuts: Sri Lanka – F.R.M.Goonatillake, R.S.Madugalle.

SRI LANKA		Runs	Balls	4/6
*B.Warnapura	c Gaekwad b Amarnath	18		
S.R.de S.Wettimuny	c Vengsarkar b Kapil Dev	67		
R.L.Dias	c and b Amarnath	50		
L.R.D.Mendis	run out	64		
R.S.Madugalle	c Khanna b Amarnath	4		
S.P.Pasqual	not out	23		
D.S.de Silva	not out	1		
†S.A.Jayasinghe				
A.R.M.Opatha				
D.L.S.de Silva				
F.R.M.Goonatillake				
Extras	(LB8, W2, NB1)	11		
TOTAL	(60 overs; 5 wickets)	238		

INDIA		Runs	Balls	4/6
S.M.Gavaskar	c Dias b Warnapura	26		
A.D.Gaekwad	c sub (G.R.A.de Silva) b D.L.S.de Silva	33		
D.B.Vengsarkar	c D.L.S.de Silva b D.S.de Silva	36		
G.R.Viswanath	run out	22		
B.P.Patel	b D.S.de Silva	10		
Kapil Dev	c Warnapura b D.L.S.de Silva	16		
M.Amarnath	b D.S.de Silva	7		
K.D.Ghavri	c Warnapura b Opatha	3		
†S.C.Khanna	c Dias b Opatha	10		
*S.Venkataraghavan	not out	9		
B.S.Bedi	c Jayasinghe b Opatha	5		
Extras	(LB10, W3, NB1)	14		
TOTAL	(54.1 overs)	191		

INDIA	O	M	R	W
Kapil Dev	12	2	53	1
Ghavri	12	0	53	0
Amarnath	12	3	40	3
Bedi	12	2	37	0
Venkataraghavan	12	0	44	0

SRI LANKA	O	M	R	W
Opatha	10.1	0	31	3
Goonatillake	9	1	34	0
Warnapura	12	0	47	1
D.L.S.de Silva	12	0	36	2
D.S.de Silva	11	1	29	3

FALL OF WICKETS		
Wkt	SL	I
1st	31	60
2nd	127	76
3rd	147	119
4th	175	132
5th	227	147
6th	–	160
7th	–	162
8th	–	170
9th	–	185
10th	–	191

Umpires: K.E.Palmer (5) and A.G.T.Whitehead (3).

WEST INDIES v NEW ZEALAND

At Trent Bridge, Nottingham, on 16 June 1979.   Toss: New Zealand.
Result: WEST INDIES won by 32 runs.   Award: C.H.Lloyd.
LOI debuts: New Zealand – E.J.Chatfield.

WEST INDIES		Runs	Balls	4/6
C.G.Greenidge	c Edgar b Coney	65		
D.L.Haynes	lbw b Hadlee	12		
I.V.A.Richards	c Burgess b Coney	9		
A.I.Kallicharran	b McKechnie	39		
*C.H.Lloyd	not out	73		
C.L.King	lbw b Cairns	12		
†D.L.Murray	c Coney b Chatfield	12		
A.M.E.Roberts	c Lees b Cairns	1		
J.Garner	not out	9		
M.A.Holding				
C.E.H.Croft				
Extras	(B5, LB7)	12		
TOTAL	(60 overs; 7 wickets)	244		

NEW ZEALAND		Runs	Balls	4/6
B.A.Edgar	run out	12		
J.G.Wright	c Lloyd b Garner	15		
J.V.Coney	c Garner b King	36		
G.M.Turner	c Lloyd b Roberts	20		
J.F.M.Morrison	c Murray b Garner	11		
*M.G.Burgess	c Richards b Roberts	35		
†W.K.Lees	b Croft	5		
R.J.Hadlee	b Roberts	42		
B.J.McKechnie	not out	13		
B.L.Cairns	b Holding	1		
E.J.Chatfield	not out	3		
Extras	(LB14, W4, NB1)	19		
TOTAL	(60 overs; 9 wickets)	212		

NEW ZEALAND	O	M	R	W		FALL OF WICKETS	
					Wkt	WI	NZ
Hadlee	11	2	41	1	1st	23	27
Chatfield	11	0	45	1	2nd	61	38
Cairns	12	1	48	2	3rd	117	90
Coney	12	0	40	2	4th	152	91
McKechnie	11	0	46	1	5th	175	138
Morrison	3	0	12	0	6th	202	143
					7th	204	160
WEST INDIES					8th	–	199
Roberts	12	2	43	3	9th	–	202
Holding	12	1	29	1	10th	–	–
Croft	12	1	38	1			
Garner	12	0	45	2			
King	12	1	38	1			

Umpires: H.D.Bird (14) and B.J.Meyer (5).

AUSTRALIA v CANADA

At Edgbaston, Birmingham, on 16 June 1979.　Toss: Australia.
Result: **AUSTRALIA** won by 7 wickets.　Award: A.G.Hurst.
LOI debuts: Canada – S.Baksh.

CANADA		Runs	Balls	4/6
G.R.Sealy	c Porter b Dymock	25	30	4
C.J.D.Chappell	lbw b Hurst	19	42	2
F.A.Dennis	lbw b Hurst	1	8	–
Tariq Javed	c Porter b Porter	8	30	1
S.Baksh	b Hurst	0	6	–
J.C.B.Vaughan	b Porter	29	43	4
*†B.M.Mauricette	c Hilditch b Cosier	5	22	–
J.M.Patel	b Cosier	2	4	–
R.G.Callender	c Wright b Hurst	0	2	–
C.C.Henry	c Hughes b Hurst	5	11	1
J.N.Valentine	not out	0	6	–
Extras	(B4, LB5, W1, NB1)	11		
TOTAL	(33.2 overs)	105		

AUSTRALIA		Runs	Balls	4/6
A.M.J.Hilditch	c Valentine b Henry	24	30	3
W.M.Darling	lbw b Valentine	13	16	2
A.R.Border	b Henry	25	53	4
*K.J.Hughes	not out	27	40	2
G.N.Yallop	not out	13	20	–
G.J.Cosier				
†K.J.Wright				
G.D.Porter				
R.M.Hogg				
G.Dymock				
A.G.Hurst				
Extras	(LB1, NB3)	4		
TOTAL	(26 overs; 3 wickets)	106		

AUSTRALIA	O	M	R	W	FALL OF WICKETS		
					Wkt	C	A
Hogg	2	0	26	0	1st	44	23
Hurst	10	3	21	5	2nd	50	53
Dymock	8	2	17	1	3rd	51	72
Porter	6	2	13	2	4th	51	–
Cosier	7.2	2	17	2	5th	78	–
					6th	97	–
CANADA					7th	97	–
Valentine	3	0	28	1	8th	98	–
Callender	3	0	12	0	9th	104	–
Henry	10	0	27	2	10th	105	–
Vaughan	6	0	15	0			
Patel	4	0	20	0			

Umpires: D.J.Constant (13) and J.G.Langridge (7).

ENGLAND v PAKISTAN

At Headingley, Leeds, on 16 June 1979.   Toss: Pakistan.
Result: **ENGLAND** won by 14 runs.   Award: M.Hendrick.
LOI debuts: None.

ENGLAND		Runs	Balls	4/6
*J.M.Brearley	c Wasim Bari b Imran	0	2	–
G.Boycott	lbw b Majid	18	54	2
D.W.Randall	c Wasim Bari b Sikander	1	5	–
G.A.Gooch	c Sadiq b Sikander	33	90	5
D.I.Gower	b Majid	27	40	3
I.T.Botham	b Majid	22	48	1/1
P.H.Edmonds	c Wasim Raja b Asif	2	23	–
†R.W.Taylor	not out	20	59	1
C.M.Old	c and b Asif	2	7	–
R.G.D.Willis	b Sikander	24	37	3
M.Hendrick	not out	1	1	–
Extras	(LB3, W7, NB5)	15		
TOTAL	(60 overs; 9 wickets)	165		

PAKISTAN		Runs	Balls	4/6
Majid Khan	c Botham b Hendrick	7	20	1
Sadiq Mohammad	b Hendrick	18	27	4
Mudassar Nazar	lbw b Hendrick	0	2	–
Zaheer Abbas	c Taylor b Botham	3	19	–
Haroon Rashid	c Brearley b Hendrick	1	2	–
Javed Miandad	lbw b Botham	0	4	–
*Asif Iqbal	c Brearley b Willis	51	104	5
Wasim Raja	lbw b Old	21	25	4
Imran Khan	not out	21	82	1
†Wasim Bari	c Taylor b Boycott	17	33	2
Sikander Bakht	c Hendrick b Boycott	2	19	–
Extras	(LB8, W1, NB1)	10		
TOTAL	(56 overs)	151		

PAKISTAN	O	M	R	W
Imran Khan	12	3	24	1
Sikander Bakht	12	3	32	3
Mudassar Nazar	12	4	30	0
Asif Iqbal	12	3	37	2
Majid Khan	12	2	27	3

FALL OF WICKETS		
Wkt	E	P
1st	0	27
2nd	4	27
3rd	51	28
4th	70	30
5th	99	31
6th	115	34
7th	115	86
8th	118	115
9th	161	145
10th	–	151

ENGLAND	O	M	R	W
Willis	11	2	37	1
Hendrick	12	6	15	4
Botham	12	3	38	2
Old	12	2	28	1
Edmonds	3	0	8	0
Boycott	5	0	14	2
Gooch	1	0	1	0

Umpires: W.L.Budd (11) and D.G.L.Evans (2).

ENGLAND v NEW ZEALAND (SEMI-FINAL)

At Old Trafford, Manchester, on 20 June 1979. Toss: New Zealand.
Result: **ENGLAND** won by 9 runs. Award: G.A.Gooch.
LOI debuts: England – W.Larkins.

ENGLAND		Runs	Balls	4/6
*J.M.Brearley	c Lees b Coney	53	115	3
G.Boycott	c Howarth b Hadlee	2	14	–
W.Larkins	c Coney b McKechnie	7	37	–
G.A.Gooch	b McKechnie	71	84	1/3
D.I.Gower	run out	1	1	–
I.T.Botham	lbw b Cairns	21	30	2
D.W.Randall	not out	42	50	1/1
C.M.Old	c Lees b Troup	0	2	–
†R.W.Taylor	run out	12	25	1
R.G.D.Willis	not out	1	2	–
M.Hendrick				
Extras	(LB8, W3)	11		
TOTAL	(60 overs; 8 wickets)	221		

NEW ZEALAND		Runs	Balls	4/6
J.G.Wright	run out	69	137	9
B.A.Edgar	lbw b Old	17	38	1
G.P.Howarth	lbw b Boycott	7	12	1
J.V.Coney	lbw b Hendrick	11	39	–
G.M.Turner	lbw b Willis	30	51	2
*M.G.Burgess	run out	10	13	–
R.J.Hadlee	b Botham	15	32	1
†W.K.Lees	b Hendrick	23	20	–/1
B.L.Cairns	c Brearley b Hendrick	14	6	1/1
B.J.McKechnie	not out	4	9	–
G.B.Troup	not out	3	3	–
Extras	(B5, W4)	9		
TOTAL	(60 overs; 9 wickets)	212		

NEW ZEALAND	O	M	R	W		FALL OF WICKETS		
Hadlee	12	4	32	1		Wkt	E	NZ
Troup	12	1	38	1		1st	13	47
Cairns	12	2	47	1		2nd	38	58
Coney	12	0	47	1		3rd	96	104
McKechnie	12	1	46	2		4th	98	112
						5th	145	132
ENGLAND						6th	177	162
Botham	12	3	42	1		7th	178	180
Hendrick	12	0	55	3		8th	219	195
Old	12	1	33	1		9th	–	208
Boycott	9	1	24	1		10th		
Gooch	3	1	8	0				
Willis	12	1	41	1				

Umpires: J.G.Langridge (8) and K.E.Palmer (6).

WEST INDIES v PAKISTAN (SEMI-FINAL)

At Kennington Oval, London, on 20 June 1979.   Toss: Pakistan.
Result: **WEST INDIES** won by 43 runs.   Award: C.G.Greenidge.
LOI debuts: None.

WEST INDIES		Runs	Balls	4/6
C.G.Greenidge	c Wasim b Asif	73	107	5/1
D.L.Haynes	c and b Asif	65	115	4
I.V.A.Richards	b Asif	42	62	1
*C.H.Lloyd	c Mudassar b Asif	37	38	3
C.L.King	c sub (Wasim Raja) b Sarfraz	34	25	3
A.I.Kallicharran	b Imran	11	14	–
A.M.E.Roberts	not out	7	4	–
J.Garner	not out	1	1	–
†D.L.Murray				
M.A.Holding				
C.E.H.Croft				
Extras	(B1, LB17, W1, NB4)	23		
TOTAL	(60 overs; 6 wickets)	293		

PAKISTAN		Runs	Balls	4/6
Majid Khan	c Kallicharran b Croft	81	124	7
Sadiq Mohammad	c Murray b Holding	2	7	–
Zaheer Abbas	c Murray b Croft	93	122	8/1
Haroon Rashid	run out	15	22	1
Javed Miandad	lbw b Croft	0	1	–
*Asif Iqbal	c Holding b Richards	17	20	1
Mudassar Nazar	c Kallicharran b Richards	2	9	–
Imran Khan	c and b Richards	6	4	1
Sarfraz Nawaz	c Haynes b Roberts	12	15	–
†Wasim Bari	c Murray b Roberts	9	12	–
Sikander Bakht	not out	1	4	–
Extras	(LB9, W2, NB1)	12		
TOTAL	(56.2 overs)	250		

PAKISTAN	O	M	R	W		FALL OF WICKETS		
Imran Khan	9	1	43	1	Wkt	WI	P	
Sarfraz Nawaz	12	1	71	1	1st	132	10	
Sikander Bakht	6	1	24	0	2nd	165	176	
Mudassar Nazar	10	0	50	0	3rd	233	187	
Majid Khan	12	2	26	0	4th	236	187	
Asif Iqbal	11	0	56	4	5th	285	208	
					6th	285	220	
WEST INDIES					7th	–	221	
Roberts	9.2	2	41	2	8th	–	228	
Holding	9	1	28	1	9th	–	246	
Croft	11	0	29	3	10th	–	250	
Garner	12	1	47	0				
King	7	0	41	0				
Richards	8	0	52	3				

Umpires: W.L.Budd (12) and D.J.Constant (14).

ENGLAND v WEST INDIES (FINAL)

At Lord's, London, on 23 June 1979.   Toss: England.
Result: **WEST INDIES** won by 92 runs.   Award: I.V.A.Richards.
LOI debuts: None.

WEST INDIES		Runs	Balls	4/6
C.G.Greenidge	run out	9	31	–
D.L.Haynes	c Hendrick b Old	20	27	3
I.V.A.Richards	not out	138	157	11/3
A.I.Kallicharran	b Hendrick	4	17	–
*C.H.Lloyd	c and b Old	13	33	2
C.L.King	c Randall b Edmonds	86	66	10/3
†D.L.Murray	c Gower b Edmonds	5	9	1
A.M.E.Roberts	c Brearley b Hendrick	0	7	–
J.Garner	c Taylor b Botham	0	5	–
M.A.Holding	b Botham	0	6	–
C.E.H.Croft	not out	0	2	–
Extras	(B1, LB10)	11		
TOTAL	(60 overs; 9 wickets)	286		

ENGLAND		Runs	Balls	4/6
*J.M.Brearley	c King b Holding	64	130	7
G.Boycott	c Kallicharran b Holding	57	105	3
D.W.Randall	b Croft	15	22	–
G.A.Gooch	b Garner	32	28	4
D.I.Gower	b Garner	0	4	–
I.T.Botham	c Richards b Croft	4	3	–
W.Larkins	b Garner	0	1	–
P.H.Edmonds	not out	5	8	–
C.M.Old	b Garner	0	2	–
†R.W.Taylor	c Murray b Garner	0	1	–
M.Hendrick	b Croft	0	5	–
Extras	(LB12, W2, NB3)	17		
TOTAL	(51 overs)	194		

ENGLAND	O	M	R	W		FALL OF WICKETS	
Botham	12	2	44	2	Wkt	WI	E
Hendrick	12	2	50	2	1st	22	129
Old	12	0	55	2	2nd	36	135
Boycott	6	0	38	0	3rd	55	183
Edmonds	12	2	40	2	4th	99	183
Gooch	4	0	27	0	5th	238	186
Larkins	2	0	21	0	6th	252	186
					7th	258	192
WEST INDIES					8th	260	192
Roberts	9	2	33	0	9th	272	194
Holding	8	1	16	2	10th	–	194
Croft	10	1	42	3			
Garner	11	0	38	5			
Richards	10	0	35	0			
King	3	0	13	0			

Umpires: H.D.Bird (15) and B.J.Meyer (6).

THE 1983 WORLD CUP

India caused one of the major sporting upsets of the century when they beat the holders and firm favourites, West Indies, by the emphatic margin of 43 runs in a low-scoring final. This was no cricketing fluke. A fortnight earlier they had beaten Clive Lloyd's team by 34 runs, successfully defending their record World Cup total of 262.

The third World Cup, the last to be sponsored by Prudential, began with another giant-killing feat when Zimbabwe beat Australia in the opening round. For the first time, all eight teams won a match. Compared with its two predecessors, this competition was almost double the size, involving 27 matches instead of the earlier 15. This was the result of expanding the programme at group stage, each team playing the others within that group twice in order to reduce the chances of a team being eliminated through ill-luck with the weather. Fortunately, after one of the wettest Mays on record, June was mainly dry and sunny and of the 27 matches staged over 16 days, only three required the assistance of the reserve day.

For the first time the World Cup was taken outside the Test match grounds, Swansea producing the then record World Cup match aggregate of 626 runs, Pakistan contributing the record total of 338 for 5 and Sri Lanka responding with the highest second innings tally of 288 for 9. Tunbridge Wells saw Kapil Dev savage its rhododendrons and the Zimbabwean bowlers with 6 sixes and 16 fours in his record World Cup innings of 175 not out. Taunton nearly reached Swansea's record aggregate when England's encounter with Sri Lanka produced 619 runs, while Leicester, Bristol, Worcester, Southampton, Derby and Chelmsford all enjoyed a unique occasion.

Again, matches were of 60 overs and bowlers were restricted to 12 apiece. To counteract negative bowling, the playing conditions empowered umpires to apply a stricter interpretation of wides and bouncers than in first-class cricket.

As before, the top two teams in each group qualified for the semi-finals, Pakistan getting the nod over New Zealand by virtue of their superior run-rate per over, both countries gaining 12 points.

GROUP A	P	W	L	Pts	R/O	GROUP B	P	W	L	Pts	R/O
ENGLAND	6	5	1	20	4.67	WEST INDIES	6	5	1	20	4.31
PAKISTAN	6	3	3	12	4.01	INDIA	6	4	2	16	3.87
New Zealand	6	3	3	12	3.93	Australia	6	2	4	8	3.81
Sri Lanka	6	1	5	4	3.75	Zimbabwe	6	1	5	4	3.49

In financial terms this was the most bountiful tournament so far, the Prudential doubling their sponsorship from £500,000, gate receipts reaching £1,195,712 from an aggregate attendance of 232,081, and a resultant surplus in excess of £1 million.

This profit inspired other countries to bid for the next World Cup and when tenders were submitted at the end of the year the fourth tournament was awarded jointly to India and Pakistan.

ENGLAND v NEW ZEALAND

At Kennington Oval, London, on 9 June 1983. Toss: England.
Result: **ENGLAND** won by 106 runs. Award: A.J.Lamb.
LOI debuts: None.

ENGLAND		Runs	Balls	4/6
G.Fowler	c Coney b Cairns	8	19	1
C.J.Tavaré	c Edgar b Chatfield	45	91	4
D.I.Gower	c Edgar b Coney	39	62	6
A.J.Lamb	b Snedden	102	105	12/2
M.W.Gatting	b Snedden	43	47	3
I.T.Botham	c Lees b Hadlee	22	16	–/1
†I.J.Gould	not out	14	12	1
G.R.Dilley	not out	31	14	4
V.J.Marks				
P.J.W.Allott				
*R.G.D.Willis				
Extras	(LB12, W1, NB5)	18		
TOTAL	(60 overs; 6 wickets)	322		

NEW ZEALAND		Runs	Balls	4/6
G.M.Turner	lbw b Willis	14	28	2
B.A.Edgar	c Gould b Willis	3	6	–
J.G.Wright	c Botham b Dilley	10	17	1
*G.P.Howarth	c Lamb b Marks	18	44	1
J.V.Coney	run out	23	52	2
M.D.Crowe	run out	97	118	8
†W.K.Lees	b Botham	8	23	–
R.J.Hadlee	c Lamb b Marks	1	9	–
B.L.Cairns	lbw b Botham	1	2	–
M.C.Snedden	c Gould b Gatting	21	34	1
E.J.Chatfield	not out	9	24	1
Extras	(B2, LB4, W4, NB1)	11		
TOTAL	(59 overs)	216		

NEW ZEALAND	O	M	R	W		FALL OF WICKETS	
					Wkt	E	NZ
Hadlee	12	4	26	1	1st	13	3
Cairns	12	4	57	1	2nd	79	28
Snedden	12	1	105	2	3rd	117	31
Chatfield	12	1	45	1	4th	232	62
Coney	6	1	20	1	5th	271	85
Crowe	6	0	51	0	6th	278	123
ENGLAND					7th	–	136
Willis	7	2	9	2	8th	–	138
Dilley	8	0	33	1	9th	–	190
Botham	12	0	42	2	10th	–	216
Allott	12	1	47	0			
Marks	12	1	39	2			
Gatting	8	1	35	1			

Umpires: B.J.Meyer (10) and D.O.Oslear (3).

PAKISTAN v SRI LANKA

At St Helen's, Swansea, on 9 June 1983.　Toss: Sri Lanka.
Result: **PAKISTAN** won by 50 runs.　Award: Mohsin Khan.
LOI debuts: Sri Lanka – M.A.R.Samarasekera.

PAKISTAN		Runs	Balls	4/6
Mudassar Nazar	c De Silva b Ratnayake	36		
Mohsin Khan	b John	82		
Zaheer Abbas	c Kuruppu b De Mel	82		
Javed Miandad	lbw b De Mel	72	54	
*Imran Khan	not out	56	33	
Ijaz Faqih	run out	2		
Tahir Naqqash	not out	0		
†Wasim Bari				
Rashid Khan				
Shahid Mahboob				
Sarfraz Nawaz				
Extras	(B4, LB4)	8		
TOTAL	(60 overs; 5 wickets)	338		

SRI LANKA		Runs	Balls	4/6
S.Wettimuny	c Rashid b Sarfraz	12		
D.S.B.P.Kuruppu	run out	72		7/2
R.L.Dias	b Rashid	5		
*L.R.D.Mendis	b Tahir	16		
A.Ranatunga	c and b Mudassar	31		
M.A.R.Samarasekera	run out	0		
D.S.de Silva	c Wasim Bari b Sarfraz	35		
A.L.F.de Mel	c Tahir b Shahid	11		
†R.G.de Alwis	not out	59		
R.J.Ratnayake	c Mudassar b Sarfraz	13		
V.B.John	not out	12		
Extras	(LB8, W10, NB4)	22		
TOTAL	(60 overs; 9 wickets)	288		

SRI LANKA	O	M	R	W
De Mel	12	2	69	2
John	12	2	58	1
Ratnayake	12	0	65	1
Ranatunga	9	0	53	0
De Silva	10	0	52	0
Samarasekera	5	0	33	0

PAKISTAN	O	M	R	W
Sarfraz Nawaz	12	1	40	3
Shahid Mahboob	11	0	48	1
Tahir Naqqash	8	0	49	1
Rashid Khan	12	1	55	1
Ijaz Faqih	12	1	52	0
Mudassar Nazar	4	0	18	1
Zaheer Abbas	1	0	4	0

FALL OF WICKETS		
Wkt	P	SL
1st	88	34
2nd	156	58
3rd	229	85
4th	325	142
5th	332	143
6th	–	157
7th	–	180
8th	–	234
9th	–	262
10th	–	–

Umpires: K.E.Palmer (9) and D.R.Shepherd (1).

AUSTRALIA v ZIMBABWE

At Trent Bridge, Nottingham, on 9 June 1983.   Toss: Australia.
Result: **ZIMBABWE** won by 13 runs.   Award: D.A.G.Fletcher.
LOI debuts: Zimbabwe – all.

ZIMBABWE		Runs	Balls	4/6
A.H.Shah	c Marsh b Lillee	16		–
G.A.Paterson	c Hookes b Lillee	27		2
J.G.Heron	c Marsh b Yallop	14		1
A.J.Pycroft	b Border	21		1
†D.L.Houghton	c Marsh b Yallop	0		–
*D.A.G.Fletcher	not out	69		5
K.M.Curran	c Hookes b Hogg	27		2
I.P.Butchart	not out	34		2
P.W.E.Rawson				
A.J.Traicos				
V.R.Hogg				
Extras	(LB18, W7, NB6)	31		
TOTAL .,	(60 overs; 6 wickets)	239		

AUSTRALIA		Runs	Balls	4/6
G.M.Wood	c Houghton b Fletcher	31		3
K.C.Wessels	run out	76		5
*K.J.Hughes	c Shah b Fletcher	0		–
D.W.Hookes	c Traicos b Fletcher	20		1
G.N.Yallop	c Pycroft b Fletcher	2		–
A.R.Border	c Pycroft b Curran	17		–
†R.W.Marsh	not out	50		3/2
G.F.Lawson	b Butchart	0		–
R.M.Hogg	not out	19		1
D.K.Lillee				
J.R.Thomson				
Extras	(B2, LB7, W2)	11		
TOTAL	(60 overs; 7 wickets)	226		

AUSTRALIA	O	M	R	W	FALL OF WICKETS		
					Wkt	A	Z
Lawson	11	2	33	0	1st	55	61
Hogg	12	3	43	1	2nd	55	63
Lillee	12	1	47	2	3rd	86	114
Thomson	11	1	46	0	4th	86	133
Yallop	9	0	28	2	5th	94	138
Border	5	0	11	1	6th	164	168
ZIMBABWE					7th	–	176
Hogg	6	2	15	0	8th	–	–
Rawson	12	1	54	0	9th	–	–
Butchart	10	0	39	1	10th	–	–
Fletcher	11	1	42	4			
Traicos	12	2	27	0			
Curran	9	0	38	1			

Umpires: D.J.Constant (19) and M.J.Kitchen (1).

WEST INDIES v INDIA

At Old Trafford, Manchester, on 9, 10 June 1983.   Toss: West Indies.
Result: **INDIA** won by 34 runs.   Award: Yashpal Sharma.
LOI debuts: None.

INDIA		Runs	Balls	4/6
S.M.Gavaskar	c Dujon b Marshall	19		
K.Srikkanth	c Dujon b Holding	14		
M.Amarnath	c Dujon b Garner	21		
S.M. Patil	b Gomes	36		
Yashpal Sharma	b Holding	89		
*Kapil Dev	c Richards b Gomes	6		
R.M.H.Binny	lbw b Marshall	27		
Madan Lal	not out	21		
†S.M.H.Kirmani	run out	1		
R.J.Shastri	not out	5		
B.S.Sandhu				
Extras	(B4, LB10, W1, NB8)	23		
TOTAL	(60 overs; 8 wickets)	262		

WEST INDIES		Runs	Balls	4/6
C.G.Greenidge	b Sandhu	24		
D.L.Haynes	run out	24		
I.V.A.Richards	c Kirmani b Binny	17		
S.F.A.F.Bacchus	b Madan Lal	14		
*C.H.Lloyd	b Binny	25		
†P.J.L.Dujon	c Sandhu b Binny	7		
H.A.Gomes	run out	8		
M.D.Marshall	st Kirmani b Shastri	2		
A.M.E.Roberts	not out	37		
M.A.Holding	b Shastri	8		
J.Garner	st Kirmani b Shastri	37		
Extras	(B4, LB17, W4)	25		
TOTAL	(54.1 overs)	228		

WEST INDIES	O	M	R	W		FALL OF WICKETS	
					Wkt	I	WI
Holding	12	3	32	2	1st	21	49
Roberts	12	1	51	0	2nd	46	56
Marshall	12	1	48	2	3rd	76	76
Garner	12	1	49	1	4th	125	96
Richards	2	0	13	0	5th	141	107
Gomes	10	0	46	2	6th	214	124
					7th	243	126
INDIA					8th	246	130
Kapil Dev	10	0	34	0	9th	–	157
Sandhu	12	1	36	1	10th	–	228
Madan Lal	12	1	34	1			
Binny	12	1	48	3			
Shastri	5.1	0	26	3			
Patil	3	0	25	0			

Umpires: B.Leadbeater (1) and A.G.T.Whitehead (6).

ENGLAND v SRI LANKA

At County Ground, Taunton, on 11 June 1983.   Toss: England.
Result: **ENGLAND** won by 47 runs.   Award: D.I.Gower.
LOI debuts: None.

ENGLAND		Runs	Balls	4/6
G. Fowler	b John	22	59	1
C.J.Tavaré	c De Alwis b Ranatunga	32	61	4
D.I.Gower	b De Mel	130	120	12/5
A.J.Lamb	b Ratnayake	53	51	4/2
M.W.Gatting	run out	7	8	–
I.T.Botham	run out	0	1	–
†I.J.Gould	c Ranatunga b Ratnayake	35	40	2
G.R.Dilley	b De Mel	29	16	5
V.J.Marks	run out	5	5	–
P.J.W.Allott	not out	0	–	–
*R.G.D.Willis				
Extras	(LB11, W9)	20		
TOTAL	(60 overs; 9 wickets)	333		

SRI LANKA		Runs	Balls	4/6
S.Wettimuny	lbw b Marks	33	66	3/1
D.S.B.P.Kuruppu	c Gatting b Dilley	4	3	1
R.L.Dias	c Botham b Dilley	2	15	–
*L.R.D.Mendis	c Willis b Marks	56	64	5/1
R.S.Madugalle	c Tavaré b Marks	12	26	1
A.Ranatunga	c Lamb b Marks	34	45	4
D.S.de Silva	st Gould b Marks	28	37	2
†R.G.de Alwis	not out	58	51	6/1
A.L.F.de Mel	c Dilley b Allott	27	26	2
R.J.Ratnayake	c Lamb b Dilley	15	18	1
V.B.John	b Dilley	0	1	–
Extras	(LB12, W2, NB3)	17		
TOTAL	(58 overs)	286		

SRI LANKA	O	M	R	W		FALL OF WICKETS	
					Wkt	E	SL
De Mel	12	3	62	2	1st	49	11
John	12	0	55	1	2nd	78	17
Ratnayake	12	0	66	2	3rd	174	92
Ranatunga	12	0	65	1	4th	193	108
De Silva	12	0	65	0	5th	194	117
					6th	292	168
ENGLAND					7th	298	192
Willis	11	3	43	0	8th	333	246
Dilley	11	0	45	4	9th	333	281
Allott	12	1	82	1	10th	–	286
Botham	12	0	60	0			
Marks	12	3	39	5			

Umpires: M.J.Kitchen (2) and K.E.Palmer (10).

NEW ZEALAND v PAKISTAN

At Edgbaston, Birmingham, on 11, 12 June 1983.   Toss: Pakistan.
Result: **NEW ZEALAND** won by 52 runs.   Award: Abdul Qadir.
LOI debuts: New Zealand – J.G.Bracewell; Pakistan – Abdul Qadir.

NEW ZEALAND		Runs	Balls	4/6
G.M.Turner	c Wasim b Rashid	27	37	5
B.A.Edgar	c Imran b Qadir	44	107	3
J.G.Wright	c Wasim b Qadir	9	14	2
B.L.Cairns	b Qadir	4	6	1
*G.P.Howarth	st Wasim b Qadir	16	35	1
J.V.Coney	c Ijaz b Shahid	33	65	3
M.D.Crowe	c Mohsin b Rashid	34	53	2
R.J.Hadlee	c Wasim b Sarfraz	13	11	1
J.G.Bracewell	lbw b Rashid	3	6	–
†W.K.Lees	not out	24	21	2
E.J.Chatfield	not out	6	8	–
Extras	(LB20, W4, NB1)	25		
TOTAL	(60 overs; 9 wickets)	238		

PAKISTAN		Runs	Balls	4/6
Mohsin Khan	lbw b Hadlee	0	3	–
Mudassar Nazar	c Lees b Cairns	0	2	–
Zaheer Abbas	b Hadlee	0	3	–
Javed Miandad	lbw b Chatfield	35	61	3
*Imran Khan	c Chatfield b Hadlee	9	26	1
Ijaz Faqih	c Edgar b Coney	12	37	1
Shahid Mahboob	c Wright b Coney	17	31	2
†Wasim Bari	c Edgar b Coney	34	71	2
Abdul Qadir	not out	41	68	2/1
Sarfraz Nawaz	c Crowe b Chatfield	13	14	2
Rashid Khan	c and b Cairns	9	21	–
Extras	(B5, LB6, W3, NB2)	16		
TOTAL	(55.2 overs)	186		

PAKISTAN	O	M	R	W		FALL OF WICKETS		
Sarfraz Nawaz	11	1	49	1		Wkt	NZ	P
Shahid Mahboob	10	2	38	1		1st	57	0
Rashid Khan	11	0	47	3		2nd	68	0
Mudassar Nazar	12	1	40	0		3rd	80	0
Abdul Qadir	12	4	21	4		4th	109	22
Ijaz Faqih	1	0	6	0		5th	120	54
Zaheer Abbas	3	0	12	0		6th	166	60
						7th	197	102
NEW ZEALAND						8th	202	131
Hadlee	9	2	20	3		9th	223	158
Cairns	9.2	3	21	2		10th	–	186
Chatfield	12	0	50	2				
Crowe	2	0	12	0				
Coney	12	3	28	3				
Bracewell	11	2	39	0				

Umpires: H.D.Bird (19) and B.Leadbeater (2).

AUSTRALIA v WEST INDIES

At Headingley, Leeds, on 11, 12 June 1983. Toss: Australia.
Result: **WEST INDIES** won by 101 runs. Award: W.W.Davis.
LOI debuts: None.

WEST INDIES		Runs	Balls	4/6
C.G.Greenidge	c Wood b Hogg	4		1
D.L.Haynes	c Marsh b Lawson	13		1
I.V.A.Richards	b Lawson	7		1
H.A.Gomes	c Marsh b Lillee	78		4
*C.H.Lloyd	lbw b Macleay	19		1/1
S.F.A.F.Bacchus	c Wessels b Yallop	47		5
†P.J.L.Dujon	lbw b Lawson	12		–
A.M.E.Roberts	c Marsh b Lillee	5		–
M.A.Holding	run out	20		2
W.W.Daniel	not out	16		2
W.W.Davis				
Extras	(B1, LB9, W10, NB11)	31		
TOTAL	(60 overs; 9 wickets)	252		

AUSTRALIA		Runs	Balls	4/6
G.M.Wood	retired hurt	2		–
K.C.Wessels	b Roberts	11		2
*K.J.Hughes	c Lloyd b Davis	18		–/2
D.W.Hookes	c Dujon b Davis	45		5
G.N.Yallop	c Holding b Davis	29		4
A.R.Border	c Lloyd b Davis	17		2
K.H.Macleay	c Haynes b Davis	1		–
†R.W.Marsh	c Haynes b Holding	8		1
G.F.Lawson	c Dujon b Davis	2		–
R.M.Hogg	not out	0		–
D.K.Lillee	b Davis	0		–
Extras	(B1, LB4, W5, NB8)	18		
TOTAL	(30.3 overs)	151		

AUSTRALIA	O	M	R	W		FALL OF WICKETS	
Lawson	12	3	29	3	Wkt	WI	A
Hogg	12	1	49	1	1st	7	18
Macleay	12	1	31	1	2nd	25	55
Lillee	12	0	55	2	3rd	32	114
Yallop	5	0	26	1	4th	78	116
Border	7	0	31	0	5th	154	126
					6th	192	137
WEST INDIES					7th	208	141
Roberts	7	0	14	1	8th	211	150
Holding	8	2	23	1	9th	252	151
Davis	10.3	0	51	7	10th	–	–
Daniel	3	0	35	0			
Gomes	2	0	10	0			

Umpires: D.J.Constant (20) and D.G.L.Evans (7).

INDIA v ZIMBABWE

At Grace Road, Leicester, on 11 June 1983.   Toss: India.
Result: **INDIA** won by 5 wickets.   Award: Madan Lal.
LOI debuts: Zimbabwe – R.D.Brown.

ZIMBABWE		Runs	Balls	4/6
A.H.Shah	c Kirmani b Sandhu	8		
G.A.Paterson	lbw b Madan Lal	22		
J.G.Heron	c Kirmani b Madan Lal	18		
A.J.Pycroft	c Shastri b Binny	14		
†D.L.Houghton	c Kirmani b Madan Lal	21		
*D.A.G.Fletcher	b Kapil Dev	13		
K.M.Curran	run out	8		
I.P.Butchart	not out	22		
R.D.Brown	c Kirmani b Shastri	6		
P.W.E.Rawson	c Kirmani b Binny	3		
A.J.Traicos	run out	2		
Extras	(LB9, W9)	18		
TOTAL	(51.4 overs)	155		

INDIA		Runs	Balls	4/6
K.Srikkanth	c Butchart b Rawson	20		
S.M.Gavaskar	c Heron b Rawson	4		
M.Amarnath	c sub (G.E.Peckover) b Traicos	44		
S.M.Patil	b Fletcher	50	50	7/1
R.J.Shastri	c Brown b Shah	17		
Yashpal Sharma	not out	18		
*Kapil.Dev	not out	2		
R.M.H.Binny				
Madan Lal				
†S.M.H.Kirmani				
B.S.Sandhu				
Extras	(W2)	2		
TOTAL	(37.3 overs; 5 wickets)	157		

INDIA	O	M	R	W	FALL OF WICKETS		
Kapil Dev	9	3	18	1	Wkt	Z	I
Sandhu	9	1	29	1	1st	13	13
Madan Lal	10.4	0	27	3	2nd	55	32
Binny	11	2	25	2	3rd	56	101
Shastri	12	1	38	1	4th	71	128
					5th	106	148
ZIMBABWE					6th	114	–
Rawson	5.1	1	11	2	7th	115	–
Curran	6.5	1	33	0	8th	139	–
Butchart	5	1	21	0	9th	148	–
Traicos	11	1	41	1	10th	155	–
Fletcher	6	1	32	1			
Shah	3.3	0	17	1			

Umpires: J.Birkenshaw (1) and R.Palmer (1).

ENGLAND v PAKISTAN

At Lord's, London, on 13 June 1983.   Toss: Pakistan.
Result: **ENGLAND** won by 8 wickets.   Award: Zaheer Abbas.
LOI debuts: None.

PAKISTAN		Runs	Balls	4/6
Mohsin Khan	c Tavaré b Willis	3	29	–
Mudassar Nazar	c Gould b Allott	26	98	2
Mansoor Akhtar	c Gould b Willis	3	15	–
Javed Miandad	c Gould b Botham	14	26	2
Zaheer Abbas	not out	83	104	7/1
*Imran Khan	run out	7	35	1
Wasim Raja	c Botham b Marks	9	19	2
Abdul Qadir	run out	0	2	–
Sarfraz Nawaz	c and b Botham	11	15	2
†Wasim Bari	not out	18	21	1
Rashid Khan				
Extras	(B5, LB8, W3, NB3)	19		
TOTAL	(60 overs; 8 wickets)	193		

ENGLAND		Runs	Balls	4/6
G.Fowler	not out	78	151	5
C.J.Tavaré	lbw b Rashid	8	21	–
D.I.Gower	c Sarfraz b Mansoor	48	72	6
A.J.Lamb	not out	48	62	5/1
M.W.Gatting				
I.T.Botham				
†I.J.Gould				
V.J.Marks				
G.R.Dilley				
P.J.W.Allott				
*R.G.D.Willis				
Extras	(B1, LB12, W2, NB2)	17		
TOTAL	(50.4 overs; 2 wickets)	199		

ENGLAND	O	M	R	W		FALL OF WICKETS		
Willis	12	4	24	2	Wkt	P	E	
Dilley	12	1	33	0	1st	29	15	
Allott	12	2	48	1	2nd	33	93	
Botham	12	3	36	2	3rd	49	–	
Marks	12	1	33	1	4th	67	–	
					5th	96	–	
PAKISTAN					6th	112	–	
Rashid Khan	7	2	19	1	7th	118	–	
Sarfraz Nawaz	11	5	22	0	8th	154	–	
Wasim Raja	3	0	14	0	9th	–	–	
Mudassar Nazar	8	0	30	0	10th	–	–	
Abdul Qadir	9.4	0	53	0				
Mansoor Akhtar	12	2	44	1				

Umpires: B.J.Meyer (11) and A.G.T.Whitehead (7).

NEW ZEALAND v SRI LANKA

At County Ground, Bristol, on 13 June 1983.　Toss: New Zealand.
Result: **NEW ZEALAND** won by 5 wickets.　Award: R.J.Hadlee.
LOI debuts: None.

SRI LANKA		Runs	Balls	4/6
S.Wettimuny	lbw b Hadlee	7	19	1
D.S.B.P.Kuruppu	c Hadlee b Chatfield	26	60	5
R.L.Dias	b Chatfield	25	43	4
*L.R.D.Mendis	b Hadlee	43	70	2
R.S.Madugalle	c Snedden b Coney	60	87	3/1
A.Ranatunga	lbw b Hadlee	0	3	–
D.S.de Silva	b Coney	13	20	–
†R.G.de Alwis	c Howarth b Snedden	16	17	2
A.L.F.de Mel	c and b Hadlee	1	6	–
R.J.Ratnayake	b Hadlee	5	9	–
V.B.John	not out	2	5	–
Extras	(LB6, W1, NB1)	8		
TOTAL	(56.1 overs)	**206**		

NEW ZEALAND		Runs	Balls	4/6
G.M.Turner	c Mendis b De Silva	50	60	8
J.G.Wright	lbw b De Mel	45	52	8
*G.P.Howarth	c Madugalle b Ratnayake	76	79	14
M.D.Crowe	c De Alwis b De Mel	0	11	–
J.J.Crowe	lbw b John	23	26	4
J.V.Coney	not out	2	10	–
†I.D.S.Smith	no. out	4	1	1
R.J.Hadlee				
B.L.Cairns				
M.C.Snedden				
E.J.Chatfield				
Extras	(LB6, W3)	9		
TOTAL	(39.2 overs; 5 wickets)	**209**		

NEW ZEALAND	O	M	R	W		FALL OF WICKETS		
Hadlee	10.1	4	25	5		Wkt	SL	NZ
Snedden	10	1	38	1		1st	16	89
Chatfield	12	4	24	2		2nd	56	99
Cairns	7	0	35	0		3rd	73	110
Coney	12	0	44	2		4th	144	176
M.D.Crowe	5	0	32	0		5th	144	205
						6th	171	–
SRI LANKA						7th	196	–
De Mel	8	2	30	2		8th	199	–
John	8.2	0	49	1		9th	199	–
Ratnayake	12	0	60	1		10th	206	–
De Silva	9	0	39	1				
Ranatunga	2	0	22	0				

Umpires: H.D.Bird (20) and D.R.Shepherd (2).

AUSTRALIA v INDIA

At Trent Bridge, Nottingham, on 13 June 1983.   Toss: Australia.
Result: **AUSTRALIA** won by 162 runs.   Award: T.M.Chappell.
LOI debuts: None.

AUSTRALIA		Runs	Balls	4/6
K.C.Wessels	b Kapil Dev	5	11	1
T.M.Chappell	c Srikkanth b Amarnath	110	131	11
*K.J.Hughes	b Madan Lal	52	86	3
D.W.Hookes	c Kapil Dev b Madan Lal	1	4	–
G.N.Yallop	not out	66	73	5
A.R.Border	c Yashpal b Binny	26	23	1
†R.W.Marsh	c Sandhu b Kapil Dev	12	15	1
K.H.Macleay	c and b Kapil Dev	4	5	–
T.G.Hogan	b Kapil Dev	11	9	–/1
G.F.Lawson	c Srikkanth b Kapil Dev	6	3	1
R.M.Hogg	not out	2	2	–
Extras	(B1, LB14, W8, NB2)	25		
TOTAL	(60 overs; 9 wickets)	320		

INDIA		Runs	Balls	4/6
R.J.Shastri	lbw b Lawson	11	18	1
K.Srikkanth	c Border b Hogan	39	63	6
M.Amarnath	run out	2	17	–
D.B.Vengsarkar	lbw b Macleay	5	14	1
S.M.Patil	b Macleay	0	7	–
Yashpal Sharma	c and b Macleay	3	11	–
*Kapil Dev	b Hogan	40	27	2/1
Madan Lal	c Hogan b Macleay	27	39	2
R.M.H.Binny	lbw b Macleay	0	6	–
†S.M.H.Kirmani	b Macleay	12	23	2
B.S.Sandhu	not out	9	12	–/1
Extras	(B1, LB4, W3, NB2)	10		
TOTAL	(37.5 overs)	158		

INDIA	O	M	R	W		FALL OF WICKETS		
Kapil Dev	12	2	43	5		Wkt	A	I
Sandhu	12	1	52	0		1st	11	38
Binny	12	0	52	1		2nd	155	43
Shastri	2	0	16	0		3rd	159	57
Madan Lal	12	0	69	2		4th	206	57
Patil	6	0	36	0		5th	254	64
Amarnath	4	0	27	1		6th	277	66
						7th	289	124
AUSTRALIA						8th	301	126
Lawson	5	1	25	1		9th	307	136
Hogg	7	2	23	0		10th	–	158
Hogan	12	1	48	2				
Macleay	11.5	3	39	6				
Border	2	0	13	0				

Umpires: D.O.Oslear (4) and R.Palmer (2).

WEST INDIES v ZIMBABWE

At New Road, Worcester, on 13 June 1983.   Toss: West Indies.
Result: **WEST INDIES** won by 8 wickets.   Award: C.G.Greenidge.
LOI debuts: Zimbabwe – G.E.Peckover.

ZIMBABWE		Runs	Balls	4/6
A.H.Shah	b Roberts	2		
G.A.Paterson	c Dujon b Holding	4		
J.G.Heron	st Dujon b Gomes	12	73	
A.J.Pycroft	run out	13		
†D.L.Houghton	c Dujon b Roberts	54		
*D.A.G.Fletcher	not out	71		
K.M.Curran	b Roberts	7		
I.P.Butchart	lbw b Holding	0		
G.E.Peckover	not out	16		
P.W.E.Rawson				
A.J.Traicos				
Extras	(B1, LB23, W7, NB7)	38		
TOTAL	(60 overs; 7 wickets)	217		

WEST INDIES		Runs	Balls	4/6
C.G.Greenidge	not out	105		5/1
D.L.Haynes	c Houghton b Rawson	2		
I.V.A.Richards	lbw b Rawson	16		
H.A.Gomes	not out	75		
S.F.A.F.Bacchus				
*C.H.Lloyd				
†P.J.L.Dujon				
A.M.E.Roberts				
M.A.Holding				
W.W.Daniel				
W.W.Davis				
Extras	(B1, LB8, W9, NB2)	20		
TOTAL	(48.3 overs; 2 wickets)	218		

WEST INDIES	O	M	R	W		FALL OF WICKETS		
					Wkt	Z	WI	
Roberts	12	4	36	3	1st	3	3	
Holding	12	2	33	2	2nd	7	23	
Daniel	12	4	21	0	3rd	35	–	
Davis	12	2	34	0	4th	65	–	
Gomes	8	0	42	1	5th	157	–	
Richards	4	1	13	0	6th	181	–	
					7th	183	–	
ZIMBABWE					8th	–	–	
Rawson	12	1	39	2	9th	–	–	
Curran	10.3	1	37	0	10th	–	–	
Butchart	9	1	40	0				
Fletcher	4	0	22	0				
Traicos	9	0	37	0				
Shah	4	0	23	0				

Umpires: J.Birkenshaw (2) and D.G.L.Evans (8).

ENGLAND v NEW ZEALAND

At Edgbaston, Birmingham, on 15 June 1983.   Toss: England.
Result: **NEW ZEALAND** won by 2 wickets.   Award: J.V.Coney.
LOI debuts: None.

ENGLAND		Runs	Balls	4/6
G.Fowler	c J.J.Crowe b Chatfield	69	112	9
C.J.Tavaré	c Cairns b Coney	18	44	1
I.T.Botham	c and b Bracewell	12	9	1/1
D.I.Gower	not out	92	96	6/4
A.J.Lamb	c J.J.Crowe b Cairns	8	14	1
M.W.Gatting	b Cairns	1	5	–
†I.J.Gould	lbw b Cairns	4	14	–
V.J.Marks	b Hadlee	5	15	–
G.R.Dilley	b Hadlee	10	19	–
P.J.W.Allott	c Smith b Hadlee	0	1	–
*R.G.D.Willis	lbw b Chatfield	0	3	–
Extras	(B4, LB10, W1)	15		
TOTAL	(55.2 overs)	234		

NEW ZEALAND		Runs	Balls	4/6
G.M.Turner	lbw b Willis	2	5	–
B.A.Edgar	c Gould b Willis	1	6	–
*G.P.Howarth	run out	60	104	5/1
J.J.Crowe	b Allott	17	46	1
M.D.Crowe	b Marks	20	40	2
J.V.Coney	not out	66	97	9
†I.D.S.Smith	b Botham	4	6	1
R.J.Hadlee	b Willis	31	45	3
B.L.Cairns	lbw b Willis	5	6	–
J.G.Bracewell	not out	4	7	1
E.J.Chatfield				
Extras	(B2, LB22, W1, NB3)	28		
TOTAL	(59.5 overs; 8 wickets)	238		

NEW ZEALAND	O	M	R	W		FALL OF WICKETS	
					Wkt	E	NZ
Hadlee	10	3	32	3			
Cairns	11	0	44	3	1st	63	2
Coney	12	2	27	1	2nd	77	3
Bracewell	12	0	66	1	3rd	117	47
Chatfield	10.2	0	50	2	4th	143	75
					5th	154	146
ENGLAND					6th	162	151
Willis	12	1	42	4	7th	203	221
Dilley	12	1	43	0	8th	233	231
Botham	12	1	47	1	9th	233	–
Allott	11.5	2	44	1	10th	234	–
Marks	12	1	34	1			

Umpires: J.Birkenshaw (3) and K.E.Palmer (11).

WEST INDIES v INDIA

At Kennington Oval, London, on 15 June 1983.　Toss: West Indies.
Result: **WEST INDIES** won by 66 runs.　Award: I.V.A.Richards.
LOI debuts: None.

WEST INDIES		Runs	Balls	4/6
C.G.Greenidge	c Vengsarkar b Kapil Dev	9		
D.L.Haynes	c Kapil Dev b Amarnath	38		
I.V.A.Richards	c Kirmani b Sandhu	119	146	6/1
*C.H.Lloyd	run out	41		
S.F.A.F.Bacchus	b Binny	8		
†P.J.L.Dujon	c Shastri b Binny	9		
H.A.Gomes	not out	27		
A.M.E.Roberts	c Patil b Binny	7		
M.D.Marshall	run out	4		
M.A.Holding	c sub (K.Azad) b Madan Lal	2		
W.W.Davis	not out	0		
Extras	(LB13, W5)	18		
TOTAL	(60 overs; 9 wickets)	282		

INDIA		Runs	Balls	4/6
K.Srikkanth	c Dujon b Roberts	2		
R.J.Shastri	c Dujon b Roberts	6		
M.Amarnath	c Lloyd b Holding	80		
D.B.Vengsarkar	retired hurt	32		
S.M.Patil	c and b Gomes	21		
Yashpal Sharma	run out	9		
*Kapil Dev	c Haynes b Holding	36		
R.M.H.Binny	lbw b Holding	1		
Madan Lal	not out	8		
†S.M.H.Kirmani	b Marshall	0		
B.S.Sandhu	run out	0		
Extras	(B3, LB13, NB5)	21		
TOTAL	(53.1 overs)	216		

INDIA	O	M	R	W		FALL OF WICKETS		
Kapil Dev	12	0	46	1		Wkt	WI	I
Sandhu	12	2	42	1		1st	17	2
Binny	12	0	71	3		2nd	118	21
Amarnath	12	0	58	1		3rd	198	130
Madan Lal	12	0	47	1		4th	213	143
						5th	239	193
WEST INDIES						6th	240	195
Roberts	9	1	29	2		7th	257	212
Holding	9.1	0	40	3		8th	270	214
Marshall	11	3	20	1		9th	280	216
Davis	12	2	51	0		10th	–	–
Gomes	12	1	55	1				

Umpires: B.J.Meyer (12) and D.R.Shepherd (3).

PAKISTAN v SRI LANKA

At Headingley, Leeds, on 16 June 1983. Toss: Sri Lanka.
Result: **PAKISTAN** won by 11 runs. Award: Abdul Qadir.
LOI debuts: None.

PAKISTAN		Runs	Balls	4/6
Mohsin Khan	c Ranatunga b De Mel	3		
Mansoor Akhtar	c De Alwis b De Mel	6		
Zaheer Abbas	c Dias b De Mel	15		
Javed Miandad	lbw b Ratnayake	7		
*Imran Khan	not out	102		
Ijaz Faqih	lbw b Ratnayake	0		
Shahid Mahboob	c De Silva b De Mel	77		
Sarfraz Nawaz	c Madugalle b De Mel	9		
Abdul Qadir	not out	5		
†Wasim Bari				
Rashid Khan				
Extras	(B1, LB4, W4, NB2)	11		
TOTAL	(60 overs; 7 wickets)	235		

SRI LANKA		Runs	Balls	4/6
S.Wettimuny	c Shahid b Rashid	50		
D.S.B.P.Kuruppu	b Rashid	12		
R.L.Dias	st Wasim b Qadir	47		
*L.R.D.Mendis	c Wasim b Qadir	33		
R.J.Ratnayake	st Wasim b Qadir	1		
R.S.Madugalle	c Qadir b Shahid	26		
A.Ranatunga	c Zaheer b Qadir	0		
D.S.de Silva	run out	1		
†R.G.de Alwis	c Miandad b Qadir	4		
A.L.F.de Mel	c Imran b Sarfraz	17		
V.B.John	not out	6		
Extras	(LB8, W17, NB2)	27		
TOTAL	(58.3 overs)	224		

SRI LANKA	O	M	R	W		FALL OF WICKETS	
De Mel	12	1	39	5	Wkt	P	SL
John	12	1	48	0	1st	6	22
Ratnayake	12	2	42	2	2nd	25	101
Ranatunga	11	0	49	0	3rd	30	162
De Silva	12	1	42	0	4th	43	162
Wettimuny	1	0	4	0	5th	43	166
					6th	187	166
PAKISTAN					7th	204	171
Rashid Khan	12	4	31	2	8th	–	193
Sarfraz Nawaz	11.3	2	25	1	9th	–	199
Shahid Mahboob	10	1	62	1	10th	–	224
Mansoor Akhtar	1	0	8	0			
Ijaz Faqih	12	0	27	0			
Abdul Qadir	12	1	44	5			

Umpires: D.O.Oslear (5) and A.G.T.Whitehead (8).

AUSTRALIA v ZIMBABWE

At County Ground, Southampton, on 16 June 1983.   Toss: Australia.
Result: **AUSTRALIA** won by 32 runs.   Award: D.L.Houghton.
LOI debuts: None.

AUSTRALIA		Runs	Balls	4/6
G.M.Wood	c Rawson b Traicos	73		5
T.M.Chappell	c Traicos b Rawson	22		4
*K.J.Hughes	b Traicos	31		2
D.W.Hookes	c Brown b Fletcher	10	14	–
G.N.Yallop	c Houghton b Curran	20		3
A.R.Border	b Butchart	43	61	2
†R.W.Marsh	not out	35		1/2
K.H.Macleay	c Rawson b Butchart	9		–/1
T.G.Hogan	not out	5		–
D.K.Lillee				
R.M.Hogg				
Extras	(LB16, W2, NB6)	24		
TOTAL	(60 overs; 7 wickets)	272		

ZIMBABWE		Runs	Balls	4/6
R.D.Brown	c Marsh b Hogan	38		4
G.A.Paterson	lbw b Hogg	17		1
J.G.Heron	run out	3		–
A.J.Pycroft	run out	13	24	1
†D.L.Houghton	c Hughes b Chappell	84	65	9/1
*D.A.G.Fletcher	b Hogan	2		–
K.M.Curran	lbw b Chappell	35		2
I.P.Butchart	lbw b Hogg	0		–
P.W.E.Rawson	lbw b Hogg	0		–
A.J.Traicos	b Chappell	19	37	2
V.R.Hogg	not out	7		–
Extras	(B1, LB10, W1, NB10)	22		
TOTAL	(59.5 overs)	240		

ZIMBABWE	O	M	R	W		FALL OF WICKETS		
Hogg	9	2	34	0	Wkt	A	Z	
Rawson	9	0	50	1	1st	46	48	
Fletcher	9	1	27	1	2nd	124	53	
Butchart	10	0	52	2	3rd	150	79	
Traicos	12	1	28	2	4th	150	97	
Curran	1	0	57	1	5th	219	109	
					6th	231	212	
AUSTRALIA					7th	249	213	
Hogg	12	0	40	3	8th	–	213	
Lillee	9	1	23	0	9th	–	213	
Hogan	12	0	33	2	10th	–	240	
Macleay	9	0	45	0				
Border	9	1	30	0				
Chappell	8.5	0	47	3				

Umpires: D.G.L.Evans (9) and R.Palmer (3).

ENGLAND v PAKISTAN

At Old Trafford, Manchester, on 18 June 1983.　Toss: Pakistan.
Result: **ENGLAND** won by 7 wickets.　Award: G.Fowler.
LOI debuts: None.

PAKISTAN		Runs	Balls	4/6
Mohsin Khan	c Marks b Allott	32	98	3
Mudassar Nazar	c Gould b Dilley	18	23	2
Zaheer Abbas	c Gould b Dilley	0	8	–
Javed Miandad	run out	67	100	6
*Imran Khan	c Willis b Marks	13	28	2
Wasim Raja	c Willis b Marks	15	24	3
Ijaz Faqih	not out	42	52	5
Sarfraz Nawaz	b Willis	17	20	1/1
Abdul Qadir	run out	6	7	–
†Wasim Bari	not out	2	3	–
Rashid Khan				
Extras	(B3, LB14, W2, NB1)	20		
TOTAL	(60 overs; 8 wickets)	232		

ENGLAND		Runs	Balls	4/6
G.Fowler	c Miandad b Mudassar	69	96	7
C.J.Tavaré	c Wasim Raja b Zaheer	58	116	5
D.I.Gower	c Zaheer b Mudassar	31	48	3
A.J.Lamb	not out	38	57	4
M.W.Gatting	not out	14	27	1
I.T.Botham				
†I.J.Gould				
V.J.Marks				
G.R.Dilley				
P.J.W.Allott				
*R.G.D.Willis				
Extras	(B1, LB15, W7)	23		
TOTAL	(57.2 overs; 3 wickets)	233		

ENGLAND	O	M	R	W		FALL OF WICKETS	
Willis	12	3	37	1	Wkt	P	E
Dilley	12	2	46	2	1st	33	115
Allott	12	1	33	1	2nd	34	165
Botham	12	1	51	0	3rd	87	181
Marks	12	0	45	2	4th	116	–
					5th	144	–
PAKISTAN					6th	169	–
Rashid Khan	11	1	58	0	7th	204	–
Sarfraz Nawaz	10.2	2	22	0	8th	221	–
Abdul Qadir	11	0	51	0	9th	–	–
Ijaz Faqih	6	0	19	0	10th	–	–
Mudassar Nazar	12	2	34	2			
Zaheer Abbas	7	0	26	1			

Umpires: H.D.Bird (21) and D.O.Oslear (6).

NEW ZEALAND v SRI LANKA

At County Ground, Derby, on 18 June 1983.　Toss: Sri Lanka.
Result: **SRI LANKA** won by 3 wickets.　Award: A.L.F.de Mel.
LOI debuts: None.

NEW ZEALAND		Runs	Balls	4/6
G.M.Turner	c Dias b De Mel	6	10	1
J.G.Wright	c De Alwis b De Mel	0	7	–
*G.P.Howarth	b Ratnayake	15	23	2
M.D.Crowe	lbw b Ratnayake	8	32	–
B.A.Edgar	c Samarasekera b De Silva	27	77	3
J.V.Coney	c sub (E.R.N.S.Fernando) b De Silva	22	50	2
R.J.Hadlee	c Madugalle b De Mel	15	39	3
†W.K.Lees	c Ranatunga b De Mel	2	16	–
B.L.Cairns	c Dias b De Mel	6	7	1
M.C.Snedden	run out	40	55	5
E.J.Chatfield	not out	19	48	2
Extras	(B4, LB5, W11, NB1)	21		
TOTAL	(58.2 overs)	181		

SRI LANKA		Runs	Balls	4/6
S.Wettimuny	b Cairns	4	30	–
D.S.B.P.Kuruppu	c and b Snedden	62	120	10
A.Ranatunga	b Crowe	15	22	2
R.L.Dias	not out	64	101	9
*L.R.D.Mendis	lbw b Chatfield	0	2	–
R.S.Madugalle	c Lees b Snedden	6	18	–
M.A.R.Samarasekera	c Lees b Hadlee	5	11	–
D.S.de Silva	run out	2	10	–
†R.G.de Alwis	not out	11	10	1
A.L.F.de Mel				
R.J.Ratnayake				
Extras	(B1, LB4, W10)	15		
TOTAL	(52.5 overs; 7 wickets)	184		

SRI LANKA	O	M	R	W		FALL OF WICKETS		
De Mel	12	4	32	5	Wkt	NZ	SL	
Ratnayake	11	4	18	2	1st	8	15	
Ranatunga	10	2	50	0	2nd	8	49	
De Silva	12	5	11	2	3rd	32	129	
Samarasekera	11.2	2	38	0	4th	47	130	
Wettimuny	2	0	11	0	5th	88	139	
					6th	91	151	
NEW ZEALAND					7th	105	161	
Hadlee	12	3	16	1	8th	115		
Cairns	10	2	35	1	9th	116		
Snedden	10.5	1	58	1	10th	181		
Chatfield	12	3	23	1				
Crowe	4	2	15	1				
Coney	4	1	20	0				

Umpires: D.J.Constant (21) and B.Leadbeater (3).

AUSTRALIA v WEST INDIES

At Lord's, London, on 18 June 1983.　Toss: Australia.
Result: **WEST INDIES** won by 7 wickets.　Award: I.V.A.Richards.
LOI debuts: None.

AUSTRALIA		Runs	Balls	4/6
G.M.Wood	b Marshall	17	24	–
T.M.Chappell	c Dujon b Marshall	5	14	1
*K.J.Hughes	b Gomes	69	124	8
D.W.Hookes	c Greenidge b Davis	56	74	4/2
G.N.Yallop	not out	52	74	3
A.R.Border	c and b Gomes	11	24	1
†R.W.Marsh	c Haynes b Holding	37	26	4/2
T.G.Hogan	not out	0	1	–
J.R.Thomson				
D.K.Lillee				
R.M.Hogg				
Extras	(B1, LB18, W6, NB1)	26		
TOTAL	(60 overs; 6 wickets)	273		

WEST INDIES		Runs	Balls	4/6
C.G.Greenidge	c Hughes b Hogg	90	140	8
D.L.Haynes	b Hogan	33	46	3
I.V.A.Richards	not out	95	117	9/3
H.A.Gomes	b Chappell	15	26	1
*C.H.Lloyd	not out	19	22	3
S.F.A.F.Bacchus				
†P.J.L.Dujon				
M.D.Marshall				
A.M.E.Roberts				
M.A.Holding				
W.W.Davis				
Extras	(B3, LB18, W1, NB2)	24		
TOTAL	(57.5 overs; 3 wickets)	276		

WEST INDIES	O	M	R	W		FALL OF WICKETS	
Roberts	12	0	51	0	Wkt	A	WI
Marshall	12	0	36	2	1st	10	79
Davis	12	0	57	1	2nd	37	203
Holding	12	1	56	1	3rd	138	228
Gomes	12	0	47	2	4th	176	–
					5th	202	–
AUSTRALIA					6th	266	–
Hogg	12	0	25	1	7th	–	–
Thomson	11	0	64	0	8th	–	–
Hogan	12	0	60	1	9th	–	–
Lillee	12	0	52	0	10th	–	–
Chappell	10.5	0	51	1			

Umpires: K.E.Palmer (12) and A.G.T.Whitehead (9).

INDIA v ZIMBABWE

At Nevill Ground, Tunbridge Wells, on 18 June 1983.   Toss: India.
Result: **INDIA** won by 31 runs.   Award: Kapil Dev.
LOI debuts: None.

INDIA		**Runs**	**Balls**	**4/6**
S.M.Gavaskar	lbw b Rawson	0		
K.Srikkanth	c Butchart b Curran	0		
M.Amarnath	c Houghton b Rawson	5		
S.M.Patil	c Houghton b Curran	1		
Yashpal Sharma	c Houghton b Rawson	9		
Kapil Dev	not out	175		16/6
*R.M.H.Binny	lbw b Traicos	22		
R.J.Shastri	c Pycroft b Fletcher	1		
Madan Lal	c Houghton b Curran	17		
†S.M.H.Kirmani	not out	24		
B.S.Sandhu				
Extras	(LB9, W3)	12		
TOTAL	(60 overs; 8 wickets)	**266**		

ZIMBABWE		**Runs**	**Balls**	**4/6**
R.D.Brown	run out	35		
G.A.Paterson	lbw b Binny	23		
J.G.Heron	run out	3		
A.J.Pycroft	c Kirmani b Sandhu	6		
†D.L.Houghton	lbw b Madan Lal	17		
*D.A.G.Fletcher	c Kapil Dev b Amarnath	13		
K.M.Curran	c Shastri b Madan Lal	73		
I.P.Butchart	b Binny	18		
G.E.Peckover	c Yashpal b Madan Lal	14		
P.W.E.Rawson	not out	2		
A.J.Traicos	c and b Kapil Dev	3		
Extras	(LB17, W7, NB4)	28		
TOTAL	(57 overs)	**235**		

ZIMBABWE	O	M	R	W		FALL OF WICKETS		
Rawson	12	4	47	3		Wkt	I	Z
Curran	12	1	65	3		1st	0	44
Butchart	12	2	38	0		2nd	6	48
Fletcher	12	2	59	1		3rd	6	61
Traicos	12	0	45	1		4th	9	86
						5th	17	103
INDIA						6th	77	113
Kapil Dev	11	1	32	1		7th	78	168
Sandhu	11	2	44	1		8th	140	189
Binny	11	2	45	2		9th	–	230
Madan Lal	11	2	42	3		10th	–	235
Amarnath	12	1	37	1				
Shastri	1	0	7	0				

Umpires: M.J.Kitchen (3) and B.J.Meyer (13).

ENGLAND v SRI LANKA

At Headingley, Leeds, on 20 June 1983.   Toss: England.
Result: **ENGLAND** won by 9 wickets.   Award: R.G.D.Willis.
LOI debuts: None.

SRI LANKA		Runs	Balls	4/6
S.Wettimuny	lbw b Botham	22	49	3
D.S.B.P.Kuruppu	c Gatting b Willis	6	36	1
A.Ranatunga	c Lamb b Botham	0	16	–
R.L.Dias	c Gould b Cowans	7	24	1
*L.R.D.Mendis	b Allott	10	38	–
R.S.Madugalle	c Gould b Allott	0	6	–
D.S.de Silva	c Gower b Marks	15	36	1
†R.G.de Alwis	c Marks b Cowans	19	20	2/1
A.L.F.de Mel	c Lamb b Marks	10	23	2
R.J.Ratnayake	not out	20	32	1/1
V.B.John	c Cowans b Allott	15	27	1
Extras	(B5, LB2, W3, NB2)	12		
TOTAL	(50.4 overs)	136		

ENGLAND		Runs	Balls	4/6
G.Fowler	not out	81	77	11
C.J.Tavaré	c De Alwis b De Mel	19	48	1/1
D.I.Gower	not out	27	24	3
A.J.Lamb				
M.W.Gatting				
I.T.Botham				
†I.J.Gould				
V.J.Marks				
P.J.W.Allott				
*R.G.D.Willis				
N.G.Cowans				
Extras	(B1, LB3, W3, NB3)	10		
TOTAL	(24.1 overs; 1 wicket)	137		

ENGLAND	O	M	R	W		FALL OF WICKETS		
Willis	9	4	9	1		Wkt	SL	E
Cowans	12	3	31	2		1st	25	68
Botham	9	4	12	2		2nd	30	–
Allott	10.4	0	41	3		3rd	32	–
Gatting	4	2	13	0		4th	40	–
Marks	6	2	18	2		5th	43	–
						6th	54	–
SRI LANKA						7th	81	–
De Mel	10	1	33	1		8th	97	–
Ratnayake	5	0	23	0		9th	103	–
John	6	0	41	0		10th	136	–
De Silva	3	0	29	0				
Ranatunga	0.1	0	1	0				

Umpires: B.Leadbeater (4) and R.Palmer (4).

NEW ZEALAND v PAKISTAN

At Trent Bridge, Nottingham, on 20 June 1983.   Toss: Pakistan.
Result: **PAKISTAN** won by 11 runs.   Award: Imran Khan.
LOI debuts: None.

PAKISTAN		Runs	Balls	4/6
Mohsin Khan	c Cairns b Coney	33	64	3
Mudassar Nazar	b Coney	15	60	–
Javed Miandad	b Hadlee	25	45	1
Zaheer Abbas	not out	103	121	6
*Imran Khan	not out	79	74	7/1
Ijaz Faqih				
Shahid Mahboob				
Sarfraz Nawaz				
Abdul Qadir				
†Wasim Bari				
Rashid Khan				
Extras	(B1, LB2, W2, NB1)	6		
TOTAL	(60 overs; 3 wickets)	261		

NEW ZEALAND		Runs	Balls	4/6
G.M.Turner	c Wasim b Sarfraz	4	16	–
J.G.Wright	c Imran b Qadir	19	57	1
*G.P.Howarth	c Miandad b Zaheer	39	51	3
M.D.Crowe	b Mudassar	43	62	4
B.A.Edgar	lbw b Shahid	6	22	–
J.V.Coney	run out	51	78	3
R.J.Hadlee	c Mohsin b Mudassar	11	20	1
B.L.Cairns	c Imran b Qadir	0	3	–
†W.K.Lees	c sub (Mansoor Akhtar) b Mudassar	26	25	4
J.G.Bracewell	c Mohsin b Sarfraz	34	24	7
E.J.Chatfield	not out	3	6	–
Extras	(LB8, W5, NB1)	14		
TOTAL	(59.1 overs)	250		

NEW ZEALAND	O	M	R	W		FALL OF WICKETS	
					Wkt	P	NZ
Hadlee	12	1	61	1	1st	48	13
Cairns	12	1	45	0	2nd	54	44
Chatfield	12	0	57	0	3rd	114	85
Coney	12	0	42	2	4th	–	102
Bracewell	12	0	50	0	5th	–	130
					6th	–	150
PAKISTAN					7th	–	152
Rashid Khan	6	1	24	0	8th	–	187
Sarfraz Nawaz	9.1	1	50	2	9th	–	246
Abdul Qadir	12	0	53	2	10th	–	250
Ijaz Faqih	6	1	21	0			
Shahid Mahboob	10	0	37	1			
Mudassar Nazar	12	0	43	3			
Zaheer Abbas	4	1	8	1			

Umpires: D.G.L.Evans (10) and M.J.Kitchen (4).

AUSTRALIA v INDIA

At County Ground, Chelmsford, on 20 June 1983.　Toss: India.
Result: **INDIA** won by 118 runs.　Award: R.M.H.Binny.
LOI debuts: None.

INDIA		Runs	Balls	4/6
S.M.Gavaskar	c Chappell b Hogg	9	10	1
K.Srikkanth	c Border b Thomson	24	22	3
M.Amarnath	c Marsh b Thomson	13	20	2
Yashpal Sharma	c Hogg b Hogan	40	40	1
S.M.Patil	c Hogan b Macleay	30	25	4
*Kapil Dev	c Hookes b Hogg	28	32	3
K.Azad	c Border b Lawson	15	18	1
R.M.H.Binny	run out	21	32	2
Madan Lal	not out	12	15	–
†S.M.H.Kirmani	lbw b Hogg	10	20	1
B.S.Sandhu	b Thomson	8	18	1
Extras	(LB13, W9, NB15)	37		
TOTAL	(55.5 overs)	247		

AUSTRALIA		Runs	Balls	4/6
T.M.Chappell	c Madan Lal b Sandhu	2	5	–
G.M.Wood	c Kirmani b Binny	21	32	2
G.N.Yallop	c and b Binny	18	30	2
*D.W.Hookes	b Binny	1	2	–
A.R.Border	b Madan Lal	36	49	5
†R.W.Marsh	lbw b Madan Lal	0	2	–
K.H.Macleay	c Gavaskar b Madan Lal	5	6	1
T.G.Hogan	c Srikkanth b Binny	8	10	2
G.F.Lawson	b Sandhu	16	20	1
R.M.Hogg	not out	8	12	1
J.R.Thomson	b Madan Lal	0	5	–
Extras	(LB5, W5, NB4)	14		
TOTAL	(38.2 overs)	129		

AUSTRALIA	O	M	R	W		FALL OF WICKETS	
Lawson	10	1	40	1	Wkt	I	A
Hogg	12	2	40	3	1st	27	3
Hogan	11	1	31	1	2nd	54	46
Thomson	10.5	0	51	3	3rd	65	48
Macleay	12	2	48	1	4th	118	52
					5th	157	52
INDIA					6th	174	69
Kapil Dev	8	2	16	0	7th	207	78
Sandhu	10	1	26	2	8th	215	115
Madan Lal	8.2	3	20	4	9th	232	129
Binny	8	2	29	4	10th	247	129
Amarnath	2	0	17	0			
Azad	2	0	7	0			

Umpires: J.Birkenshaw (4) and D.R.Shepherd (4).

WEST INDIES v ZIMBABWE

At Edgbaston, Birmingham, on 20 June 1983.　Toss: Zimbabwe.
Result: **WEST INDIES** won by 10 wickets.　Award: S.F.A.F.Bacchus.
LOI debuts: None.

ZIMBABWE		Runs	Balls	4/6
R.D.Brown	c Lloyd b Marshall	14		
G.A.Paterson	c Richards b Garner	6		
J.G.Heron	c Dujon b Garner	0		
A.J.Pycroft	c Dujon b Marshall	4		
†D.L.Houghton	c Lloyd b Daniel	0		
*D.A.G.Fletcher	b Richards	23		
K.M.Curran	b Daniel	62		
I.P.Butchart	c Haynes b Richards	8		
G.E.Peckover	c and b Richards	3		
P.W.E.Rawson	b Daniel	19		
A.J.Traicos	not out	1		
Extras	(B4, LB13, W7, NB7)	31		
TOTAL	(60 overs)	171		

WEST INDIES		Runs	Balls	4/6
D.L.Haynes	not out	88		
S.F.A.F.Bacchus	not out	80		
A.L.Logie				
I.V.A.Richards				
H.A.Gomes				
*C.H.Lloyd				
†P.J.L.Dujon				
M.D.Marshall				
J.Garner				
W.W.Daniel				
W.W.Davis				
Extras	(LB1, W3)	4		
TOTAL	(45.1 overs; 0 wickets)	172		

WEST INDIES	O	M	R	W		FALL OF WICKETS		
Marshall	12	3	19	2	Wkt	Z	WI	
Garner	7	4	13	2	1st	17	–	
Davis	8	2	13	0	2nd	17	–	
Daniel	9	2	28	3	3rd	41	–	
Gomes	12	2	26	0	4th	42	–	
Richards	12	1	41	3	5th	42	–	
					6th	79	–	
ZIMBABWE					7th	104	–	
Rawson	12	3	38	0	8th	115	–	
Butchart	4	0	23	0	9th	170	–	
Traicos	12	2	24	0	10th	171	–	
Curran	9	0	44	0				
Fletcher	8.1	0	39	0				

Umpires: H.D.Bird (22) and D.J.Constant (22).

ENGLAND v INDIA (SEMI-FINAL)

At Old Trafford, Manchester, on 22 June 1983.   Toss: England.
Result: **INDIA** won by 6 wickets.   Award: M.Amarnath.
LOI debuts: None.

ENGLAND		Runs	Balls	4/6
G.Fowler	b Binny	33	59	3
C.J.Tavaré	c Kirmani b Binny	32	51	4
D.I.Gower	c Kirmani b Amarnath	17	30	1
A.J.Lamb	run out	29	58	1
M.W.Gatting	b Amarnath	18	46	1
I.T.Botham	b Azad	6	26	–
†I.J.Gould	run out	13	36	–
V.J.Marks	b Kapil Dev	8	18	–
G.R.Dilley	not out	20	26	2
P.J.W.Allott	c Patil b Kapil Dev	8	14	–
*R.G.D.Willis	b Kapil Dev	0	2	–
Extras	(B1, LB17, W7, NB4)	29		
TOTAL	(60 overs)	213		

INDIA		Runs	Balls	4/6
S.M.Gavaskar	c Gould b Allott	25	41	3
K.Srikkanth	c Willis b Botham	19	44	3
M.Amarnath	run out	46	92	4/1
Yashpal Sharma	c Allott b Willis	61	115	3/2
S.M.Patil	not out	51	32	8
*Kapil Dev	not out	1	6	–
K.Azad				
R.M.H.Binny				
Madan Lal				
†S.M.H.Kirmani				
B.S.Sandhu				
Extras	(B5, LB6, W1, NB2)	14		
TOTAL	(54.4 overs; 4 wickets)	217		

INDIA	O	M	R	W		FALL OF WICKETS	
					Wkt	E	I
Kapil Dev	11	1	35	3	1st	69	46
Sandhu	8	1	36	0	2nd	84	50
Binny	12	1	43	2	3rd	107	142
Madan Lal	5	0	15	0	4th	141	205
Azad	12	1	28	1	5th	150	–
Amarnath	12	1	27	2	6th	160	–
					7th	175	–
ENGLAND					8th	177	–
Willis	10.4	2	42	1	9th	202	–
Dilley	11	0	43	0	10th	213	–
Allott	10	3	40	1			
Botham	11	4	40	1			
Marks	12	1	38	0			

Umpires: D.G.L.Evans (11) and D.O.Oslear (7).

PAKISTAN v WEST INDIES (SEMI-FINAL)

At Kennington Oval, London, on 22 June 1983.   Toss: West Indies.
Result: **WEST INDIES** won by 8 wickets.   Award: I.V.A.Richards.
LOI debuts: None.

PAKISTAN		Runs	Balls	4/6
Mohsin Khan	b Roberts	70		1
Mudassar Nazar	c and b Garner	11		
Ijaz Faqih	c Dujon b Holding	5		
Zaheer Abbas	b Gomes	30		
*Imran Khan	c Dujon b Marshall	17		
Wasim Raja	lbw b Marshall	0		
Shahid Mahboob	c Richards b Marshall	6		
Sarfraz Nawaz	c Holding b Roberts	3		
Abdul Qadir	not out	10		
†Wasim Bari	not out	4		
Rashid Khan				
Extras	(B6, LB13, W4, NB5)	28		
TOTAL	(60 overs; 8 wickets)	184		

WEST INDIES		Runs	Balls	4/6
C.G.Greenidge	lbw b Rashid	17		
D.L.Haynes	b Qadir	29		
I.V.A.Richards	not out	80		11/1
H.A.Gomes	not out	50		3
*C.H.Lloyd				
S.F.A.F.Bacchus				
†P.J.L.Dujon				
M.D.Marshall				
A.M.E.Roberts				
J.Garner				
M.A.Holding				
Extras	(B2, LB6, W4)	12		
TOTAL	(48.4 overs; 2 wickets)	188		

WEST INDIES	O	M	R	W	FALL OF WICKETS		
					Wkt	P	WI
Roberts	12	3	25	2	1st	23	34
Garner	12	1	31	1	2nd	34	56
Marshall	12	2	28	3	3rd	88	–
Holding	12	1	25	1	4th	139	–
Gomes	7	0	29	1	5th	139	–
Richards	5	0	18	0	6th	159	–
					7th	164	–
PAKISTAN					8th	171	–
Rashid Khan	12	2	32	1	9th	–	–
Sarfraz Nawaz	8	0	23	0	10th	–	–
Abdul Qadir	11	1	42	1			
Shahid Mahboob	11	1	43	0			
Wasim Raja	1	0	9	0			
Zaheer Abbas	4.4	1	24	0			
Mohsin Khan	1	0	3	0			

Umpires: D.J.Constant (23) and A.G.T.Whitehead (10).

WEST INDIES v INDIA (FINAL)

At Lord's, London, on 25 June 1983.　　Toss: West Indies.
Result: **INDIA** won by 43 runs.　　Award: M.Amarnath.
LOI debuts: None.

INDIA		Runs	Balls	4/6
S.M.Gavaskar	c Dujon b Roberts	2	12	–
K.Srikkanth	lbw b Marshall	38	57	7/1
M.Amarnath	b Holding	26	80	3
Yashpal Sharma	c sub (A.L.Logie) b Gomes	11	32	1
S.M.Patil	c Gomes b Garner	27	29	–/1
*Kapil Dev	c Holding b Gomes	15	8	3
K.Azad	c Garner b Roberts	0	3	–
R.M.H.Binny	c Garner b Roberts	2	8	–
Madan Lal	b Marshall	17	27	–/1
†S.M.H.Kirmani	b Holding	14	43	–
B.S.Sandhu	not out	11	30	1
Extras	(B5, LB5, W9, NB1)	20		
TOTAL	(54.4 overs)	**183**		

WEST INDIES		Runs	Balls	4/6
C.G.Greenidge	b Sandhu	1	12	–
D.L.Haynes	c Binny b Madan Lal	13	33	2
I.V.A.Richards	c Kapil Dev b Madan Lal	33	28	7
*C.H.Lloyd	c Kapil Dev b Binny	8	17	1
H.A.Gomes	c Gavaskar b Madan Lal	5	16	–
S.F.A.F.Bacchus	c Kirmani b Sandhu	8	25	–
†P.J.L.Dujon	b Amarnath	25	73	–/1
M.D.Marshall	c Gavaskar b Amarnath	18	51	–
A.M.E.Roberts	lbw b Kapil Dev	4	14	–
J.Garner	not out	5	19	–
M.A.Holding	lbw b Amarnath	6	24	–
Extras	(LB4, W10)	14		
TOTAL	(52 overs)	**140**		

WEST INDIES	O	M	R	W
Roberts	10	3	32	3
Garner	12	4	24	1
Marshall	11	1	24	2
Holding	9.4	2	26	2
Gomes	11	1	49	2
Richards	1	0	8	0
INDIA				
Kapil Dev	11	4	21	1
Sandhu	9	1	32	2
Madan Lal	12	2	31	3
Binny	10	1	23	1
Amarnath	7	0	12	3
Azad	3	0	7	0

FALL OF WICKETS		
Wkt	I	WI
1st	2	5
2nd	59	50
3rd	90	57
4th	92	66
5th	110	66
6th	111	76
7th	130	119
8th	153	124
9th	161	126
10th	183	140

Umpires: H.D.Bird (23) and B.J.Meyer (14).

THE 1987 WORLD CUP

Cricket's first oriental World Cup was a resounding success, the Indo-Pakistan Joint Management Committee overcoming the enormous logistical problems created by spreading the 27 matches around 21 venues scattered throughout an area roughly the size of the present European Community. Officially known as the Reliance Cup, this fourth world tournament began with its closest finishes to date, Australia defeating India in Madras by a single run, New Zealand scraping home by three runs against Zimbabwe despite Dave Houghton's record innings of 142, and England storming home against West Indies with two wickets and three balls to spare despite chasing 35 runs off the last three overs.

This tournament was also the longest, taking six weeks, much of the time spent travelling, many of them in airport transit lounges awaiting delayed flights. Sri Lanka had the worst deal, four of their successive journeys each involving two days of travel: from Peshawar in Pakistan's North-West Frontier Province, they went to Kanpur in central India, before crossing back to Faisalabad and finally returning to Poona.

Because of the fewer daylight hours, matches were of 50 overs per innings. Despite the early starts (9am), morning dew appeared to pose few batting problems and 19 of the 27 games were won by the team batting first. So batting friendly were the pitches that many totals reached the norm for the 60-over contests of the England-based World Cups. Indeed, West Indies against Sri Lanka in Karachi broke the team (360 for 4) and individual (Viv Richards 181) World Cup records. Rain interrupted only one match, Australia and New Zealand being reduced to 30 overs apiece in Indore. The new ruling that matches could not be carried over into a second day was never brought to trial.

GROUP A	P	W	L	Pts	R/O	GROUP B	P	W	L	Pts	R/O
INDIA	6	5	1	20	5.39	PAKISTAN	6	5	1	20	5.01
AUSTRALIA	6	5	1	20	5.19	ENGLAND	6	4	2	16	5.12
New Zealand	6	2	4	8	4.88	West Indies	6	3	3	12	5.16
Zimbabwe	6	0	6	0	3.76	Sri Lanka	6	0	6	0	4.04

Co-hosts India and Pakistan had been expected to meet in the final but neither survived the previous stage, England trouncing India by 35 runs in Bombay thanks to a masterly innings by Graham Gooch who swept the spinners to distraction during his 136-ball innings of 115. Australia had a closer encounter in Lahore before a decisive burst of fast bowling by Craig McDermott condemned Pakistan to their third successive semi-final defeat. Attempts to arrange a third-place play-off between India and Pakistan were aborted as a result of excessive financial demands by key players.

Calcutta's vast Eden Gardens Stadium staged the most colourful and noisy final so far, crammed with a crowd three times the capacity of Lord's. Australia took full advantage of winning the toss, compiling a total of 253 for 5 thereby setting England a target in excess of any so far achieved in the second innings of a final. Despite a late assault from Phillip DeFreitas, 17 were wanted off McDermott's concluding over. An outstanding team effort had brought deserved success for Australia and they delighted the crowd with their lap of honour, the captain, Allan Border, being borne aloft clutching the golden Reliance Cup.

PAKISTAN v SRI LANKA

At Niaz Stadium, Hyderabad, Pakistan, on 8 October 1987.　Toss: Pakistan.
Result: **PAKISTAN** won by 15 runs.　Award: Javed Miandad.
LOI debuts: None.

PAKISTAN		Runs	Balls	4/6
Ramiz Raja	c Ratnayake b Anurasiri	76	115	3
Ijaz Ahmed	c Kuruppu b Ratnayake	16	34	2
Mansoor Akhtar	c Ratnayake b Ratnayeke	12	23	–
Javed Miandad	b Ratnayeke	103	100	6
Wasim Akram	run out	14	14	–
Salim Malik	not out	18	12	1
*Imran Khan	b Ratnayeke	2	4	–
†Salim Yousuf	not out	1	1	–
Mudassar Nazar				
Abdul Qadir				
Tausif Ahmed				
Extras	(LB15, W9, NB1)	25		
TOTAL	(50 overs; 6 wickets)	267		

SRI LANKA		Runs	Balls	4/6
†D.S.B.P.Kuruppu	c Salim Yousuf b Imran	9	24	1
R.S.Mahanama	c Miandad b Mansoor	89	117	7/1
R.L.Dias	b Qadir	5	21	–
A. Ranatunga	b Tausif	24	29	3
*L.R.D.Mendis	run out	1	6	–
A.P.Gurusinha	b Qadir	37	39	2/1
P.A.de Silva	b Imran	42	32	3/1
J.R.Ratnayeke	c Salim Yousuf b Wasim	7	13	–
R.J.Ratnayake	c Mudassar b Wasim	8	9	–
V.B.John	not out	1	4	–
S.D.Anurasiri	run out	0	3	–
Extras	(B7, LB14, W7, NB1)	29		
TOTAL	(49.2 overs)	252		

SRI LANKA	O	M	R	W		FALL OF WICKETS	
John	10	2	37	0	Wkt	P	SL
Ratnayake	10	0	64	2	1st	48	29
Ratnayeke	9	0	47	2	2nd	67	57
De Silva	10	0	44	0	3rd	180	100
Anurasiri	10	0	52	1	4th	226	103
Gurusinha	1	0	8	0	5th	259	182
					6th	266	190
PAKISTAN					7th	–	209
Imran Khan	10	2	42	2	8th	–	223
Wasim Akram	9.2	1	41	2	9th	–	251
Mudassar Nazar	9	0	63	0	10th	–	252
Abdul Qadir	10	1	30	2			
Tausif Ahmed	10	0	48	1			
Mansoor Akhtar	1	0	7	1			

Umpires: V.K.Ramaswamy (*India*) (4) and S.J.Woodward (*New Zealand*) (7).

ENGLAND v WEST INDIES

At Municipal Stadium, Gujranwala, Pakistan, on 9 October 1987.   Toss: England.
Result: **ENGLAND** won by 2 wickets.   Award: A.J.Lamb.
LOI debuts: None.

WEST INDIES		Runs	Balls	4/6
D.L.Haynes	run out	19	45	1
C.A.Best	b DeFreitas	5	15	–
R.B.Richardson	b Foster	53	80	8
*I.V.A.Richards	b Foster	27	36	3
†P.J.L.Dujon	run out	46	76	3
A.L.Logie	b Foster	49	41	3/1
R.A.Harper	b Small	24	10	3/1
C.L.Hooper	not out	1	2	–
W.K.M.Benjamin	not out	7	2	1
C.A.Walsh				
B.P.Patterson				
Extras	(LB9, NB3)	12		
TOTAL	(50 overs; 7 wickets)	243		

ENGLAND		Runs	Balls	4/6
G.A.Gooch	c Dujon b Hooper	47	93	3
B.C.Broad	c Dujon b Walsh	3	12	–
R.T.Robinson	run out	12	35	1
*M.W.Gatting	b Hooper	25	23	3
A.J.Lamb	not out	67	68	5/1
D.R.Pringle	c Best b Hooper	12	23	–
†P.R.Downton	run out	3	4	–
J.E.Emburey	b Patterson	22	15	2/1
P.A.J.DeFreitas	b Patterson	23	21	2
N.A.Foster	not out	9	6	1
G.C.Small				
Extras	(LB14, W6, NB3)	23		
TOTAL	(49.3 overs; 8 wickets)	246		

ENGLAND	O	M	R	W		FALL OF WICKETS	
DeFreitas	10	2	31	1	Wkt	WI	E
Foster	10	0	53	3	1st	8	14
Emburey	10	1	22	0	2nd	53	40
Small	10	0	45	1	3rd	105	98
Pringle	10	0	83	0	4th	122	99
					5th	205	123
WEST INDIES					6th	235	131
Patterson	10	0	49	2	7th	235	162
Walsh	9.3	0	65	1	8th	–	209
Harper	10	0	44	0	9th	–	–
Benjamin	10	2	32	0	10th	–	–
Hooper	10	0	42	3			

Umpires: A.R.Crafter (*Australia*) (53) and R.B.Gupta (*India*) (4).

INDIA v AUSTRALIA

At Chidambaram Stadium, Madras, India, on 9 October 1987. Toss: India.
Result: **AUSTRALIA** won by 1 run. Award: G.R.Marsh.
LOI debuts: India – N.S.Sidhu; Australia – T.M.Moody.

AUSTRALIA		Runs	Balls	4/6
D.C.Boon	lbw b Shastri	49	68	5
G.R.Marsh	c Azharuddin b Prabhakar	110	141	7/1
D.M.Jones	c Sidhu b Maninder	39	35	2/2
*A.R.Border	b Binny	16	22	–
T.M.Moody	c Kapil Dev b Prabhakar	8	13	1
S.R.Waugh	not out	19	17	–
S.P.O'Donnell	run out	7	10	–
†G.C.Dyer				
P.L.Taylor				
C.J.McDermott				
B.A.Reid				
Extras	(LB18, W2, NB2)	22		
TOTAL	(50 overs; 6 wickets)	270		

INDIA		Runs	Balls	4/6
K.Srikkanth	lbw b Waugh	70	83	7
S.M.Gavaskar	c Reid b Taylor	37	32	6/1
N.S.Sidhu	b McDermott	73	79	4/5
D.B.Vengsarkar	c Jones b McDermott	29	45	2
M.Azharuddin	b McDermott	10	14	1
*Kapil Dev	c Boon b O'Donnell	6	10	–
R.J.Shastri	c and b McDermott	12	11	1
†K.S.More	not out	12	14	2
R.M.H.Binny	run out	0	3	–
M.Prabhakar	run out	5	7	–
Maninder Singh	b Waugh	4	5	–
Extras	(B2, LB7, W2)	11		
TOTAL	(49.5 overs)	269		

INDIA	O	M	R	W		FALL OF WICKETS	
					Wkt	A	I
Kapil Dev	10	0	41	0			
Prabhakar	10	0	47	2	1st	110	69
Binny	7	0	46	1	2nd	174	131
Maninder	10	0	48	1	3rd	228	207
Shastri	10	0	50	1	4th	237	229
Azharuddin	3	0	20	0	5th	251	232
					6th	270	246
AUSTRALIA					7th	–	256
McDermott	10	0	56	4	8th	–	256
Reid	10	2	35	0	9th	–	265
O'Donnell	9	1	32	1	10th	–	269
Taylor	5	0	46	1			
Waugh	9.5	0	52	2			
Border	6	0	39	0			

Umpires: D.M.Archer (*West Indies*) (11) and H.D.Bird (*England*) (45).

NEW ZEALAND v ZIMBABWE

At Lal Bahadur Stadium, Hyderabad, India, on 10 October 1987.   Toss: Zimbabwe.
Result: **NEW ZEALAND** won by 3 runs.   Award: D.L.Houghton.
LOI debuts: New Zealand – A.H.Jones; Zimbabwe – E.A.Brandes, A.C.Waller.

NEW ZEALAND		Runs	Balls	4/6
M.C.Snedden	c Waller b Rawson	64	96	3
J.G.Wright	c Houghton b Traicos	18	40	1
M.D.Crowe	c and b Rawson	72	88	5/1
A.H.Jones	c Brandes b Shah	0	6	–
*J.J.Crowe	c Brown b Curran	31	35	2
D.N.Patel	lbw b Shah	0	2	–
J.G.Bracewell	not out	13	20	–
†D.S.Smith	c Brown b Curran	29	20	2/1
S.L.Boock	not out	0	–	–
W.Watson				
E.J.Chatfield				
Extras	(B4, LB4, W4, NB3)	15		
TOTAL	(50 overs; 7 wickets)	242		

ZIMBABWE		Runs	Balls	4/6
R.D.Brown	c J.J.Crowe b Chatfield	1	10	–
A.H.Shah	lbw b Snedden	5	13	–
†D.L.Houghton	c M.D.Crowe b Snedden	142	137	13/6
A.J.Pycroft	run out	12	22	2
K.M.Curran	c Boock b Watson	4	8	–
A.C.Waller	c Smith b Watson	5	14	–
G.A.Paterson	c Smith b Boock	2	11	–
P.W.E.Rawson	lbw b Boock	1	10	–
I.P.Butchart	run out	54	70	2/1
E.A.Brandes	run out	0	–	–
*A.J.Traicos	not out	4	6	–
Extras	(LB7, W1, NB1)	9		
TOTAL	(49.4 overs)	239		

ZIMBABWE	O	M	R	W		FALL OF WICKETS		
					Wkt	NZ	Z	
Curran	10	0	51	2	1st	59	8	
Rawson	10	0	62	2	2nd	143	10	
Brandes	7	2	24	0	3rd	145	61	
Traicos	10	2	28	1	4th	166	67	
Butchart	4	0	27	0	5th	169	86	
Shah	9	0	42	2	6th	205	94	
NEW ZEALAND					7th	240	104	
Chatfield	10	2	26	1	8th	–	221	
Snedden	9	0	53	2	9th	–	221	
Watson	10	2	36	2	10th	–	239	
Bracewell	7	0	48	0				
Patel	5	0	27	0				
Boock	8.4	0	42	2				

Umpires: Mahboob Shah (*Pakistan*) (9) and P.W.Vidanagamage (*Sri Lanka*) (15).

PAKISTAN v ENGLAND

At Pindi Club Ground, Rawalpindi, Pakistan, on 12 (*no play*), 13 October 1987.
Toss: England.
Result: **PAKISTAN** won by 18 runs.   Award: Abdul Qadir.
LOI debuts: None.

PAKISTAN		Runs	Balls	4/6
Mansoor Akhtar	c Downton b Foster	6	24	1
Ramiz Raja	run out	15	40	1
Salim Malik	c Downton b DeFreitas	65	80	8
Javed Miandad	lbw b DeFreitas	23	50	3
Ijaz Ahmed	c Robinson b Small	59	59	4/1
*Imran Khan	b Small	22	32	2
Wasim Akram	b DeFreitas	5	3	1
†Salim Yousuf	not out	16	10	–
Abdul Qadir	not out	12	7	1/1
Tausif Ahmed				
Salim Jaffer				
Extras	(LB10, W3, NB3)	16		
TOTAL	(50 overs; 7 wickets)	239		

ENGLAND		Runs	Balls	4/6
G.A.Gooch	b Qadir	21	41	3
B.C.Broad	b Tausif	36	78	2
R.T.Robinson	b Qadir	33	62	1
*M.W.Gatting	b Salim Jaffer	43	47	4
A.J.Lamb	lbw b Qadir	30	38	3
D.R.Pringle	run out	8	14	–
J.E.Emburey	run out	1	1	–
†P.R.Downton	c Salim Yousuf b Qadir	0	2	–
P.A.J.DeFreitas	not out	3	3	–
N.A.Foster	run out	6	5	–
G.C.Small	lbw b Salim Jaffer	0	1	–
Extras	(B6, LB26, W8)	40		
TOTAL	(48.4 overs)	221		

ENGLAND	O	M	R	W		FALL OF WICKETS		
DeFreitas	10	1	42	3	Wkt	P	E	
Foster	10	1	35	1	1st	13	52	
Small	10	1	47	2	2nd	51	92	
Pringle	10	0	54	0	3rd	112	141	
Emburey	10	0	51	0	4th	123	186	
					5th	202	206	
PAKISTAN					6th	210	207	
Wasim Akram	9	0	32	0	7th	210	207	
Salim Jaffer	9.4	0	42	2	8th	–	213	
Tausif Ahmed	10	0	39	1	9th	–	221	
Abdul Qadir	10	0	31	4	10th	–	221	
Salim Malik	7	0	29	0				
Mansoor Akhtar	3	0	16	0				

Umpires: A.R.Crafter (*Australia*) (54) and R.B.Gupta (*India*) (5).

AUSTRALIA v ZIMBABWE

At Chidambaram Stadium, Madras, India, on 13 October 1987. Toss: Zimbabwe.
Result: **AUSTRALIA** won by 96 runs.   Award: S.R.Waugh.
LOI debuts: Australia – T.B.A.May; Zimbabwe – M.P.Jarvis.

AUSTRALIA		Runs	Balls	4/6
G.R.Marsh	c Curran b Shah	62	101	8
D.C.Boon	c Houghton b Curran	2	15	–
D.M.Jones	run out	2	12	–
*A.R.Border	c Shah b Butchart	67	88	8
S.R.Waugh	run out	45	41	3/2
S.P.O'Donnell	run out	3	11	–
†G.C.Dyer	c Paterson b Butchart	27	20	1/2
P.L.Taylor	not out	17	13	1
C.J.McDermott	c Brown b Curran	1	3	–
T.B.A.May	run out	1	1	–
B.A.Reid				
Extras	(W8)	8		
TOTAL	(50 overs; 9 wickets)	235		

ZIMBABWE		Runs	Balls	4/6
R.D.Brown	b O'Donnell	3	30	–
G.A.Paterson	run out	16	53	1
†D.L.Houghton	c O'Donnell b May	11	22	1
A.J.Pycroft	run out	9	29	1
K.M.Curran	b O'Donnell	30	38	1/3
A.C.Waller	c and b May	19	22	1/1
A.H.Shah	b McDermott	2	9	–
P.W.E.Rawson	b Reid	15	14	2
I.P.Butchart	c Jones b O'Donnell	18	32	2
*A.J.Traicos	c and b O'Donnell	6	5	1
M.P.Jarvis	not out	1	1	–
Extras	(B2, LB3, W3, NB1)	9		
TOTAL	(42.4 overs)	139		

ZIMBABWE	O	M	R	W		FALL OF WICKETS	
					Wkt	A	Z
Curran	8	0	29	2	1st	10	13
Jarvis	10	0	40	0	2nd	20	27
Rawson	6	0	39	0	3rd	133	41
Butchart	10	1	59	2	4th	143	44
Traicos	10	0	36	0	5th	155	79
Shah	6	0	32	1	6th	202	97
					7th	228	97
AUSTRALIA					8th	230	124
McDermott	7	1	13	1	9th	235	137
Reid	7	1	21	1	10th	–	139
O'Donnell	9.4	0	39	4			
Waugh	6	3	7	0			
May	8	0	29	2			
Taylor	5	0	25	0			

Umpires: Khizer Hayat (*Pakistan*) (13) and D.R.Shepherd (*England*) (21).

WEST INDIES v SRI LANKA

At National Stadium, Karachi, Pakistan, on 13 October 1987.　Toss: Sri Lanka.
Result: **WEST INDIES** won by 191 runs.　Award: I.V.A.Richards.
LOI debuts: None.

WEST INDIES		Runs	Balls	4/6
D.L.Haynes	b Gurusinha	105	109	9/1
C.A.Best	b Ratnayeke	18		
R.B.Richardson	c Kuruppu b Ratnayeke	0		
*I.V.A.Richards	c Mahanama b De Mel	181	125	16/6
A.L.Logie	not out	31		
R.A.Harper	not out	5		
C.L.Hooper				
†P.J.L.Dujon				
W.K.M.Benjamin				
C.A.Walsh				
B.P.Patterson				
Extras	(B4, LB8, W4, NB4)	20		
TOTAL	(50 overs; 4 wickets)	360		

SRI LANKA		Runs	Balls	4/6
R.S.Mahanama	c Dujon b Walsh	12		
†D.S.B.P.Kuruppu	lbw b Patterson	14		
A.P.Gurusinha	b Hooper	36		
P.A.de Silva	c Dujon b Hooper	9		
A.Ranatunga	not out	52		
*L.R.D.Mendis	not out	37		
R.S.Madugalle				
J.R.Ratnayeke				
A.L.F.de Mel				
V.B.John				
S.D.Anurasiri				
Extras	(B1, LB2, W6)	9		
TOTAL	(50 overs; 4 wickets)	169		

SRI LANKA	O	M	R	W		FALL OF WICKETS	
John	10	1	48	0	Wkt	WI	SL
Ratnayeke	8	0	68	2	1st	45	24
Anurasiri	10	0	39	0	2nd	45	31
De Mel	10	0	97	1	3rd	227	57
De Silva	6	0	35	0	4th	343	112
Ranatunga	2	0	18	0	5th	–	–
Gurusinha	4	0	43	1	6th	–	–
					7th	–	–
WEST INDIES					8th	–	–
Patterson	7	0	32	1	9th	–	–
Walsh	7	2	23	1	10th	–	–
Harper	10	2	15	0			
Benjamin	4	0	11	0			
Hooper	10	0	39	2			
Richards	8	0	22	0			
Richardson	4	0	24	0			

Umpires: V.K.Ramaswamy (*India*) (5) and S.J.Woodward (*New Zealand*) (8).

INDIA v NEW ZEALAND

At Chinnaswamy Stadium, Bangalore, India, on 14 October 1987.　Toss: New Zealand.
Result: **INDIA** won by 16 runs.　Award: Kapil Dev.
LOI debuts: None.

INDIA		Runs	Balls	4/6
K.Srikkanth	run out	9	19	1
S.M.Gavaskar	run out	2	14	–
N.S.Sidhu	c Jones b Patel	75	71	4/4
D.B.Vengsarkar	c and b Watson	0	8	–
M.Azharuddin	c Boock b Patel	21	57	1
R.J.Shastri	c and b Patel	22	44	–/1
*Kapil Dev	not out	72	58	4/1
M.Prabhakar	c and b Chatfield	3	5	–
†K.S.More	not out	42	26	5
L.Sivaramakrishnan				
Maninder Singh				
Extras	(LB4, W2)	6		
TOTAL	(50 overs; 7 wickets)	252		

NEW ZEALAND		Runs	Balls	4/6
M.C.Snedden	c Shastri b Azharuddin	33	63	2
K.R.Rutherford	c Srikkanth b Shastri	75	95	6/2
M.D.Crowe	st More b Maninder	9	12	1
A.H.Jones	run out	64	86	2
*J.J.Crowe	c Vengsarkar b Maninder	7	11	–
D.N.Patel	run out	1	3	–
J.G.Bracewell	c Maninder b Shastri	8	14	–
†D.S.Smith	b Prabhakar	10	5	–
S.L.Boock	not out	7	8	–
W.Watson	not out	2	3	–
E.J.Chatfield				
Extras	(B5, LB9, W5, NB1)	20		
TOTAL	(50 overs; 8 wickets)	236		

NEW ZEALAND	O	M	R	W		FALL OF WICKETS	
Chatfield	10	1	39	1	Wkt	I	NZ
Snedden	10	1	56	0	1st	11	67
Watson	9	0	59	1	2nd	16	86
Boock	4	0	26	0	3rd	21	146
Bracewell	7	0	32	0	4th	86	168
Patel	10	0	36	3	5th	114	170
					6th	165	189
INDIA					7th	170	206
Kapil Dev	10	1	54	0	8th	–	225
Prabhakar	8	0	38	1	9th	–	–
Azharuddin	4	0	11	1	10th	–	–
Sivaramakrishnan	8	0	34	0			
Maninder	10	0	40	2			
Shastri	10	0	45	2			

Umpires: D.M Archer (*West Indies*) (12) and H.D.Bird (*England*) (46).

PAKISTAN v WEST INDIES

At Gaddafi Stadium, Lahore, Pakistan, on 16 October 1987.   Toss: West Indies.
Result: **PAKISTAN** won by 1 wicket.   Award: Salim Yousuf.
LOI debuts: West Indies – P.V.Simmons.

WEST INDIES		Runs	Balls	4/6
D.L.Haynes	b Salim Jaffer	37	81	3
P.V.Simmons	c and b Tausif	50	57	8
R.B.Richardson	c Ijaz b Salim Jaffer	11	22	1
*I.V.A.Richards	c Salim Malik b Imran	51	52	4/1
A.L.Logie	c Mansoor b Salim Jaffer	2	4	–
C.L.Hooper	lbw b Wasim	22	37	2
†P.J.L.Dujon	lbw b Wasim	5	12	–
R.A.Harper	c Mansoor b Imran	0	1	–
E.A.E.Baptiste	b Imran	14	20	1
C.A.Walsh	lbw b Imran	7	6	1
B.P.Patterson	not out	0	4	–
Extras	(B1, LB14, W2)	17		
TOTAL	(49.3 overs)	216		

PAKISTAN		Runs	Balls	4/6
Ramiz Raja	c Richards b Harper	42	87	1
Mansoor Akhtar	b Patterson	10	24	2
Salim Malik	c Baptiste b Walsh	4	7	1
Javed Miandad	c and b Hooper	33	72	1
Ijaz Ahmed	b Walsh	6	14	–
*Imran Khan	c Logie b Walsh	18	26	–
†Salim Yousuf	c Hooper b Walsh	56	49	7
Wasim Akram	c Richardson b Patterson	7	8	–
Abdul Qadir	not out	16	9	–/1
Tausif Ahmed	run out	0	1	–
Salim Jaffer	not out	1	3	–
Extras	(B5, LB12, W7)	24		
TOTAL	(50 overs; 9 wickets)	217		

PAKISTAN	O	M	R	W
Imran Khan	8.3	2	37	4
Wasim Akram	10	0	45	2
Abdul Qadir	8	0	42	0
Tausif Ahmed	10	2	35	1
Salim Jaffer	10	0	30	3
Salim Malik	3	0	12	0

WEST INDIES	O	M	R	W
Patterson	10	1	51	2
Walsh	10	1	40	4
Baptiste	8	1	33	0
Harper	10	0	28	1
Hooper	10	0	38	1
Richards	2	0	10	0

FALL OF WICKETS		
Wkt	WI	P
1st	91	23
2nd	97	28
3rd	118	92
4th	121	104
5th	169	110
6th	184	183
7th	184	200
8th	196	202
9th	207	203
10th	216	–

Umpires: A.R.Crafter (*Australia*) (55) and S.J.Woodward (*New Zealand*) (9).

ENGLAND v SRI LANKA

At Shahi Bagh Stadium, Peshawar, Pakistan, on 17 October 1987.   Toss: England.
Result: **ENGLAND** won on faster scoring rate.   Award: A.J.Lamb.
LOI debuts: None.

ENGLAND		Runs	Balls	4/6
G.A.Gooch	c and b Anurasiri	84	100	8
B.C.Broad	c De Silva b Ratnayeke	28	60	1
*M.W.Gatting	b Ratnayeke	58	63	3
A.J.Lamb	c De Silva b Ratnayeke	76	58	3/2
J.E.Emburey	not out	30	19	3/1
C.W.J.Athey	not out	2	2	–
†P.R.Downton				
P.A.J.DeFreitas				
D.R.Pringle				
E.E.Hemmings				
G.C.Small				
Extras	(LB13, W5)	18		
TOTAL	(50 overs; 4 wickets)	296		

SRI LANKA		Runs	Balls	4/6
R.S.Mahanama	c Gooch b Pringle	11	39	2
†D.S.B.P.Kuruppu	c Hemmings b Emburey	13	26	1
A.P.Gurusinha	run out	1	12	–
R.S.Madugalle	b Hemmings	30	49	3
A.Ranatunga	lbw b DeFreitas	40	67	4
*L.R.D.Mendis	run out	14	33	1
P.A.de Silva	c Emburey b Hemmings	6	14	–
J.R.Ratnayeke	c Broad b Emburey	1	5	–
R.J.Ratnayake	not out	14	22	1
V.B.John	not out	8	7	1
S.D.Anurasiri				
Extras	(B2, LB9, W6, NB3)	20		
TOTAL	(45 overs; 8 wickets)	158		

SRI LANKA	O	M	R	W		FALL OF WICKETS		
Ratnayeke	9	0	62	2		Wkt	E	SL
John	10	0	44	0		1st	89	31
De Silva	7	0	33	0		2nd	142	32
Ratnayake	10	0	60	1		3rd	218	37
Anurasiri	8	0	44	1		4th	287	99
Ranatunga	6	0	40	0		5th	–	105
						6th	–	113
ENGLAND						7th	–	119
DeFreitas	9	2	24	1		8th	–	137
Small	7	0	27	0		9th	–	–
Pringle	4	0	11	1		10th	–	–
Emburey	10	1	26	2				
Hemmings	10	1	31	2				
Gooch	2	0	9	0				
Athey	1	0	10	0				
Broad	1	0	6	0				
Lamb	1	0	3	0				

Umpires: R.B.Gupta (*India*) (6) and V.K.Ramaswamy (*India*) (6).

INDIA v ZIMBABWE

At Wankhede Stadium, Bombay, India, on 17 October 1987.   Toss: Zimbabwe.
Result: **INDIA** won by 8 wickets.   Award: M.Prabhakar.
LOI debuts: Zimbabwe – K.J.Arnott, M.A.Meman.

ZIMBABWE		Runs	Balls	4/6
G.A.Paterson	b Prabhakar	6		
K.J.Arnott	lbw b Prabhakar	1		
†D.L.Houghton	b Prabhakar	0		
A.J.Pycroft	st More b Shastri	61	102	2
K.M.Curran	c More b Prabhakar	0		
A.C.Waller	st More b Maninder	16		
I.P.Butchart	c Sivaramakrishnan b Maninder	10		
A.H.Shah	c More b Maninder	0		
M.A.Meman	run out	19		
*A.J.Traicos	c Gavaskar b Sivaramakrishnan	0		
M.P.Jarvis	not out	8		
Extras	(B2, LB6, W6)	14		
TOTAL	(44.2 overs)	135		

INDIA		Runs	Balls	4/6
K.Srikkanth	c Paterson b Traicos	31		
S.M.Gavaskar	st Houghton b Traicos	43	51	9
M.Prabhakar	not out	11		
D.B.Vengsarkar	not out	46		
N.S.Sidhu				
M.Azharuddin				
*Kapil Dev				
R.J.Shastri				
†K.S.More				
L.Sivaramakrishnan				
Maninder Singh				
Extras	(LB1, W4)	5		
TOTAL	(27.5 overs; 2 wickets)	136		

INDIA	O	M	R	W		FALL OF WICKETS	
Kapil Dev	8	1	17	0	Wkt	Z	I
Prabhakar	8	1	19	4	1st	3	76
Maninder	10	0	21	3	2nd	12	80
Azharuddin	1	0	6	0	3rd	13	–
Sivaramakrishnan	9	0	36	1	4th	13	–
Shastri	8.2	0	28	1	5th	47	–
					6th	67	–
ZIMBABWE					7th	67	–
Curran	6	0	32	0	8th	98	–
Jarvis	4	0	22	0	9th	99	–
Butchart	3	0	20	0	10th	135	–
Traicos	8	0	27	2			
Meman	6.5	0	34	0			

Umpires: Mahboob Shah (*Pakistan*) (10) and D.R.Shepherd (*England*) (22).

AUSTRALIA v NEW ZEALAND

At Nehru Stadium, Indore, India, on 18 (*no play*), 19 October 1987.　Toss: New Zealand.
Result: **AUSTRALIA** won by 3 runs.　Award: D.C.Boon.
LOI debuts: None.

AUSTRALIA		Runs	Balls	4/6
D.C.Boon	c Wright b Snedden	87	96	5/2
G.R.Marsh	c J.J.Crowe b Snedden	5	9	–
D.M.Jones	c Rutherford b Patel	52	48	1/3
*A.R.Border	c M.D.Crowe b Chatfield	34	28	3
S.R.Waugh	not out	13	8	1/1
T.M.Moody	not out	0	3	–
S.P.O'Donnell				
†G.C.Dyer				
T.B.A.May				
C.J.McDermott				
B.A.Reid				
Extras	(B1, LB5, W2)	8		
TOTAL	(30 overs; 4 wickets)	199		

NEW ZEALAND		Runs	Balls	4/6
K.R.Rutherford	b O'Donnell	37	38	2/2
J.G.Wright	c Dyer b O'Donnell	47	44	1/2
M.D.Crowe	c Marsh b Waugh	58	48	5
A.H.Jones	c Marsh b McDermott	15	23	–
*J.J.Crowe	c and b Reid	3	10	–
D.N.Patel	run out	13	9	1
J.G.Bracewell	c and b Reid	6	4	1
†I.D.S.Smith	b Waugh	1	2	–
M.C.Snedden	run out	1	1	–
W.Watson	not out	2	3	–
E.J.Chatfield	not out	0	–	–
Extras	(B4, LB5, W4)	13		
TOTAL	(30 overs; 9 wickets)	196		

NEW ZEALAND	O	M	R	W		FALL OF WICKETS		
Snedden	6	0	36	2		Wkt	A	NZ
Chatfield	6	0	27	1		1st	17	83
Watson	6	0	34	0		2nd	134	94
Patel	6	0	45	1		3rd	171	133
Bracewell	6	0	51	0		4th	196	140
						5th	–	165
						6th	–	183
AUSTRALIA						7th	–	193
McDermott	6	0	30	1		8th	–	193
Reid	6	0	38	2		9th	–	195
May	6	0	39	0		10th	–	–
O'Donnell	6	0	44	2				
Waugh	6	0	36	2				

Umpires: D.M.Archer (*West Indies*) (13) and Khizer Hayat (*Pakistan*) (14).

PAKISTAN v ENGLAND

At National Stadium, Karachi, Pakistan, on 20 October 1987.　Toss: Pakistan.
Result: **PAKISTAN** won by 7 wickets.　Award: Imran Khan.
LOI debuts: None.

ENGLAND		Runs	Balls	4/6
G.A.Gooch	c Wasim b Imran	16	27	2
R.T.Robinson	b Qadir	16	26	1
C.W.J.Athey	b Tausif	86	104	6/2
*M.W.Gatting	c Salim Yousuf b Qadir	60	65	3/1
A.J.Lamb	b Imran	9	15	–
J.E.Emburey	lbw b Qadir	3	11	–
†P.R.Downton	c Salim Yousuf b Imran	6	13	–
P.A.J.DeFreitas	c Salim Yousuf b Imran	13	15	1
N.A.Foster	not out	20	20	–
G.C.Small	run out	0	1	–
E.E.Hemmings	not out	4	3	2
Extras	(LB7, W4)	11		
TOTAL	(50 overs; 9 wickets)	244		

PAKISTAN		Runs	Balls	4/6
Ramiz Raja	c Gooch b DeFreitas	113	148	5
Mansoor Akhtar	run out	29	49	3
Salim Malik	c Athey b Emburey	88	92	7
Javed Miandad	not out	6	3	1
Ijaz Ahmed	not out	4	2	1
*Imran Khan				
†Salim Yousuf				
Wasim Akram				
Abdul Qadir				
Tausif Ahmed				
Salim Jaffer				
Extras	(LB6, W1)	7		
TOTAL	(49 overs; 3 wickets)	247		

PAKISTAN	O	M	R	W
Imran Khan	9	0	37	4
Wasim Akram	8	0	44	0
Tausif Ahmed	10	0	46	1
Abdul Qadir	10	0	31	3
Salim Jaffer	8	0	44	0
Salim Malik	5	0	35	0

ENGLAND	O	M	R	W
DeFreitas	8	2	41	1
Foster	10	0	51	0
Hemmings	10	1	40	0
Emburey	10	0	34	1
Small	9	0	63	0
Gooch	2	0	12	0

FALL OF WICKETS		
Wkt	E	P
1st	26	61
2nd	52	228
3rd	187	243
4th	187	–
5th	192	–
6th	203	–
7th	206	–
8th	230	–
9th	230	–
10th	–	–

Umpires: A.R.Crafter (*Australia*) (56) and V.K.Ramaswamy (*India*) (7).

WEST INDIES v SRI LANKA

At Modi Stadium, Green Park, Kanpur, India, on 21 October 1987.   Toss: Sri Lanka.
Result: **WEST INDIES** won by 25 runs.   Award: P.V.Simmons.
LOI debuts: None.

WEST INDIES		Runs	Balls	4/6
D.L.Haynes	b Anurasiri	24		
P.V.Simmons	c Madugalle b Ratnayeke	89		11
R.B.Richardson	c Mahanama b Jeganathan	4		
*I.V.A.Richards	c Ratnayake b De Silva	14		
A.L.Logie	not out	65		
C.L.Hooper	st Kuruppu b De Silva	6		
†P.J.L.Dujon	c Kuruppu b Ratnayeke	6		
R.A.Harper	b Ratnayeke	3		
W.K.M.Benjamin	b Ratnayeke	0		
C.A.Walsh	not out	9		
B.P.Patterson				
Extras	(B2, LB7, W7)	16		
TOTAL	(50 overs; 8 wickets)	236		

SRI LANKA		Runs	Balls	4/6
R.S.Mahanama	b Patterson	0		
†D.S.B.P.Kuruppu	c and b Hooper	33		
J.R.Ratnayeke	lbw b Benjamin	15		
R.S.Madugalle	c Haynes b Harper	18		
A.Ranatunga	not out	86		
*L.R.D.Mendis	b Walsh	19		
P.A.de Silva	b Patterson	8		
R.J.Ratnayake	c Walsh b Patterson	5		
S.Jeganathan	run out	3		
V.B.John	not out	1		
S.D.Anurasiri				
Extras	(B2, LB11, NB10)	23		
TOTAL	(50 overs; 8 wickets)	211		

SRI LANKA	O	M	R	W		FALL OF WICKETS	
Ratnayeke	10	1	41	3	Wkt	WI	SL
John	5	1	25	0	1st	62	2
Ratnayake	5	0	39	1	2nd	80	28
Jeganathan	10	1	33	1	3rd	115	66
Anurasiri	10	1	46	1	4th	155	86
De Silva	10	0	43	2	5th	168	156
					6th	199	184
WEST INDIES					7th	213	200
Patterson	10	0	31	3	8th	214	209
Walsh	9	2	43	1	9th	–	–
Benjamin	10	0	43	1	10th	–	–
Harper	10	1	29	1			
Hooper	8	0	35	1			
Richards	3	0	17	0			

Umpires: Amanullah Khan (*Pakistan*) (10) and Mahboob Shah (*Pakistan*) (11).

INDIA v AUSTRALIA

At Feroz Shah Kotla, Delhi, India, on 22 October 1987.　Toss: Australia.
Result: **INDIA** won by 56 runs.　Award: M.Azharuddin.
LOI debuts: Australia – A.K.Zesers.

INDIA		Runs	Balls	4/6
K.Srikkanth	c Dyer b McDermott	26	37	3
S.M.Gavaskar	b O'Donnell	61	72	7
N.S.Sidhu	c Moody b McDermott	51	70	2
D.B.Vengsarkar	c O'Donnell b Reid	63	60	3/2
*Kapil Dev	c Dyer b McDermott	3	5	–
M.Azharuddin	not out	54	45	5/1
R.J.Shastri	c and b Waugh	8	7	1
†K.S.More	not out	5	4	–
M.Prabhakar				
C.Sharma				
Maninder Singh				
Extras	(B1, LB6, W11)	18		
TOTAL	(50 overs; 6 wickets)	289		

AUSTRALIA		Runs	Balls	4/6
G.R.Marsh	st More b Maninder	33	56	2
D.C.Boon	c More b Shastri	62	59	7
D.M.Jones	c Kapil Dev b Maninder	36	55	–
*A.R.Border	c Prabhakar b Maninder	12	24	–
S.R.Waugh	c Sidhu b Kapil Dev	42	52	3
T.M.Moody	run out	2	6	–
S.P.O'Donnell	b Azharuddin	5	10	–
†G.C.Dyer	c Kapil Dev b Prabhakar	15	12	–/1
C.J.McDermott	c and b Azharuddin	4	5	–
A.K.Zesers	not out	2	11	–
B.A.Reid	c Sidhu b Azharuddin	1	6	–
Extras	(LB11, W8)	19		
TOTAL	(49 overs)	233		

AUSTRALIA	O	M	R	W		FALL OF WICKETS	
O'Donnell	9	1	45	1	Wkt	I	A
Reid	10	0	65	1	1st	50	88
Waugh	10	0	59	1	2nd	125	104
McDermott	10	0	61	3	3rd	167	135
Moody	2	0	15	0	4th	178	164
Zesers	9	1	37	0	5th	243	167
					6th	274	182
INDIA					7th	–	214
Kapil Dev	8	1	41	1	8th	–	227
Prabhakar	10	0	56	1	9th	–	231
Maninder	10	0	34	3	10th	–	233
Shastri	10	0	35	1			
Sharma	7.1	0	37	0			
Azharuddin	3.5	0	19	3			

Umpires: Khalid Aziz (*Pakistan*) (4) and D.R.Shepherd (*England*) (23).

NEW ZEALAND v ZIMBABWE

At Eden Gardens, Calcutta, India, on 23 October 1987.   Toss: New Zealand.
Result: **NEW ZEALAND** won by 4 wickets.   Award: J.J.Crowe.
LOI debuts: None.

ZIMBABWE		Runs	Balls	4/6
G.A.Paterson	run out	0		
A.H.Shah	c M.D.Crowe b Watson	41		
K.J.Arnott	run out	51		
†D.L.Houghton	c M.D.Crowe b Boock	50	58	
A.J.Pycroft	not out	52		
K.M.Curran	b Boock	12		
A.C.Waller	not out	8		
I.P.Butchart				
E.A.Brandes				
*A.J.Traicos				
M.P.Jarvis				
Extras	(LB7, W6)	13		
TOTAL	(50 overs; 5 wickets)	227		

NEW ZEALAND		Runs	Balls	4/6
K.R.Rutherford	b Brandes	22		
J.G.Wright	b Shah	12		
M.D.Crowe	c Butchart b Shah	58	58	8
D.N.Patel	c Arnott b Brandes	1		
*J.J.Crowe	not out	88	105	8
A.H.Jones	c Jarvis b Traicos	15		
M.C.Snedden	b Jarvis	4		
†I.D.S.Smith	not out	17		
S.L.Boock				
E.J.Chatfield				
W.Watson				
Extras	(B1, LB5, W4, NB1)	11		
TOTAL	(47.4 overs; 6 wickets)	228		

NEW ZEALAND	O	M	R	W	FALL OF WICKETS		
Chatfield	10	2	47	0	Wkt	Z	NZ
Snedden	10	2	32	0	1st	1	37
Watson	10	1	45	1	2nd	82	53
Boock	10	1	43	2	3rd	121	56
Patel	10	1	53	0	4th	180	125
					5th	216	158
ZIMBABWE					6th	–	182
Curran	2	0	12	0	7th	–	–
Jarvis	7.4	0	39	1	8th	–	–
Brandes	10	1	44	2	9th	–	–
Shah	10	0	34	2	10th	–	–
Traicos	10	0	43	1			
Butchart	8	0	50	0			

Umpires: Khizer Hayat (*Pakistan*) (15) and P.W.Vidanagamage (*Sri Lanka*) (16).

PAKISTAN v SRI LANKA

At Iqbal Stadium, Faisalabad, Pakistan, on 25 October 1987.   Toss: Pakistan.
Result: **PAKISTAN** won by 113 runs.   Award: Salim Malik
LOI debuts: None.

PAKISTAN

		Runs	Balls	4/6
Ramiz Raja	c and b Anurasiri	32	49	2
Mansoor Akhtar	b Jeganathan	33	61	2
Salim Malik	b Ratnayeke	100	95	10
Javed Miandad	run out	1	8	–
Wasim Akram	c Ranatunga b De Silva	39	40	2/2
Ijaz Ahmed	c and b John	30	18	5
*Imran Khan	run out	39	20	5/1
Manzoor Elahi	not out	4	6	–
†Salim Yousuf	not out	11	6	–/1
Abdul Qadir				
Tausif Ahmed				
Extras	(LB6, W2)	8		
TOTAL	(50 overs; 7 wickets)	297		

SRI LANKA

		Runs	Balls	4/6
R.S.Mahanama	run out	8	13	1
†D.S.B.P.Kuruppu	c Salim Yousuf b Imran	0	1	–
J.R.Ratnayeke	run out	22	60	2
R.S.Madugalle	c Salim Yousuf b Manzoor	15	38	2
A.Ranatunga	c and b Qadir	50	66	4
*L.R.D.Mendis	b Qadir	58	65	6
P.A.de Silva	not out	13	35	–
A.L.F.de Mel	b Qadir	0	3	–
S.Jeganathan	c Salim Yousuf b Miandad	1	11	–
V.B.John	not out	1	12	–
S.D.Anurasiri				
Extras	(B4, LB4, W6, NB2)	16		
TOTAL	(50 overs; 8 wickets)	184		

SRI LANKA	O	M	R	W
Ratnayeke	10	0	58	1
John	8	1	53	1
De Mel	10	0	53	0
Jeganathan	9	1	45	1
Anurasiri	7	0	45	1
De Silva	6	0	37	1

PAKISTAN	O	M	R	W
Imran Khan	3.2	1	13	1
Wasim Akram	7	0	34	0
Manzoor Elahi	9.4	0	32	1
Tausif Ahmed	10	1	23	0
Abdul Qadir	10	0	40	3
Salim Malik	7	1	29	0
Javed Miandad	3	0	5	1

FALL OF WICKETS		
Wkt	P	SL
1st	64	4
2nd	72	11
3rd	77	41
4th	137	70
5th	197	150
6th	264	173
7th	285	173
8th	–	179
9th	–	–
10th	–	–

Umpires: R.B.Gupta (*India*) (7) and S.J.Woodward (*New Zealand*) (10).

ENGLAND v WEST INDIES

At Sawai Mansingh Stadium, Jaipur, India, on 26 October 1987.   Toss: West Indies.
Result: **ENGLAND** won by 34 runs.   Award: G.A.Gooch.
LOI debuts: None.

ENGLAND		Runs	Balls	4/6
G.A.Gooch	c Harper b Patterson	92	137	7
R.T.Robinson	b Patterson	13	19	2
C.W.J.Athey	c Patterson b Harper	21	44	3
*M.W.Gatting	lbw b Richards	25	24	1
A.J.Lamb	c Richardson b Patterson	40	52	3
J.E.Emburey	not out	24	16	4
P.A.J.DeFreitas	not out	16	9	3
†P.R.Downton				
N.A.Foster				
G.C.Small				
E.E.Hemmings				
Extras	(B5, LB10, W22, NB1)	38		
TOTAL	(50 overs; 5 wickets)	269		

WEST INDIES		Runs	Balls	4/6
D.L.Haynes	c Athey b DeFreitas	9	14	2
P.V.Simmons	b Emburey	25	28	5
R.B.Richardson	c Downton b Small	93	130	8/1
*I.V.A.Richards	b Hemmings	51	51	4/3
A.L.Logie	c Hemmings b Emburey	22	21	3
C.L.Hooper	c Downton b DeFreitas	8	11	1
†P.J.L.Dujon	c Downton b Foster	1	4	–
R.A.Harper	run out	3	4	–
W.K.M.Benjamin	c Foster b DeFreitas	8	16	–
C.A.Walsh	b Hemmings	2	3	–
B.P.Patterson	not out	4	8	–
Extras	(LB7, W1, NB1)	9		
TOTAL	(48.1 overs)	235		

WEST INDIES	O	M	R	W
Patterson	9	0	56	3
Walsh	10	0	24	0
Benjamin	10	0	63	0
Harper	10	1	52	1
Hooper	3	0	27	0
Richards	8	0	32	1

ENGLAND	O	M	R	W
DeFreitas	9.1	2	28	3
Foster	10	0	52	1
Emburey	9	0	41	2
Small	10	0	61	1
Hemmings	10	0	46	2

FALL OF WICKETS		
Wkt	E	WI
1st	35	18
2nd	90	65
3rd	154	147
4th	209	182
5th	250	208
6th	–	211
7th	–	219
8th	–	221
9th	–	224
10th	–	235

Umpires: Mahboob Shah (*Pakistan*) (12) and P.W.Vidanagamage (*Sri Lanka*) (17).

INDIA v ZIMBABWE

At Gujarat Stadium, Ahmedabad, India, on 26 October 1987. Toss: India.
Result: **INDIA** won by 7 wickets.   Award: Kapil Dev.
LOI debuts: None.

ZIMBABWE		Runs	Balls	4/6
R.D.Brown	c More b Sharma	13		
A.H.Shah	run out	0		
K.J.Arnott	b Kapil Dev	60		
A.J.Pycroft	c More b Sharma	2		
†D.L.Houghton	c Kapil Dev b Shastri	22		
A.C.Waller	c Shastri b Maninder	39		
I.P.Butchart	b Kapil Dev	13		
P.W.E.Rawson	not out	16		
E.A.Brandes	not out	3		
M.P.Jarvis				
*A.J.Traicos				
Extras	(B1, LB12, W9, NB1)	23		
TOTAL	(50 overs; 7 wickets)	191		

INDIA		Runs	Balls	4/6
K.Srikkanth	lbw b Jarvis	6		
S.M.Gavaskar	c Butchart b Rawson	50		
N.S.Sidhu	c Brandes b Rawson	55		
D.B.Vengsarkar	not out	33		
*Kapil Dev	not out	41		
M.Azharuddin				
R.J.Shastri				
†K.S.More				
M.Prabhakar				
C.Sharma				
Maninder Singh				
Extras	(LB6, W3)	9		
TOTAL	(42 overs; 3 wickets)	194		

INDIA	O	M	R	W		FALL OF WICKETS	
Kapil Dev	10	2	44	2	Wkt	Z	I
Prabhakar	7	2	12	0	1st	4	11
Sharma	10	0	41	2	2nd	36	105
Maninder	10	1	32	1	3rd	40	132
Shastri	10	0	35	1	4th	83	–
Azharuddin	3	0	14	0	5th	150	–
					6th	155	–
ZIMBABWE					7th	184	–
Brandes	6	0	28	0	8th	–	–
Jarvis	8	1	21	1	9th	–	–
Shah	8	0	40	0	10th	–	–
Traicos	10	0	39	0			
Rawson	8	0	46	2			
Butchart	2	0	14	0			

Umpires: D.M.Archer (*West Indies*) (14) and H.D.Bird (*England*) (47).

AUSTRALIA v NEW ZEALAND

At Sector 16 Stadium, Chandigarh, India, on 27 October 1987. Toss: Australia.
Result: **AUSTRALIA** won by 17 runs. Award: G.R.Marsh.
LOI debuts: None.

AUSTRALIA		Runs	Balls	4/6
G.R.Marsh	not out	126	149	12/3
D.C.Boon	run out	14	28	1
D.M.Jones	c Smith b Watson	56	80	1/2
*A.R.Border	b Snedden	1	4	–
M.R.J.Veletta	run out	0	1	–
S.R.Waugh	b Watson	1	7	–
†G.C.Dyer	b Chatfield	8	10	–
C.J.McDermott	lbw b Chatfield	5	7	–
T.B.A.May	run out	15	10	1
A.K.Zesers	not out	8	3	1
B.A.Reid				
Extras	(LB10, W7)	17		
TOTAL	(50 overs; 8 wickets)	251		

NEW ZEALAND		Runs	Balls	4/6
M.C.Snedden	b Waugh	32	56	3
J.G.Wright	c and b Zesers	61	82	4
M.D.Crowe	run out	4	5	–
K.R.Rutherford	c Jones b McDermott	44	57	4
*J.J.Crowe	c and b Border	27	28	3
D.N.Patel	st Dyer b Border	3	10	–
J.G.Bracewell	run out	12	20	–
†I.D.S.Smith	c Boon b Waugh	12	15	–
S.L.Boock	run out	12	8	1
W.Watson	run out	8	8	–/1
E.J.Chatfield	not out	5	6	–
Extras	(B1, LB7, W4, NB2)	14		
TOTAL	(48.4 overs)	234		

NEW ZEALAND	O	M	R	W		FALL OF WICKETS		
					Wkt	A	NZ	
Snedden	10	0	48	1	1st	25	72	
Chatfield	10	2	52	2	2nd	151	82	
Boock	10	1	45	0	3rd	158	127	
Bracewell	4	0	24	0	4th	158	173	
Watson	8	0	46	2	5th	175	179	
Patel	8	0	26	0	6th	193	186	
					7th	201	206	
AUSTRALIA					8th	228	208	
McDermott	10	1	43	1	9th	–	221	
Reid	6	0	30	0	10th	–	234	
Waugh	9.4	0	37	2				
Zesers	6	0	37	1				
May	10	0	52	0				
Border	7	0	27	2				

Umpires: Khizer Hayat (*Pakistan*) (16) and D.R.Shepherd (*England*) (24).

AUSTRALIA v ZIMBABWE

At Barabati Stadium, Cuttack, India, on 30 October 1987.   Toss: Zimbabwe.
Result: AUSTRALIA won by 70 runs.   Award: D.C.Boon.
LOI debuts: None.

AUSTRALIA		Runs	Balls	4/6
D.C.Boon	c Houghton b Butchart	93	101	9/1
G.R.Marsh	run out	37	65	1
D.M.Jones	not out	58	72	1/1
C.J.McDermott	c Rawson b Traicos	9	10	–/1
*A.R.Border	st Houghton b Traicos	4	6	
M.R.J.Veletta	run out	43	39	3
S.R.Waugh	not out	10	14	1
S.P.O'Donnell				
†G.C.Dyer				
T.B.A.May				
B.A.Reid				
Extras	(B3, LB3, W6)	12		
TOTAL	(50 overs; 5 wickets)	266		

ZIMBABWE		Runs	Balls	4/6
A.H.Shah	b Waugh	32	90	4
A.C.Waller	c Waugh b McDermott	38	83	2
K.M.Curran	c Waugh b May	29	57	2
A.J.Pycroft	c Dyer b McDermott	38	46	2
†D.L.Houghton	lbw b May	1	11	–
I.P.Butchart	st Dyer b Border	3	5	–
P.W.E.Rawson	not out	24	29	2/1
E.A.Brandes	not out	18	11	1/2
K.J.Arnott				
M.P.Jarvis				
*A.J.Traicos				
Extras	(LB5, W6, NB2)	13		
TOTAL	(50 overs; 6 wickets)	196		

ZIMBABWE	O	M	R	W		FALL OF WICKETS	
Rawson	9	0	41	0	Wkt	A	Z
Jarvis	6	0	33	0	1st	90	55
Shah	7	0	31	0	2nd	148	89
Brandes	10	1	58	0	3rd	159	92
Traicos	10	0	45	2	4th	170	97
Butchart	8	0	52	1	5th	248	139
					6th	–	156
AUSTRALIA					7th	–	–
McDermott	10	0	43	2	8th	–	–
Reid	9	2	30	0	9th	–	–
Waugh	4	0	9	1	10th	–	–
O'Donnell	7	1	21	0			
May	10	1	30	2			
Border	8	0	36	1			
Jones	1	0	5	0			
Boon	1	0	17	0			

Umpires: Mahboob Shah (*Pakistan*) (13) and P.W.Vidanagamage (*Sri Lanka*) (18).

ENGLAND v SRI LANKA

At Nehru Stadium, Poona (Pune), India, on 30 October 1987.   Toss: Sri Lanka.
Result: **ENGLAND** won by 8 wickets.   Award: G.A.Gooch.
LOI debuts: None.

SRI LANKA		Runs	Balls	4/6
R.S.Mahanama	c Emburey b DeFreitas	14	28	1
J.R.Ratnayeke	lbw b Small	7	26	–
†A.P.Gurusinha	run out	34	63	3
R.L.Dias	st Downton b Hemmings	80	105	6/3
*L.R.D.Mendis	b DeFreitas	7	11	1
R.S.Madugalle	c sub (P.W.Jarvis) b Hemmings	22	38	–/1
P.A.de Silva	not out	23	18	2
A.L.F.de Mel	c Lamb b Hemmings	0	2	–
S.Jeganathan	not out	20	15	2/1
V.B.John				
S.D.Anurasiri				
Extras	(LB3, W3, NB5)	11		
TOTAL	(50 overs; 7 wickets)	218		

ENGLAND		Runs	Balls	4/6
G.A.Gooch	c and b Jeganathan	61	79	7
R.T.Robinson	b Jeganathan	55	75	7
C.W.J.Athey	not out	40	55	–
*M.W.Gatting	not out	46	40	4
A.J.Lamb				
†P.R.Downton				
J.E.Emburey				
P.A.J.DeFreitas				
N.A.Foster				
G.C.Small				
E.E.Hemmings				
Extras	(B1, LB13, W3)	17		
TOTAL	(41.2 overs; 2 wickets)	219		

ENGLAND	O	M	R	W	FALL OF WICKETS		
					Wkt	SL	E
DeFreitas	10	2	46	2	1st	23	123
Small	10	1	33	1	2nd	25	132
Foster	10	0	37	0	3rd	113	–
Emburey	10	1	42	0	4th	125	–
Hemmings	10	0	57	3	5th	170	–
					6th	177	–
SRI LANKA					7th	180	–
Ratnayeke	8	1	37	0	8th	–	–
John	6	2	19	0	9th	–	–
De Mel	4.2	0	34	0	10th	–	–
Jeganathan	10	0	45	2			
Anurasiri	10	0	45	0			
De Silva	3	0	25	0			

Umpires: D.M.Archer (*West Indies*) (15) and Khizer Hayat (*Pakistan*) (17).

PAKISTAN v WEST INDIES

At National Stadium, Karachi, Pakistan, on 30 October 1987.　Toss: West Indies.
Result: **WEST INDIES** won by 28 runs.　Award: R.B.Richardson.
LOI debuts: None.

WEST INDIES		Runs	Balls	4/6
D.L.Haynes	c Imran b Mudassar	25	52	1
P.V.Simmons	b Wasim	6	9	1
R.B.Richardson	c Qadir b Imran	110	135	8/2
*I.V.A.Richards	b Wasim	67	75	2/2
A.L.Logie	c Mudassar b Imran	12	17	–
R.A.Harper	b Wasim	2	7	–
C.L.Hooper	not out	5	7	–
W.K.M.Benjamin	c Mudassar b Imran	0	1	–
†P.J.L.Dujon	not out	1	1	–
C.A.Walsh				
B.P.Patterson				
Extras	(B3, LB10, W16, NB1)	30		
TOTAL	(50 overs; 7 wickets)	258		

PAKISTAN		Runs	Balls	4/6
Mudassar Nazar	b Harper	40	55	3
Ramiz Raja	c Hooper b Patterson	70	111	3
Salim Malik	c Richards b Walsh	23	37	–
Javed Miandad	b Benjamin	38	38	3
Ijaz Ahmed	b Benjamin	6	10	–
*Imran Khan	c Harper b Walsh	8	11	–
†Salim Yousuf	b Patterson	7	11	–
Wasim Akram	lbw b Patterson	0	2	–
Abdul Qadir	not out	8	11	–
Shoaib Mohammad	b Benjamin	0	1	–
Salim Jaffer	not out	8	16	–
Extras	(B4, LB6, W10, NB2)	22		
TOTAL	(50 overs; 9 wickets)	230		

PAKISTAN	O	M	R	W		FALL OF WICKETS		
					Wkt	WI	P	
Imran Khan	9	0	57	3	1st	19	78	
Wasim Akram	10	0	45	3	2nd	84	128	
Abdul Qadir	10	1	29	0	3rd	221	147	
Mudassar Nazar	10	0	47	1	4th	242	167	
Salim Jaffer	6	0	37	0	5th	248	186	
Salim Malik	5	0	30	0	6th	255	202	
					7th	255	202	
WEST INDIES					8th	–	208	
Patterson	10	1	34	3	9th	–	208	
Walsh	10	1	34	2	10th	–	–	
Harper	10	0	38	1				
Benjamin	10	0	69	3				
Richards	10	0	45	0				

Umpires: R.B.Gupta (*India*) (8) and V.K.Ramaswamy (*India*) (8).

INDIA v NEW ZEALAND

At Vidarbha CA Ground, Nagpur, India, on 31 October 1987.   Toss: New Zealand.
Result: **INDIA** won by 9 wickets.   Award: S.M.Gavaskar.
LOI debuts: New Zealand – D.K.Morrison.

NEW ZEALAND		Runs	Balls	4/6
J.G.Wright	run out	35	59	4
P.A.Horne	b Prabhakar	18	35	1
M.D.Crowe	c Pandit b Azharuddin	21	24	2
K.R.Rutherford	b Sharma	26	54	1
*J.J.Crowe	b Maninder	24	24	3
D.N.Patel	c Kapil Dev b Shastri	40	51	3
M.C.Snedden	run out	23	28	2
†I.D.S.Smith	b Sharma	0	1	–
E.J.Chatfield	b Sharma	0	1	–
W.Watson	not out	12	25	1
D.K.Morrison				
Extras	(LB14, W7, NB1)	22		
TOTAL	(50 overs; 9 wickets)	221		

INDIA		Runs	Balls	4/6
K.Srikkanth	c Rutherford b Watson	75	58	9/3
S.M.Gavaskar	not out	103	88	10/3
M.Azharuddin	not out	41	51	5
N.S.Sidhu				
D.B.Vengsarkar				
*Kapil Dev				
R.J.Shastri				
†C.S.Pandit				
M.Prabhakar				
C.Sharma				
Maninder Singh				
Extras	(LB1, W2, NB2)	5		
TOTAL	(32.1 overs; 1 wicket)	224		

INDIA	O	M	R	W		FALL OF WICKETS	
					Wkt	NZ	I
Kapil Dev	6	0	24	0			
Prabhakar	7	0	23	1	1st	46	136
Sharma	10	2	51	3‡	2nd	84	–
Maninder	10	0	51	1	3rd	90	–
Shastri	10	1	32	1	4th	122	–
Azharuddin	7	0	26	1	5th	181	–
					6th	182	–
NEW ZEALAND					7th	182	–
Morrison	10	0	69	0	8th	182	–
Chatfield	4.1	1	39	0	9th	221	–
Snedden	4	0	29	0	10th	–	–
Watson	10	0	50	1			
Patel	4	0	36	0			

Umpires: H.D.Bird (*England*) (48) and D.R.Shepherd (*England*) (25).

‡ (including a hat-trick)

PAKISTAN v AUSTRALIA (SEMI-FINAL)

At Gaddafi Stadium, Lahore, Pakistan, on 4 November 1987.   Toss: Australia.
Result: **AUSTRALIA** won by 18 runs.   Award: C.J.McDermott.
LOI debuts: None.

AUSTRALIA		Runs	Balls	4/6
G.R.Marsh	run out	31	57	2
D.C.Boon	st Miandad b Salim Malik	65	91	4
D.M.Jones	b Tausif	38	45	3
*A.R.Border	run out	18	22	2
M.R.J.Veletta	b Imran	48	50	2
S.R.Waugh	not out	32	28	4/1
S.P.O'Donnell	run out	0	2	–
†G.C.Dyer	b Imran	0	1	–
C.J.McDermott	b Imran	1	3	–
T.B.A.May	not out	0	2	–
B.A.Reid				
Extras	(B1, LB19, W13, NB1)	34		
TOTAL	(50 overs; 8 wickets)	267		

PAKISTAN		Runs	Balls	4/6
Ramiz Raja	run out	1	1	–
Mansoor Akhtar	b McDermott	9	19	–
Salim Malik	c McDermott b Waugh	25	31	3
Javed Miandad	b Reid	70	103	4
*Imran Khan	c Dyer b Border	58	84	4
Wasim Akram	b McDermott	20	13	–/2
Ijaz Ahmed	c Jones b Reid	8	7	1
†Salim Yousuf	c Dyer b McDermott	21	15	2
Abdul Qadir	not out	20	16	2
Salim Jaffer	c Dyer b McDermott	0	2	–
Tausif Ahmed	c Dyer b McDermott	1	3	–
Extras	(LB6, W10)	16		
TOTAL	(49 overs)	249		

PAKISTAN	O	M	R	W
Imran Khan	10	1	36	3
Salim Jaffer	6	0	57	0
Wasim Akram	10	0	54	0
Abdul Qadir	10	0	39	0
Tausif Ahmed	10	1	39	1
Salim Malik	4	0	22	1

AUSTRALIA	O	M	R	W
McDermott	10	0	44	5
Reid	10	2	41	2
Waugh	9	1	51	1
O'Donnell	10	1	45	0
May	6	0	36	0
Border	4	0	26	1

FALL OF WICKETS		
Wkt	A	P
1st	73	2
2nd	155	37
3rd	155	38
4th	215	150
5th	236	177
6th	236	192
7th	241	212
8th	249	236
9th	–	247
10th	–	249

Umpires: H.D.Bird (*England*) (49) and D.R.Shepherd (*England*) (26).

INDIA v ENGLAND (SEMI-FINAL)

At Wankhede Stadium, Bombay, India, on 5 November 1987. Toss: India.
Result: **ENGLAND** won by 35 runs.   Award: G.A.Gooch.
LOI debuts: None.

ENGLAND		Runs	Balls	4/6
G.A.Gooch	c Srikkanth b Maninder	115	136	11
R.T.Robinson	st More b Maninder	13	36	2
C.W.J.Athey	c More b Sharma	4	17	–
*M.W.Gatting	b Maninder	56	62	5
A.J.Lamb	not out	32	29	2
J.E.Emburey	lbw b Kapil Dev	6	10	–
P.A.J.DeFreitas	b Kapil Dev	7	8	1
†P.R.Downton	not out	1	5	–
N.A.Foster				
G.C.Small				
E.E.Hemmings				
Extras	(B1, LB18, W1)	20		
TOTAL	(50 overs; 6 wickets)	254		

INDIA		Runs	Balls	4/6
K.Srikkanth	b Foster	31	55	4
S.M.Gavaskar	b DeFreitas	4	7	1
N.S.Sidhu	c Athey b Foster	22	40	–
M.Azharuddin	lbw b Hemmings	64	74	7
C.S.Pandit	lbw b Foster	24	30	3
*Kapil Dev	c Gatting b Hemmings	30	22	3
R.J.Shastri	c Downton b Hemmings	21	32	2
†K.S.More	c and b Emburey	0	5	–
M.Prabhakar	c Downton b Small	4	11	–
C.Sharma	c Lamb b Hemmings	0	1	–
Maninder Singh	not out	0	–	–
Extras	(B1, LB9, W6, NB3)	19		
TOTAL	(45.3 overs)	219		

INDIA	O	M	R	W		FALL OF WICKETS		
					Wkt	E	I	
Kapil Dev	10	1	38	2	1st	40	7	
Prabhakar	9	1	40	0	2nd	79	58	
Maninder	10	0	54	3	3rd	196	73	
Sharma	9	0	41	1	4th	203	121	
Shastri	10	0	49	0	5th	219	168	
Azharuddin	2	0	13	0	6th	231	204	
					7th	–	205	
ENGLAND					8th	–	218	
DeFreitas	7	0	37	1	9th	–	219	
Small	6	0	22	1	10th	–	219	
Emburey	10	1	35	1				
Foster	10	0	47	3				
Hemmings	9.3	1	52	4				
Gooch	3	0	16	0				

Umpires: A.R.Crafter (*Australia*) (57) and S.J.Woodward (*New Zealand*) (11).

ENGLAND v AUSTRALIA (FINAL)

At Eden Gardens, Calcutta, India, on 8 November 1987.   Toss: Australia.
Result: **AUSTRALIA** won by 7 runs.   Award: D.C.Boon.
LOI debuts: None.

AUSTRALIA		Runs	Balls	4/6
D.C.Boon	c Downton b Hemmings	75	125	7
G.R.Marsh	b Foster	24	49	3
D.M.Jones	c Athey b Hemmings	33	57	1/1
C.J.McDermott	b Gooch	14	8	2
*A.R.Border	run out	31	31	3
M.R.J.Veletta	not out	45	31	6
S.R.Waugh	not out	5	4	
S.P.O'Donnell				
†G.C.Dyer				
T.B.A.May				
B.A.Reid				
Extras	(B1, LB13, W5, NB7)	26		
TOTAL	(50 overs; 5 wickets)	253		

ENGLAND		Runs	Balls	4/6
G.A.Gooch	lbw b O'Donnell	35	57	4
R.T.Robinson	lbw b McDermott	0	1	
C.W.J.Athey	run out	58	103	2
*M.W.Gatting	c Dyer b Border	41	45	3/1
A.J.Lamb	b Waugh	45	45	4
†P.R.Downton	c O'Donnell b Border	9	8	1
J.E.Emburey	run out	10	16	
P.A.J.DeFreitas	c Reid b Waugh	17	10	2/1
N.A.Foster	not out	7	6	
G.C.Small	not out	3	3	
E.E.Hemmings				
Extras	(B1, LB14, W2, NB4)	21		
TOTAL	(50 overs; 8 wickets)	246		

ENGLAND	O	M	R	W
DeFreitas	6	1	34	0
Small	6	0	33	0
Foster	10	0	38	1
Hemmings	10	1	48	2
Emburey	10	0	44	0
Gooch	8	1	42	1

AUSTRALIA	O	M	R	W
McDermott	10	1	51	1
Reid	10	0	43	0
Waugh	9	0	37	2
O'Donnell	10	1	35	1
May	4	0	27	0
Border	7	0	38	2

FALL OF WICKETS		
Wkt	A	E
1st	75	1
2nd	151	66
3rd	166	135
4th	168	170
5th	241	188
6th	–	218
7th	–	220
8th	–	235
9th	–	–
10th	–	–

Umpires: R.B.Gupta (9) and Mahboob Shah (*Pakistan*) (14).

THE 1992 WORLD CUP

The fifth World Cup was the largest ever, its 39 matches exceeding even the 37 scheduled for the 1996 competition, 14 of them being staged in New Zealand and the remaining 25 in Australia, ten of the latter being day/night games. This was the first World Cup to involve floodlit cricket with its full panoply of coloured clothing, white balls and white sightscreens.

Matches were again 50 overs per innings and, despite there being a dozen more games than in the Reliance Cup, it was completed in 33 days as opposed to six weeks. It was also the fairest in that instead of being divided into groups, each side played the others once before the top four in the qualifying table played off in the semi-finals.

The competition's only major fault, and it was a vital one, concerned the new rules governing rain-interrupted matches. To accommodate such a compressed schedule of matches and allowing for travelling time involved in an itinerary stretching from Perth to Dunedin, no spare days were allowed. To overcome the imperfection of a straight run-rate calculation when a second innings had to be shortened after rain, the organising committee employed a method whereby the reduction in the target would be proportionate to the lowest-scoring overs of the side batting first. England's encounters with South Africa were the worst affected. At Melbourne, rain deprived England of 9 overs but their target of 237 was reduced by only 11 runs. Thanks to a remarkable innings of 75 not out by Neil Fairbrother, England won by three wickets off the penultimate ball. Their meeting in the Sydney semi-final was again interrupted, a 12-minute downpour arriving when South Africa wanted 22 from 13 balls. At first their target was reduced to 22 from seven but, as the teams took the field, the scoreboard showed that it had been adjusted to 21 from one! England were embarrassed, South Africa distraught and the crowd in uproar. In the case of the final rounds a second day had been put aside and the match could easily have been completed then without reducing the overs, as would have been the case in England. The demands of television proved paramount and the rules quite inflexible. It was an especially unfortunate end for South Africa, newly restored to the fold and slotted into the tournament at the last moments. This was the first tournament to involve nine teams – the eight current full members plus aspiring Zimbabwe, winners of the ICC Trophy.

QUALIFYING TABLE	P	W	L	NR	Points	Net Run-rate†
NEW ZEALAND	8	7	1	0	14	0.59
ENGLAND	8	5	2	1	11	0.47
SOUTH AFRICA	8	5	3	0	10	0.13
PAKISTAN	8	4	3	1	9	0.16
Australia	8	4	4	0	8	0.20
West Indies	8	4	4	0	8	0.07
India	8	2	5	1	5	0.14
Sri Lanka	8	2	5	1	5	-0.68
Zimbabwe	8	1	7	0	2	-1.14

† *Calculated by subtracting runs conceded per over from runs scored per over, revising figures in shortened matches and discounting those matches not played to a result.*

After three semi-final defeats and a disastrous start in this tournament, Pakistan won the Benson and Hedges World Cup, defeating England by 22 runs at the MCG before a record Australian limited-overs crowd of 87,182 (receipts \$A2 million (£880,000)).

NEW ZEALAND v AUSTRALIA

At Eden Park, Auckland, New Zealand, on 22 February 1992.   Toss: New Zealand.
Result: **NEW ZEALAND** won by 37 runs.   Award: M.D.Crowe.
LOI debuts: None.

NEW ZEALAND		Runs	Balls	4/6
J.G.Wright	b McDermott	0	1	–
R.T.Latham	c Healy b Moody	26	44	4
A.H.Jones	lbw b Reid	4	14	1
*M.D.Crowe	not out	100	134	11
K.R.Rutherford	run out	57	71	6
C.Z.Harris	run out	14	15	2
†I.D.S.Smith	c Healy b McDermott	14	14	1
C.L.Cairns	not out	16	11	2
D.N.Patel				
G.R.Larsen				
W.Watson				
Extras	(LB6, W7, NB4)	17		
TOTAL	(50 overs; 6 wickets)	248		

AUSTRALIA		Runs	Balls	4/6
D.C.Boon	run out	100	131	11
G.R.Marsh	c Latham b Larsen	19	56	2
D.M.Jones	run out	21	27	3
*A.R.Border	c Cairns b Patel	3	11	–
T.M.Moody	c and b Latham	7	11	–
M.E.Waugh	lbw b Larsen	2	5	–
S.R.Waugh	c and b Larsen	38	34	3/1
†I.A.Healy	not out	7	9	–
C.J.McDermott	run out	1	1	–
P.L.Taylor	c Rutherford b Watson	1	2	–
B.A.Reid	c Jones b Harris	3	4	–
Extras	(LB6, W2, NB1)	9		
TOTAL	(48.1 overs)	211		

AUSTRALIA	O	M	R	W		FALL OF WICKETS		
McDermott	10	1	43	2	Wkt	NZ	A	
Reid	10	0	39	1	1st	2	62	
Moody	9	1	37	1	2nd	13	92	
S.R.Waugh	10	0	60	0	3rd	53	104	
Taylor	7	0	36	0	4th	171	120	
M.E.Waugh	4	0	27	0	5th	191	125	
					6th	215	199	
NEW ZEALAND					7th	–	200	
Cairns	4	0	30	0	8th	–	205	
Patel	10	1	36	1	9th	–	206	
Watson	9	1	39	1	10th	-	211	
Larsen	10	1	30	3				
Harris	7.1	0	35	1				
Latham	8	0	35	1				

Umpires: Khizer Hayat (*Pakistan*) (38) and D.R.Shepherd (*England*) (41).

ENGLAND v INDIA

At WACA Ground, Perth, Australia, on 22 February 1992.   Toss: England.
Result: **ENGLAND** won by 9 runs.   Award: I.T.Botham.
LOI debuts: None.

ENGLAND		Runs	Balls	4/6
*G.A.Gooch	c Tendulkar b Shastri	51	89	1
I.T.Botham	c More b Kapil Dev	9	21	1
R.A.Smith	c Azharuddin b Prabhakar	91	108	8/2
G.A.Hick	c More b Banerjee	5	6	1
N.H.Fairbrother	c Srikkanth b Srinath	24	34	1
†A.J.Stewart	b Prabhakar	13	15	1
C.C.Lewis	c Banerjee b Kapil Dev	10	6	1
D.R.Pringle	c Srikkanth b Srinath	1	3	–
D.A.Reeve	not out	8	8	–
P.A.J.DeFreitas	run out	1	5	–
P.C.R.Tufnell	not out	3	5	–
Extras	(B1, LB6, W13)	20		
TOTAL	(50 overs; 9 wickets)	236		

INDIA		Runs	Balls	4/6
R.J.Shastri	run out	57	112	2
K.Srikkanth	c Botham b DeFreitas	39	50	7
*M.Azharuddin	c Stewart b Reeve	0	1	–
S.R.Tendulkar	c Stewart b Botham	35	44	5
V.G.Kambli	c Hick b Botham	3	11	–
P.K.Amre	run out	22	31	–
Kapil Dev	c DeFreitas b Reeve	17	18	2
S.T.Banerjee	not out	25	16	1/1
†K.S.More	run out	1	4	–
M.Prabhakar	b Reeve	0	2	–
J.Srinath	run out	11	8	–
Extras	(LB9, W7, NB1)	17		
TOTAL	(49.2 overs)	227		

INDIA	O	M	R	W		FALL OF WICKETS		
Kapil Dev	10	0	38	2	Wkt	E	I	
Prabhakar	10	3	34	2	1st	21	63	
Srinath	9	1	47	2	2nd	131	63	
Banerjee	7	0	45	1	3rd	137	126	
Tendulkar	10	0	37	0	4th	197	140	
Shastri	4	0	28	1	5th	198	149	
					6th	214	187	
ENGLAND					7th	222	194	
Pringle	10	0	53	0	8th	223	200	
Lewis	9.2	0	36	0	9th	224	201	
DeFreitas	10	0	39	1	10th	–	227	
Reeve	6	0	38	3				
Botham	10	0	27	2				
Tufnell	4	0	25	0				

Umpires: J.D.Buultjens (*Sri Lanka*) (13) and P.J.McConnell (63).

SRI LANKA v ZIMBABWE

At Pukekura Park, New Plymouth, New Zealand, on 23 February 1992.
Toss: Sri Lanka.
Result: **SRI LANKA** won by 3 wickets.   Award: A.Flower.
LOI debuts: Zimbabwe – K.G.Duers, A.Flower, W.R.James.

ZIMBABWE		Runs	Balls	4/6
†A.Flower	not out	115	152	8/1
W.R.James	c Tillekeratne b Wickremasinghe	17	21	3
A.J.Pycroft	c Ramanayake b Gurusinha	5	22	–
*D.L.Houghton	c Tillekeratne b Gurusinha	10	19	1
K.J.Arnott	c Tillekeratne b Wickremasinghe	52	56	4/1
A.C.Waller	not out	83	45	9/3
I.P.Butchart				
E.A.Brandes				
K.G.Duers				
M.P.Jarvis				
A.J.Traicos				
Extras	(B2, LB6, W13, NB9)	30		
TOTAL	(50 overs; 4 wickets)	312		

SRI LANKA		Runs	Balls	4/6
R.S.Mahanama	c Arnott b Brandes	59	89	4
M.A.R.Samarasekera	c Duers b Traicos	75	61	11/1
*P.A.de Silva	c Houghton b Brandes	14	28	1
A.P.Gurusinha	run out	5	6	–
A.Ranatunga	not out	88	61	9/1
S.T.Jayasuriya	c Flower b Houghton	32	23	2/2
†H.P.Tillekeratne	b Jarvis	18	12	1/1
R.S.Kalpage	c Houghton b Brandes	11	14	1
C.P.H.Ramanayake	not out	1	1	–
K.I.W.Wijegunawardene				
G.P.Wickremasinghe				
Extras	(LB5, W5)	10		
TOTAL	(49.2 overs; 7 wickets)	313		

SRI LANKA	O	M	R	W		FALL OF WICKETS	
					Wkt	Z	SL
Ramanayake	10	0	59	0	1st	30	128
Wijegunawardene	7	0	54	0	2nd	57	144
Wickremasinghe	10	1	50	2	3rd	82	155
Gurusinha	10	0	72	2	4th	167	167
Kalpage	10	0	51	0	5th	–	212
Jayasuriya	3	0	18	0	6th	–	273
					7th	–	308
ZIMBABWE					8th	–	–
Jarvis	9.2	0	51	1	9th	–	–
Brandes	10	0	70	3	10th	–	–
Duers	10	0	72	0			
Butchart	8	0	63	0			
Traicos	10	1	33	1			
Houghton	2	0	19	1			

Umpires: P.D.Reporter (*India*) (13) and S.J.Woodward (24).

LOI No. 717/57

WEST INDIES v PAKISTAN

At Melbourne Cricket Ground, Australia, on 23 February 1992. Toss: West Indies.
Result: **WEST INDIES** won by 10 wickets. Award: B.C.Lara.
LOI debuts: Pakistan – Iqbal Sikander, Wasim Haider.

PAKISTAN		Runs	Balls	4/6
Ramiz Raja	not out	102	158	4
Aamir Sohail	c Logie b Benjamin	23	44	3
Inzamam-ul-Haq	c Hooper b Harper	27	39	–
*Javed Miandad	not out	57	61	5
Salim Malik				
Ijaz Ahmed				
Wasim Akram				
Iqbal Sikander				
Wasim Haider				
†Moin Khan				
Aqib Javed				
Extras	(B1, LB3, W5, NB2)	11		
TOTAL	(50 overs; 2 wickets)	220		

WEST INDIES		Runs	Balls	4/6
D.L.Haynes	not out	93	144	7
B.C.Lara	retired hurt	88	101	11
*R.B.Richardson	not out	20	40	1
C.L.Hooper				
A.L.Logie				
K.L.T.Arthurton				
R.A.Harper				
M.D.Marshall				
W.K.M.Benjamin				
†D.Williams				
C.E.L.Ambrose				
Extras	(B2, LB8, W7, NB3)	20		
TOTAL	(46.5 overs; 0 wickets)	221		

WEST INDIES	O	M	R	W		FALL OF WICKETS		
						Wkt	P	WI
Marshall	10	1	53	0		1st	45	–
Ambrose	10	0	40	0		2nd	97	–
Benjamin	10	0	49	1		3rd	–	–
Hooper	10	0	41	0		4th	–	–
Harper	10	0	33	1		5th	–	–
						6th	–	–
PAKISTAN						7th	–	–
Wasim Akram	10	0	37	0		8th	–	–
Aqib Javed	8.5	0	42	0		9th	–	–
Wasim Haider	8	0	42	0		10th	–	–
Ijaz Ahmed	6	1	29	0				
Iqbal Sikander	8	1	26	0				
Aamir Sohail	6	0	35	0				

Umpires: S.G.Randell (43) and I.D.Robinson (*Zimbabwe*) (1).

NEW ZEALAND v SRI LANKA

At Trust Bank Park, Hamilton, New Zealand, on 25 February 1992.   Toss: New Zealand.
Result: **NEW ZEALAND** won by 6 wickets.   Award: K.R.Rutherford.
LOI debuts: None.

SRI LANKA		Runs	Balls	4/6
R.S.Mahanama	c and b Harris	80	131	6
M.A.R.Samarasekera	c Wright b Watson	9	20	1
A.P.Gurusinha	c Smith b Harris	9	33	1
*P.A.de Silva	run out	31	45	2
A.Ranatunga	c Rutherford b Harris	20	26	2
S.T.Jayasuriya	run out	5	7	–
†H.P.Tillekeratne	c Crowe b Watson	8	19	–
R.S.Kalpage	c Larsen b Watson	11	17	–
C.P.H.Ramanayake	run out	2	1	–
S.D.Anurasiri	not out	3	2	–
G.P.Wickremasinghe	not out	3	4	–
Extras	(B1, LB15, W4, NB5)	25		
TOTAL	(50 overs; 9 wickets)	206		

NEW ZEALAND		Runs	Balls	4/6
J.G.Wright	c and b Kalpage	57	76	9
R.T.Latham	b Kalpage	20	41	3
A.H.Jones	c Jayasuriya b Gurusinha	49	77	4
*M.D.Crowe	c Ramanayake b Wickremasinghe	5	23	–
K.R.Rutherford	not out	65	71	6/1
C.Z.Harris	not out	5	5	–
†I.D.S.Smith				
D.N.Patel				
D.K.Morrison				
G.R.Larsen				
W.Watson				
Extras	(LB3, W3, NB3)	9		
TOTAL	(48.2 overs; 4 wickets)	210		

NEW ZEALAND	O	M	R	W		FALL OF WICKETS	
					Wkt	SL	NZ
Morrison	8	0	36	0	1st	18	77
Watson	10	0	37	3	2nd	50	90
Larsen	10	1	29	0	3rd	120	105
Harris	10	0	43	3	4th	172	186
Latham	3	0	13	0	5th	172	–
Patel	9	0	32	0	6th	181	–
					7th	195	–
SRI LANKA					8th	199	–
Ramanayake	9.2	0	46	0	9th	202	–
Wickremasinghe	8	1	40	1	10th	–	–
Anurasiri	10	1	27	0			
Kalpage	10	0	33	2			
Gurusinha	4	0	19	1			
Ranatunga	4	0	22	0			
Jayasuriya	2	0	14	0			
De Silva	3	0	6	0			

Umpires: P.D.Reporter (*India*) (14) and D.R.Shepherd (*England*) (42).

AUSTRALIA v SOUTH AFRICA

At Sydney Cricket Ground, Australia, on 26 February 1992.   Toss: Australia.
Result: **SOUTH AFRICA won by 9 wickets.**   Award: K.C.Wessels.
LOI debuts: South Africa – W.J.Cronje, M.W.Pringle, J.N.Rhodes.

AUSTRALIA		Runs	Balls	4/6
G.R.Marsh	c Richardson b Kuiper	25	72	1
D.C.Boon	run out	27	32	4
D.M.Jones	c Richardson b McMillan	24	51	1
*A.R.Border	b Kuiper	0	1	–
T.M.Moody	lbw b Donald	10	33	–
S.R.Waugh	c Cronje b McMillan	27	51	1
†I.A.Healy	c McMillan b Donald	16	24	2
P.L.Taylor	b Donald	4	9	–
C.J.McDermott	run out	6	12	–
M.R.Whitney	not out	9	15	1
B.A.Reid	not out	5	10	–
Extras	(LB2, W11, NB4)	17		
TOTAL	(49 overs; 9 wickets)	**170**		

SOUTH AFRICA		Runs	Balls	4/6
*K.C.Wessels	not out	81	148	9
A.C.Hudson	b Taylor	28	52	3
P.N.Kirsten	not out	49	88	1
A.P.Kuiper				
J.N.Rhodes				
W.J.Cronje				
B.M.McMillan				
†D.J.Richardson				
R.P.Snell				
M.W.Pringle				
A.A.Donald				
Extras	(LB5, W6, NB2)	13		
TOTAL	(46.5 overs; 1 wicket)	**171**		

SOUTH AFRICA	O	M	R	W		FALL OF WICKETS		
Donald	10	0	34	3		Wkt	A	SA
Pringle	10	0	52	0		1st	42	74
Snell	9	1	15	0		2nd	76	–
McMillan	10	0	35	2		3rd	76	–
Kuiper	5	0	15	2		4th	97	–
Cronje	5	1	17	0		5th	108	–
						6th	143	–
AUSTRALIA						7th	146	–
McDermott	10	1	23	0		8th	156	–
Reid	8.5	0	41	0		9th	161	–
Whitney	6	0	26	0		10th	–	–
Waugh	4	1	16	0				
Taylor	10	1	32	1				
Border	4	0	13	0				
Moody	4	0	15	0				

Umpires: B.L.Aldridge (*New Zealand*) (19) and S.A.Bucknor (*West Indies*) (4).

PAKISTAN v ZIMBABWE

At Bellerive Oval, Hobart, Australia, on 27 February 1992.   Toss: Zimbabwe.
Result: **PAKISTAN** won by 53 runs.   Award: Aamir Sohail.
LOI debuts: None.

PAKISTAN		Runs	Balls	4/6
Ramiz Raja	c Flower b Jarvis	9	16	1
Aamir Sohail	c Pycroft b Butchart	114	136	12
Inzamam-ul-Haq	c Brandes b Butchart	14	43	–
Javed Miandad	lbw b Butchart	89	94	5
Salim Malik	not out	14	12	–
Wasim Akram	not out	1	1	–
*Imran Khan				
Mushtaq Ahmed				
Iqbal Sikander				
†Moin Khan				
Aqib Javed				
Extras	(LB9, NB4)	13		
TOTAL	(50 overs; 4 wickets)	254		

ZIMBABWE		Runs	Balls	4/6
K.J.Arnott	c Wasim b Iqbal	7	61	–
†A.Flower	c Inzamam b Wasim	6	21	–
A.J.Pycroft	b Wasim	0	4	–
*D.L.Houghton	c Ramiz b Aamir	44	82	3
A.H.Shah	b Aamir	33	58	2
A.C.Waller	b Wasim	44	36	3/1
I.P.Butchart	c Miandad b Aqib	33	27	4
E.A.Brandes	not out	2	3	–
A.J.Traicos	not out	8	7	–
W.R.James				
M.P.Jarvis				
Extras	(B3, LB15, W6)	24		
TOTAL	(50 overs; 7 wickets)	201		

ZIMBABWE	O	M	R	W		FALL OF WICKETS		
Brandes	10	1	49	0		Wkt	P	Z
Jarvis	10	1	52	1		1st	29	14
Shah	10	1	24	0		2nd	63	14
Butchart	10	0	57	3		3rd	208	33
Traicos	10	0	63	0		4th	253	103
						5th	–	108
PAKISTAN						6th	–	187
Wasim Akram	10	2	21	3		7th	–	190
Aqib Javed	10	1	49	1		8th	–	–
Iqbal Sikander	10	1	35	1		9th	–	–
Mushtaq Ahmed	10	1	34	0		10th	–	–
Aamir Sohail	6	1	26	2				
Salim Malik	4	0	18	0				

Umpires: J.D.Buultjens (*Sri Lanka*) (14) and S.G.Randell (44).

ENGLAND v WEST INDIES

At Melbourne Cricket Ground, Australia, on 27 February 1992.   Toss: England.
Result: **ENGLAND** won by 6 wickets.   Award: C.C.Lewis.
LOI debuts: None.

WEST INDIES		Runs	Balls	4/6
D.L.Haynes	c Fairbrother b DeFreitas	38	68	5
B.C.Lara	c Stewart b Lewis	0	2	–
*R.B.Richardson	c Botham b Lewis	5	17	1
C.L.Hooper	c Reeve b Botham	5	20	–
K.L.T.Arthurton	c Fairbrother b DeFreitas	54	101	2/2
A.L.Logie	run out	20	27	–/1
R.A.Harper	c Hick b Reeve	3	14	–
M.D.Marshall	run out	3	8	–
†D.Williams	c Pringle b DeFreitas	6	19	–
C.E.L.Ambrose	c DeFreitas b Lewis	4	6	–
W.K.M.Benjamin	not out	11	15	1
Extras	(LB4, W3, NB1)	8		
TOTAL	(49.2 overs)	157		

ENGLAND		Runs	Balls	4/6
*G.A.Gooch	st Williams b Hooper	65	101	7
I.T.Botham	c Williams b Benjamin	8	28	1
R.A.Smith	c Logie b Benjamin	8	28	–
G.A.Hick	c and b Harper	54	55	3/1
N.H.Fairbrother	not out	13	28	1
†A.J.Stewart	not out	0	1	–
D.A.Reeve				
C.C.Lewis				
D.R.Pringle				
P.A.J.DeFreitas				
P.C.R.Tufnell				
Extras	(LB7, W4, NB1)	12		
TOTAL	(39.5 overs; 4 wickets)	160		

ENGLAND	O	M	R	W		FALL OF WICKETS		
Pringle	7	3	16	0	Wkt	WI	E	
Lewis	8.2	1	30	3	1st	0	50	
DeFreitas	9	2	34	3	2nd	22	71	
Botham	10	0	30	1	3rd	36	126	
Reeve	10	1	23	1	4th	55	156	
Tufnell	5	0	20	0	5th	91	–	
					6th	102	–	
WEST INDIES					7th	116	–	
Ambrose	8	1	26	0	8th	131	–	
Marshall	8	0	37	0	9th	145	–	
Benjamin	9.5	2	22	2	10th	157	–	
Hooper	10	1	38	1				
Harper	4	0	30	1				

Umpires: K.E.Liebenberg (*South Africa*) (1) and S.J.Woodward (*New Zealand*) (25).

INDIA v SRI LANKA

At Harrup Park, Mackay, Queensland, Australia, on 28 February 1992.   Toss: Sri Lanka.
NO RESULT.   No award.
LOI debuts: India – A.D.Jadeja.

INDIA		Runs	Balls	4/6
K.Srikkanth	not out	1	2	–
Kapil Dev	not out	0	–	–
*M.Azharuddin				
S.R.Tendulkar				
V.G.Kambli				
P.K.Amre				
A.D.Jadeja				
†K.S.More				
M.Prabhakar				
J.Srinath				
S.L.V.Raju				
Extras		–		
TOTAL	(0.2 overs; 0 wickets)	1		

SRI LANKA		Runs	Balls	4/6
R.S.Mahanama				
U.C.Hathurusinghe				
A.P.Gurusinha				
*P.A.de Silva				
A.Ranatunga				
S.T.Jayasuriya				
†H.P.Tillekeratne				
R.S.Kalpage				
C.P.H.Ramanayake				
K.I.W.Wijegunawardene				
G.P.Wickremasinghe				
Extras				
TOTAL				

SRI LANKA	O	M	R	W
Ramanayake	0.2	0	1	0

Umpires: I.D.Robinson (*Zimbabwe*) (2) and D.R.Shepherd (*England*) (43).

NEW ZEALAND v SOUTH AFRICA

At Eden Park, Auckland, New Zealand, on 29 February 1992. Toss: South Africa.
Result: **NEW ZEALAND** won by 7 wickets. Award: M.J.Greatbatch.
LOI debuts: South Africa – T.Bosch.

SOUTH AFRICA		Runs	Balls	4/6
*K.C.Wessels	c Smith b Watson	3	18	–
A.C.Hudson	b Patel	1	16	–
P.N.Kirsten	c Cairns b Watson	90	129	10
W.J.Cronje	c Smith b Harris	7	22	–
†D.J.Richardson	c Larsen b Cairns	28	53	1
A.P.Kuiper	run out	2	2	–
J.N.Rhodes	c Crowe b Cairns	6	13	–
B.M.McMillan	not out	33	40	1
R.P.Snell	not out	11	8	1
A.A.Donald				
T.Bosch				
Extras	(LB8, NB1)	9		
TOTAL	(50 overs; 7 wickets)	190		

NEW ZEALAND		Runs	Balls	4/6
M.J.Greatbatch	b Kirsten	68	60	9/3
R.T.Latham	c Wessels b Snell	60	69	7
A.H.Jones	not out	34	63	4
†I.D.S.Smith	c Kirsten b Donald	19	8	4
*M.D.Crowe	not out	3	9	–
K.R.Rutherford				
C.Z.Harris				
C.L.Cairns				
D.N.Patel				
G.R.Larsen				
W.Watson				
Extras	(B1, W5, NB1)	7		
TOTAL	(34.3 overs; 3 wickets)	191		

NEW ZEALAND	O	M	R	W		FALL OF WICKETS		
Watson	10	2	30	2	Wkt	SA	NZ
Patel	10	1	28	1	1st	8	114
Larsen	10	1	29	0	2nd	10	155
Harris	10	2	33	1	3rd	29	179
Latham	2	0	19	0	4th	108	–
Cairns	8	0	43	2	5th	111	–
					6th	121	–
SOUTH AFRICA					7th	162	–
Donald	10	0	38	1	8th	–	–
McMillan	5	1	23	0	9th	–	–
Snell	7	0	56	1	10th	–	–
Bosch	2.3	0	19	0			
Cronje	2	0	14	0			
Kuiper	1	0	18	0			
Kirsten	7	1	22	1			

Umpires: Khizer Hayat (*Pakistan*) (39) and P.D.Reporter (*India*) (15).

WEST INDIES v ZIMBABWE

At Woolloongabba, Brisbane, Australia, on 29 February 1992. Toss: Zimbabwe.
Result: **WEST INDIES** won by 75 runs.   Award: B.C.Lara.
LOI debuts: Zimbabwe – A.D.R.Campbell.

WEST INDIES		Runs	Balls	4/6
P.V.Simmons	b Brandes	21	45	3
B.C.Lara	c Houghton b Shah	72	71	12
*R.B.Richardson	c Brandes b Jarvis	56	76	2/2
C.L.Hooper	c Pycroft b Traicos	63	67	5/1
K.L.T.Arthurton	b Duers	26	18	2/2
A.L.Logie	run out	5	6	–
M.D.Marshall	c Houghton b Brandes	2	10	–
†D.Williams	not out	8	6	1
W.K.M.Benjamin	b Brandes	1	4	–
A.C.Cummins				
B.P.Patterson				
Extras	(B1, LB6, W2, NB1)	10		
TOTAL	(50 overs; 8 wickets)	264		

ZIMBABWE		Runs	Balls	4/6
K.J.Arnott	retired hurt	16	36	1
†A.Flower	b Patterson	6	20	–
A.J.Pycroft	c Williams b Benjamin	10	24	–
*D.L.Houghton	c Patterson b Hooper	55	88	3
A.C.Waller	c Simmons b Benjamin	0	9	–
A.D.R.Campbell	c Richardson b Hooper	1	18	–
A.H.Shah	not out	60	87	4
E.A.Brandes	c and b Benjamin	6	9	–
A.J.Traicos	run out	8	19	–
M.P.Jarvis	not out	5	4	1
K.G.Duers				
Extras	(LB9, W5, NB8)	22		
TOTAL	(50 overs; 7 wickets)	189		

ZIMBABWE	O	M	R	W		FALL OF WICKETS		
Brandes	10	1	45	3	Wkt	WI	Z	
Jarvis	10	1	71	1	1st	78	21	
Duers	10	0	52	1	2nd	103	43	
Shah	10	2	39	1	3rd	220	48	
Traicos	10	0	50	1	4th	221	63	
					5th	239	132	
WEST INDIES					6th	254	161	
Patterson	10	0	25	1	7th	255	181	
Marshall	6	0	23	0	8th	264	–	
Benjamin	10	2	27	3	9th	–	–	
Cummins	10	0	33	0	10th	–	–	
Hooper	10	0	47	2				
Arthurton	4	0	25	0				

Umpires: K.E.Liebenberg (*South Africa*) (2) and S.J.Woodward (*New Zealand*) (26).

AUSTRALIA v INDIA

At Woolloongabba, Brisbane, Australia, on 1 March 1992.   Toss: Australia.
Result: **AUSTRALIA** won by 1 run (*target revised to 236 from 47 overs*).
Award: D.M.Jones.
LOI debuts: None.

AUSTRALIA		Runs	Balls	4/6
M.A.Taylor	c More b Kapil Dev	13	22	–
G.R.Marsh	b Kapil Dev	8	29	1
†D.C.Boon	c Shastri b Raju	43	61	4
D.M.Jones	c and b Prabhakar	90	109	6/2
S.R.Waugh	b Srinath	29	48	1
T.M.Moody	b Prabhakar	25	23	3
*A.R.Border	c Jadeja b Kapil Dev	10	10	–
C.J.McDermott	c Jadeja b Prabhakar	2	5	–
P.L.Taylor	run out	1	1	–
M.G.Hughes	not out	0	4	–
M.R.Whitney				
Extras	(LB7, W5, NB4)	16		
TOTAL	(50 overs; 9 wickets)	237		

INDIA		Runs	Balls	4/6
R.J.Shastri	c Waugh b Moody	25	70	1
K.Srikkanth	b McDermott	0	11	–
*M.Azharuddin	run out	93	103	10
S.R.Tendulkar	c Waugh b Moody	11	19	1
Kapil Dev	lbw b Waugh	21	21	3
S.V.Manjrekar	run out	47	42	3/1
A.D.Jadeja	b Hughes	1	4	–
†K.S.More	b Moody	14	8	2
J.Srinath	not out	8	8	–
M.Prabhakar	run out	1	1	–
S.L.V.Raju	run out	0	–	–
Extras	(LB8, W5)	13		
TOTAL	(47 overs)	234		

INDIA	O	M	R	W	FALL OF WICKETS		
Kapil Dev	10	2	41	3	Wkt	A	I
Prabhakar	10	0	41	3	1st	18	6
Srinath	8	0	48	1	2nd	31	53
Tendulkar	5	0	29	0	3rd	102	86
Raju	10	0	37	1	4th	156	128
Jadeja	7	0	34	0	5th	198	194
					6th	230	199
AUSTRALIA					7th	235	216
McDermott	9	1	35	1	8th	236	231
Whitney	10	2	36	0	9th	237	232
Hughes	9	1	49	1	10th	–	234
Moody	9	0	56	3			
Waugh	10	0	50	1			

Umpires: B.L.Aldridge (*New Zealand*) (20) and I.D.Robinson (*Zimbabwe*) (3).

FIFTH WORLD CUP (13th Match) LOI No. 726/30

ENGLAND v PAKISTAN

At Adelaide Oval, Australia, on 1 March 1992. Toss: England.
NO RESULT. No award.
LOI debuts: None.

PAKISTAN		Runs	Balls	4/6
Ramiz Raja	c Reeve b DeFreitas	1	10	–
Aamir Sohail	c and b Pringle	9	39	–
Inzamam-ul-Haq	c Stewart b DeFreitas	0	1	–
*Javed Miandad	b Pringle	3	22	–
Salim Malik	c Reeve b Botham	17	20	3
Ijaz Ahmed	c Stewart b Small	0	15	–
Wasim Akram	b Botham	1	13	–
†Moin Khan	c Hick b Small	2	14	–
Wasim Haider	c Stewart b Reeve	13	46	1
Mushtaq Ahmed	c Reeve b Pringle	17	42	1
Aqib Javed	not out	1	21	–
Extras	(LB1, W8, NB1)	10		
TOTAL	(40.2 overs)	74		

ENGLAND		Runs	Balls	4/6
*G.A.Gooch	c Moin b Wasim Akram	3	14	–
I.T.Botham	not out	6	22	–
R.A.Smith	not out	5	13	1
G.A.Hick				
N.H.Fairbrother				
†A.J.Stewart				
C.C.Lewis				
D.A.Reeve				
D.R.Pringle				
P.A.J.DeFreitas				
G.C.Small				
Extras	(B1, LB3, W5, NB1)	10		
TOTAL	(8 overs; 1 wicket)	24		

ENGLAND	O	M	R	W	FALL OF WICKETS		
Pringle	8.2	5	8	3	Wkt	P	E
DeFreitas	7	1	22	2	1st	5	14
Small	10	1	29	2	2nd	5	–
Botham	10	4	12	2	3rd	14	–
Reeve	5	3	2	1	4th	20	–
					5th	32	–
PAKISTAN					6th	35	–
Wasim Akram	3	0	7	1	7th	42	–
Aqib Javed	3	1	7	0	8th	47	–
Wasim Haider	1	0	1	0	9th	62	–
Ijaz Ahmed	1	0	5	0	10th	74	–

Umpires: S.A.Bucknor (*West Indies*) (5) and P.J.McConnell (64).

SOUTH AFRICA v SRI LANKA

At Basin Reserve, Wellington, New Zealand, on 2 March 1992.   Toss: Sri Lanka.
Result: **SRI LANKA** won by 3 wickets.   Award: A.Ranatunga.
LOI debuts: South Africa – O.Henry, M.W.Rushmere.

SOUTH AFRICA		Runs	Balls	4/6
*K.C.Wessels	c and b Ranatunga	40	94	4
A.P.Kuiper	b Anurasiri	18	44	3
P.N.Kirsten	c Hathurusinghe b Kalpage	47	81	5/1
J.N.Rhodes	c Jayasuriya b Wickremasinghe	28	21	2
M.W.Rushmere	c Jayasuriya b Ranatunga	4	9	–
W.J.Cronje	st Tillekeratne b Anurasiri	3	6	–
B.M.McMillan	not out	18	22	–
R.P.Snell	b Anurasiri	9	5	2
†D.J.Richardson	run out	0		–
O.Henry	c Kalpage b Ramanayake	11	13	–
A.A.Donald	run out	3	6	–
Extras	(LB9, W4, NB1)	14		
TOTAL	(50 overs)	195		

SRI LANKA		Runs	Balls	4/6
R.S.Mahanama	c Richardson b McMillan	68	121	6
U.C.Hathurusinghe	c Wessels b Donald	5	9	1
A.P.Gurusinha	lbw b Donald	0	4	–
*P.A.de Silva	b Donald	7	16	1
†H.P.Tillekeratne	c Rushmere b Henry	17	63	–
A.Ranatunga	not out	64	73	6
S.T.Jayasuriya	st Richardson b Kirsten	3	7	–
R.S.Kalpage	run out	5	11	–
C.P.H.Ramanayake	not out	4	2	1
S.D.Anurasiri				
G.P.Wickremasinghe				
Extras	(B1, LB7, W13, NB4)	25		
TOTAL	(49.5 overs; 7 wickets)	198		

SRI LANKA	O	M	R	W
Ramanayake	9	2	19	1
Wickremasinghe	7	0	32	1
Anurasiri	10	1	41	3
Gurusinha	8	0	30	0
Kalpage	10	0	38	1
Ranatunga	6	0	26	2

SOUTH AFRICA	O	M	R	W
McMillan	10	2	34	1
Donald	9.5	0	42	3
Snell	10	1	33	0
Henry	10	0	31	1
Kuiper	5	0	25	0
Kirsten	5	0	25	1

FALL OF WICKETS		
Wkt	SA	SL
1st	27	11
2nd	114	12
3rd	114	35
4th	128	87
5th	149	154
6th	153	168
7th	165	189
8th	165	–
9th	186	–
10th	195	–

Umpires: Khizer Hayat (*Pakistan*) (40) and S.J.Woodward (27).

NEW ZEALAND v ZIMBABWE

At McLean Park, Napier, New Zealand, on 3 March 1992.　Toss: Zimbabwe.
Result: **NEW ZEALAND** won by 48 runs (*target revised to 154 from 18 overs*).
Award: M.D.Crowe.
LOI debuts: Zimbabwe – M.G.Burmester.

NEW ZEALAND		Runs	Balls	4/6
M.J.Greatbatch	b Duers	15	16	2
R.T.Latham	b Brandes	2	6	–
A.H.Jones	c Waller b Butchart	57	58	9
*M.D.Crowe	not out	74	44	8/2
C.L.Cairns	not out	1	2	–
K.R.Rutherford				
C.Z.Harris				
†D.S.Smith				
D.N.Patel				
D.K.Morrison				
G.R.Larsen				
Extras	(B6, LB7)	13		
TOTAL	(20.5 overs; 3 wickets)	162		

ZIMBABWE		Runs	Balls	4/6
†A.Flower	b Larsen	30	27	5
A.C.Waller	b Morrison	11	11	1/1
*D.L.Houghton	b Larsen	10	14	2
I.P.Butchart	c Cairns b Larsen	3	7	–
E.A.Brandes	b Harris	6	8	–
A.J.Pycroft	not out	13	20	–
A.D.R.Campbell	c Crowe b Harris	8	9	1
A.H.Shah	b Harris	7	8	1
M.G.Burmester	not out	4	8	–
A.J.Traicos				
K.G.Duers				
Extras	(LB9, W3, NB1)	13		
TOTAL	(18 overs; 7 wickets)	105		

ZIMBABWE	O	M	R	W		FALL OF WICKETS	
Brandes	5	1	28	1	Wkt	NZ	Z
Duers	6	0	17	1	1st	9	22
Shah	4	0	34	0	2nd	25	40
Butchart	4	0	53	1	3rd	154	63
Burmester	1.5	0	17	0	4th	–	63
					5th	–	75
NEW ZEALAND					6th	–	86
Morrison	4	0	14	1	7th	–	97
Cairns	2	0	27	0	8th	–	–
Larsen	4	0	16	3	9th	–	–
Harris	4	0	15	3	10th	–	–
Latham	3	0	18	0			
Crowe	1	0	6	0			

Umpires: J.D.Buultjens (*Sri Lanka*) (15) and K.E.Liebenberg (*South Africa*) (3).

INDIA v PAKISTAN

At Sydney Cricket Ground, Australia, on 4 March 1992.   Toss: India.
Result: INDIA won by 43 runs.   Award: S.R.Tendulkar.
LOI debuts: None.

INDIA		Runs	Balls	4/6
A.D.Jadeja	c Zahid b Wasim Haider	46	81	2
K.Srikkanth	c Moin b Aqib	5	40	–
*M.Azharuddin	c Moin b Mushtaq	32	51	4
V.G.Kambli	c Inzamam b Mushtaq	24	42	–
S.R.Tendulkar	not out	54	62	3
S.V.Manjrekar	b Mushtaq	0	1	–
Kapil Dev	c Imran b Aqib	35	26	2/1
†K.S.More	run out	4	4	–
M.Prabhakar	not out	2	1	–
J.Srinath				
S.L.V.Raju				
Extras	(LB3, W9, NB2)	14		
TOTAL	(49 overs; 7 wickets)	216		

PAKISTAN		Runs	Balls	4/6
Aamir Sohail	c Srikkanth b Tendulkar	62	103	6
Inzamam-ul-Haq	lbw b Kapil Dev	2	7	–
Zahid Fazal	c More b Prabhakar	2	10	–
Javed Miandad	b Srinath	40	113	2
Salim Malik	c More b Prabhakar	12	9	2
*Imran Khan	run out	0	5	–
Wasim Akram	st More b Raju	4	8	–
Wasim Haider	b Srinath	13	25	–
†Moin Khan	c Manjrekar b Kapil Dev	12	12	1
Mushtaq Ahmed	run out	3	4	–
Aqib Javed	not out	1	12	–
Extras	(LB6, W15, NB1)	22		
TOTAL	(48.1 overs)	173		

PAKISTAN	O	M	R	W	FALL OF WICKETS		
					Wkt	I	P
Wasim Akram	10	0	45	0	1st	25	8
Aqib Javed	8	2	28	2	2nd	86	17
Imran Khan	8	0	25	0	3rd	101	105
Wasim Haider	10	1	36	1	4th	147	127
Mushtaq Ahmed	10	0	59	3	5th	148	130
Aamir Sohail	3	0	20	0	6th	208	141
					7th	213	141
INDIA					8th	–	161
Kapil Dev	10	0	30	2	9th	–	166
Prabhakar	10	1	22	2	10th	–	173
Srinath	8.1	0	37	2			
Tendulkar	10	0	37	1			
Raju	10	1	41	1			

Umpires: P.J.McConnell (65) and D.R.Shepherd (*England*) (44).

SOUTH AFRICA v WEST INDIES

At Lancaster Park, Christchurch, New Zealand, on 5 March 1992.　Toss: West Indies.
Result: **SOUTH AFRICA** won by 64 runs.　Award: M.W.Pringle.
LOI debuts: None.

SOUTH AFRICA		Runs	Balls	4/6
*K.C.Wessels	c Haynes b Marshall	1	9	–
A.C.Hudson	c Lara b Cummins	22	60	3
P.N.Kirsten	c Williams b Marshall	56	91	2
M.W.Rushmere	st Williams b Hooper	10	24	–
A.P.Kuiper	b Ambrose	23	29	–/1
J.N.Rhodes	c Williams b Cummins	22	27	–
B.M.McMillan	c Lara b Benjamin	20	29	2
†D.J.Richardson	not out	20	26	1
R.P.Snell	c Haynes b Ambrose	3	6	–
M.W.Pringle	not out	5	6	–
A.A.Donald				
Extras	(LB8, W3, NB7)	18		
TOTAL	(50 overs; 8 wickets)	**200**		

WEST INDIES		Runs	Balls	4/6
D.L.Haynes	c Richardson b Kuiper	30	83	3
B.C.Lara	c Rhodes b Pringle	9	13	2
*R.B.Richardson	lbw b Pringle	1	3	–
C.L.Hooper	c Wessels b Pringle	0	4	–
K.L.T.Arthurton	c Wessels b Pringle	0	4	–
A.L.Logie	c Pringle b Kuiper	61	69	9/1
M.D.Marshall	c Rhodes b Snell	6	10	1
†D.Williams	c Richardson b Snell	0	3	–
C.E.L.Ambrose	run out	12	15	2
A.C.Cummins	c McMillan b Donald	6	24	–
W.K.M.Benjamin	not out	1	4	–
Extras	(LB9, W1)	10		
TOTAL	(38.4 overs)	**136**		

WEST INDIES	O	M	R	W
Ambrose	10	1	34	2
Marshall	10	1	26	2
Hooper	10	0	45	1
Cummins	10	0	40	2
Benjamin	10	0	47	1

SOUTH AFRICA	O	M	R	W
Donald	6.4	2	13	1
Pringle	8	4	11	4
Snell	7	2	16	2
McMillan	8	2	36	0
Kuiper	9	0	51	2

FALL OF WICKETS		
Wkt	SA	WI
1st	8	10
2nd	51	19
3rd	73	19
4th	119	19
5th	127	70
6th	159	70
7th	181	116
8th	187	117
9th	–	132
10th	–	136

Umpires: B.L.Aldridge (21) and S.G.Randell (*Australia*) (45).

AUSTRALIA v ENGLAND

At Sydney Cricket Ground, Australia, on 5 March 1992.   Toss: Australia.
Result: **ENGLAND** won by 8 wickets.   Award: I.T.Botham.
LOI debuts: None.

AUSTRALIA		Runs	Balls	4/6
T.M.Moody	b Tufnell	51	91	3
M.A.Taylor	lbw b Pringle	0	11	–
D.C.Boon	run out	18	27	2
D.M.Jones	c Lewis b DeFreitas	22	50	2
S.R.Waugh	run out	27	43	2
*A.R.Border	b Botham	16	22	1
†I.A.Healy	c Fairbrother b Botham	9	7	–/1
P.L.Taylor	lbw b Botham	0	2	–
C.J.McDermott	c DeFreitas b Botham	0	2	–
M.R.Whitney	not out	8	27	–1
B.A.Reid	b Reeve	1	22	–
Extras	(B2, LB8, W5, NB4)	19		
TOTAL	(49 overs)	171		

ENGLAND		Runs	Balls	4/6
*G.A.Gooch	b Waugh	58	115	7
I.T.Botham	c Healy b Whitney	53	79	6
R.A.Smith	not out	30	60	3
G.A.Hick	not out	7	5	1
N.H.Fairbrother				
†A.J.Stewart				
C.C.Lewis				
D.A.Reeve				
D.R.Pringle				
P.A.J.DeFreitas				
P.C.R.Tufnell				
Extras	(LB13, W8, NB4)	25		
TOTAL	(40.5 overs; 2 wickets)	173		

ENGLAND	O	M	R	W		FALL OF WICKETS		
Pringle	9	1	24	1		Wkt	A	E
Lewis	10	2	28	0		1st	5	107
DeFreitas	10	3	23	1		2nd	35	153
Botham	10	1	31	4		3rd	106	–
Tufnell	9	0	52	1		4th	114	–
Reeve	1	0	3	1		5th	145	–
						6th	155	–
AUSTRALIA						7th	155	–
McDermott	10	1	29	0		8th	155	–
Reid	7.5	0	49	0		9th	164	–
Whitney	10	2	28	1		10th	171	–
Waugh	6	0	29	1				
P.L.Taylor	3	0	7	0				
Moody	4	0	18	0				

Umpires: S.A.Bucknor (*West Indies*) (6) and Khizer Hayat (*Pakistan*) (41).

INDIA v ZIMBABWE

At Trust Bank Park, Hamilton, New Zealand, on 7 March 1992.   Toss: India.
Result: **INDIA** won by 55 runs (*totals revised to 158 and 103 respectively*).
Award: S.R.Tendulkar.
LOI debuts: None.

INDIA		Runs	Balls	4/6
K.Srikkanth	b Burmester	32	32	5
Kapil Dev	lbw b Brandes	10	14	–/1
*M.Azharuddin	c Flower b Burmester	12	15	2
S.R.Tendulkar	c Campbell b Burmester	81	77	8/1
S.V.Manjrekar	c Duers b Traicos	34	34	2
V.G.Kambli	b Traicos	1	2	–
A.D.Jadeja	c Shah b Traicos	6	6	–
†K.S.More	not out	15	8	–/1
J.Srinath	not out	6	4	1
M.Prabhakar				
S.L.V.Raju				
Extras	(LB3, W3)	6		
TOTAL	(32 overs; 7 wickets)	203		

ZIMBABWE		Runs	Balls	4/6
A.H.Shah	b Tendulkar	31	51	3
†A.Flower	not out	43	56	3
A.C.Waller	not out	13	7	2
A.J.Pycroft				
*D.L.Houghton				
A.D.R.Campbell				
I.P.Butchart				
E.A.Brandes				
M.G.Burmester				
A.J.Traicos				
K.G.Duers				
Extras	(B1, LB11, W5)	17		
TOTAL	(19.1 overs; 1 wicket)	104		

ZIMBABWE	O	M	R	W		FALL OF WICKETS		
Brandes	7	0	43	1		Wkt	I	Z
Duers	7	0	48	0		1st	23	79
Burmester	6	0	36	3		2nd	43	–
Shah	6	1	38	0		3rd	69	–
Traicos	6	0	35	3		4th	168	–
						5th	170	–
INDIA						6th	182	–
Kapil Dev	4	0	6	0		7th	184	–
Prabhakar	3	0	14	0		8th	–	–
Srinath	4	0	20	0		9th	–	–
Tendulkar	6	0	35	1		10th	–	–
Raju	2.1	0	17	0				

Umpires: J.D.Buultjens (*Sri Lanka*) (16) and S.G.Randell (*Australia*) (46).

AUSTRALIA v SRI LANKA

At Adelaide Oval, Australia, on 7 March 1992.   Toss: Australia.
Result: **AUSTRALIA** won by 7 wickets.   Award: T.M.Moody.
LOI debuts: None.

SRI LANKA		Runs	Balls	4/6
R.S.Mahanama	run out	7	10	1
M.A.R.Samarasekera	c Healy b Taylor	34	63	3
A.P.Gurusinha	lbw b Whitney	5	23	1
*P.A.de Silva	c Moody b McDermott	62	83	2
A.Ranatunga	c Jones b Taylor	23	52	–
S.T.Jayasuriya	lbw b Border	15	29	1
†H.P.Tillekeratne	run out	5	13	–
R.S.Kalpage	run out	14	15	1
C.P.H.Ramanayake	run out	5	10	–
S.D.Anurasiri	not out	4	4	–
G.P.Wickremasinghe				
Extras	(B3, LB6, W5, NB1)	15		
TOTAL	(50 overs; 9 wickets)	**189**		

AUSTRALIA		Runs	Balls	4/6
T.M.Moody	c Mahanama b Wickremasinghe	57	86	4
G.R.Marsh	c Anurasiri b Kalpage	60	113	3/1
M.E.Waugh	c Mahanama b Wickremasinghe	26	26	–/2
D.C.Boon	not out	27	37	1
D.M.Jones	not out	12	8	–/1
S.R.Waugh				
*A.R.Border				
†I.A.Healy				
P.L.Taylor				
C.J.McDermott				
M.R.Whitney				
Extras	(LB2, W3, NB3)	8		
TOTAL	(44 overs; 3 wickets)	**190**		

AUSTRALIA	O	M	R	W		FALL OF WICKETS	
					Wkt	SL	A
McDermott	10	0	28	1	1st	8	120
S.R.Waugh	7	0	34	0	2nd	28	130
Whitney	10	3	26	1	3rd	72	165
Moody	3	0	18	0	4th	123	–
Taylor	10	0	34	2	5th	151	–
Border	10	0	40	1	6th	163	–
					7th	166	–
SRI LANKA					8th	182	–
Wickremasinghe	10	3	29	2	9th	189	–
Ramanayake	9	1	44	0	10th	–	–
Anurasiri	10	0	43	0			
Gurusinha	6	0	20	0			
Kalpage	8	0	41	1			
Ranatunga	1	0	11	0			

Umpires: P.D.Reporter (*India*) (16) and I.D.Robinson (*Zimbabwe*) (4).

NEW ZEALAND v WEST INDIES

At Eden Park, Auckland, New Zealand, on 8 March 1992.   Toss: New Zealand.
Result: **NEW ZEALAND** won by 5 wickets.   Award: M.D.Crowe.
LOI debuts: None.

WEST INDIES		Runs	Balls	4/6
D.L.Haynes	c and b Harris	22	61	–/1
B.C.Lara	c Rutherford b Larsen	52	81	7
*R.B.Richardson	c Smith b Watson	29	54	1
C.L.Hooper	c Greatbatch b Patel	2	9	–
K.L.T.Arthurton	b Morrison	40	54	3
A.L.Logie	b Harris	3	4	–
M.D.Marshall	b Larsen	5	14	–
†D.Williams	not out	32	24	5
W.K.M.Benjamin	not out	2	1	–
C.E.L.Ambrose				
A.C.Cummins				
Extras	(LB8, W7, NB1)	16		
TOTAL	(50 overs; 7 wickets)	203		

NEW ZEALAND		Runs	Balls	4/6
M.J.Greatbatch	c Haynes b Benjamin	63	77	7/3
R.T.Latham	c Williams b Cummins	14	27	1
A.H.Jones	c Williams b Benjamin	10	35	–
*M.D.Crowe	not out	81	81	12
K.R.Rutherford	c Williams b Ambrose	8	32	1
C.Z.Harris	c Williams b Cummins	7	23	–
D.N.Patel	not out	10	18	–
†I.D.S.Smith				
D.K.Morrison				
G.R.Larsen				
W.Watson				
Extras	(LB7, W5, NB1)	13		
TOTAL	(48.3 overs; 5 wickets)	206		

NEW ZEALAND	O	M	R	W		FALL OF WICKETS		
Morrison	9	1	33	1	Wkt	WI	NZ	
Patel	10	2	19	1	1st	65	67	
Watson	10	2	56	1	2nd	95	97	
Larsen	10	0	41	2	3rd	100	100	
Harris	10	2	32	2	4th	136	135	
Latham	1	0	14	0	5th	142	174	
					6th	156	–	
WEST INDIES					7th	201	–	
Ambrose	10	1	41	1	8th	–	–	
Marshall	9	1	35	0	9th	–	–	
Cummins	10	0	53	2	10th	–	–	
Hooper	10	0	36	0				
Benjamin	9.3	3	34	2				

Umpires: K.E.Liebenberg (*South Africa*) (4) and P.J.McConnell (*Australia*) (66).

SOUTH AFRICA v PAKISTAN

At Woolloongabba, Brisbane, Australia, on 8 March 1992. Toss: Pakistan.
Result: **SOUTH AFRICA** won by 20 runs (*target revised to 194 from 36 overs*).
Award: A.C.Hudson.
LOI debuts: None.

SOUTH AFRICA		Runs	Balls	4/6
A.C.Hudson	c Ijaz b Imran	54	81	8
*K.C.Wessels	c Moin b Aqib	7	26	–
M.W.Rushmere	c Aamir b Mushtaq	35	70	2
A.P.Kuiper	c Moin b Imran	5	12	–
J.N.Rhodes	lbw b Iqbal	5	17	–
W.J.Cronje	not out	47	53	4
B.M.McMillan	b Wasim	33	44	1
†D.J.Richardson	b Wasim	5	10	–
R.P.Snell	not out	1	1	–
M.W.Pringle				
A.A.Donald				
Extras	(LB8, W9, NB2)	19		
TOTAL	(50 overs; 7 wickets)	211		

PAKISTAN		Runs	Balls	4/6
Aamir Sohail	b Snell	23	53	2
Zahid Fazal	c Richardson b McMillan	11	46	1
Inzamam-ul-Haq	run out	48	45	5
*Imran Khan	c Richardson b McMillan	34	53	5
Salim Malik	c Donald b Kuiper	12	11	–
Wasim Akram	c Snell b Kuiper	9	8	1
Ijaz Ahmed	c Rhodes b Kuiper	6	3	1
†Moin Khan	not out	5	5	–
Mushtaq Ahmed	run out	4	4	–
Iqbal Sikander	not out	1	3	–
Aqib Javed				
Extras	(LB2, W17, NB1)	20		
TOTAL	(36 overs; 8 wickets)	173		

PAKISTAN	O	M	R	W
Wasim Akram	10	0	42	2
Aqib Javed	7	1	36	1
Imran Khan	10	0	34	2
Iqbal Sikander	8	0	30	1
Ijaz Ahmed	7	0	26	0
Mushtaq Ahmed	8	1	35	1

SOUTH AFRICA	O	M	R	W
Donald	7	1	31	0
Pringle	7	0	31	0
Snell	8	2	26	1
McMillan	7	0	34	2
Kuiper	6	0	40	3
Cronje	1	0	9	0

FALL OF WICKETS		
Wkt	SA	P
1st	31	50
2nd	98	50
3rd	110	135
4th	111	136
5th	127	156
6th	198	157
7th	207	163
8th	–	171
9th	–	–
10th	–	–

Umpires: B.L.Aldridge (*New Zealand*) (22) and S.A.Bucknor (*West Indies*) (7).

ENGLAND v SRI LANKA

At Eastern Oval, Ballarat, Australia, on 9 March 1992.   Toss: England.
Result: **ENGLAND** won by 106 runs.   Award: C.C.Lewis.
LOI debuts: None.

ENGLAND		Runs	Balls	4/6
*G.A.Gooch	b Labrooy	8	28	1
I.T.Botham	b Anurasiri	47	63	5/2
R.A.Smith	run out	19	39	2
G.A.Hick	b Ramanayake	41	62	3
N.H.Fairbrother	c Ramanayake b Gurusinha	63	70	2/2
†A.J.Stewart	c Jayasuriya b Gurusinha	59	36	7/1
C.C.Lewis	not out	20	6	1/2
D.R.Pringle	not out	0	–	–
D.A.Reeve				
P.A.J.DeFreitas				
R.K.Illingworth				
Extras	(B1, LB9, W9, NB4)	23		
TOTAL	(50 overs; 6 wickets)	280		

SRI LANKA		Runs	Balls	4/6
R.S.Mahanama	c Botham b Lewis	9	19	1
M.A.R.Samarasekera	c Illingworth b Lewis	23	29	4
A.P.Gurusinha	c and b Lewis	7	9	–
*P.A.de Silva	c Fairbrother b Lewis	7	10	1
A.Ranatunga	c Stewart b Botham	36	51	6
†H.P.Tillekeratne	run out	4	30	–
S.T.Jayasuriya	c DeFreitas b Illingworth	19	16	2
G.F.Labrooy	c Smith b Illingworth	19	34	1
C.P.H.Ramanayake	c and b Reeve	12	38	–
S.D.Anurasiri	lbw b Reeve	11	19	–
G.P.Wickremasinghe	not out	6	16	–
Extras	(LB7, W8, NB6)	21		
TOTAL	(44 overs)	174		

SRI LANKA	O	M	R	W		FALL OF WICKETS		
Wickremasinghe	9	0	54	0		Wkt	E	SL
Ramanayake	10	1	42	1		1st	44	33
Labrooy	10	1	68	1		2nd	80	46
Anurasiri	10	1	27	1		3rd	105	56
Gurusinha	10	0	67	2		4th	164	60
Jayasuriya	1	0	12	0		5th	244	91
						6th	268	119
ENGLAND						7th	–	123
Pringle	7	1	27	0		8th	–	156
Lewis	8	0	30	4		9th	–	158
DeFreitas	5	1	31	0		10th	–	174
Botham	10	0	33	1				
Illingworth	10	0	32	2				
Reeve	4	0	14	2				

Umpires: Khizer Hayat (*Pakistan*) (42) and P.D.Reporter (*India*) (17).

WEST INDIES v INDIA

At Basin Reserve, Wellington, New Zealand, on 10 March 1992.　Toss: India.
Result: **WEST INDIES** won by 5 wickets (*target revised to 195 from 46 overs*).
Award: A.C.Cummins.
LOI debuts: None.

INDIA		Runs	Balls	4/6
A.D.Jadeja	c Benjamin b Simmons	27	61	2
K.Srikkanth	c Logie b Hooper	40	70	2
*M.Azharuddin	c Ambrose b Cummins	61	84	4
S.R.Tendulkar	c Williams b Ambrose	4	11	–
S.V.Manjrekar	run out	27	40	–
Kapil Dev	c Haynes b Cummins	3	4	–
P.K.Amre	c Hooper b Ambrose	4	8	–
†K.S.More	c Hooper b Cummins	5	5	1
M.Prabhakar	c Richardson b Cummins	8	10	1
J.Srinath	not out	5	5	–
S.L.V.Raju	run out	1	1	–
Extras	(LB6, W5, NB1)	12		
TOTAL	(49.4 overs)	197		

WEST INDIES		Runs	Balls	4/6
D.L.Haynes	c Manjrekar b Kapil Dev	16	16	3
B.C.Lara	c Manjrekar b Srinath	41	37	6/1
P.V.Simmons	c Tendulkar b Prabhakar	22	20	2/1
*R.B.Richardson	c Srikkanth b Srinath	3	8	–
K.L.T.Arthurton	not out	58	99	3
A.L.Logie	c More b Raju	7	10	1
C.L.Hooper	not out	34	57	3
†D.Williams				
W.K.M.Benjamin				
C.E.L.Ambrose				
A.C.Cummins				
Extras	(LB8, W2, NB4)	14		
TOTAL	(40.2 overs; 5 wickets)	195		

WEST INDIES	O	M	R	W		FALL OF WICKETS		
Ambrose	10	1	24	2	Wkt	I	WI	
Benjamin	9.4	0	35	0	1st	56	57	
Cummins	10	0	33	4	2nd	102	82	
Simmons	9	0	48	1	3rd	115	88	
Hooper	10	0	46	1	4th	166	98	
Arthurton	1	0	5	0	5th	171	112	
					6th	172	–	
INDIA					7th	180	–	
Kapil Dev	8	0	45	1	8th	186	–	
Prabhakar	9	0	55	1	9th	193	–	
Raju	10	2	32	1	10th	197	–	
Srinath	9	2	23	2				
Tendulkar	3	0	20	0				
Srikkanth	1	0	7	0				
Jadeja	0.2	0	5	0				

Umpires: S.G.Randell (*Australia*) (47) and S.J.Woodward (28).

SOUTH AFRICA v ZIMBABWE

At Manuka Oval, Canberra, Australia, on 10 March 1992.   Toss: South Africa.
Result: **SOUTH AFRICA** won by 7 wickets.   Award: P.N.Kirsten.
LOI debuts: None.

ZIMBABWE		Runs	Balls	4/6
W.R.James	lbw b Pringle	5	12	1
†A.Flower	c Richardson b Cronje	19	44	–
A.J.Pycroft	c Wessels b McMillan	19	47	–
*D.L.Houghton	c Cronje b Kirsten	15	53	–
A.C.Waller	c Cronje b Kirsten	15	28	1
A.H.Shah	c Wessels b Kirsten	3	4	–
E.A.Brandes	c Richardson b McMillan	20	28	1/1
M.G.Burmester	c Kuiper b Cronje	1	10	–
A.J.Traicos	not out	16	40	1
M.P.Jarvis	c and b McMillan	17	21	1/1
K.G.Duers	b Donald	5	10	–
Extras	(LB11, W13, NB4)	28		
TOTAL	(48.3 overs)	163		

SOUTH AFRICA		Runs	Balls	4/6
*K.C.Wessels	b Shah	70	137	6
A.C.Hudson	b Jarvis	13	22	1
P.N.Kirsten	not out	62	103	3
A.P.Kuiper	c Burmester b Brandes	7	9	–
J.N.Rhodes	not out	3	3	–
W.J.Cronje				
B.M.McMillan				
†D.J.Richardson				
R.P.Snell				
M.W.Pringle				
A.A.Donald				
Extras	(LB4, W2, NB3)	9		
TOTAL	(45.1 overs; 3 wickets)	164		

SOUTH AFRICA	O	M	R	W		FALL OF WICKETS	
					Wkt	Z	SA
Donald	9.3	1	25	1	1st	7	27
Pringle	9	0	25	1	2nd	51	139
Snell	10	3	24	0	3rd	72	151
Cronje	5	0	17	2	4th	80	–
Kirsten	5	0	31	3	5th	80	–
McMillan	10	1	30	3	6th	115	–
					7th	117	–
ZIMBABWE					8th	123	–
Brandes	9.1	0	40	1	9th	151	–
Jarvis	9	2	23	1	10th	163	–
Burmester	5	0	20	0			
Shah	8	2	32	1			
Duers	8	1	19	0			
Traicos	6	0	26	0			

Umpires: S.A.Bucknor (*West Indies*) (8) and D.R.Shepherd (*England*) (45).

AUSTRALIA v PAKISTAN

At WACA Ground, Perth, Australia, on 11 March 1992.   Toss: Pakistan.
Result: **PAKISTAN** won by 48 runs.   Award: Aamir Sohail.
LOI debuts: None.

PAKISTAN		Runs	Balls	4/6
Aamir Sohail	c Healy b Moody	76	106	8
Ramiz Raja	c Border b Whitney	34	61	4
Salim Malik	b Moody	0	6	–
Javed Miandad	c Healy b S.R.Waugh	46	75	3
*Imran Khan	c Moody b S.R.Waugh	13	22	–/1
Inzamam-ul-Haq	run out	16	16	–
Ijaz Ahmed	run out	0	2	–
Wasim Akram	c M.E.Waugh b S.R.Waugh	0	1	–
†Moin Khan	c Healy b McDermott	5	8	–
Mushtaq Ahmed	not out	3	5	–
Aqib Javed				
Extras	(LB9, W16, NB2)	27		
TOTAL	(50 overs; 9 wickets)	220		

AUSTRALIA		Runs	Balls	4/6
T.M.Moody	c Salim b Aqib	4	18	–
G.R.Marsh	c Moin b Imran	39	91	1
D.C.Boon	c Mushtaq b Aqib	5	15	1
D.M.Jones	c Aqib b Mushtaq	47	79	2
M.E.Waugh	c Ijaz b Mushtaq	30	42	2
*A.R.Border	c Ijaz b Mushtaq	1	4	–
S.R.Waugh	c Moin b Imran	5	6	1
†I.A.Healy	c Ijaz b Aqib	8	15	–
C.J.McDermott	lbw b Wasim	0	2	–
M.R.Whitney	b Wasim	5	9	–
B.A.Reid	not out	0		–
Extras	(LB7, W14, NB7)	28		
TOTAL	(45.2 overs)	172		

AUSTRALIA	O	M	R	W		FALL OF WICKETS	
McDermott	10	0	33	1	Wkt	P	A
Reid	9	0	37	0	1st	78	13
S.R.Waugh	10	0	36	3	2nd	80	31
Whitney	10	1	50	1	3rd	157	116
Moody	10	0	42	1	4th	193	122
M.E.Waugh	1	0	13	0	5th	194	123
					6th	205	130
PAKISTAN					7th	205	156
Wasim Akram	7.2	0	28	2	8th	214	162
Aqib Javed	8	1	21	3	9th	220	167
Imran Khan	10	1	32	2	10th	–	172
Ijaz Ahmed	10	0	43	0			
Mushtaq Ahmed	10	0	41	3			

Umpires: K.E.Liebenberg (*South Africa*) (5) and P.D.Reporter (*India*) (18).

NEW ZEALAND v INDIA

At Carisbrook, Dunedin, New Zealand, on 12 March 1992.   Toss: India.
Result: **NEW ZEALAND** won by 4 wickets.   Award: M.J.Greatbatch.
LOI debuts: None.

INDIA		Runs	Balls	4/6
A.D.Jadeja	retired hurt	13	32	1
K.Srikkanth	c Latham b Patel	0	3	–
*M.Azharuddin	c Greatbatch b Patel	55	98	3/1
S.R.Tendulkar	c Smith b Harris	84	107	6
S.V.Manjrekar	c and b Harris	18	25	–
Kapil Dev	c Larsen b Harris	33	16	5
S.T.Banerjee	c Greatbatch b Watson	11	9	1
†K.S.More	not out	2	8	–
J.Srinath	not out	4	3	–
M.Prabhakar				
S.L.V.Raju				
Extras	(B1, LB4, W4, NB1)	10		
TOTAL	(50 overs; 6 wickets)	230		

NEW ZEALAND		Runs	Balls	4/6
M.J.Greatbatch	c Banerjee b Raju	73	77	5/4
R.T.Latham	b Prabhakar	8	22	1
A.H.Jones	not out	67	107	8
*M.D.Crowe	run out	26	28	3/1
†I.D.S.Smith	c sub b Prabhakar	9	8	1
K.R.Rutherford	lbw b Raju	21	22	3/1
C.Z.Harris	b Prabhakar	4	17	–
C.L.Cairns	not out	4	5	1
D.N.Patel				
G.R.Larsen				
W.Watson				
Extras	(B4, LB3, W4, NB8)	19		
TOTAL	(47.1 overs; 6 wickets)	231		

NEW ZEALAND	O	M	R	W	FALL OF WICKETS		
					Wkt	I	NZ
Cairns	8	1	40	0			
Patel	10	0	29	2	1st	4	36
Watson	10	1	34	1	2nd	149	118
Larsen	9	0	43	0	3rd	166	162
Harris	9	0	55	3	4th	201	172
Latham	4	0	24	0	5th	222	206
					6th	223	225
INDIA					7th	–	–
Kapil Dev	10	0	55	0	8th	–	–
Prabhakar	10	0	46	3	9th	–	–
Banerjee	6	1	40	0	10th	–	–
Srinath	9	0	35	0			
Raju	10	0	38	2			
Tendulkar	1	0	2	0			
Srikkanth	1.1	0	8	0			

Umpires: P.J.McConnell (*Australia*) (67) and I.D.Robinson (*Zimbabwe*) (5).

ENGLAND v SOUTH AFRICA

At Melbourne Cricket Ground, Australia, on 12 March 1992.   Toss: England.
Result: **ENGLAND** won by 3 wickets (*target revised to 226 from 41 overs*).
Award: A.J.Stewart.
LOI debuts: None.

SOUTH AFRICA		Runs	Balls	4/6
*K.C.Wessels	c Smith b Hick	85	126	6
A.C.Hudson	c and b Hick	79	115	7
P.N.Kirsten	c Smith b DeFreitas	11	12	–/1
J.N.Rhodes	run out	18	23	–
A.P.Kuiper	not out	15	12	1
W.J.Cronje	not out	13	15	–
B.M.McMillan				
†D.J.Richardson				
R.P.Snell				
M.W.Pringle				
A.A.Donald				
Extras	(B4, LB4, W4, NB3)	15		
TOTAL	(50 overs; 4 wickets)	236		

ENGLAND		Runs	Balls	4/6
*†A.J.Stewart	run out	77	88	7
I.T.Botham	b McMillan	22	30	1
R.A.Smith	c Richardson b McMillan	0	2	–
G.A.Hick	c Richardson b Snell	1	4	–
N.H.Fairbrother	not out	75	83	6
D.A.Reeve	c McMillan b Snell	10	15	–
C.C.Lewis	run out	33	22	4
D.R.Pringle	c Kuiper b Snell	1	3	–
P.A.J.DeFreitas	not out	1	1	–
R.K.Illingworth				
G.C.Small				
Extras	(LB3, W1, NB2)	6		
TOTAL	(40.5 overs; 7 wickets)	226		

ENGLAND	O	M	R	W		FALL OF WICKETS	
Pringle	9	2	34	0	Wkt	SA	E
DeFreitas	10	1	41	1	1st	151	63
Botham	8	0	37	0	2nd	170	63
Small	2	0	14	0	3rd	201	64
Illingworth	10	0	43	0	4th	205	132
Reeve	2.4	0	15	0	5th	–	166
Hick	8.2	0	44	2	6th	–	216
					7th	–	225
SOUTH AFRICA					8th	–	–
Donald	9	1	43	0	9th	–	–
Pringle	8	0	44	0	10th	–	–
Snell	7.5	0	42	3			
McMillan	8	1	39	2			
Kuiper	4	0	32	0			
Cronje	3	0	14	0			
Kirsten	1	0	9	0			

Umpires: B.L.Aldridge (*New Zealand*) (23) and J.D.Buultjens (*Sri Lanka*) (17).

WEST INDIES v SRI LANKA

At Berri Oval, South Australia, Australia, on 13 March 1992.   Toss: Sri Lanka.
Result: **WEST INDIES** won by 91 runs.   Award: P.V.Simmons.
LOI debuts: None.

WEST INDIES		Runs	Balls	4/6
D.L.Haynes	c Tillekeratne b Ranatunga	38	47	3/1
B.C.Lara	c and b Ramanayake	1	6	–
P.V.Simmons	c Wickremasinghe b Hathurusinghe	110	125	8/2
*R.B.Richardson	run out	8	23	–
K.L.T.Arthurton	c Tillekeratne b Hathurusinghe	40	54	1
A.L.Logie	b Anurasiri	0	2	–
C.L.Hooper	c Gurusinha b Hathurusinghe	12	12	1
†D.Williams	c Tillekeratne b Hathurusinghe	2	3	–
C.E.L.Ambrose	not out	15	14	–/1
W.K.M.Benjamin	not out	24	20	1
A.C.Cummins				
Extras	(LB9, W3, NB6)	18		
TOTAL	(50 overs; 8 wickets)	268		

SRI LANKA		Runs	Balls	4/6
R.S.Mahanama	c Arthurton b Cummins	11	50	–
M.A.R.Samarasekera	lbw b Hooper	40	41	4/1
U.C.Hathurusinghe	run out	16	25	–
*P.A.de Silva	c and b Hooper	11	19	–
A.Ranatunga	c Benjamin b Arthurton	24	40	–/1
A.P.Gurusinha	c Richardson b Ambrose	10	30	–
†H.P.Tillekeratne	b Ambrose	3	9	–
R.S.Kalpage	not out	13	40	–
C.P.H.Ramanayake	b Arthurton	1	13	–
S.D.Anurasiri	b Benjamin	3	11	–
G.P.Wickremasinghe	not out	21	21	1
Extras	(LB8, W14, NB2)	24		
TOTAL	(50 overs; 9 wickets)	177		

SRI LANKA	O	M	R	W
Wickremasinghe	7	0	30	0
Ramanayake	7	1	17	1
Anurasiri	10	0	46	1
Gurusinha	1	0	10	0
Ranatunga	7	0	35	1
Kalpage	10	0	64	0
Hathurusinghe	8	0	57	4

WEST INDIES	O	M	R	W
Ambrose	10	2	24	2
Benjamin	10	0	34	1
Cummins	9	0	49	1
Hooper	10	1	19	2
Arthurton	10	0	40	2
Simmons	1	0	3	0

FALL OF WICKETS		
Wkt	WI	SL
1st	6	56
2nd	72	80
3rd	103	86
4th	194	99
5th	195	130
6th	217	135
7th	223	137
8th	228	139
9th	–	149
10th	–	–

Umpires: D.R.Shepherd (*England*) (46) and S.J.Woodward (*New Zealand*) (29).

AUSTRALIA v ZIMBABWE

At Bellerive Oval, Hobart, Australia, on 14 March 1992.   Toss: Zimbabwe.
Result: **AUSTRALIA** won by 128 runs.   Award: S.R.Waugh.
LOI debuts: None.

AUSTRALIA		Runs	Balls	4/6
T.M.Moody	run out	6	8	–
D.C.Boon	b Shah	48	84	4
D.M.Jones	b Burmester	54	71	4
*A.R.Border	st Flower b Traicos	22	29	2
M.E.Waugh	not out	66	39	5/2
S.R.Waugh	b Brandes	55	43	4
†I.A.Healy	lbw b Duers	0	2	–
P.L.Taylor	not out	1	1	–
C.J.McDermott				
M.R.Whitney				
B.A.Reid				
Extras	(B2, LB8, W2, NB1)	13		
TOTAL	(46 overs; 6 wickets)	265		

ZIMBABWE		Runs	Balls	4/6
A.H.Shah	run out	23	47	2
†A.Flower	c Border b S.R.Waugh	20	49	1
A.D.R.Campbell	c M.E.Waugh b Whitney	4	20	1
A.J.Pycroft	c M.E.Waugh b S.R.Waugh	0	1	–
*D.L.Houghton	b McDermott	2	10	–
A.C.Waller	c Taylor b Moody	18	39	2
K.J.Arnott	b Whitney	8	15	–
E.A.Brandes	c McDermott b Taylor	23	28	3
M.G.Burmester	c Border b Reid	12	24	–
A.J.Traicos	c Border b Taylor	3	9	–
K.G.Duers	not out	2	10	–
Extras	(LB12, W8, NB2)	22		
TOTAL	(41.4 overs)	137		

ZIMBABWE	O	M	R	W	FALL OF WICKETS		
					Wkt	A	Z
Brandes	9	0	59	1	1st	8	47
Duers	9	1	48	1	2nd	102	51
Burmester	9	0	65	1	3rd	134	51
Shah	9	0	53	1	4th	144	57
Traicos	10	0	30	1	5th	257	69
					6th	258	88
AUSTRALIA					7th	–	97
McDermott	8	0	26	1	8th	–	117
Reid	9	2	17	1	9th	–	132
S.R.Waugh	7	0	28	2	10th	–	137
Whitney	10	3	15	2			
Moody	4	0	25	1			
Taylor	3.4	0	14	2			

Umpires: B.L.Aldridge (*New Zealand*) (24) and S.A.Bucknor (*West Indies*) (9).

NEW ZEALAND v ENGLAND

At Basin Reserve, Wellington, New Zealand, on 15 March 1992.   Toss: New Zealand.
Result: **NEW ZEALAND** won by 7 wickets.   Award: A.H.Jones.
LOI debuts: None.

ENGLAND		Runs	Balls	4/6
*†A.J.Stewart	c Harris b Patel	41	59	7
I.T.Botham	b Patel	8	25	1
G.A.Hick	c Greatbatch b Harris	56	70	6/1
R.A.Smith	c Patel b Jones	38	72	3
A.J.Lamb	c Cairns b Watson	12	29	–
C.C.Lewis	c and b Watson	0	1	–
D.A.Reeve	not out	21	27	1
D.R.Pringle	c sub (R.T.Latham) b Jones	10	16	–
P.A.J.DeFreitas	c Cairns b Harris	0	1	–
R.K.Illingworth	not out	2	2	–
G.C.Small				
Extras	(B1, LB7, W4)	12		
TOTAL	(50 overs; 8 wickets)	200		

NEW ZEALAND		Runs	Balls	4/6
M.J.Greatbatch	c DeFreitas b Botham	35	37	4/1
J.G.Wright	b DeFreitas	1	5	–
A.H.Jones	run out	78	113	13
*M.D.Crowe	not out	73	81	6
K.R.Rutherford	not out	3	12	–
C.Z.Harris				
C.L.Cairns				
†I.D.S.Smith				
D.N.Patel				
G.R.Larsen				
W.Watson				
Extras	(LB9, W1, NB1)	11		
TOTAL	(40.5 overs; 3 wickets)	201		

NEW ZEALAND	O	M	R	W		FALL OF WICKETS		
Patel	10	1	26	2		Wkt	E	NZ
Harris	8	0	39	2		1st	25	5
Watson	10	0	40	2		2nd	95	62
Cairns	3	0	21	0		3rd	135	171
Larsen	10	3	24	0		4th	162	–
Jones	9	0	42	2		5th	162	–
						6th	169	–
ENGLAND						7th	189	–
Pringle	6.2	1	34	0		8th	195	–
DeFreitas	8.3	1	45	1		9th	–	–
Botham	4	0	19	1		10th	–	–
Illingworth	9	1	46	0				
Hick	6	0	26	0				
Reeve	3	0	9	0				
Small	4	0	13	0				

Umpires: S.G.Randell (*Australia*) (48) and I.D.Robinson (*Zimbabwe*) (6).

SOUTH AFRICA v INDIA

At Adelaide Oval, Australia, on 15 March 1992.   Toss: South Africa.
Result: **SOUTH AFRICA** won by 6 wickets.   Award: P.N.Kirsten.
LOI debuts: None.

INDIA		Runs	Balls	4/6
K.Srikkanth	c Kirsten b Donald	0	5	–
S.V.Manjrekar	b Kuiper	28	53	–
*M.Azharuddin	c Kuiper b Pringle	79	77	6
S.R.Tendulkar	c Wessels b Kuiper	14	14	1
Kapil Dev	b Donald	42	29	3/1
V.G.Kambli	run out	1	3	–
P.K.Amre	not out	1	1	–
J.Srinath	not out	0	–	–
†K.S.More				
M.Prabhakar				
S.L.V.Raju				
Extras	(LB7, W6, NB2)	15		
TOTAL	(30 overs; 6 wickets)	180		

SOUTH AFRICA		Runs	Balls	4/6
A.C.Hudson	b Srinath	53	73	4
P.N.Kirsten	b Kapil Dev	84	86	7
A.P.Kuiper	run out	7	6	–
J.N.Rhodes	c Raju b Prabhakar	7	3	–/1
*K.C.Wessels	not out	9	6	1
W.J.Cronje	not out	8	6	1
B.M.McMillan				
†D.J.Richardson				
R.P.Snell				
M.W.Pringle				
A.A.Donald				
Extras	(LB10, NB3)	13		
TOTAL	(29.1 overs; 4 wickets)	181		

SOUTH AFRICA	O	M	R	W		FALL OF WICKETS	
Donald	6	0	34	2	Wkt	I	SA
Pringle	6	0	37	1	1st	1	128
Snell	6	1	46	0	2nd	79	149
McMillan	6	0	28	0	3rd	103	157
Kuiper	6	0	28	2	4th	174	163
					5th	177	–
INDIA					6th	179	–
Kapil Dev	6	0	36	1	7th	–	–
Prabhakar	5.1	1	33	1	8th	–	–
Tendulkar	6	0	20	0	9th	–	–
Srinath	6	0	39	1	10th	–	–
Raju	6	0	43	0			

Umpires: J.D.Buultjens (*Sri Lanka*) (18) and Khizer Hayat (*Pakistan*) (43).

PAKISTAN v SRI LANKA

At WACA Ground, Perth, Australia, on 15 March 1992.   Toss: Sri Lanka.
Result: **PAKISTAN** won by 4 wickets.   Award: Javed Miandad.
LOI debuts: None.

SRI LANKA		Runs	Balls	4/6
R.S.Mahanama	b Wasim	12	36	1
M.A.R.Samarasekera	st Moin b Mushtaq	38	59	1
U.C.Hathurusinghe	b Mushtaq	5	29	–
*P.A.de Silva	c Aamir b Ijaz	43	56	2
A.P.Gurusinha	c Salim b Imran	37	54	2
A.Ranatunga	c sub (Zahid Fazal) b Aamir	7	19	–
†H.P.Tillekeratne	not out	25	34	3
R.S.Kalpage	not out	13	14	–
C.P.H.Ramanayake				
K.I.W.Wijegunawardene				
G.P.Wickremasinghe				
Extras	(LB15, W11, NB6)	32		
TOTAL	(50 overs; 6 wickets)	212		

PAKISTAN		Runs	Balls	4/6
Aamir Sohail	c Mahanama b Ramanayake	1	10	–
Ramiz Raja	c Gurusinha b Wickremasinghe	32	56	3
*Imran Khan	c De Silva b Hathurusinghe	22	69	2
Javed Miandad	c Wickremasinghe b Gurusinha	57	84	3
Salim Malik	c Kalpage b Ramanayake	51	66	2
Inzamam-ul-Haq	run out	11	11	–
Ijaz Ahmed	not out	8	6	1
Wasim Akram	not out	5	5	1
†Moin Khan				
Mushtaq Ahmed				
Aqib Javed				
Extras	(LB12, W9, NB8)	29		
TOTAL	(49.1 overs; 6 wickets)	216		

PAKISTAN	O	M	R	W	FALL OF WICKETS		
					Wkt	SL	P
Wasim Akram	10	0	37	1	1st	29	7
Aqib Javed	10	0	39	0	2nd	48	68
Imran Khan	8	1	36 /	1	3rd	99	84
Mushtaq Ahmed	10	0	43	2	4th	132	185
Ijaz Ahmed	8	0	28	1	5th	158	201
Aamir Sohail	4	0	14	1	6th	187	205
SRI LANKA					7th	–	–
Wijegunawardene	10	1	34	0	8th	–	–
Ramanayake	10	1	37	2	9th	–	–
Wickremasinghe	9.1	0	41	1	10th	–	–
Gurusinha	9	0	38	1			
Hathurusinghe	9	0	40	1			
Kalpage	2	0	14	0			

Umpires: K.E.Liebenberg (*South Africa*) (6) and P.J.McConnell (68).

NEW ZEALAND v PAKISTAN

At Lancaster Park, Christchurch, New Zealand, on 18 March 1992.   Toss: Pakistan.
Result: **PAKISTAN** won by 7 wickets.   Award: Mushtaq Ahmed.
LOI debuts: None.

NEW ZEALAND		Runs	Balls	4/6
M.J.Greatbatch	c Salim b Mushtaq	42	67	5/1
R.T.Latham	c Inzamam b Aqib	6	9	1
A.H.Jones	lbw b Wasim	2	3	–
*M.D.Crowe	c Aamir b Wasim	3	20	–
K.R.Rutherford	run out	8	35	–
C.Z.Harris	st Moin b Mushtaq	1	6	–
D.N.Patel	c Mushtaq b Aamir	7	13	–
†I.D.S.Smith	b Imran	1	4	–
G.R.Larsen	b Wasim	37	80	3
D.K.Morrison	c Inzamam b Wasim	12	45	1
W.Watson	not out	5	13	–
Extras	(B3, LB23, W12, NB4)	42		
TOTAL	(48.2 overs)	166		

PAKISTAN		Runs	Balls	4/6
Aamir Sohail	c Patel b Morrison	0	1	–
Ramiz Raja	not out	119	155	16
Inzamam-ul-Haq	b Morrison	5	8	1
Javed Miandad	lbw b Morrison	30	85	1
Salim Malik	not out	9	23	1
*Imran Khan				
Wasim Akram				
Ijaz Ahmed				
†Moin Khan				
Mushtaq Ahmed				
Aqib Javed				
Extras	(LB1, W1, NB2)	4		
TOTAL	(44.4 overs; 3 wickets)	167		

PAKISTAN	O	M	R	W		FALL OF WICKETS		
Wasim Akram	9.2	0	32	4	Wkt	NZ	P	
Aqib Javed	10	1	34	1	1st	23	0	
Mushtaq Ahmed	10	0	18	2	2nd	26	9	
Imran Khan	8	0	22	1	3rd	39	124	
Aamir Sohail	10	1	29	1	4th	85	–	
Ijaz Ahmed	1	0	5	0	5th	88	–	
					6th	93	–	
NEW ZEALAND					7th	96	–	
Morrison	10	0	42	3	8th	106	–	
Patel	10	2	25	0	9th	150	–	
Watson	10	3	26	0	10th	166	–	
Harris	4	0	18	0				
Larsen	3	0	16	0				
Jones	3	0	10	0				
Latham	2	0	13	0				
Rutherford	1.4	0	11	0				
Greatbatch	1	0	5	0				

Umpires: S.A.Bucknor (*West Indies*) (10) and S.G.Randell (*Australia*) (49).

212

ENGLAND v ZIMBABWE

At Lavington Sports Ground, Albury, Australia, on 18 March 1992.　Toss: England.
Result: **ZIMBABWE** won by 9 runs.　Award: E.A.Brandes.
LOI debuts: None.

ZIMBABWE		Runs	Balls	4/6
W.R.James	c and b Illingworth	13	46	1
†A.Flower	b DeFreitas	7	16	1
A.J.Pycroft	c Gooch b Botham	3	13	–
K.J.Arnott	lbw b Botham	11	33	–
*D.L.Houghton	c Fairbrother b Small	29	74	2
A.C.Waller	b Tufnell	8	16	1
A.H.Shah	c Lamb b Tufnell	3	16	–
I.P.Butchart	c Fairbrother b Botham	24	36	2
E.A.Brandes	st Stewart b Illingworth	14	24	1
A.J.Traicos	not out	0	6	–
M.P.Jarvis	lbw b Illingworth	6	6	–
Extras	(LB8, W8)	16		
TOTAL	(46.1 overs)	134		

ENGLAND		Runs	Balls	4/6
*G.A.Gooch	lbw b Brandes	0	1	–
I.T.Botham	c Flower b Shah	18	34	4
A.J.Lamb	c James b Brandes	17	26	2
R.A.Smith	b Brandes	2	13	–
G.A.Hick	b Brandes	0	6	–
N.H.Fairbrother	c Flower b Butchart	20	77	–
†A.J.Stewart	c Waller b Shah	29	96	3
P.A.J.DeFreitas	c Flower b Butchart	4	17	–
R.K.Illingworth	run out	11	20	–
G.C.Small	c Pycroft b Jarvis	5	18	–
P.C.R.Tufnell	not out	0	–	–
Extras	(B4, LB3, W11, NB1)	19		
TOTAL	(49.1 overs)	125		

ENGLAND	O	M	R	W	FALL OF WICKETS		
					Wkt	Z	E
DeFreitas	8	1	14	1	1st	12	0
Small	9	1	20	1	2nd	19	32
Botham	10	2	23	3	3rd	30	42
Illingworth	9.1	0	33	3	4th	52	42
Tufnell	10	2	36	2	5th	65	43
ZIMBABWE					6th	77	95
Brandes	10	4	21	4	7th	96	101
Jarvis	9.1	0	32	1	8th	127	108
Shah	10	3	17	2	9th	127	124
Traicos	10	4	16	0	10th	134	125
Butchart	10	1	32	2			

Umpires: B.L.Aldridge (*New Zealand*) (25) and Khizer Hayat (*Pakistan*) (44).

AUSTRALIA v WEST INDIES

At Melbourne Cricket Ground, Australia, on 18 March 1992.   Toss: Australia.
Result: **AUSTRALIA** won by 57 runs.   Award: D.C.Boon.
LOI debuts: None.

AUSTRALIA		Runs	Balls	4/6
T.M.Moody	c Benjamin b Simmons	42	70	3
D.C.Boon	c Williams b Cummins	100	147	8
D.M.Jones	c Williams b Cummins	6	14	–
*A.R.Border	lbw b Simmons	8	10	1
M.E.Waugh	st Williams b Hooper	21	31	–
S.R.Waugh	b Cummins	6	14	–
†I.A.Healy	not out	11	11	–
P.L.Taylor	not out	10	6	1
C.J.McDermott				
M.R.Whitney				
B.A.Reid				
Extras	(LB3, W3, NB6)	12		
TOTAL	(50 overs; 6 wickets)	216		

WEST INDIES		Runs	Balls	4/6
D.L.Haynes	c Jones b McDermott	14	24	2
B.C.Lara	run out	70	97	3
P.V.Simmons	lbw b McDermott	0	1	–
*R.B.Richardson	c Healy b Whitney	10	44	–
K.L.T.Arthurton	c McDermott b Whitney	15	15	2
A.L.Logie	c Healy b Whitney	5	15	–
C.L.Hooper	c M.E.Waugh b Whitney	4	11	–
†D.Williams	c Border b Reid	4	15	–
W.K.M.Benjamin	lbw b S.R.Waugh	15	21	1
C.E.L.Ambrose	run out	2	7	–
A.C.Cummins	not out	5	10	–
Extras	(B3, LB5, W3, NB4)	15		
TOTAL	(42.4 overs)	159		

WEST INDIES	O	M	R	W		FALL OF WICKETS	
Ambrose	10	0	46	0	Wkt	A	WI
Benjamin	10	1	49	0	1st	107	27
Cummins	10	1	38	3	2nd	128	27
Hooper	10	0	40	1	3rd	141	59
Simmons	10	1	40	2	4th	185	83
					5th	189	99
AUSTRALIA					6th	200	117
McDermott	6	1	29	2	7th	–	128
Reid	10	1	26	1	8th	–	137
Whitney	10	1	34	4	9th	–	150
S.R.Waugh	6.4	0	24	1	10th	–	159
Taylor	4	0	24	0			
Moody	6	1	14	0			

Umpires: P.D.Reporter (*India*) (19) and D.R.Shepherd (*England*) (47).

NEW ZEALAND v PAKISTAN (SEMI-FINAL)

At Eden Park, Auckland, New Zealand, on 21 March 1992.   Toss: New Zealand.
Result: **PAKISTAN** won by 4 wickets.   Award: Inzamam-ul-Haq.
LOI debuts: None.

NEW ZEALAND		Runs	Balls	4/6
M.J.Greatbatch	b Aqib	17	22	–/2
J.G.Wright	c Ramiz b Mushtaq	13	44	1
A.H.Jones	lbw b Mushtaq	21	53	2
*M.D.Crowe	run out	91	83	7/3
K.R.Rutherford	c Moin b Wasim	50	68	5/1
C.Z.Harris	st Moin b Iqbal	13	12	1
†I.D.S.Smith	not out	18	10	3
D.N.Patel	lbw b Wasim	8	6	1
G.R.Larsen	not out	8	6	1
D.K.Morrison				
W.Watson				
Extras	(LB11, W8, NB4)	23		
TOTAL	(50 overs; 7 wickets)	262		

PAKISTAN		Runs	Balls	4/6
Aamir Sohail	c Jones b Patel	14	20	1
Ramiz Raja	c Morrison b Watson	44	55	6
*Imran Khan	c Larsen b Harris	44	93	1/2
Javed Miandad	not out	57	69	4
Salim Malik	c sub (R.T.Latham) b Larsen	1	2	–
Inzamam-ul-Haq	run out	60	37	7/1
Wasim Akram	b Watson	9	8	1
†Moin Khan	not out	20	11	2/1
Mushtaq Ahmed				
Iqbal Sikander				
Aqib Javed				
Extras	(B4, LB10, W1)	15		
TOTAL	(49 overs; 6 wickets)	264		

PAKISTAN	O	M	R	W		FALL OF WICKETS		
Wasim Akram	10	1	40	2	Wkt	NZ	P	
Aqib Javed	10	2	45	1	1st	35	30	
Mushtaq Ahmed	10	0	40	2	2nd	39	84	
Imran Khan	10	0	59	0	3rd	87	134	
Iqbal Sikander	9	0	56	1	4th	194	140	
Aamir Sohail	1	0	11	0	5th	214	227	
					6th	221	238	
NEW ZEALAND					7th	244		
Patel	10	1	50	1	8th	–	–	
Morrison	9	0	55	0	9th	–	–	
Watson	10	2	39	2	10th	–	–	
Larsen	10	1	34	1				
Harris	10	0	72	1				

Umpires: S.A.Bucknor (*West Indies*) (11) and D.R.Shepherd (*England*) (48).

ENGLAND v SOUTH AFRICA (SEMI-FINAL)

At Sydney Cricket Ground, Australia, on 22 March 1992.   Toss: South Africa.
Result: **ENGLAND** won by 19 runs (*target revised to 252 runs off 43 overs*).
Award: G.A.Hick.
LOI debuts: None.

ENGLAND		Runs	Balls	4/6
*G.A.Gooch	c Richardson b Donald	2	8	–
I.T.Botham	b Pringle	21	27	3
†A.J.Stewart	c Richardson b McMillan	33	58	4
G.A.Hick	c Rhodes b Snell	83	90	9
N.H.Fairbrother	b Pringle	28	50	1
A.J.Lamb	c Richardson b Donald	19	22	1
C.C.Lewis	not out	18	17	2
D.A.Reeve	not out	25	14	4
P.A.J.DeFreitas				
G.C.Small				
R.K.Illingworth				
Extras	(B1, LB7, W9, NB6)	23		
TOTAL	(45 overs; 6 wickets)	252		

SOUTH AFRICA		Runs	Balls	4/6
*K.C.Wessels	c Lewis b Botham	17	23	1
A.C.Hudson	lbw b Illingworth	46	53	6
P.N.Kirsten	b DeFreitas	11	26	–
A.P.Kuiper	b Illingworth	36	44	5
W.J.Cronje	c Hick b Small	24	46	1
J.N.Rhodes	c Lewis b Small	43	39	3
B.M.McMillan	not out	21	21	–
†D.J.Richardson	not out	13	10	1
R.P.Snell				
M.W.Pringle				
A.A.Donald				
Extras	(LB17, W4)	21		
TOTAL	(43 overs; 6 wickets)	232		

SOUTH AFRICA	O	M	R	W		FALL OF WICKETS		
Donald	10	0	69	2	Wkt	E	SA	
Pringle	9	2	36	2	1st	20	26	
Snell	8	0	52	1	2nd	39	61	
McMillan	9	0	47	1	3rd	110	90	
Kuiper	5	0	26	0	4th	183	131	
Cronje	4	0	14	0	5th	187	176	
					6th	221	206	
ENGLAND					7th	–	–	
Botham	10	0	52	1	8th	–	–	
Lewis	5	0	38	0	9th	–	–	
DeFreitas	8	1	28	1	10th	–	–	
Illingworth	10	1	46	2				
Small	10	1	51	2				

Umpires: B.L.Aldridge (*New Zealand*) (26) and S G.Randell (50).

ENGLAND v PAKISTAN (FINAL)

At Melbourne Cricket Ground, Australia, on 25 March 1992.   Toss: Pakistan.
Result: **PAKISTAN** won by 22 runs.   Award: Wasim Akram.
LOI debuts: None.

PAKISTAN		Runs	Balls	4/6
Aamir Sohail	c Stewart b Pringle	4	19	–
Ramiz Raja	lbw b Pringle	8	26	1
*Imran Khan	c Illingworth b Botham	72	110	5/1
Javed Miandad	c Botham b Illingworth	58	98	4
Inzamam-ul-Haq	b Pringle	42	35	4
Wasim Akram	run out	33	19	4
Salim Malik	not out	0	1	
Ijaz Ahmed				
†Moin Khan				
Mushtaq Ahmed				
Aqib Javed				
Extras	(LB19, W6, NB7)	32		
TOTAL	(50 overs; 6 wickets)	249		

ENGLAND		Runs	Balls	4/6
*G.A.Gooch	c Aqib b Mushtaq	29	66	1
I.T.Botham	c Moin b Wasim	0	6	–
†A.J.Stewart	c Moin b Aqib	7	16	1
G.A.Hick	lbw b Mushtaq	17	36	1
N.H.Fairbrother	c Moin b Aqib	62	70	3
A.J.Lamb	b Wasim	31	41	2
C.C.Lewis	b Wasim	0	1	–
D.A.Reeve	c Ramiz b Mushtaq	15	32	–
D.R.Pringle	not out	18	16	1
P.A.J.DeFreitas	run out	10	8	–
R.K.Illingworth	c Ramiz b Imran	14	11	2
Extras	(LB5, W13, NB6)	24		
TOTAL	(49.2 overs)	227		

ENGLAND	O	M	R	W		FALL OF WICKETS	
Pringle	10	2	22	3	Wkt	P	E
Lewis	10	2	52	0	1st	20	6
Botham	7	0	42	1	2nd	24	21
DeFreitas	10	1	42	0	3rd	163	59
Illingworth	10	0	50	1	4th	197	69
Reeve	3	0	22	0	5th	249	141
					6th	249	141
PAKISTAN					7th	–	180
Wasim Akram	10	0	49	3	8th	–	183
Aqib Javed	10	2	27	2	9th	–	208
Mushtaq Ahmed	10	1	41	3	10th	–	227
Ijaz Ahmed	3	0	13	0			
Imran Khan	6.2	0	43	1			
Aamir Sohail	10	0	49	0			

Umpires: B.L.Aldridge (*New Zealand*) (27) and S.A.Bucknor (*West Indies*) (12).

INDEX OF WORLD CUP CRICKETERS

ENGLAND (52 players)

Allott, P.J.W. (7): 197, 201, 205, 209, 213, 217, 221.
Amiss, D.L. (4): 19, 23, 27, 31.
Arnold, G.G. (3): 19, 23, 31.
Athey, C.W.J. (6): 460, 463, 468, 472, 476, 477.
Botham, I.T. (22): 63, 67, 71, 72, 74, 197, 201, 205, 209, 213, 217, 221, 715, 721, 726, 731, 736, 741, 744, 748, 751, 752.
Boycott, G. (5): 63, 67, 71, 72, 74.
Brearley, J.M. (5): 63, 67, 71, 72, 74.
Broad, B.C. (3): 452, 455, 460.
Cowans, N.G. (1): 217.
DeFreitas, P.A.J. (18): 452, 455, 460, 463, 468, 472, 476, 477, 715, 721, 726, 731, 736, 741, 744, 748, 751, 752.
Denness, M.H. (4): 19, 23, 27, 31.
Dilley, G.R. (6): 197, 201, 205, 209, 213, 221.
Downton, P.R. (8): 452, 455, 460, 463, 468, 472, 476, 477.
Edmonds, P.H. (3): 63, 71, 74.
Emburey, J.E. (8): 452, 455, 460, 463, 468, 472, 476, 477.
Fairbrother, N.H. (9): 715, 721, 726, 731, 736, 741, 748, 751, 752.
Fletcher, K.W.R. (4): 19, 23, 27, 31.
Foster, N.A. (7): 452, 455, 463, 468, 472, 476, 477.
Fowler, G. (7): 197, 201, 205, 209, 213, 217, 221.
Gatting, M.W. (15): 197, 201, 205, 209, 213, 217, 221, 452, 455, 460, 463, 468, 472, 476, 477.
Gooch, G.A. (21): 63, 67, 71, 72, 74, 452, 455, 460, 463, 468, 472, 476, 477, 715, 721, 726, 731, 736, 748, 751, 752.
Gould, I.J. (7): 197, 201, 205, 209, 213, 217, 221.
Gower, D.I. (12): 63, 67, 71, 72, 74, 197, 201, 205, 209, 213, 217, 221.
Greig, A.W. (4): 19, 23, 27, 31.
Hayes, F.C. (3): 23, 27, 31.
Hemmings, E.E. (6): 460, 463, 468, 472, 476, 477.
Hendrick, M. (5): 63, 67, 71, 72, 74.
Hick, G.A. (10): 715, 721, 726, 731, 736, 741, 744, 748, 751, 752.
Illingworth, R.K. (6): 736, 741, 744, 748, 751, 752.
Jameson, J.A. (2): 19, 23.
Knott, A.P.E. (4): 19, 23, 27, 31.
Lamb, A.J. (19): 197, 201, 205, 209, 213, 217, 221, 452, 455, 460, 463, 468, 472, 476, 477, 744, 748, 751, 752.
Larkins, W. (2): 72, 74.
Lever, P. (4): 19, 23, 27, 31.
Lewis, C.C. (9): 715, 721, 726, 731, 736, 741, 744, 751, 752.
Marks, V.J. (7): 197, 201, 205, 209, 213, 217, 221.
Miller, G. (1): 67.
Old, C.M. (9): 19, 23, 27, 31, 63, 67, 71, 72, 74.
Pringle, D.R. (11): 452, 455, 460, 715, 721, 726, 731, 736, 741, 744, 752.
Randall, D.W. (5): 63, 67, 71, 72, 74.
Reeve, D.A. (9): 715, 721, 726, 731, 736, 741, 744, 751, 752.
Robinson, R.T. (7): 452, 455, 463, 468, 472, 476, 477.
Small, G.C. (13): 452, 455, 460, 463, 468, 472, 476, 477, 726, 741, 744, 748, 751.
Smith, R.A. (8): 715, 721, 726, 731, 736, 741, 744, 748.
Snow, J.A. (3): 19, 23, 31.
Stewart, A.J. (10): 715, 721, 726, 731, 736, 741, 744, 748, 751, 752.
Tavaré, C.J. (7): 197, 201, 205, 209, 213, 217, 221.

Taylor, R.W. (5): 63, 67, 71, 72, 74.
Tufnell, P.C.R. (4): 715, 721, 731, 748.
Underwood, D.L. (2): 23, 27.
Willis, R.G.D. (11): 63, 67, 71, 72, 197, 201, 205, 209, 213, 217, 221.
Wood, B. (3): 19, 27, 31.

AUSTRALIA (50 players)

Boon, D.C. (16): 453, 456, 462, 465, 470, 471, 475, 477, 714, 719, 725, 731, 733, 739,
   743, 749.
Border, A.R. (25): 63, 66, 70, 199, 203, 207, 212, 215, 219, 453, 456, 462, 465, 470, 471,
   475, 477, 714, 719, 725, 731, 733, 739, 743, 749.
Chappell, G.S. (5): 21, 25, 29, 31, 33.
Chappell, I.M. (5): 21, 25, 29, 31, 33.
Chappell, T.M. (4): 207, 212, 215, 219.
Cosier, G.J. (3): 63, 66, 70.
Darling, W.M. (3): 63, 66, 70.
Dyer, G.C. (8): 453, 456, 462, 465, 470, 471, 475, 477.
Dymock, G. (3): 63, 66, 70.
Edwards, R. (5): 21, 25, 29, 31, 33.
Gilmour, G.J. (2): 31, 33.
Healy, I.A. (7): 714, 719, 731, 733, 739, 743, 749.
Hilditch, A.M.J. (3): 63, 66, 70.
Hogan, T.G. (4): 207, 212, 215, 219.
Hogg, R.M. (8): 63, 70, 199, 203, 207, 212, 215, 219.
Hookes, D.W. (6): 199, 203, 207, 212, 215, 219.
Hughes, K.J. (8): 63, 66, 70, 199, 203, 207, 212, 215.
Hughes, M.G. (1): 725.
Hurst, A.G. (3): 63, 66, 70.
Jones, D.M. (16): 453, 456, 462, 465, 470, 471, 475, 477, 714, 719, 725, 731, 733, 739,
   743, 749.
Laughlin, T.J. (1): 63.
Lawson, G.F. (4): 199, 203, 207, 219.
Lillee, D.K. (9): 21, 25, 29, 31, 33, 199, 203, 212, 215.
McCosker, R.B. (5): 21, 25, 29, 31, 33.
McDermott, C.J. (16): 453, 456, 462, 465, 470, 471, 475, 477, 714, 719, 725, 731, 733,
   739, 743, 749.
Macleay, K.H. (4): 203, 207, 212, 219.
Mallett, A.A. (3): 21, 25, 29.
Marsh, G.R. (13): 453, 456, 462, 465, 470, 471, 475, 477, 714, 719, 725, 733, 739.
Marsh, R.W. (11): 21, 25, 29, 31, 33, 199, 203, 207, 212, 215, 219.
May, T.B.A. (6): 456, 462, 470, 471, 475, 477.
Moody, T.M. (11): 453, 462, 465, 714, 719, 725, 731, 733, 739, 743, 749.
Moss, J.K. (1): 66.
O'Donnell, S.P. (7): 453, 456, 462, 465, 471, 475, 477.
Porter, G.D. (2): 66, 70.
Reid, B.A. (14): 453, 456, 462, 465, 470, 471, 475, 477, 714, 719, 731, 739, 743, 749.
Taylor, M.A. (2): 725, 731.
Taylor, P.L. (9): 453, 456, 714, 719, 725, 731, 733, 743, 749.
Thomson, J.R. (8): 21, 25, 29, 31, 33, 199, 215, 219.
Turner, A. (5): 21, 25, 29, 31, 33.
Veletta, M.R.J. (4): 470, 471, 475, 477.
Walker, M.H.N. (5): 21, 25, 29, 31, 33.
Walters, K.D. (5): 21, 25, 29, 31, 33.
Waugh, M.E. (5): 714, 733, 739, 743, 749.
Waugh, S.R. (16): 453, 456, 462, 465, 470, 471, 475, 477, 714, 719, 725, 731, 733, 739,
   743, 749.

Wessels, K.C. (3): 199, 203, 207. (*Also 9 matches for South Africa: 719, 723, 727, 730, 735, 738, 741, 745, 751*).
Whitney, M.R. (7): 719, 725, 731, 733, 739, 743, 749.
Wood, G.M. (5): 199, 203, 212, 215, 219.
Wright, K.J. (3): 63, 66, 70.
Yallop, G.N. (9): 63, 66, 70, 199, 203, 207, 212, 215, 219.
Zesers, A.K. (2): 465, 470.

SOUTH AFRICA (14 players)

Bosch, T. (1): 723.
Cronje, W.J. (8): 719, 723, 727, 735, 738, 741, 745, 751.
Donald, A.A. (9): 719, 723, 727, 730, 735, 738, 741, 745, 751.
Henry, O. (1): 727.
Hudson, A.C. (8): 719, 723, 730, 735, 738, 741, 745, 751.
Kirsten, P.N. (8): 719, 723, 727, 730, 738, 741, 745, 751.
Kuiper, A.P. (9): 719, 723, 727, 730, 735, 738, 741, 745, 751.
McMillan, B.M. (9): 719, 723, 727, 730, 735, 738, 741, 745, 751.
Pringle, M.W. (7): 719, 730, 735, 738, 741, 745, 751.
Rhodes, J.N. (9): 719, 723, 727, 730, 735, 738, 741, 745, 751.
Richardson, D.J. (9): 719, 723, 727, 730, 735, 738, 741, 745, 751.
Rushmere, M.W. (3): 727, 730, 735.
Snell, R.P. (9): 719, 723, 727, 730, 735, 738, 741, 745, 751.
Wessels, K.C. (9): 719, 723, 727, 730, 735, 738, 741, 745, 751. (*Also 3 matches for Australia: 199, 203, 207*).

WEST INDIES (38 players)

Ambrose, C.E.L. (7): 717, 721, 730, 734, 737, 742, 749.
Arthurton, K.L.T. (8): 717, 721, 724, 730, 734, 737, 742, 749.
Bacchus, S.F.A.F. (8): 200, 203, 208, 210, 215, 220, 222, 223.
Baptiste, E.A.E. (1): 459.
Benjamin, W.K.M. (13): 452, 457, 464, 468, 473, 717, 721, 724, 730, 734, 737, 742, 749.
Best, C.A. (2): 452, 457.
Boyce, K.D. (5): 22, 26, 29, 32, 33.
Croft, C.E.H. (4): 61, 69, 73, 74.
Cummins, A.C. (6): 724, 730, 734, 737, 742, 749.
Daniel, W.W. (3): 203, 208, 220.
Davis, W.W. (5): 203, 208, 210, 215, 220.
Dujon, P.J.L. (14): 200, 203, 208, 210, 215, 220, 222, 223, 452, 457, 459, 464, 468, 473.
Fredericks, R.C. (5): 22, 26, 29, 32, 33.
Garner, J. (8): 61, 69, 73, 74, 200, 220, 222, 223.
Gibbs, L.R. (1): 22.
Gomes, H.A. (8): 200, 203, 208, 210, 215, 220, 222, 223.
Greenidge, C.G. (15): 26, 29, 32, 33, 61, 69, 73, 74, 200, 203, 208, 210, 215, 222, 223.
Harper, R.A. (8): 452, 457, 459, 464, 468, 473, 717, 721.
Haynes, D.L. (25): 61, 69, 73, 74, 200, 203, 208, 210, 215, 220, 222, 223, 452, 457, 459, 464, 468, 473, 717, 721, 730, 734, 737, 742, 749.
Holder, V.A. (5): 22, 26, 29, 32, 33.
Holding, M.A. (11): 61, 69, 73, 74, 200, 203, 208, 210, 215, 222, 223.
Hooper, C.L. (14): 452, 457, 459, 464, 468, 473, 717, 721, 724, 730, 734, 737, 742, 749.
Julien, B.D. (5): 22, 26, 29, 32, 33.
Kallicharran, A.I. (9): 22, 26, 29, 32, 33, 61, 69, 73, 74.
Kanhai, R.B. (5): 22, 26, 29, 32, 33.
King, C.L. (4): 61, 69, 73, 74.
Lara, B.C. (8): 717, 721, 724, 730, 734, 737, 742, 749.
Lloyd, C.H. (17): 22, 26, 29, 32, 33, 61, 69, 73, 74, 200, 203, 208, 210, 215, 220, 222, 223.

Logie, A.L. (15): 220, 452, 457, 459, 464, 468, 473, 717, 721, 724, 730, 734, 737, 742, 749.
Marshall, M.D. (11): 200, 210, 215, 220, 222, 223, 717, 721, 724, 730, 734.
Murray, D.L. (9): 22, 26, 29, 32, 33, 61, 69, 73, 74.
Patterson, B.P. (7): 452, 457, 459, 464, 468, 473, 724.
Richards, I.V.A. (23): 22, 26, 29, 32, 33, 61, 69, 73, 74, 200, 203, 208, 210, 215, 220, 222, 223, 452, 457, 459, 464, 468, 473.
Richardson, R.B. (14): 452, 457, 459, 464, 468, 473, 717, 721, 724, 730, 734, 737, 742, 749.
Roberts, A.M.E. (16): 22, 26, 29, 32, 33, 61, 69, 73, 74, 200, 203, 208, 210, 215, 222, 223.
Simmons, P.V. (8): 459, 464, 468, 473, 724, 737, 742, 749.
Walsh, C.A. (6): 452, 457, 459, 464, 468, 473.
Williams, D. (8): 717, 721, 724, 730, 734, 737, 742, 749.

NEW ZEALAND (38 players)

Boock, S.L. (4): 454, 458, 466, 470.
Bracewell, J.G. (7): 202, 209, 218, 454, 458, 462, 470.
Burgess, M.G. (4): 62, 65, 69, 72.
Cairns, B.L. (11): 32, 62, 65, 69, 72, 197, 202, 206, 209, 214, 218.
Cairns, C.L. (5): 714, 723, 728, 740, 744.
Chatfield, E.J. (13): 69, 197, 202, 206, 209, 214, 218, 454, 458, 462, 466, 470, 474.
Collinge, R.O. (4): 20, 23, 28, 32.
Coney, J.V. (10): 62, 65, 69, 72, 197, 202, 206, 209, 214, 218.
Crowe, J.J. (8): 206, 209, 454, 458, 462, 466, 470, 474.
Crowe, M.D. (21): 197, 202, 206, 209, 214, 218, 454, 458, 462, 466, 470, 474, 714, 718, 723, 728, 734, 740, 744, 747, 750.
Edgar, B.A. (8): 65, 69, 72, 197, 202, 209, 214, 218.
Greatbatch, M.J. (7): 723, 728, 734, 740, 744, 747, 750.
Hadlee, B.G. (1): 23.
Hadlee, D.R. (4): 20, 23, 28, 32.
Hadlee, R.J. (13): 20, 23, 28, 62, 65, 69, 72, 197, 202, 206, 209, 214, 218.
Harris, C.Z. (9): 714, 718, 723, 728, 734, 740, 744, 747, 750.
Hastings, B.F. (4): 20, 23, 28, 32.
Horne, P.A. (1): 474.
Howarth, G.P. (11): 20, 28, 32, 62, 72, 197, 202, 206, 209, 214, 218.
Howarth, H.J. (4): 20, 23, 28, 32.
Jones, A.H. (13): 454, 458, 462, 466, 714, 718, 723, 728, 734, 740, 744, 747, 750.
Larsen, G.R. (9): 714, 718, 723, 728, 734, 740, 744, 747, 750.
Latham, R.T. (7): 714, 718, 723, 728, 734, 740, 747.
Lees, W.K. (8): 62, 65, 69, 72, 197, 202, 214, 218.
McKechnie, B.J. (8): 20, 23, 28, 32, 62, 65, 69, 72.
Morrison, D.K. (6): 474, 718, 728, 734, 747, 750.
Morrison, J.F.M. (6): 20, 23, 28, 32, 65, 69.
Parker, J.M. (4): 20, 23, 28, 32.
Patel, D.N. (15): 454, 458, 462, 466, 470, 474, 714, 718, 723, 728, 734, 740, 744, 747, 750.
Rutherford, K.R. (14): 458, 462, 466, 470, 474, 714, 718, 723, 728, 734, 740, 744, 747, 750.
Smith, I.D.S. (17): 206, 209, 454, 458, 462, 466, 470, 474, 714, 718, 723, 728, 734, 740, 744, 747, 750.
Snedden, M.C. (9): 197, 206, 214, 454, 458, 462, 466, 470, 474.
Stott, L.W. (1): 62.
Troup, G.B. (3): 62, 65, 72.
Turner, G.M. (14): 20, 23, 28, 32, 62, 65, 69, 72, 197, 202, 206, 209, 214, 218.
Wadsworth, K.J. (4): 20, 23, 28, 32.
Watson, W. (14): 454, 458, 462, 466, 470, 474, 714, 718, 723, 734, 740, 744, 747, 750.

Wright, J.G. (18): 62, 65, 69, 72, 197, 202, 206, 214, 218, 454, 462, 466, 470, 474, 714, 718, 744, 750.

INDIA (39 players)

Abid Ali, S. (3): 19, 24, 28.
Amarnath, M. (14): 19, 24, 28, 61, 65, 68, 200, 204, 207, 210, 216, 219, 221, 223.
Amre, P.K. (4): 715, 722, 737, 745.
Azad, K. (3): 219, 221, 223.
Azharuddin, M. (15): 453, 458, 461, 465, 469, 474, 476, 715, 722, 725, 729, 732, 737, 740, 745.
Banerjee, S.T. (2): 715, 740.
Bedi, B.S. (5): 24, 28, 61, 65, 68.
Binny, R.M.H. (9): 200, 204, 207, 210, 216, 219, 221, 223, 453.
Engineer, F.M. (3): 19, 24, 28.
Gaekwad, A.D. (6): 19, 24, 28, 61, 65, 68.
Gavaskar, S.M. (19): 19, 24, 28, 61, 65, 68, 200, 204, 216, 219, 221, 223, 453, 458, 461, 465, 469, 474, 476.
Ghavri, K.D. (4): 19, 61, 65, 68.
Jadeja, A.D. (6): 722, 725, 729, 732, 737, 740.
Kambli, V.G. (5): 715, 722, 729, 732, 745.
Kapil Dev (26): 61, 65, 68, 200, 204, 207, 210, 216, 219, 221, 223, 453, 458, 461, 465, 469, 474, 476, 715, 722, 725, 729, 732, 737, 740, 745.
Khanna, S.C. (3): 61, 65, 68.
Kirmani, S.M.H. (8): 200, 204, 207, 210, 216, 219, 221, 223.
Madan Lal (11): 19, 24, 28, 200, 204, 207, 210, 216, 219, 221, 223.
Maninder Singh (7): 453, 458, 461, 465, 469, 474, 476.
Manjrekar, S.V. (6): 725, 729, 732, 737, 740, 745.
More, K.S. (14): 453, 458, 461, 465, 469, 476, 715, 722, 725, 729, 732, 737, 740, 745.
Pandit, C.S. (2): 474, 476.
Patel, B.P. (6): 19, 24, 28, 61, 65, 68.
Patil, S.M. (8): 200, 204, 207, 210, 216, 219, 221, 223.
Prabhakar, M. (15): 453, 458, 461, 465, 469, 474, 476, 715, 722, 725, 729, 732, 737, 740, 745.
Raju, S.L.V. (7): 722, 725, 729, 732, 737, 740, 745.
Sandu, B.S. (8): 200, 204, 207, 210, 216, 219, 221, 223.
Sharma, C, (4): 465, 469, 474, 476.
Shastri, R.J. (14): 200, 204, 207, 210, 216, 453, 458, 461, 465, 469, 474, 476, 715, 725.
Sidhu, N.S. (7): 453, 458, 461, 465, 469, 474, 476.
Sivaramakrishnan, L. (2): 458, 461.
Solkar, E.D. (3): 19, 24, 28.
Srikkanth, K. (23): 200, 204, 207, 210, 216, 219, 221, 223, 453, 458, 461, 465, 469, 474, 476, 715, 722, 725, 729, 732, 737, 740, 745.
Srinath, J. (8): 715, 722, 725, 729, 732, 737, 740, 745.
Tendulkar, S.R. (8): 715, 722, 725, 729, 732, 737, 740, 745.
Vengsarkar, D.B. (11): 61, 65, 68, 207, 210, 453, 458, 461, 465, 469, 474.
Venkataraghavan, S. (6): 19, 24, 28, 61, 65, 68.
Viswanath, G.R. (6): 19, 24, 28, 61, 65, 68.
Yashpal Sharma (8): 200, 204, 207, 210, 216, 219, 221, 223.

PAKISTAN (40 players)

Aamir Sohail (10): 717, 720, 726, 729, 735, 739, 746, 747, 750, 752.
Abdul Qadir (13): 202, 205, 211, 213, 218, 222, 451, 455, 459, 463, 467, 473, 475.
Aqib Javed (10): 717, 720, 726, 729, 735, 739, 746, 747, 750, 752.
Asif Iqbal (5): 21, 64, 66, 71, 73.
Asif Masood (3): 21, 26, 30.

Haroon Rashid (4): 64, 66, 71, 73.
Ijaz Ahmed, sr (14): 451, 455, 459, 463, 467, 473, 475, 717, 726, 735, 739, 746, 747, 752.
Ijaz Faqih (6): 198, 202, 211, 213, 218, 222.
Imran Khan (28): 21, 30, 64, 66, 71, 73, 198, 202, 205, 211, 213, 218, 222, 451, 455, 459, 463, 467, 473, 475, 720, 729, 735, 739, 746, 747, 750, 752.
Inzamam-ul-Haq (10): 717, 720, 726, 729, 735, 739, 746, 747, 750, 752.
Iqbal Sikander (4): 717, 720, 735, 750.
Javed Miandad (28): 26, 30, 64, 66, 71, 73, 198, 202, 205, 211, 213, 218, 451, 455, 459, 463, 467, 473, 475, 717, 720, 726, 729, 739, 746, 747, 750, 752.
Majid Khan (7): 21, 26, 30, 64, 66, 71, 73.
Mansoor Akhtar (8): 205, 211, 451, 455, 459, 463, 467, 475.
Manzoor Elahi (1): 467.
Mohsin Khan (7): 198, 202, 205, 211, 213, 218, 222.
Moin Khan (10): 717, 720, 726, 729, 735, 739, 746, 747, 750, 752.
Mudassar Nazar (12): 64, 66, 71, 73, 198, 202, 205, 213, 218, 222, 451, 473.
Mushtaq Ahmed (9): 720, 726, 729, 735, 739, 746, 747, 750, 752.
Mushtaq Mohammad (3): 21, 26, 30.
Naseer Malik (3): 21, 26, 30.
Parvez Mir (2): 26, 30.
Ramiz Raja (15): 451, 455, 459, 463, 467, 473, 475, 717, 720, 726, 739, 746, 747, 750, 752.
Rashid Khan (7): 198, 202, 205, 211, 213, 218, 222.
Sadiq Mohammad (7): 21, 26, 30, 64, 66, 71, 73.
Salim Jaffer (5): 455, 459, 463, 473, 475.
Salim Malik (17): 451, 455, 459, 463, 467, 473, 475, 717, 720, 726, 729, 735, 739, 746, 747, 750, 752.
Salim Yousuf (7): 451, 455, 459, 463, 467, 473, 475.
Sarfraz Nawaz (11): 21, 26, 64, 73, 198, 202, 205, 211, 213, 218, 222.
Shahid Mahboob (5): 198, 202, 211, 218, 222.
Shoaib Mohammad (1): 473.
Sikander Bakht (4): 64, 66, 71, 73.
Tahir Naqqash (1): 198.
Tausif Ahmed (6): 451, 455, 459, 463, 467, 475.
Wasim Akram (17): 451, 455, 459, 463, 467, 473, 475, 717, 720, 726, 729, 735, 739, 746, 747, 750, 752.
Wasim Bari (14): 21, 26, 30, 64, 66, 71, 73, 198, 202, 205, 211, 213, 218, 222.
Wasim Haider (3): 717, 726, 729.
Wasim Raja (8): 21, 26, 30, 66, 71, 205, 213, 222.
Zaheer Abbas (14): 21, 26, 30, 64, 66, 71, 73, 198, 202, 205, 211, 213, 218, 222.
Zahid Fazal (2): 729, 735.

SRI LANKA (41 players)

Anurasiri, S.D. (11): 451, 457, 460, 464, 467, 472, 718, 727, 733, 736, 742.
De Alwis, R.G. (6): 198, 201, 206, 211, 214, 217.
De Mel, A.L.F. (9): 198, 201, 206, 211, 214, 217, 457, 467, 472.
De Silva, D.L.S. (2): 62, 68.
De Silva, D.S. (11): 22, 25, 30, 62, 68, 198, 201, 206, 211, 214, 217.
De Silva, G.R.A. (2): 30, 62.
De Silva, P.A. (14): 451, 457, 460, 464, 467, 472, 716, 718, 722, 727, 733, 736, 742, 746.
Dias, R.L. (10): 62, 68, 198, 201, 206, 211, 214, 217, 451, 472.
Fernando, E.R. (3): 22, 25, 30.
Goonatillake, F.R.M. (1): 68.
Gurusinha, A.P. (12): 451, 457, 460, 472, 716, 718, 722, 727, 733, 736, 742, 746.
Hathurusingh, U.C. (4): 722, 727, 742, 746.
Heyn, P.D. (2): 22, 30.
Jayasinghe, S.A. (2): 62, 68.

Jayasuriya, S.T. (6): 716, 718, 722, 727, 733, 736.
Jeganathan, S. (3): 464, 467, 472.
John, V.B. (11): 198, 201, 206, 211, 217, 451, 457, 460, 464, 467, 472.
Kalpage, R.S. (7): 716, 718, 722, 727, 733, 742, 746.
Kaluperuma, L.W.S. (3): 22, 25, 30.
Kuruppu, D.S.B.P. (11): 198, 201, 206, 211, 214, 217, 451, 457, 460, 464, 467.
Labrooy, G.F. (1): 736.
Madugalle, R.S. (11): 68, 201, 206, 211, 214, 217, 457, 460, 464, 467, 472.
Mahanama, R.S. (14): 451, 457, 460, 464, 467, 472, 716, 718, 722, 727, 733, 736, 742, 746.
Mendis, L.R.D. (16): 22, 25, 62, 68, 198, 201, 206, 211, 214, 217, 451, 457, 460, 464, 467, 472.
Opatha, A.R.M. (5): 22, 25, 30, 62, 68.
Pasqual, S.P. (2): 62, 68.
Pieris, H.S.M. (3): 22, 25, 30.
Ramanayake, C.P.H. (8): 716, 718, 722, 727, 733, 736, 742, 746.
Ranasinghe, A.N, (3): 22, 25, 30.
Ranatunga, A. (19): 198, 201, 206, 211, 214, 217, 451, 457, 460, 464, 467, 716, 718, 722, 727, 733, 736, 742, 746.
Ratnayake, R.J. (9): 198, 201, 206, 211, 214, 217, 451, 460, 464.
Ratnayeke, J.R. (6): 451, 457, 460, 464, 467, 472.
Samarasekera, M.A.R. (8): 198, 214, 716, 718, 733, 736, 742, 746.
Tennekoon, A.P.B. (4): 22, 25, 30, 62.
Tillekeratne, H.P. (8): 716, 718, 722, 727, 733, 736, 742, 746.
Tissera, M.H. (3): 22, 25, 30.
Warnapura, B. (5): 22, 25, 30, 62, 68.
Wettimuny, S. (6): 198, 201, 206, 211, 214, 217.
Wettimuny, S.R.de S. (3): 25, 62, 68.
Wickremasinghe, G.P. (8): 716, 718, 722, 727, 733, 736, 742, 746.
Wijegunawardene, K.I.W. (3): 716, 722, 746.

ZIMBABWE (23 players)

Arnott, K.J. (9): 461, 466, 469, 471, 716, 720, 724, 743, 748.
Brandes, E.A. (12): 454, 466, 469, 471, 716, 720, 724, 728, 732, 738, 743, 748.
Brown, R.D. (7): 204, 212, 216, 220, 454, 456, 469.
Burmester, M.G. (4): 728, 732, 738, 743.
Butchart, I.P. (17): 199, 204, 208, 212, 216, 220, 454, 456, 461, 466, 469, 471, 716, 720, 728, 732, 748.
Campbell, A.D.R. (4): 724, 728, 732, 743.
Curran, K.M. (11): 199, 204, 208, 212, 216, 220, 454, 456, 461, 466, 471.
Duers, K.G. (6): 716, 724, 728, 732, 738, 743.
Fletcher, D.A.G. (6): 199, 204, 208, 212, 216, 220.
Flower, A. (8): 716, 720, 724, 728, 732, 738, 743, 748.
Heron, J.G. (6): 199, 204, 208, 212, 216, 220.
Hogg, V.R. (2): 199, 212.
Houghton, D.L. (20): 199, 204, 208, 212, 216, 220, 454, 456, 461, 466, 469, 471, 716, 720, 724, 728, 732, 738, 743, 748.
James, W.R. (4): 716, 720, 738, 748.
Jarvis, M.P. (10): 456, 461, 466, 469, 471, 716, 720, 724, 738, 748.
Meman, M.A. (1): 461.
Paterson, G.A. (10): 199, 204, 208, 212, 216, 220, 454, 456, 461, 466.
Peckover, G.E. (3): 208, 216, 220.
Pycroft, A.J. (20): 199, 204, 208, 212, 216, 220, 454, 456, 461, 466, 469, 471, 716, 720, 724, 728, 732, 738, 743, 748.
Rawson, P.W.E. (10): 199, 204, 208, 212, 216, 220, 454, 456, 469, 471.
Shah, A.H. (*registered as Omarshah*) (16): 199, 204, 208, 454, 456, 461, 466, 469, 471, 720, 724, 728, 732, 738, 743, 748.

Traicos, A.J. (20): 199, 204, 208, 212, 216, 220, 454, 456, 461, 466, 469, 471, 716, 720,
    724, 728, 732, 738, 743, 748.
Waller, A.C. (14): 454, 456, 461, 466, 469, 471, 716, 720, 724, 728, 732, 738, 743, 748.

CANADA (13 players)

Baksh, S. (1): 70.
Callender, R.G. (2): 67, 70.
Chappell, C.J.D. (3): 64, 67, 70.
Dennis, F.A. (3): 64, 67, 70.
Henry, C.C. (2): 64, 70.
Marshall, C.A. (2): 64, 67.
Mauricette, B.M. (3): 64, 67, 70.
Patel, J.M. (3): 64, 67, 70.
Sealy, G.R. (3): 64, 67, 70.
Stead, M.P. (2): 64, 67.
Tariq Javed (3): 64, 67, 70.
Valentine, J.N. (3): 64, 67, 70.
Vaughan, J.C.B. (3): 64, 67, 70.

EAST AFRICA (14 players)

Frasat Ali (3): 20, 24, 27.
Harilal R. Shah (3): 20, 24, 27.
Jawahir Shah (3): 20, 24, 27.
McLeod, H. (2): 20, 27.
Mehmood Quaraishy (3): 20, 24, 27.
Nagenda, J. (1): 20.
Nana, P.G. (3): 20, 24, 27.
Praful Mehta (1): 24.
Pringle, D. (2): 24, 27.
Ramesh Sethi (3): 20, 24, 27.
Shiraz Sumar (1): 20.
Walusimba, S. (3): 20, 24, 27.
Yunus Badat (2): 24, 27.
Zulfiqar Ali (3): 20, 24, 27.

WORLD CUP RECORDS 1975-92

RESULTS SUMMARY

	Played	Won	Lost	No Result
England	34	23	10	1
West Indies	32	22	9	1
Australia	30	17	13	–
Pakistan	31	17	13	1
New Zealand	29	16	13	–
India	29	14	14	1
South Africa	9	5	4	–
Sri Lanka	26	4	20	2
Zimbabwe	20	2	18	–
Canada	3	–	3	–
East Africa	3	–	3	–

WORLD CUP FINALS

1975	WEST INDIES (291-8) beat Australia (274) by 17 runs	Lord's
1979	WEST INDIES (286-9) beat England (194) by 92 runs	Lord's
1983	INDIA (183) beat West Indies (140) by 43 runs	Lord's
1987-88	AUSTRALIA (253-5) beat England (246-8) by 7 runs	Calcutta
1991-92	PAKISTAN (249-6) beat England (227) by 22 runs	Melbourne

TEAM RECORDS

HIGHEST TOTAL
| 360-4 | West Indies v Sri Lanka | Karachi | 1987-88 |

HIGHEST TOTAL – BATTING SECOND
| 313-7 | Sri Lanka v Zimbabwe | New Plymouth | 1991-92 |

LOWEST TOTAL
| 45 | Canada v England | Manchester | 1979 |

HIGHEST MATCH AGGREGATE
| 626 | Pakistan v Sri Lanka | Swansea | 1983 |

LARGEST MARGINS OF VICTORY
10 wkts	India beat East Africa	Leeds	1975
10 wkts	West Indies beat Zimbabwe	Birmingham	1983
10 wkts	West Indies beat Pakistan	Melbourne	1991-92
202 runs	England beat India	Lord's	1975

NARROWEST MARGINS OF VICTORY
1 wkt	West Indies beat Pakistan	Birmingham	1975
1 wkt	Pakistan beat West Indies	Lahore	1987-88
1 run	Australia beat India	Madras	1987-88
1 run	Australia beat India	Brisbane	1991-92

INDIVIDUAL RECORDS – BATTING

MOST RUNS

		M	I	NO	HS	Runs	Avge	100
Javed Miandad	P	28	27	4	103	**1029**	44.73	1
I.V.A.Richards	WI	23	21	5	181	**1013**	63.31	3
G.A.Gooch	E	21	21	1	115	**897**	44.85	1
M.D.Crowe	NZ	21	21	5	100*	**880**	55.00	1
D.L.Haynes	WI	25	25	2	105	**854**	37.13	1
D.C.Boon	A	16	16	1	100	**815**	54.33	2

HIGHEST INDIVIDUAL SCORE

181	I.V.A.Richards	West Indies v Sri Lanka	Karachi	1987-88

HUNDRED BEFORE LUNCH

101	A.Turner	Australia v Sri Lanka	The Oval	1975

MOST HUNDREDS

3   I.V.A.Richards (West Indies), Ramiz Raja (Pakistan)

HIGHEST PARTNERSHIP FOR EACH WICKET

1st	182	R.B.McCosker/A.Turner	A v SL	The Oval	1975
2nd	176	D.L.Amiss/K.W.R.Fletcher	E v I	Lord's	1975
3rd	195*	C.G.Greenidge/H.A.Gomes	WI v Z	Worcester	1983
4th	149	R.B.Kanhai/C.H.Lloyd	WI v I	Lord's	1975
5th	145*	A.Flower/A.C.Waller	Z v SL	New Plymouth	1991-92
6th	144	Imran Khan/Shahid Mahboob	P v SL	Leeds	1983
7th	75*	D.A.G.Fletcher/I.P.Butchart	Z v A	Nottingham	1983
8th	117	D.L.Houghton/I.P.Butchart	Z v NZ	Hyderabad	1987-88
9th	126*	Kapil Dev/S.M.H.Kirmani	I v Z	Tunbridge Wells	1983
10th	71	A.M.E.Roberts/J.Garner	WI v I	Manchester	1983

INDIVIDUAL RECORDS – BOWLING

MOST WICKETS

		Balls	Runs	Wkts	Avge	Best	4w
Imran Khan	P	1017	655	**34**	19.26	4-37	2
I.T.Botham	E	1332	762	**30**	25.40	4-31	1
Kapil Dev	I	1422	892	**28**	31.85	5-43	1
A.M.E.Roberts	WI	1021	552	**26**	21.23	3-32	–
C.J.McDermott	A	876	587	**26**	22.57	5-44	2
Wasim Akram	P	918	633	**25**	25.32	4-32	1

BEST ANALYSIS

7-51	W.W.Davis	West Indies v Australia	Leeds	1983

HAT-TRICK

	C.Sharma	India v New Zealand	Nagpur	1987-88

MOST ECONOMICAL BOWLING

12-8-6-1	B.S.Bedi	India v East Africa	Leeds	1975

MOST EXPENSIVE BOWLING

12-1-105-2	M.C.Snedden	New Zealand v England	The Oval	1983

INDIVIDUAL RECORDS – WICKET-KEEPING

MOST DISMISSALS

22	(18ct, 4st)	Wasim Bari	Pakistan
20	(19ct, 1st)	P.J.L.Dujon	West Indies
18	(17ct, 1st)	R.W.Marsh	Australia
18	(12ct, 6st)	K.S.More	India
16	(16ct)	D.L.Murray	West Indies
15	(14ct, 1st)	D.J.Richardson	South Africa

MOST DISMISSALS IN AN INNINGS

5 (5ct)	S.M.H.Kirmani	India v Zimbabwe	Leicester	1983

INDIVIDUAL RECORDS – FIELDING

MOST CATCHES

12	C.H.Lloyd	West Indies
12	Kapil Dev	India
12	D.L.Haynes	West Indies
10	I.T.Botham	England
10	A.R.Border	Australia

MOST CATCHES IN AN INNINGS

3	C.H.Lloyd	West Indies v Sri Lanka	Manchester	1975
3	D.A.Reeve	England v Pakistan	Adelaide	1991-92
3	Ijaz Ahmed, sr	Pakistan v Australia	Perth	1991-92
3	A.R.Border	Australia v Zimbabwe	Hobart	1991-92

INDIVIDUAL RECORDS – GENERAL

MOST APPEARANCES

28	Imran Khan (Pakistan), Javed Miandad (Pakistan)
26	Kapil Dev (India)
25	A.R.Border (Australia), D.L.Haynes (West Indies)

WORLD CUP RECORDS

ENGLAND

	Opponents	Venue	Tournament

HIGHEST TOTAL

334-4 (60 overs) — India — Lord's — 1975

LOWEST TOTAL

93 (36.2 overs) — Australia — Leeds — 1975

HUNDREDS (5)

137	D.L.Amiss	India	Lord's	1975
131	K.W.R.Fletcher	New Zealand	Nottingham	1975
130	D.I.Gower	Sri Lanka	Taunton	1983
115	G.A.Gooch	India	Bombay	1987-88
102	A.J.Lamb	New Zealand	The Oval	1983

HIGHEST PARTNERSHIP FOR EACH WICKET

1st	158	B.Wood, D.L.Amiss	East Africa	Birmingham	1975
2nd	176	D.L.Amiss, K.W.R.Fletcher	India	Lord's	1975
3rd	135	C.W.J.Athey, M.W.Gatting	Pakistan	Karachi	1987-88
4th	115	A.J.Lamb, M.W.Gatting	New Zealand	The Oval	1983
5th	89*	M.H.Denness, C.M.Old	India	Lord's	1975
6th	98	D.I.Gower, I.J.Gould	Sri Lanka	Taunton	1983
7th	44*	I.J.Gould, G.R.Dilley	New Zealand	The Oval	1983
8th	47	A.J.Lamb, P.A.J.DeFreitas	West Indies	Gujranwala	1987-88
9th	43	R.W.Taylor, R.G.D.Willis	Pakistan	Leeds	1979
10th	20	G.G.Arnold, P.Lever	Australia	Leeds	1975

FOUR OR MORE WICKETS

5-39	V.J.Marks	Sri Lanka	Taunton	1983
4- 8	C.M.Old	Canada	Manchester	1979
4-11	J.A.Snow	East Africa	Birmingham	1975
4-11	R.G.D.Willis	Canada	Manchester	1979
4-15	M.Hendrick	Pakistan	Leeds	1979
4-30	C.C.Lewis	Sri Lanka	Ballarat	1991-92
4-31	I.T.Botham	Australia	Sydney	1991-92
4-42	R.G.D.Willis	New Zealand	Birmingham	1983
4-45	A.W.Greig	New Zealand	Nottingham	1975
4-45	G.R.Dilley	Sri Lanka	Taunton	1983
4-52	E.E.Hemmings	India	Bombay	1987-88

AUSTRALIA

		Opponents	Venue	Tournament
HIGHEST TOTAL				
328-5 (60 overs)		Sri Lanka	The Oval	1975

LOWEST TOTAL

| 129 (38.2 overs) | | India | Chelmsford | 1983 |

HUNDREDS (6)

126*	G.R.Marsh	New Zealand	Chandigarh	1987-88
110	T.M.Chappell	India	Nottingham	1983
110	G.R.Marsh	India	Madras	1987-88
101	A.Turner	Sri Lanka	The Oval	1975
100	D.C.Boon	New Zealand	Auckland	1991-92
100	D.C.Boon	West Indies	Melbourne	1991-92

HIGHEST PARTNERSHIP FOR EACH WICKET

1st	182	R.B.McCosker, A.Turner	Sri Lanka	The Oval	1975
2nd	144	T.M.Chappell, K.J.Hughes	India	Nottingham	1983
3rd	113	G.R.Marsh, A.R.Border	Zimbabwe	Madras	1987-88
4th	117	G.S.Chappell, K.D.Walters	Sri Lanka	The Oval	1975
5th	113	M.E.Waugh, S.R.Waugh	Zimbabwe	Hobart	1991-92
6th	99	R.Edwards, R.W.Marsh	West Indies	The Oval	1975
7th	55*	K.D.Walters, G.J.Gilmour	England	Leeds	1975
8th	50*	R.W.Marsh, R.M.Hogg	Zimbabwe	Nottingham	1983
9th	23*	G.R.Marsh, A.K.Zesers	New Zealand	Chandigarh	1987-88
10th	41	J.R.Thomson, D.K.Lillee	West Indies	Lord's	1975

FOUR OR MORE WICKETS

6-14	G.J.Gilmour	England	Leeds	1975
6-39	K.H.Macleay	India	Nottingham	1983
5-21	A.G.Hurst	Canada	Birmingham	1979
5-34	D.K.Lillee	Pakistan	Leeds	1975
5-44	C.J.McDermott	Pakistan	Lahore	1987
5-48	G.J.Gilmour	West Indies	Lord's	1975
4-34	M.R.Whitney	West Indies	Melbourne	1991-92
4-39	S.P.O'Donnell	Zimbabwe	Madras	1987-88
4-56	C.J.McDermott	India	Madras	1987-88

SOUTH AFRICA

			Opponents	Venue	Tournament

HIGHEST TOTAL

236-4 (50 overs) — England — Melbourne — 1991-92

LOWEST TOTAL

195 (50 overs) — Sri Lanka — Wellington — 1991-92

HUNDREDS (0)

Highest Score
90 P.N.Kirsten — New Zealand — Auckland — 1991-92

HIGHEST PARTNERSHIP FOR EACH WICKET

1st	151	K.C.Wessels, A.C.Hudson	England	Melbourne	1991-92
2nd	112	K.C.Wessels, P.N.Kirsten	Zimbabwe	Canberra	1991-92
3rd	31	K.C.Wessels, J.N.Rhodes	England	Melbourne	1991-92
4th	79	P.N.Kirsten, D.J.Richardson	New Zealand	Auckland	1991-92
5th	45	A.C.Hudson, J.N.Rhodes	England	Sydney	1991-92
6th	71	W.J.Cronje, B.M.McMillan	Pakistan	Brisbane	1991-92
7th	41	P.N.Kirsten, B.M.McMillan	New Zealand	Auckland	1991-92
8th	28*	B.M.McMillan, R.P.Snell	New Zealand	Auckland	1991-92
9th	21	B.M.McMillan, O.Henry	Sri Lanka	Wellington	1991-92
10th	9	B.M.McMillan, A.A.Donald	Sri Lanka	Wellington	1991-92

FOUR OR MORE WICKETS

4-11 M.W.Pringle — West Indies — Christchurch — 1991-92

WEST INDIES

	Opponents	Venue	Tournament
HIGHEST TOTAL			
360-4 (50 overs)	Sri Lanka	Karachi	1987-88
LOWEST TOTAL			
136 (38.4 overs)	South Africa	Christchurch	1991-92

HUNDREDS (9)

181	I.V.A.Richards	Sri Lanka	Karachi	1987-88
138*	I.V.A.Richards	England	Lord's	1979
119	I.V.A.Richards	India	The Oval	1983
110	R.B.Richardson	Pakistan	Karachi	1987-88
110	P.V.Simmons	Sri Lanka	Berri	1991-92
106*	C.G.Greenidge	India	Birmingham	1979
105*	C.G.Greenidge	Zimbabwe	Worcester	1983
105	D.L.Haynes	Sri Lanka	Karachi	1987-88
102	C.H.Lloyd	Australia	Lord's	1975

HIGHEST PARTNERSHIP FOR EACH WICKET

1st	175*	D.L.Haynes, B.C.Lara	Pakistan	Melbourne	1991-92
2nd	125	C.G.Greenidge, A.I.Kallicharran	New Zealand	The Oval	1975
3rd	195*	C.G.Greenidge, H.A.Gomes	Zimbabwe	Worcester	1983
4th	149	R.B.Kanhai, C.H.Lloyd	Australia	Lord's	1975
5th	139	I.V.A.Richards, C.L.King	England	Lord's	1979
6th	83*	K.L.T.Arthurton, C.L.Hooper	India	Wellington	1991-92
7th	52	C.H.Lloyd, B.D.Julien	Australia	Lord's	1975
8th	40*	C.H.Lloyd, J.Garner	New Zealand	Nottingham	1979
9th	41	S.F.A.F.Bacchus, W.W.Daniel	Australia	Leeds	1983
10th	71	A.M.E.Roberts, J.Garner	India	Manchester	1983

Although the first wicket added 221 v Pakistan at Melbourne in 1991-92, this consisted of two partnerships: D.L.Haynes added 175* with B.C.Lara (retired hurt), and a further 46 with R.B.Richardson.*

FOUR OR MORE WICKETS

7-51	W.W.Davis	Australia	Leeds	1983
5-38	J.Garner	England	Lord's	1979
4-20	B.D.Julien	Sri Lanka	Manchester	1975
4-27	B.D.Julien	New Zealand	The Oval	1975
4-33	M.A.Holding	India	Birmingham	1979
4-33	A.C.Cummins	India	Wellington	1991-92
4-40	C.A.Walsh	Pakistan	Lahore	1987-88
4-50	K.D.Boyce	Australia	Lord's	1975

NEW ZEALAND

			Opponents	Venue	Tournament

HIGHEST TOTAL

309-5 (60 overs)			East Africa	Birmingham	1975

LOWEST TOTAL

158 (52.2 overs)			West Indies	The Oval	1975

HUNDREDS (3)

			Opponents	Venue	Tournament
171*		G.M.Turner	East Africa	Birmingham	1975
114*		G.M.Turner	India	Manchester	1975
100*		M.D.Crowe	Australia	Auckland	1991-92

HIGHEST PARTNERSHIP FOR EACH WICKET

			Opponents	Venue	Tournament
1st	114	M.J.Greatbatch, R.T.Latham	South Africa	Auckland	1991-92
2nd	126*	G.M.Turner, G.P.Howarth	Sri Lanka	Nottingham	1979
3rd	149	G.M.Turner, J.M.Parker	East Africa	Birmingham	1975
4th	118	M.D.Crowe, K.R.Rutherford	Australia	Auckland	1991-92
5th	71	G.P.Howarth, J.V.Coney	England	Birmingham	1983
6th	46	J.V.Coney, M.D.Crowe	Pakistan	Birmingham	1983
7th	70	J.V.Coney, R.J.Hadlee	England	Birmingham	1983
8th	48	B.J.McKechnie, D.R.Hadlee	England	Nottingham	1975
9th	59	W.K.Lees, J.G.Bracewell	Pakistan	Nottingham	1983
10th	65	M.C.Snedden, E.J.Chatfield	Sri Lanka	Derby	1983

FOUR OR MORE WICKETS

		Opponents	Venue	Tournament
5-25	R.J.Hadlee	Sri Lanka	Bristol	1983

INDIA

		Opponents	Venue	Tournament

HIGHEST TOTAL

289-6 (50 overs) | | Australia | Delhi | 1987-88

LOWEST TOTAL

158 (37.5 overs) | | Australia | Nottingham | 1983

HUNDREDS (2)

| 175* | Kapil Dev | Zimbabwe | Tunbridge Wells | 1983 |
| 103* | S.M.Gavaskar | New Zealand | Nagpur | 1987-88 |

HIGHEST PARTNERSHIP FOR EACH WICKET

1st	136	K.Srikkanth, S.M.Gavaskar	New Zealand	Nagpur	1987-88
2nd	127	M.Azharuddin, S.R.Tendulkar	New Zealand	Dunedin	1991-92
3rd	92	M.Amarnath, Yashpal Sharma	England	Manchester	1983
4th	99	S.R.Tendulkar, S.V.Manjrekar	Zimbabwe	Hamilton	1991-92
5th	66	M.Azharuddin, S.V.Manjrekar	Australia	Brisbane	1991-92
6th	73	Yashpal Sharma, R.M.H.Binny	West Indies	Manchester	1983
7th	58	Kapil Dev, Madan Lal	Australia	Nottingham	1983
8th	82*	Kapil Dev, K.S.More	New Zealand	Bangalore	1987-88
9th	126*	Kapil Dev, S.M.H.Kirmani	Zimbabwe	Tunbridge Wells	1983
10th	27	S.Venkataraghavan, B.S.Bedi	West Indies	Birmingham	1979

Although the second wicket added 145 v New Zealand at Dunedin in 1991-92, this consisted of two partnerships: M.Azharuddin added 18 with A.D.Jadeja (retired hurt), and a further 127 with S.R.Tendulkar.

Although the third wicket added 109 v West Indies at The Oval in 1983, this consisted of two partnerships: M.Amarnath added 67 with D.B.Vengsarkar (retired hurt), and a further 42 with S.M.Patil.

FOUR OR MORE WICKETS

5-43	Kapil Dev	Australia	Nottingham	1983
4-19	M.Prabhakar	Zimbabwe	Bombay	1987-88
4-20	Madan Lal	Australia	Chelmsford	1983
4-29	R.M.H.Binny	Australia	Chelmsford	1983

PAKISTAN

		Opponents	Venue	Tournament
HIGHEST TOTAL				
338-5 (60 overs)		Sri Lanka	Swansea	1983

LOWEST TOTAL

74 (40.2 overs)		England	Adelaide	1991-92

HUNDREDS (8)

119*	Ramiz Raja	New Zealand	Christchurch	1991-92
114	Aamir Sohail	Zimbabwe	Hobart	1991-92
113	Ramiz Raja	England	Karachi	1987-88
103*	Zaheer Abbas	New Zealand	Nottingham	1983
103	Javed Miandad	Sri Lanka	Hyderabad	1987-88
102*	Imran Khan	Sri Lanka	Leeds	1983
102*	Ramiz Raja	West Indies	Melbourne	1991-92
100	Salim Malik	Sri Lanka	Faisalabad	1987-88

HIGHEST PARTNERSHIP FOR EACH WICKET

1st	159	Sadiq Mohammad, Majid Khan	Sri Lanka	Nottingham	1975
2nd	167	Ramiz Raja, Salim Malik	England	Karachi	1987-88
3rd	145	Aamir Sohail, Javed Miandad	Zimbabwe	Hobart	1991-92
4th	147*	Zaheer Abbas, Imran Khan	New Zealand	Nottingham	1983
5th	87	Majid Khan, Asif Iqbal	Australia	Nottingham	1979
	87	Javed Miandad, Inzamam-ul-Haq	New Zealand	Auckland	1991-92
6th	144	Imran Khan, Shahid Mahboob	Sri Lanka	Leeds	1983
7th	52	Asif Iqbal, Wasim Raja	England	Leeds	1979
8th	36	Zaheer Abbas, Sarfraz Nawaz	England	Lord's	1983
9th	39*	Zaheer Abbas, Wasim Bari	England	Lord's	1983
10th	28	Abdul Qadir, Rashid Khan	New Zealand	Birmingham	1983

FOUR OR MORE WICKETS

5-44	Abdul Qadir	Sri Lanka	Leeds	1983
4-21	Abdul Qadir	New Zealand	Birmingham	1983
4-31	Abdul Qadir	England	Rawalpindi	1987-88
4-32	Wasim Akram	New Zealand	Christchurch	1991-92
4-37	Imran Khan	West Indies	Lahore	1987-88
4-37	Imran Khan	England	Karachi	1987-88
4-44	Sarfraz Nawaz	West Indies	Birmingham	1975
4-56	Asif Iqbal	West Indies	The Oval	1979

SRI LANKA

	Opponents	Venue	Tournament
HIGHEST TOTAL			
313-7 (49.2 overs)	Zimbabwe	New Plymouth	1991-92

LOWEST TOTAL

| 86 (37.2 overs) | West Indies | Manchester | 1975 |

HUNDREDS (0)

Highest Score

| 89 | R.S.Mahanama | Pakistan | Hyderabad | 1987-88 |

HIGHEST PARTNERSHIP FOR EACH WICKET

1st	128	R.S.Mahanama, M.A.R.Samarasekera	Zimbabwe	New Plymouth	1991-92
2nd	96	S.R.de S.Wettimuny, R.L.Dias	India	Manchester	1979
3rd	88	A.P.Gurusinha, R.L.Dias	England	Poona	1987-88
4th	71	L.R.D.Mendis, R.S.Madugalle	New Zealand	Bristol	1983
5th	80	A.Ranatunga, L.R.D.Mendis	Pakistan	Faisalabad	1987-88
6th	61	A.Ranatunga, H.P.Tillekeratne	Zimbabwe	New Plymouth	1991-92
7th	36	A.Ranatunga, R.S.Kalpage	Zimbabwe	New Plymouth	1991-92
8th	54	D.S.de Silva, R.G.de Alwis	Pakistan	Swansea	1983
	54	D.S.de Silva, R.G.de Alwis	England	Taunton	1983
9th	35	R.G.de Alwis, A.L.F.de Mel	England	Taunton	1983
10th	33	R.J.Ratnayake, V.B.John	England	Leeds	1983

Although the third wicket added 162 v Australia at The Oval in 1975, this consisted of three partnerships between S.R.de S.Wettimuny (retired hurt), L.R.D.Mendis (retired hurt), A.P.B.Tennekoon and M.H.Tissera.

FOUR OR MORE WICKETS

5-32	A.L.F.de Mel	New Zealand	Derby	1983
5-39	A.L.F.de Mel	Pakistan	Leeds	1983
4-57	U.C.Hathurusinghe	West Indies	Berri	1991-92

ZIMBABWE

	Opponents	Venue	Tournament

HIGHEST TOTAL

312-4 (50 overs) — Sri Lanka — New Plymouth 1991-92

LOWEST TOTAL

134   (46.1 overs) — England — Albury — 1991-92

HUNDREDS (2)

| 142 | D.L.Houghton | New Zealand | Hyderabad | 1987-88 |
| 115* | A.Flower | Sri Lanka | New Plymouth | 1991-92 |

HIGHEST PARTNERSHIP FOR EACH WICKET

1st	79	A.H.Shah, A.Flower	India	Hamilton	1991-92
2nd	81	A.H.Shah, K.J.Arnott	New Zealand	Calcutta	1987-88
3rd	51	D.L.Houghton, A.J.Pycroft	New Zealand	Hyderabad	1987-88
4th	85	A.Flower, K.J.Arnott	Sri Lanka	New Plymouth	1991-92
5th	145*	A.Flower, A.C.Waller	Sri Lanka	New Plymouth	1991-92
6th	103	D.L.Houghton, K.M.Curran	Australia	Southampton	1983
7th	75*	D.A.G.Fletcher, I.P.Butchart	Australia	Nottingham	1983
8th	117	D.L.Houghton, I.P.Butchart	New Zealand	Hyderabad	1987-88
9th	55	K.M.Curran, P.W.E.Rawson	West Indies	Birmingham	1983
10th	36	A.J.Pycroft, M.P.Jarvis	India	Bombay	1987-88

FOUR OR MORE WICKETS

4-21	E.A.Brandes	England	Albury	1991-92
4-42	D.A.G.Fletcher	Australia	Nottingham	1983

LIMITED-OVERS INTERNATIONALS RESULTS SUMMARY

1970-71 to 1995 inclusive

Opponents	Matches	Won by													Tied	NR
		E	A	SA	WI	NZ	I	P	SL	Z	B	C	EA	UAE		
England Australia	57	26	29	–	–	–	–	–	–	–	–	–	–	–	1	1
South Africa	4	4	–	0	–	–	–	–	–	–	–	–	–	–	–	–
West Indies	51	22	–	–	27	–	–	–	–	–	–	–	–	–	–	2
New Zealand	41	21	–	–	–	17	–	–	–	–	–	–	–	–	–	3
India	29	16	–	–	–	–	13	–	–	–	–	–	–	–	–	–
Pakistan	36	23	–	–	–	–	–	12	–	–	–	–	–	–	–	1
Sri Lanka	11	8	–	–	–	–	–	–	3	–	–	–	–	–	–	–
Zimbabwe	3	1	–	–	–	–	–	–	–	2	–	–	–	–	–	–
Canada	1	1	–	–	–	–	–	–	–	–	0	–	–	–	–	–
East Africa	1	1	–	–	–	–	–	–	–	–	–	0	–	–	–	–
Australia South Africa	20	–	12	8	–	–	–	–	–	–	–	–	–	–	–	–
West Indies	74	–	27	–	45	–	–	–	–	–	–	–	–	–	1	1
New Zealand	62	–	43	–	–	17	–	–	–	–	–	–	–	–	–	2
India	43	–	24	–	–	–	16	–	–	–	–	–	–	–	–	3
Pakistan	42	–	21	–	–	–	–	18	–	–	–	–	–	–	1	2
Sri Lanka	26	–	18	–	–	–	–	–	6	–	–	–	–	–	–	2
Zimbabwe	7	–	6	–	–	–	–	–	–	1	–	–	–	–	–	–
Bangladesh	1	–	1	–	–	–	–	–	–	–	0	–	–	–	–	–
Canada	1	–	1	–	–	–	–	–	–	–	–	0	–	–	–	–
S Africa West Indies	8	–	–	4	4	–	–	–	–	–	–	–	–	–	–	–
New Zealand	7	–	–	3	–	4	–	–	–	–	–	–	–	–	–	–
India	14	–	–	8	–	–	6	–	–	–	–	–	–	–	–	–
Pakistan	11	–	–	4	–	–	–	7	–	–	–	–	–	–	–	–
Sri Lanka	7	–	–	3	–	–	–	–	3	–	–	–	–	–	–	1
Zimbabwe	2	–	–	1	–	–	–	–	–	0	–	–	–	–	–	1
W Indies New Zealand	19	–	–	–	15	2	–	–	–	–	–	–	–	–	–	2
India	50	–	–	–	32	–	17	–	–	–	–	–	–	–	1	–
Pakistan	73	–	–	–	50	–	–	21	–	–	–	–	–	–	2	–
Sri Lanka	19	–	–	–	16	–	–	–	2	–	–	–	–	–	–	1
Zimbabwe	4	–	–	–	4	–	–	–	–	0	–	–	–	–	–	–
N Zealand India	36	–	–	–	–	16	20	–	–	–	–	–	–	–	–	–
Pakistan	36	–	–	–	–	14	–	20	–	–	–	–	–	–	1	1
Sri Lanka	32	–	–	–	–	22	–	–	8	–	–	–	–	–	–	2
Zimbabwe	5	–	–	–	–	5	–	–	–	0	–	–	–	–	–	–
Bangladesh	1	–	–	–	–	1	–	–	–	–	0	–	–	–	–	–
East Africa	1	–	–	–	–	1	–	–	–	–	–	0	–	–	–	–
India Pakistan	41	–	–	–	–	–	12	27	–	–	–	–	–	–	–	2
Sri Lanka	37	–	–	–	–	–	24	–	11	–	–	–	–	–	–	2
Zimbabwe	10	–	–	–	–	–	9	–	–	0	–	–	–	1	–	–
Bangladesh	3	–	–	–	–	–	3	–	–	–	0	–	–	–	–	–
East Africa	1	–	–	–	–	–	1	–	–	–	–	0	–	–	–	–
U A Emirates	1	–	–	–	–	–	1	–	–	–	–	–	0	–	–	–
Pakistan Sri Lanka	49	–	–	–	–	–	–	38	10	–	–	–	–	–	1	–
Zimbabwe	9	–	–	–	–	–	–	7	–	1	–	–	–	–	–	1
Bangladesh	3	–	–	–	–	–	–	3	–	–	0	–	–	–	–	–
Canada	1	–	–	–	–	–	–	1	–	–	–	0	–	–	–	–
U A Emirates	1	–	–	–	–	–	–	1	–	–	–	–	0	–	–	–
Sri Lanka Zimbabwe	6	–	–	–	–	–	–	–	5	1	–	–	–	–	–	–
Bangladesh	4	–	–	–	–	–	–	–	4	–	0	–	–	–	–	–
	1001	123	182	31	193	99	122	155	52	5	0	0	0	0	9	30

LEAGUE TABLE OF ALL LIMITED-OVERS INTERNATIONALS

1970-71 to 1995 inclusive

	Matches	Won	Lost	Tied	No Result	% Won (exc NR)
West Indies	298	193	95	4	6	66.09
Australia	333	182	137	3	11	56.52
England	234	123	103	1	7	54.18
Pakistan	302	155	135	5	7	52.54
India	265	122	134	2	7	47.28
South Africa	73	31	40	–	2	43.66
New Zealand	240	99	130	1	10	43.04
Sri Lanka	191	52	130	–	9	28.57
Zimbabwe	46	5	38	2	1	11.11
United Arab Emirates	2	–	2	–	–	–
Canada	3	–	3	–	–	–
East Africa	3	–	3	–	–	–
Bangladesh	12	–	12	–	–	–

LIMITED-OVERS INTERNATIONAL RECORDS

To the end of the 1995 season

TEAM RECORDS

HIGHEST TOTALS

363-7	(55 overs)	England v Pakistan	Nottingham	1992
360-4	(50 overs)	West Indies v Sri Lanka	Karachi	1987-88
338-4	(50 overs)	New Zealand v Bangladesh	Sharjah	1989-90
338-5	(60 overs)	Pakistan v Sri Lanka	Swansea	1983
334-4	(60 overs)	England v India	Lord's	1975
333-8	(45 overs)	West Indies v India	Jamshedpur	1983-84
333-9	(60 overs)	England v Sri Lanka	Taunton	1983
332-3	(50 overs)	Australia v Sri Lanka	Sharjah	1989-90
330-6	(60 overs)	Pakistan v Sri Lanka	Nottingham	1975

Highest Totals by other ICC Full Members:

314-7	(50 overs)	South Africa v New Zealand	Verwoerdburg	1994-95
313-7	(49.2 overs)	Sri Lanka v Zimbabwe	New Plymouth	1991-92
312-4	(50 overs)	Zimbabwe v Sri Lanka	New Plymouth	1991-92
299-4	(40 overs)	India v Sri Lanka	Bombay	1986-87

HIGHEST TOTALS BATTING SECOND

WINNING

313-7	(49.2 overs)	Sri Lanka v Zimbabwe	New Plymouth	1991-92
298-6	(54.5 overs)	New Zealand v England	Leeds	1990
297-6	(48.5 overs)	New Zealand v England	Adelaide	1982-83

LOSING

289-7	(40 overs)	Sri Lanka v India	Bombay	1986-87
288-9	(60 overs)	Sri Lanka v Pakistan	Swansea	1983
288-8	(50 overs)	Sri Lanka v Pakistan	Adelaide	1989-90
288-8	(50 overs)	Sri Lanka v Zimbabwe	Harare	1994-95

HIGHEST MATCH AGGREGATES

626-14	(120 overs)	Pakistan v Sri Lanka	Swansea	1983
625-11	(99.2 overs)	Sri Lanka v Zimbabwe	New Plymouth	1991-92
619-19	(118 overs)	England v Sri Lanka	Taunton	1983
604-9	(120 overs)	Australia v Sri Lanka	The Oval	1975
603-11	(100 overs)	Pakistan v Sri Lanka	Adelaide	1989-90

LOWEST TOTALS†

43	(19.5 overs)	Pakistan v West Indies	Cape Town	1992-93
45	(40.3 overs)	Canada v England	Manchester	1979
55	(28.3 overs)	Sri Lanka v West Indies	Sharjah	1986-87
63	(25.5 overs)	India v Australia	Sydney	1980-81
64	(35.5 overs)	New Zealand v Pakistan	Sharjah	1985-86
69	(28 overs)	South Africa v Australia	Sydney	1993-94
70	(25.2 overs)	Australia v England	Birmingham	1977
70	(26.3 overs)	Australia v New Zealand	Adelaide	1985-86

Lowest Totals by other ICC Full Members:

87	(29.3 overs)	West Indies v Australia	Sydney	1992-93
93	(36.2 overs)	England v Australia	Leeds	1975
99	(36.3 overs)	Zimbabwe v West Indies	Hyderabad (Ind)	1993-94

† Excluding instances when the number of overs was reduced after play began.

LOWEST MATCH AGGREGATE

88-13	(32.2 overs)	West Indies v Pakistan	Cape Town	1992-93

The match was completed before lunch.

LARGEST MARGINS OF VICTORY

232 runs	Australia beat Sri Lanka	Adelaide	1984-85
206 runs	New Zealand beat Australia	Adelaide	1985-86
202 runs	England beat India	Lord's	1975
10 wickets	Nine instances		

TIED MATCHES

Australia	222-9 (50)	West Indies	222-5 (50)	Melbourne	1983-84
England	226-5 (55)	Australia	226-8 (55)	Nottingham	1989
West Indies	186-5 (39)	Pakistan	186-9 (39)	Lahore	1991-92
India	126 (47.4)	West Indies	126 (41)	Perth	1991-92
Australia	228-7 (50)	Pakistan	228-9 (50)	Hobart	1992-93
Pakistan	244-6 (50)	West Indies	244-5 (50)	Georgetown	1992-93
India	248-5 (50)	Zimbabwe	248 (50)	Indore	1993-94
Pakistan	161-9 (50)	New Zealand	161 (49.4)	Auckland	1993-94

INDIVIDUAL RECORDS – BATTING

4000 RUNS IN LIMITED-OVERS INTERNATIONALS

		LOI	I	NO	HS	Runs	Avge	100	50
D.L.Haynes	WI	238	237	28	152*	**8648**	41.37	17	57
Javed Miandad	P	228	215	40	119*	**7327**	41.86	8	50
I.V.A.Richards	WI	187	167	24	189*	**6721**	47.00	11	45
A.R.Border	A	273	252	39	127*	**6524**	30.62	3	39
D.M.Jones	A	164	161	25	145	**6068**	44.61	7	46
D.C.Boon	A	181	177	16	122	**5964**	37.04	5	37
R.B.Richardson	WI	206	199	27	122	**5689**	33.07	5	41
M.Azharuddin	I	194	179	35	108*	**5288**	36.72	3	29
Salim Malik	P	210	190	27	102	**5271**	32.33	5	33
C.G.Greenidge	WI	128	127	13	133*	**5134**	45.03	11	31
Ramiz Raja	P	159	158	11	119*	**4915**	33.43	8	29
A.Ranatunga	SL	164	157	29	101*	**4536**	35.43	1	31
M.D.Crowe	NZ	139	137	18	105*	**4517**	37.95	3	33
P.A.de Silva	SL	156	152	14	107*	**4389**	31.80	3	32
G.R.Marsh	A	117	115	6	126*	**4357**	39.97	9	22
G.A.Gooch	E	125	122	6	142	**4290**	36.98	8	23
K.Srikkanth	I	146	145	4	123	**4092**	29.02	4	27
A.J.Lamb	E	122	118	16	118	**4010**	39.31	4	26

Highest aggregates for other ICC Full Members:

W.J.Cronje	SA	68	65	11	112	**1975**	36.57	2	10
D.L.Houghton	Z	45	43	1	142	**1246**	29.66	1	10

HIGHEST INDIVIDUAL SCORES

189*	I.V.A.Richards	West Indies v England	Manchester	1984
181	I.V.A.Richards	West Indies v Sri Lanka	Karachi	1987-88
175*	Kapil Dev	India v Zimbabwe	Tunbridge Wells	1983
171*	G.M.Turner	New Zealand v East Africa	Birmingham	1975
169*	D.J.Callaghan	South Africa v New Zealand	Verwoerdburg	1994-95
167*	R.A.Smith	England v Australia	Birmingham	1993
158	D.I.Gower	England v New Zealand	Brisbane	1982-83
153*	I.V.A.Richards	West Indies v Australia	Melbourne	1979-80
153	B.C.Lara	West Indies v Pakistan	Sharjah	1993-94
152*	D.L.Haynes	West Indies v India	Georgetown	1988-89

Highest individual scores for other ICC Full Members:

145	D.M.Jones	Australia v England	Brisbane	1990-91
142	D.L.Houghton	Zimbabwe v New Zealand	Hyderabad (Ind)	1987-88
140	S.T.Jayasuriya	Sri Lanka v New Zealand	Bloemfontein	1994-95
137*	Inzamam-ul-Haq	Pakistan v New Zealand	Sharjah	1993-94

MOST HUNDREDS

						Opponents					
		100	E	A	WI	NZ	I	P	SA	SL	Z
D.L.Haynes	WI	**17**	2	6	–	2	2	4	–	1	–
C.G.Greenidge	WI	**11**	–	1	–	3	3	2	–	1	1
I.V.A.Richards	WI	**11**	3	3	–	1	3	–	–	1	–
G.R.Marsh	A	**9**	1	–	2	2	3	1	–	–	–
G.A.Gooch	E	**8**	–	4	1	1	1	1	–	–	–
Javed Miandad	P	**8**	1	–	1	4	1	–	–	1	2
Ramiz Raja	P	**8**	1	–	1	3	–	–	–	3	–
Saeed Anwar	P	**8**	–	1	1	1	1	–	–	4	1
D.I.Gower	E	**7**	–	3	1	–	3	–	–	–	–
D.M.Jones	A	**7**	3	–	–	2	–	1	–	1	–
Zaheer Abbas	P	**7**	–	2	–	1	3	–	–	1	–

241

VIV RICHARDS'S 189 NOT OUT

WORLD RECORD SCORE IN LIMITED-OVERS INTERNATIONALS

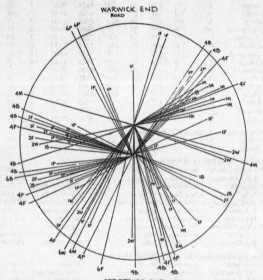

| BOWLER | SYMBOL | BALLS | R U N S | | | | | TOTAL | PER 100 BALLS |
			1	2	3	4	6		
WILLIS	W	29	4	5	·	1	1	24	82·7
BOTHAM	B	41	6	2	·	9	1	52	126·8
FOSTER	F	37	13	6	·	5	1	51	137·8
MILLER	M	29	9	1	·	2	-	19	65·5
PRINGLE	P	34	9	3	·	4	2	43	126·4
TOTALS		170	41	17	·	21	5	189	111·1

ENGLAND v WEST INDIES
INAUGURAL TEXACO TROPHY MATCH
AT OLD TRAFFORD, MANCHESTER
ON THURSDAY, 31 MAY 1984

© BILL FRINDALL 1984

HIGHEST PARTNERSHIP FOR EACH WICKET

1st	212	G.R.Marsh/D.C.Boon	A v I	Jaipur	1986-87
2nd	263	Aamir Sohail/Inzamam-ul-Haq	P v NZ	Sharjah	1993-94
3rd	224*	D.M.Jones/A.R.Border	A v SL	Adelaide	1984-85
4th	173	D.M.Jones/S.R.Waugh	A v P	Perth	1986-87
5th	152	I.V.A.Richards/C.H.Lloyd	WI v SL	Brisbane	1984-85
6th	154	R.B.Richardson/P.J.L.Dujon	WI v P	Sharjah	1991-92
7th	115	P.J.L.Dujon/M.D.Marshall	WI v P	Gujranwala	1986-87
8th	119	P.R.Reiffel/S.K.Warne	A v SA	Port Elizabeth	1993-94
9th	126*	Kapil Dev/S.M.H.Kirmani	I v Z	Tunbridge Wells	1983
10th	106*	I.V.A.Richards/M.A.Holding	WI v E	Manchester	1984

INDIVIDUAL RECORDS – BOWLING

100 WICKETS IN LIMITED-OVERS INTERNATIONALS

		LOI	O	R	W	Avge	Best	4w
Wasim Akram	P	189	1633.2	6164	273	22.57	5-15	15
Kapil Dev	I	224	1867	6946	253	27.45	5-43	4
C.J.McDermott	A	129	1170.3	4733	190	24.91	5-44	5
Imran Khan	P	175	1243.3	4845	182	26.62	6-14	4
Waqar Younis	P	104	871.5	3800	176	21.59	6-26	15
S.R.Waugh	A	185	1222	5415	162	33.42	4-33	2
R.J.Hadlee	NZ	115	1030.2	3407	158	21.56	5-25	6
C.A.Walsh	WI	142	1245	4778	158	30.24	5- 1	6
M.D.Marshall	WI	136	1195.5	4233	157	26.96	4-18	6
C.E.L.Ambrose	WI	114	1015.5	3571	154	23.18	5-17	8
M.Prabhakar	I	120	993	4188	147	28.48	5-35	5
J.Garner	WI	98	888.2	2752	146	18.84	5-31	5
I.T.Botham	E	116	1045.1	4139	145	28.54	4-31	3
M.A.Holding	WI	102	912.1	3034	142	21.36	5-26	6
E.J.Chatfield	NZ	114	1010.5	3621	140	25.86	5-34	4
Abdul Qadir	P	104	850	3453	132	26.15	5-44	6
R.J.Shastri	I	150	1102.1	4650	129	36.04	5-15	3
C.L.Hooper	WI	133	899.4	3921	126	31.11	4-34	1
Aqib Javed	P	110	928.4	3760	123	30.56	7-37	3
I.V.A.Richards	WI	187	940.4	4228	118	35.83	6-41	3
M.C.Snedden	NZ	93	753.1	3235	114	28.37	4-34	1
J.Srinath	I	77	656.5	2814	112	25.12	5-24	3
Mudassar Nazar	P	122	809.1	3431	111	30.90	5-28	2
S.P.O'Donnell	A	87	725	3102	108	28.72	5-13	6
P.A.J.DeFreitas	E	93	868.5	3401	105	32.39	4-35	1
D.K.Lillee	A	63	598.5	2145	103	20.82	5-34	6
C.Pringle	NZ	64	552.2	2455	103	23.83	5-45	3
W.K.M.Benjamin	WI	85	740.2	3079	100	30.79	5-22	1

Highest aggregates for other ICC Full Members:

J.R.Ratnayeke	SL	78	595.3	2866	85	33.71	4-23	1
A.A.Donald	SA	50	443.2	1764	67	26.32	5-29	1
E.A.Brandes	Z	24	205.5	1016	29	35.03	4-21	1

BEST ANALYSES

7-37	Aqib Javed	Pakistan v India	Sharjah	1991-92
7-51	W.W.Davis	West Indies v Australia	Leeds	1983
6-12	A.Kumble	India v West Indies	Calcutta	1993-94
6-14	G.J.Gilmour	Australia v England	Leeds	1975
6-14	Imran Khan	Pakistan v India	Sharjah	1984-85
6-15	C.E.H.Croft	West Indies v England	Arnos Vale	1980-81
6-26	Waqar Younis	Pakistan v Sri Lanka	Sharjah	1989-90
6-29	B.P.Patterson	West Indies v India	Nagpur	1987-88
6-29	S.T.Jayasuriya	Sri Lanka v England	Moratuwa	1992-93
6-30	Waqar Younis	Pakistan v New Zealand	Auckland	1993-94
6-39	K.H.Macleay	Australia v India	Nottingham	1983
6-41	I.V.A.Richards	West Indies v India	Delhi	1989-90
6-50	A.H.Gray	West Indies v Australia	Port-of-Spain	1990-91

Best analyses for other ICC Full Members:

5-20	V.J.Marks	England v New Zealand	Wellington	1983-84
5-22	M.N.Hart	New Zealand v West Indies	Margao	1994-95
5-29	A.A.Donald	South Africa v India	Calcutta	1991-92
4-21	E.A.Brandes	Zimbabwe v England	Albury	1991-92

HAT-TRICKS

Jalaluddin	Pakistan v Australia	Hyderabad	1982-83
B.A.Reid	Australia v New Zealand	Sydney	1985-86
C.Sharma	India v New Zealand	Nagpur	1987-88
Wasim Akram	Pakistan v West Indies	Sharjah	1989-90
Wasim Akram	Pakistan v Australia	Sharjah	1989-90
Kapil Dev	India v Sri Lanka	Calcutta	1990-91
Aqib Javed	Pakistan v India	Sharjah	1991-92
D.K.Morrison	New Zealand v India	Napier	1993-94
Waqar Younis	Pakistan v New Zealand	East London	1994-95

INDIVIDUAL RECORDS – WICKET-KEEPING

MOST DISMISSALS IN LIMITED-OVERS INTERNATIONALS

		LOI	Ct	St	Dis
P.J.L.Dujon	West Indies	169	183	21	**204**
I.A.Healy	Australia	129	155	27	**182**
R.W.Marsh	Australia	92	120	4	**124**
Salim Yousuf	Pakistan	86	81	22	**103**
D.J.Richardson	South Africa	69	83	12	**95**
K.S.More	India	94	63	27	**90**
I.D.S.Smith	New Zealand	98	81	5	**86**
Rashid Latif	Pakistan	66	64	18	**82**

MOST DISMISSALS IN AN INNINGS

5 (all ct)	R.W.Marsh	Australia v England	Leeds	1981
5 (all ct)	R.G.de Alwis	Sri Lanka v Australia	Colombo (PSS)	1982-83
5 (all ct)	S.M.H.Kirmani	India v Zimbabwe	Leicester	1983
5 (3ct, 2st)	S.Viswanath	India v England	Sydney	1984-85
5 (all ct)	K.S.More	India v New Zealand	Sharjah	1987-88
5 (all ct)	H.P.Tillekeratne	Sri Lanka v Pakistan	Sharjah	1990-91
5 (3ct, 2st)	N.R.Mongia	India v New Zealand	Auckland	1993-94
5 (3ct, 2st)	A.C.Parore	New Zealand v West Indies	Margao	1994-95
5 (all ct)	D.J.Richardson	South Africa v Pakistan	Johannesburg	1994-95
5 (all ct)	Moin Khan	Pakistan v Zimbabwe	Harare	1994-95
5 (4ct, 1st)	R.S.Kaluwitharana	Sri Lanka v Pakistan	Sharjah	1994-95

INDIVIDUAL RECORDS – FIELDING

MOST CATCHES IN LIMITED-OVERS INTERNATIONALS

		LOI	Ct
A.R.Border	Australia	273	127
I.V.A.Richards	West Indies	187	101
M.Azharuddin	India	194	80
Kapil Dev	India	224	71
R.B.Richardson	West Indies	206	70

MOST CATCHES IN AN INNINGS

5	J.N.Rhodes	South Africa v West Indies	Bombay	1993-94
4	Salim Malik	Pakistan v New Zealand	Sialkot	1984-85
4	S.M.Gavaskar	India v Pakistan	Sharjah	1984-85
4	R.B.Richardson	West Indies v England	Birmingham	1991
4	K.C.Wessels	South Africa v West Indies	Kingston	1991-92
4	M.A.Taylor	Australia v West Indies	Sydney	1992-93
4	C.L.Hooper	West Indies v Pakistan	Durban	1992-93
4	K.R.Rutherford	New Zealand v India	Napier	1994-95

Most Catches in an Innings by a Substitute

4	J.G.Bracewell	New Zealand v Australia	Adelaide	1980-81

INDIVIDUAL RECORDS – ALL-ROUND PERFORMANCES

1000 RUNS AND 100 WICKETS

		LOI	Runs	Wkts
I.T.Botham	England	116	2113	145
R.J.Hadlee	New Zealand	115	1749	158
C.L.Hooper	West Indies	133	3071	126
Imran Khan	Pakistan	175	3709	182
Kapil Dev	India	224	3783	253
Mudassar Nazar	Pakistan	122	2624	111
S.P.O'Donnell	Australia	87	1242	108
M.Prabhakar	India	120	1699	147
I.V.A.Richards	West Indies	187	6721	118
R.J.Shastri	India	150	3108	129
Wasim Akram	Pakistan	189	1680	273
S.R.Waugh	Australia	185	3852	162

1000 RUNS AND 100 DISMISSALS

		LOI	Runs	Dis
P.J.L.Dujon	West Indies	169	1945	204
I.A.Healy	Australia	129	1341	182
R.W.Marsh	Australia	92	1225	124

INDIVIDUAL RECORDS – GENERAL

MOST APPEARANCES

		Total	E	A	SA	WI	NZ	I	P	SL	Z	C	B	UAE
A.R.Border	A	273	43	–	15	61	52	38	34	23	5	1	1	–
D.L.Haynes	WI	238	35	64	8	–	13	36	65	14	3	–	–	–
Javed Miandad	P	228	26	35	3	64	23	34	–	35	6	1	1	–
Kapil Dev	I	224	23	41	13	42	29	–	32	33	9	–	2	–
Salim Malik	P	210	21	24	11	45	31	28	–	40	8	–	1	1
R.B.Richardson	WI	206	35	46	8	14	11	31	59	14	2	–	–	–

Most Appearances for other ICC Full Members:

		Total	E	A	SA	WI	NZ	I	P	SL	Z	C	B	UAE
A.Ranatunga	SL	164	9	21	7	15	27	33	43	–	6	–	3	–
J.G.Wright	NZ	149	30	42	–	11	–	21	18	24	2	–	1	–
G.A.Gooch	E	125	–	32	1	32	16	18	16	6	3	1	–	–
D.J.Richardson	SA	69	4	20	–	6	6	14	10	7	2	–	–	–
D.L.Houghton	Z	45	2	7	2	4	5	10	9	6	–	–	–	–

ENGLAND

BEST PERFORMANCES IN LIMITED-OVERS INTERNATIONALS

v AUSTRALIA
Highest Total	320-8	(55 overs)	Birmingham	1980
Lowest Total	93	(36.2 overs)	Leeds	1975
Highest Score	167*	R.A.Smith	Birmingham	1993
Best Bowling	5-31	M.Hendrick	The Oval	1980

v SOUTH AFRICA
Highest Total	252-6	(45 overs)	Sydney	1991-92
Lowest Total	236-4	(50 overs)	Melbourne	1991-92
Highest Score	83	G.A.Hick	Sydney	1991-92
Best Bowling	3-32	C.C.Lewis	Birmingham	1994

v WEST INDIES
Highest Total	306-5	(55 overs)	The Oval	1995
Lowest Total	114	(39 overs)	Bridgetown	1985-86
Highest Score	129*	G.A.Gooch	Port-of-Spain	1985-86
Best Bowling	4-23	G.R.Dilley	Brisbane	1986-87

v NEW ZEALAND
Highest Total	322-6	(60 overs)	The Oval	1983
Lowest Total	127	(40.1 overs)	Christchurch	1982-83
Highest Score	158	D.I.Gower	Brisbane	1982-83
Best Bowling	5-20	V.J.Marks	Wellington	1983-84

v INDIA
Highest Total	334-4	(60 overs)	Lord's	1975
Lowest Total	149	(41.4 overs)	Sydney	1984-85
Highest Score	137	D.L.Amiss	Lord's	1975
Best Bowling	5-35	P.W.Jarvis	Bangalore	1992-93

v PAKISTAN
Highest Total	363-7	(55 overs)	Nottingham	1992
Lowest Total	122	(31.6 8-ball overs)	Lahore	1977-78
Highest Score	142	G.A.Gooch	Karachi	1987-88
Best Bowling	4-15	R.G.D.Willis	Manchester	1978

v SRI LANKA
Highest Total	333-9	(60 overs)	Taunton	1983
Lowest Total	170	(36.1 overs)	Colombo (RPS)	1992-93
Highest Score	130	D.I.Gower	Taunton	1983
Best Bowling	5-39	V.J.Marks	Taunton	1983

v ZIMBABWE
Highest Total	200-8	(50 overs)	Brisbane	1994-95
Lowest Total	125	(49.1 overs)	Albury	1991-92
Highest Score	89	G.P.Thorpe	Brisbane	1994-95
Best Bowling	5-44	D.Gough	Sydney	1994-95

HIGHEST PARTNERSHIP FOR EACH WICKET

1st	193	G.A.Gooch, C.W.J.Athey	New Zealand	Manchester	1986
2nd	202	G.A.Gooch, D.I.Gower	Australia	Lord's	1985
3rd	213	G.A.Hick, N.H.Fairbrother	West Indies	Lord's	1991
4th	139	A.J.Lamb, D.W.Randall	Australia	Melbourne	1982-83
5th	142	R.A.Smith, G.P.Thorpe	Australia	Birmingham	1993
6th	98	D.I.Gower, I.J.Gould	Sri Lanka	Taunton	1983
7th	86*	M.W.Gatting, P.R.Downton	India	Poona	1984-85
8th	55	D.W.Randall, R.D.Jackman	West Indies	Lord's	1976
	55	C.M.Old, J.K.Lever	Australia	Birmingham	1977
9th	47	A.J.Lamb, N.A.Foster	West Indies	Manchester	1984
10th	43*	A.R.C.Fraser, P.C.R.Tufnell	Australia	Melbourne	1990-91

AUSTRALIA

BEST PERFORMANCES IN LIMITED-OVERS INTERNATIONALS

v ENGLAND

Highest Total	283-5	(50 overs)	Brisbane	1990-91
Lowest Total	70	(25.2 overs)	Birmingham	1977
Highest Score	145	D.M.Jones	Brisbane	1990-91
Best Bowling	6-14	G.J.Gilmour	Leeds	1975

v SOUTH AFRICA

Highest Total	281-6	(50 overs)	Port Elizabeth	1993-94
Lowest Total	126	(41 overs)	Perth	1993-94
Highest Score	107	M.E.Waugh	Sydney	1993-94
Best Bowling	4-13	P.R.Reiffel	Sydney	1993-94

v WEST INDIES

Highest Total	286-9	(50 overs)	Georgetown	1994-95
Lowest Total	91	(35.4 overs)	Perth	1986-87
Highest Score	127*	A.R.Border	Sydney	1984-85
Best Bowling	5-24	M.E.Waugh	Melbourne	1992-93

v NEW ZEALAND

Highest Total	302-8	(50 overs)	Melbourne	1982-83
Lowest Total	70	(26.3 overs)	Adelaide	1985-86
Highest Score	138*	G.S.Chappell	Sydney	1980-81
Best Bowling	5-13	S.P.O'Donnell	Christchurch	1989-90

v INDIA

Highest Total	320-9	(60 overs)	Nottingham	1983
Lowest Total	101	(37.5 overs)	Perth	1991-92
Highest Score	125	G.R.Marsh	Sydney	1985-86
Best Bowling	6-39	K.H.Macleay	Nottingham	1983

v PAKISTAN

Highest Total	300-5	(50 overs)	Brisbane	1989-90
Lowest Total	139	(43.2 overs)	Bombay	1989-90
Highest Score	125*	G.R.Marsh	Melbourne	1988-89
Best Bowling	5-16	C.G.Rackemann	Adelaide	1983-84

v SRI LANKA

Highest Total	332-3	(50 overs)	Sharjah	1989-90
Lowest Total	168-9	(45 overs)	Colombo (PSS)	1982-83
Highest Score	122	D.C.Boon	Adelaide	1987-88
Best Bowling	5-21	A.I.C.Dodemaide	Perth	1987-88

v ZIMBABWE

Highest Total	272-7	(60 overs)	Southampton	1983
Lowest Total	226-7	(60 overs)	Nottingham	1983
Highest Score	110	S.G.Law	Hobart	1994-95
Best Bowling	4-39	S.P.O'Donnell	Madras	1993-94

HIGHEST PARTNERSHIP FOR EACH WICKET

1st	212	G.R.Marsh, D.C.Boon	India	Jaipur	1986-87
2nd	185	G.R.Marsh, D.M.Jones	England	Brisbane	1990-91
3rd	224*	D.M.Jones, A.R.Border	Sri Lanka	Adelaide	1984-85
4th	173	D.M.Jones, S.R.Waugh	Pakistan	Perth	1986-87
5th	115*	B.M.Laird, A.R.Border	New Zealand	Dunedin	1981-82
6th	112	M.E.Waugh, S.P.O'Donnell	England	Sydney	1990-91
7th	102*	S.R.Waugh, G.C.Dyer	India	Delhi	1986-87
8th	119	P.R.Reiffel, S.K.Warne	South Africa	Port Elizabeth	1993-94
9th	52	S.P.O'Donnell, R.J.McCurdy	West Indies	Sydney	1984-85
10th	45	T.J.Laughlin, M.H.N.Walker	England	Sydney	1979-80

SOUTH AFRICA
BEST PERFORMANCES IN LIMITED-OVERS INTERNATIONALS

v ENGLAND

Highest Total	236-4	(50 overs)	Melbourne	1991-92
Lowest Total	181-9	(55 overs)	Manchester	1994
Highest Score	85	K.C.Wessels	Melbourne	1991-92
Best Bowling	5-40	R.P.Snell	Melbourne	1993-94

v AUSTRALIA

Highest Total	265-5	(50 overs)	Verwoerdburg	1993-94
Lowest Total	69	(28 overs)	Sydney	1993-94
Highest Score	112*	G.Kirsten	Melbourne	1993-94
Best Bowling	4-40	A.A.Donald	Sydney	1993-94

v WEST INDIES

Highest Total	200-8	(50 overs)	Christchurch	1991-92
Lowest Totals	140-9	(50 overs)	Cape Town	1992-93
	152†	(43.4 overs)	Port-of-Spain	1991-92
Highest Score	70*	D.J.Cullinan	Bombay	1993-94
Best Bowling	4-11	M.W.Pringle	Christchurch	1991-92

v NEW ZEALAND

Highest Total	314-7	(50 overs)	Verwoerdburg	1994-95
Lowest Totals	147-7	(50 overs)	Hobart	1993-94
	203†	(47 overs)	Christchurch	1994-95
Highest Score	169*	D.J.Callaghan	Verwoerdburg	1994-95
Best Bowling	4-38	C.R.Matthews	Hobart	1993-94

v INDIA

Highest Total	288-2	(46.4 overs)	Delhi	1991-92
Lowest Total	178-9	(50 overs)	Chandigarh	1993-94
Highest Score	108	A.C.Hudson	Bloemfontein	1992-93
Best Bowling	5-29	A.A.Donald	Calcutta	1991-92

v PAKISTAN

Highest Total	266-5	(50 overs)	Johannesburg	1994-95
Lowest Total	162	(30.1 overs)	East London	1992-93
Highest Score	106	M.J.R.Rindel	Johannesburg	1994-95
Best Bowling	4-27	P.S.de Villiers	East London	1992-93

v SRI LANKA

Highest Total	237-8	(50 overs)	Port Elizabeth	1994-95
Lowest Total	154	(46.1 overs)	Colombo (RPS)	1993-94
Highest Score	63	D.J.Cullinan	Port Elizabeth	1994-95
Best Bowling	4-12	R.P.Snell	Gauhati	1993-94

v ZIMBABWE

Highest Total	164-3	(45.1 overs)	Canberra	1991-92
Lowest Total	–			
Highest Score	70	K.C.Wessels	Canberra	1991-92
Best Bowling	3-30	B.M.McMillan	Canberra	1991-92

† *Lowest total for which the whole team was out and lowest total when the overs were complete.*

HIGHEST PARTNERSHIP FOR EACH WICKET

1st	190	G.Kirsten, M.J.R.Rindel	Pakistan	Johannesburg	1994-95
2nd	149	D.J.Callaghan, W.J.Cronje	New Zealand	Verwoerdburg	1994-95
3rd	106	W.J.Cronje, J.N.Rhodes	Australia	Johannesburg	1993-94
4th	119	D.J.Cullinan, J.N.Rhodes	Sri Lanka	Port Elizabeth	1994-95
5th	91	J.N.Rhodes, W.J.Cronje	India	East London	1992-93
6th	88	J.N.Rhodes, D.J.Richardson	Pakistan	Durban	1993-94
7th	46	D.J.Richardson, E.O.Simons	New Zealand	Cape Town	1994-95
8th	44	B.M.McMillan, D.J.Richardson	India	Calcutta	1993-94
9th	30	D.J.Richardson, P.S.de Villiers	Australia	Sydney	1993-94
10th	51	R.P.Snell, P.S.de Villiers	Sri Lanka	Colombo (RPS)	1993-94

WEST INDIES

BEST PERFORMANCES IN LIMITED-OVERS INTERNATIONALS

v ENGLAND
Highest Total	313-6	(50 overs)	Arnos Vale	1993-94
Lowest Total	127	(47.2 overs)	Arnos Vale	1980-81
Highest Score	189*	I.V.A.Richards	Manchester	1984
Best Bowling	6-15	C.E.H.Croft	Arnos Vale	1980-81

v AUSTRALIA
Highest Total	313-9	(50 overs)	St John's	1977-78
Lowest Total	87	(29.3 overs)	Sydney	1992-93
Highest Score	153*	I.V.A.Richards	Melbourne	1979-80
Best Bowling	7-51	W.W.Davis	Leeds	1983

v SOUTH AFRICA
Highest Total	287-6	(50 overs)	Kingston	1991-92
Lowest Totals	136	(38.4 overs)	Christchurch	1991-92
	136	(47 overs)	Cape Town	1992-93
Highest Score	122	P.V.Simmons	Kingston	1991-92
Best Bowling	3-24	C.E.L.Ambrose	Port-of-Spain	1991-92

v NEW ZEALAND
Highest Total	306-6	(50 overs)	Gauhati	1994-95
Lowest Total	123	(39.1 overs)	Margao	1994-95
Highest Score	145*	D.L.Haynes	Berbice	1984-85
Best Bowling	5-41	I.V.A.Richards	Dunedin	1986-87

v INDIA
Highest Total	333-8	(45 overs)	Jamshedpur	1983-84
Lowest Total	123	(40.1 overs)	Calcutta	1993-94
Highest Score	152*	D.L.Haynes	Georgetown	1988-89
Best Bowling	6-29	B.P.Patterson	Nagpur	1987-88

v PAKISTAN
Highest Total	315-4	(47 overs)	Port-of-Spain	1987-88
Lowest Total	111	(41.4 overs)	Melbourne	1983-84
Highest Score	153	B.C.Lara	Sharjah	1993-94
Best Bowling	5-25	I.R.Bishop	Brisbane	1992-93

v SRI LANKA
Highest Total	360-4	(50 overs)	Karachi	1987-88
Lowest Total	176-9	(50 overs)	Rajkot	1989-90
Highest Score	181	I.V.A.Richards	Karachi	1987-88
Best Bowling	5-1	C.A.Walsh	Sharjah	1986-87

v ZIMBABWE
Highest Total	264-8	(50 overs)	Brisbane	1991-92
Lowest Total	233-9	(50 overs)	Hyderabad (Ind)	1993-94
Highest Score	105*	C.G.Greenidge	Worcester	1983
Best Bowling	3-23	P.V.Simmons	Hyderabad (Ind)	1993-94

HIGHEST PARTNERSHIP FOR EACH WICKET

1st	192*	C.G.Greenidge, D.L.Haynes	Pakistan	Melbourne	1991-92
2nd	221	C.G.Greenidge, D.L.Haynes	India	Jamshedpur	1983-84
3rd	195*	C.G.Greenidge, H.A.Gomes	Zimbabwe	Worcester	1983
4th	149	R.B.Kanhai, C.H.Lloyd	Australia	Lord's	1975
5th	152	I.V.A.Richards, C.H.Lloyd	Sri Lanka	Brisbane	1984-85
6th	154	R.B.Richardson, P.J.L.Dujon	Pakistan	Sharjah	1991-92
7th	115	P.J.L.Dujon, M.D.Marshall	Pakistan	Gujranwala	1986-87
8th	65	C.L.Hooper, W.K.M.Benjamin	India	Nagpur	1987-88
9th	63	M.D.Marshall, J.Garner	Australia	Sydney	1984-85
10th	106*	I.V.A.Richards, M.A.Holding	England	Manchester	1984

West Indies scored 221 runs for the first wicket in unbroken partnerships involving D.L.Haynes, B.C.Lara and R.B.Richardson v Pakistan at Melbourne in 1991-92.

NEW ZEALAND

BEST PERFORMANCES IN LIMITED-OVERS INTERNATIONALS

v ENGLAND

Highest Total	298-6	(54.5 overs)	Leeds	1990
Lowest Total	134	(42.1 overs)	Christchurch	1983-84
Highest Score	111	M.J.Greatbatch	The Oval	1990
Best Bowling	5-28	B.L.Cairns	Scarborough	1978

v AUSTRALIA

Highest Total	276-7	(50 overs)	Adelaide	1985-86
Lowest Total	74	(29 overs)	Wellington	1981-82
Highest Score	104	K.J.Wadsworth	Christchurch	1973-74
Best Bowling	5-26	R.J.Hadlee	Sydney	1980-81

v SOUTH AFRICA

Highest Total	256-7	(50 overs)	Brisbane	1993-94
Lowest Total	134	(39.5 overs)	Cape Town	1994-95
Highest Score	108	A.C.Parore	Verwoerdburg	1994-95
Best Bowling	4-59	M.L.Su'a	Verwoerdburg	1994-95

v WEST INDIES

Highest Total	213	(50 overs)	Auckland	1986-87
Lowest Total	116	(42.2 overs)	Port-of-Spain	1984-85
Highest Score	81*	M.D.Crowe	Auckland	1991-92
Best Bowling	5-22	M.N.Hart	Margao	1994-95

v INDIA

Highest Total	278-3	(50 overs)	Baroda	1988-89
Lowest Totals	132-8	(44 overs)	Sharjah	1985-86
	142	(49.4 overs)	Auckland	1993-94
Highest Score	114*	G.M.Turner	Manchester	1975
Best Bowling	5-23	R.O.Collinge	Christchurch	1975-76

v PAKISTAN

Highest Total	277-6	(50 overs)	Napier	1984-85
Lowest Total	64	(35.5 overs)	Sharjah	1985-86
Highest Score	91	M.D.Crowe	Auckland	1991-92
Best Bowling	5-38	R.J.Hadlee	Dunedin	1988-89

v SRI LANKA

Highest Total	304-5	(50 overs)	Auckland	1982-83
Lowest Total	116	(34 overs)	Moratuwa	1983-84
Highest Score	140	G.M.Turner	Auckland	1982-83
Best Bowling	5-25	R.J.Hadlee	Bristol	1983

v ZIMBABWE

Highest Total	272-6	(46.5 overs)	Harare	1992-93
Lowest Total	242-7	(50 overs)	Hyderabad (Ind)	1987-88
Highest Score	94	M.D.Crowe	Harare	1992-93
Best Bowling	3-15	C.Z.Harris	Napier	1991-92

HIGHEST PARTNERSHIP FOR EACH WICKET

1st	158	M.D.Crowe, J.G.Wright	Bangladesh	Sharjah	1989-90
2nd	130	B.A.Edgar, M.D.Crowe	India	Brisbane	1985-86
3rd	181	A.C.Parore, K.R.Rutherford	India	Baroda	1994-95
4th	152	M.D.Crowe, K.R.Rutherford	India	Dunedin	1989-90
5th	113	M.D.Crowe, J.J.Crowe	England	Manchester	1986
6th	130	K.J.Wadsworth, B.E.Congdon	Australia	Christchurch	1973-74
7th	79	M.G.Burgess, B.L.Cairns	India	Adelaide	1980-81
8th	68	B.E.Congdon, B.L.Cairns	England	Scarborough	1978
9th	63	R.J.Hadlee, G.B.Troup	England	Brisbane	1982-83
10th	65	M.C.Snedden, E.J.Chatfield	Sri Lanka	Derby	1983

INDIA

BEST PERFORMANCES IN LIMITED-OVERS INTERNATIONALS

v ENGLAND

Highest Total	282-5	(53 overs)	Nottingham	1990
Lowest Totals	132-3	(60 overs)	Lord's	1975
	171*	(47.3 overs)	The Oval	1974
Highest Score	134*	N.S.Sidhu	Gwalior	1992-93
Best Bowling	5-41	J.Srinath	Bangalore	1992-93

v AUSTRALIA

Highest Total	289-6	(50 overs)	Delhi	1987-88
Lowest Total	63	(25.5 overs)	Sydney	1980-81
Highest Score	110	S.R.Tendulkar	Colombo (PSS)	1994-95
Best Bowling	5-15	R.J.Shastri	Perth	1991-92

v SOUTH AFRICA

Highest Total	287-4	(50 overs)	Delhi	1991-92
Lowest Total	147	(49.4 overs)	Port Elizabeth	1992-93
Highest Score	114	W.V.Raman	Verwoerdberg	1992-93
Best Bowling	4-40	A.Kumble	Hamilton	1994-95

v WEST INDIES

Highest Total	282-5	(47 overs)	Berbice	1982-83
Lowest Total	100	(28.3 overs)	Ahmedabad	1993-94
Highest Score	114*	N.S.Sidhu	Vishakhapatnam	1994-95
Best Bowling	6-12	A.Kumble	Calcutta	1993-94

v NEW ZEALAND

Highest Total	289-3	(50 overs)	Delhi	1994-95
Lowest Total	113	(44.2 overs)	Perth	1985-86
Highest Score	115	S.R.Tendulkar	Baroda	1994-95
Best Bowling	5-27	K.Srikkanth	Indore	1988-89

v PAKISTAN

Highest Total	273-4	(46 overs)	Sharjah	1989-90
Lowest Total	79	(34.2 overs)	Sialkot	1978-79
Highest Score	123	K.Srikkanth	Calcutta	1986-87
Best Bowling	5-21	Arshad Ayub	Dacca	1988-89

v SRI LANKA

Highest Total	299-4	(40 overs)	Bombay	1986-87
Lowest Total	78	(24.1 overs)	Kanpur	1986-87
Highest Score	112*	S.R.Tendulkar	Sharjah	1994-95
Best Bowling	5-24	J.Srinath	Kanpur	1993-94

v ZIMBABWE

Highest Total	266-8	(60 overs)	Tunbridge Wells	1983
Lowest Total	239	(49.4 overs)	Harare	1992-93
Highest Score	175*	Kapil Dev	Tunbridge Wells	1983
Best Bowling	4-19	M.Prabhakar	Bombay	1987-88

HIGHEST PARTNERSHIP FOR EACH WICKET

1st	188	K.Srikkanth, R.J.Shastri	England	Cuttack	1984-85
2nd	175	R.J.Shastri, S.V.Manjrekar	South Africa	Delhi	1991-92
3rd	175*	N.S.Sidhu, M.Azharuddin	Sri Lanka	Sharjah	1994-95
4th	164*	V.G.Kambli, S.R.Tendulkar	England	Jaipur	1992-93
5th	112	R.Lamba, R.J.Shastri	Pakistan	Hyderabad	1986-87
6th	127	M.Azharuddin, A.K.Sharma	New Zealand	Baroda	1988-89
7th	92	S.M.Patil, S.M.H.Kirmani	Australia	Melbourne	1980-81
8th	82*	Kapil Dev, K.S.More	New Zealand	Bangalore	1987-88
9th	126*	Kapil Dev, S.M.H.Kirmani	Zimbabwe	Tunbridge Wells	1983
10th	53	R.J.Shastri, N.D.Hirwani	West Indies	Gwalior	1987-88

PAKISTAN

BEST PERFORMANCES IN LIMITED-OVERS INTERNATIONALS

v ENGLAND

Highest Total	263	(50.5 overs)	The Oval	1992
Lowest Total	74	(40.2 overs)	Adelaide	1991-92
Highest Score	113	Javed Miandad	The Oval	1987
Best Bowling	4-31	Abdul Qadir	Rawalpindi	1987-88

v AUSTRALIA

Highest Total	286-7	(60 overs)	Nottingham	1979
Lowest Total	140	(49 overs)	Adelaide	1983-84
Highest Score	109	Zaheer Abbas	Lahore	1982-83
Best Bowling	5-21	Wasim Akram	Melbourne	1984-85

v SOUTH AFRICA

Highest Total	249-6	(50 overs)	Rawalpindi	1994-95
Lowest Total	109	(32.3 overs)	Johannesburg	1994-95
Highest Score	114*	Ijaz Ahmed, sr	Durban	1994-95
Best Bowling	5-16	Wasim Akram	East London	1992-93

v WEST INDIES

Highest Total	294-6	(50 overs)	Sharjah	1988-89
Lowest Total	43	(19.5 overs)	Cape Town	1992-93
Highest Score	131	Saeed Anwar	Sharjah	1993-94
Best Bowling	5-28	Mudassar Nazar	Melbourne	1984-85

v NEW ZEALAND

Highest Total	328-2	(50 overs)	Sharjah	1993-94
Lowest Totals	136-8	(42 overs)	Napier	1992-93
	139	(47.4 overs)	Auckland	1992-93
Highest Score	137*	Inzamam-ul-Haq	Sharjah	1993-94
Best Bowling	6-30	Waqar Younis	Auckland	1993-94

v INDIA

Highest Total	286-6	(44 overs)	Nagpur	1986-87
Lowest Total	87	(32.5 overs)	Sharjah	1984-85
Highest Score	119*	Javed Miandad	Lahore	1982-83
Best Bowling	7-37	Aqib Javed	Sharjah	1991-92

v SRI LANKA

Highest Total	338-5	(60 overs)	Swansea	1983
Lowest Total	170	(43 overs)	Sharjah	1990-91
Highest Score	126	Saeed Anwar	Adelaide	1989-90
Best Bowling	6-26	Waqar Younis	Sharjah	1989-90

v ZIMBABWE

Highest Total	262-8	(50 overs)	Sharjah	1992-93
Lowest Total	148	(43.3 overs)	Harare	1994-95
Highest Score	114	Aamir Sohail	Hobart	1991-92
Best Bowling	5-15	Wasim Akram	Karachi	1993-94

HIGHEST PARTNERSHIP FOR EACH WICKET

1st	204	Saeed Anwar, Ramiz Raja	Sri Lanka	Sharjah	1992-93
2nd	263	Aamir Sohail, Inzamam-ul-Haq	New Zealand	Sharjah	1993-94
3rd	206	Moin-ul-Atiq, Ijaz Ahmed, sr	Bangladesh	Chittagong	1988-89
4th	172	Salim Malik, Basit Ali	West Indies	Sharjah	1993-94
5th	152	Inzamam-ul-Haq, Ijaz Ahmed, sr	Zimbabwe	Harare	1994-95
6th	144	Imran Khan, Shahid Mahboob	Sri Lanka	Leeds	1983
7th	108	Ramiz Raja, Anil Dalpat	New Zealand	Christchurch	1984-85
8th	64	Ramiz Raja, Tahir Naqqash	New Zealand	Auckland	1984-85
9th	44	Salim Yousuf, Waqar Yousuf	Australia	Sydney	1989-90
10th	35*	Javed Miandad, Salim Jaffer	England	Perth	1986-87
	35*	Imran Khan, Mohsin Khan	England	Birmingham	1987

SRI LANKA

BEST PERFORMANCES IN LIMITED-OVERS INTERNATIONALS

v ENGLAND
Highest Total	286	(58 overs)	Taunton	1983
Lowest Total	136	(50.4 overs)	Leeds	1983
Highest Score	86*	S.Wettimuny	Colombo (SSC)	1981-82
Best Bowling	6-29	S.T.Jayasuriya	Moratuwa	1992-93

v AUSTRALIA
Highest Total	276-4	(60 overs)	The Oval	1975
Lowest Total	91	(35.5 overs)	Adelaide	1984-85
Highest Score	105	P.A.de Silva	Colombo (PSS)	1992-93
Best Bowling	4-39	G.F.Labrooy	Melbourne	1987-88

v SOUTH AFRICA
Highest Total	226-8	(50 overs)	Bloemfontein	1994-95
Lowest Total	98	(34 overs)	Colombo (RPS)	1993-94
Highest Score	73	P.A.de Silva	Bloemfontein	1994-95
Best Bowling	4-17	C.P.H.Ramanayake	Colombo (RPS)	1993-94

v WEST INDIES
Highest Total	230-7	(48.1 overs)	Colombo (RPS)	1993-94
Lowest Total	55	(28.3 overs)	Sharjah	1986-87
Highest Score	104	H.P.Tillekeratne	Bombay	1993-94
Best Bowling	4-45	R.S.Kalpage	Colombo (RPS)	1993-94

v NEW ZEALAND
Highest Total	288-4	(50 overs)	Bloemfontein	1994-95
Lowest Totals	114-9	(39 overs)	Moratuwa	1984-85
	115	(38.1 overs)	Colombo (PSS)	1983-84
Highest Score	140	S.T.Jayasuriya	Bloemfontein	1994-95
Best Bowling	5-26	U.S.H.Karnain	Moratuwa	1983-84

v INDIA
Highest Total	289-7	(40 overs)	Bombay	1986-87
Lowest Total	96	(41 overs)	Sharjah	1983-84
Highest Score	121	R.L.Dias	Bangalore	1982-83
Best Bowling	5-57	G.F.Labrooy	Baroda	1986-87

v PAKISTAN
Highest Total	288-8	(50 overs)	Adelaide	1989-90
Lowest Total	116	(33.5 overs)	Colombo (PSS)	1985-86
Highest Score	101*	A.Ranatunga	Durban	1994-95
Best Bowling	5-32	R.J.Ratnayake	Sharjah	1990-91

v ZIMBABWE
Highest Total	313-7	(49.2 overs)	New Plymouth	1991-92
Lowest Total	256-5	(50 overs)	Harare	1994-95
Highest Score	119*	R.S.Mahanama	Harare	1994-95
Best Bowling	4-19	S.T.Jayasuriya	Patna	1993-94

HIGHEST PARTNERSHIP FOR EACH WICKET

1st	128	R.S.Mahanama, M.A.R.Samarasekera	Zimbabwe	New Plymouth	1991-92
2nd	170	S.Wettimuny, R.L.Dias	India	Delhi	1982-83
3rd	150	H.P.Tillekeratne, P.A.de Silva	Pakistan	Lucknow	1989-90
4th	143	P.A.de Silva, A.Ranatunga	Zimbabwe	Harare	1994-95
5th	139	L.R.D.Mendis, P.A.de Silva	Australia	Sydney	1984-85
6th	132	A.Ranatunga, R.S.Kalpage	India	Hyderabad	1993-94
7th	90*	A.Ranatunga, U.S.H.Karnain	West Indies	Perth	1984-85
8th	56	J.R.Ratnayeke, D.S.de Silva	New Zealand	Napier	1982-83
9th	76	R.S.Kalpage, W.P.U.C.J.Vaas	Pakistan	Colombo (SSC)	1994-95
10th	33	R.J.Ratnayake, V.B.John	England	Leeds	1983

Sri Lanka's third wicket added 162 runs in partnerships involving S.Wettimuny, L.R.D.Mendis, A.P.B.Tennekoon and M.H.Tissera v Australia at The Oval in 1975.

ZIMBABWE

BEST PERFORMANCES IN LIMITED-OVERS INTERNATIONALS

v ENGLAND
Highest Total	205	(49.3 overs)	Sydney	1994-95
Lowest Total	134	(46.1 overs)	Albury	1991-92
Highest Score	84*	G.W.Flower	Sydney	1994-95
Best Bowling	4-21	E.A.Brandes	Albury	1991-92

v AUSTRALIA
Highest Total	240	(59.5 overs)	Southampton	1983
Lowest Total	137	(41.4 overs)	Hobart	1991-92
Highest Score	84	D.L.Houghton	Southampton	1983
Best Bowling	4-42	D.A.G.Fletcher	Nottingham	1983

v SOUTH AFRICA
Highest Total	163	(48.3 overs)	Canberra	1991-92
Lowest Total	–			
Highest Score	20	E.A.Brandes	Canberra	1991-92
Best Bowling	1-12	D.H.Brain	Bangalore	1993-94

v WEST INDIES
Highest Total	217-7	(60 overs)	Worcester	1983
Lowest Total	99	(36.3 overs)	Hyderabad (Ind)	1993-94
Highest Score	71*	D.A.G.Fletcher	Worcester	1983
Best Bowling	3-45	E.A.Brandes	Brisbane	1991-92

v NEW ZEALAND
Highest Total	271-6	(50 overs)	Harare	1992-93
Lowest Totals	239	(49.4 overs)	Hyderabad (Ind)	1987-88
	222-9	(50 overs)	Bulawayo	1992-93
Highest Score	142	D.L.Houghton	Hyderabad (Ind)	1987-88
Best Bowling	3-39	G.W.Flower	Bulawayo	1992-93

v INDIA
Highest Total	248	(50 overs)	Indore	1993-94
Lowest Total	135	(44.2 overs)	Bombay	1987-88
Highest Score	73	K.M.Curran	Tunbridge Wells	1983
Best Bowling	4-26	G.J.Crocker	Harare	1992-93

v PAKISTAN
Highest Total	222-9	(50 overs)	Harare	1994-95
Lowest Totals	141-9	(40 overs)	Lahore	1993-94
	143	(38 overs)	Karachi	1993-94
Highest Score	74	A.D.R.Campbell	Rawalpindi	1993-94
Best Bowling	4-36	B.C.Strang	Harare	1994-95

v SRI LANKA
Highest Total	312-4	(50 overs)	New Plymouth	1991-92
Lowest Total	105	(48.1 overs)	Harare	1994-95
Highest Score	131*	A.D.R.Campbell	Harare	1994-95
Best Bowling	4-44	H.H.Streak	Harare	1994-95

HIGHEST PARTNERSHIP FOR EACH WICKET

1st	124	A.Flower, G.W.Flower	New Zealand	Harare	1992-93
2nd	104	A.Flower, M.G.Burmester	Pakistan	Harare	1994-95
3rd	102	A.D.R.Campbell, D.L.Houghton	Pakistan	Rawalpindi	1993-94
4th	110	G.W.Flower, D.L.Houghton	England	Sydney	1994-95
5th	145*	A.Flower, A.C.Waller	Sri Lanka	New Plymouth	1991-92
6th	103	D.L.Houghton, K.M.Curran	Australia	Southampton	1983
7th	75*	D.A.G.Fletcher, I.P.Butchart	Australia	Nottingham	1983
8th	117	D.L.Houghton, I.P.Butchart	New Zealand	Hyderabad	1987-88
9th	55	K.M.Curran, P.W.E.Rawson	West Indies	Birmingham	1983
10th	36	M.A.Meman, M.P.Jarvis	India	Bombay	1987-88

WORLD CUP FIXTURES

FEBRUARY

Sun	11	Calcutta, India	Opening Ceremony
Wed	14	Ahmedabad, India	England v New Zealand
Thu	15	Rawalpindi, Pakistan	South Africa v UAE
Fri	16	Hyderabad, India	West Indies v Zimbabwe
Sat	17	Baroda, India	New Zealand v Holland
		Colombo (RPS), Sri Lanka	Sri Lanka v Australia
Sun	18	Peshawar, Pakistan	India v Kenya
		Cuttack, India	England v UAE
Tue	20	Faisalabad, Pakistan	South Africa v New Zealand
Wed	21	Gwalior, India	India v West Indies
		Colombo (SSC), Sri Lanka	Sri Lanka v Zimbabwe
Thu	22	Peshawar, Pakistan	England v Holland
Fri	23	Vishakhapatnam, India	Australia v Kenya
Sat	24	Gujranwala, Pakistan	Pakistan v UAE
Sun	25	Rawalpindi, Pakistan	England v South Africa
		Colombo (RPS), Sri Lanka	Sri Lanka v West Indies
Mon	26	Lahore, Pakistan	Pakistan v Holland
		Patna, India	Zimbabwe v Kenya
Tue	27	Bombay, India	India v Australia
		Faisalabad, Pakistan	New Zealand v UAE
Thu	29	Karachi, Pakistan	Pakistan v South Africa
		Poona, India	West Indies v Kenya

MARCH

Fri	1	Nagpur, India	Australia v Zimbabwe
		Lahore, Pakistan	Holland v UAE
Sat	2	Delhi, India	India v Sri Lanka
Sun	3	Karachi, Pakistan	Pakistan v England
Mon	4	Jaipur, India	Australia v West Indies
Tue	5	Rawalpindi, Pakistan	South Africa v Holland
Wed	6	Kanpur, India	Pakistan v New Zealand
		Lahore, Pakistan	India v Zimbabwe
		Kandy, Sri Lanka	Sri Lanka v Kenya

QUARTER-FINALS

Sat	9	Faisalabad, Pakistan	1st in Group A v 4th in Group B
		Bangalore, India	3rd in Group A v 2nd in Group B
Mon	11	Karachi, Pakistan	1st in Group B v 4th in Group A
		Madras, India	3rd in Group B v 2nd in Group A

SEMI-FINALS

Wed	13	Calcutta, India	(Faisalabad winners v Bangalore winners)
Thu	14	Mohali, Chandigarh, India	(Karachi winners v Madras winners)

FINAL

Sun	**17**	**Lahore, Pakistan**

Key to Colombo Grounds:

RPS	R.Premadasa Stadium, Khettarama
SSC	Sinhalese Sports Club Ground